MEL Scripting for Maya Animators, 2e

Reading and following the lessons of this book provides one of the best ways for a casual Maya user to elevate their skills to a professional level. The fundamental techniques developed in MEL Scripting for Maya Animators *are critical for visual effects artists to learn.*

—Scott Stokdyk, Visual Effects Supervisor, Sony Pictures Imageworks

While the first edition opened the doors to MEL scripting for interested Maya users, this expanded and updated second edition delves deeper into important programming concepts, and new features in Maya released since the original edition. No longer just for the first steps in MEL programming, this edition takes the reader into the depths of advanced topics such as user interface layout and web panels that are sure to make this book a frequently used and a welcome addition to any technical director's bookshelf.

—Doug Cooper, Visual Effects Supervisor, DreamWorks Animation

MEL Scripting for Maya Animators is the set of keys you need to get under the hood of Maya. The book is well written for both technical and non-technical animators. It is an essential tool in making sophisticated animation not only possible but also practical.

—Henry LaBounta, Senior Art Director, Electronic Arts

MEL Scripting
for Maya Animators

Second Edition

The Morgan Kaufmann Series in Computer Graphics and Geometric Modeling

MEL Scripting for Maya Animators

for Maya

Animators

Second Edition

Mark R. Wilkins
Chris Kazmier

with a contribution by

Stephan Osterburg

AMSTERDAM • BOSTON • HEIDELBERG • LONDON
NEW YORK • OXFORD • PARIS • SAN DIEGO
SAN FRANCISCO • SINGAPORE • SYDNEY • TOKYO

Morgan Kaufmann Publishers is an imprint of Elsevier

ELSEVIER

MORGAN KAUFMANN PUBLISHERS

Senior Editor	Tim Cox
Publishing Services Manager	Simon Crump
Project Manager	Brandy Lilly
Assistant Editor	Richard Camp
Editorial Assistant	Jessica Evans
Cover Designer	Hannus Design
Cover Image	Guatemala, Pacific Slope, Finca El Baul, half-buried stone head. Copyright Getty Images/Stone Collection/David Hiser.
Composition	SPI Publisher Services
Technical Illustration	Dartmouth Publishing Services
Copyeditor	SPI USA
Proofreader	SPI USA
Indexer	SPI USA
Interior printer	The Maple-Vail Book Manufacturing Group
Cover printer	Phoenix Color

Morgan Kaufmann Publishers is an imprint of Elsevier.
500 Sansome Street, Suite 400, San Francisco, CA 94111

This book is printed on acid-free paper.

Library of Congress Cataloging-in-Publication Data
Wilkins, Mark R.
  MEL scripting for Maya animators / Mark R. Wilkins and Chris Kazmier.–2nd ed.
    p. cm.
  Includes index.
  ISBN-13: 978-0-12-088793-4   ISBN-10: 0-12-088793-2
  1. Computer animation. 2. Maya (Computer file) 3. Computer graphics. I. Kazmier, Chris. II. Title.
  TR897.7.W555 2005
  006.6'96–dc22

ISBN-13: 978-0-12-088793-4   2005015610
ISBN-10: 0-12-088793-2

For information on all Morgan Kaufmann publications,
visit our Web site at www.mkp.com or www.books.elsevier.com

Printed in the United States of America
08 09   5 4 3

Working together to grow
libraries in developing countries

www.elsevier.com | www.bookaid.org | www.sabre.org

ELSEVIER   BOOK AID
            International   Sabre Foundation

About the Authors

Mark R. Wilkins is a technical director at DreamWorks Animation SKG, where he helped develop a production pipeline using Maya for effects and character animation. Mark also provides training and technical assistance to animators using Maya. He previously worked at Walt Disney Feature Animation in a variety of positions including software engineer and scene setup supervisor. He has contributed to a number of films, including *Dinosaur*, *Mission: Impossible 2*, *Minority Report*, and *Madagascar*. Mark holds a degree in physics from Harvey Mudd College.

Chris Kazmier is a senior technical director at Sony Pictures Imageworks, where he creates computer-generated effects for live-action films. He has worked on projects ranging from *The Haunted Mansion* to Sony's first all 3D feature animation *Open Season*. Previously, Chris worked at DreamWorks on *Sinbad* and at PDI/DreamWorks on the Intel Aliens ad campaign. Credits also include Fox Animation Studio's *Titan AE* and *Anastasia*.

Contents

Chapter 3   Using Expressions   37

Example 1:   Eyes   50

Chapter 4   Controlling Particles with Expressions   61

Chapter 12 Designing MEL User Interfaces   205

Chapter 13 Simple MEL User Interfaces   213

Chapter 14 Custom Dialog Boxes   231

Chapter 17 Improving Performance with Utility Nodes   295

Chapter 18 Installing MEL Scripts   303

Chapter 19 Examples Using MEL with Particle Dynamics   309

Chapter 20 Examples Using MEL with Solid Body Dynamics   351

Preface

In the last three years, the pace of updates to Maya has accelerated. New features seem to appear every few months. However, the foundation of Maya, consisting of MEL and the dependency graph, remains largely unchanged.

This second edition serves to bring *MEL Scripting for Maya Animators* up to date with the interface changes that have taken place between Maya 4.5, with which the first edition was written, and Maya 6. Certain regrettable omissions, such as a chapter on formLayout, have been corrected. Known errors have been fixed. Also, new chapters on utility nodes and Maya's Web Panel feature provide some new ideas for how to use MEL in one's applications.

More than anything else, feedback from people who have used the book to learn or teach MEL has spurred us on. To the contributors of these thoughts and perspectives, thank you!

Acknowledgments

Along the way to getting this book into your hands we've had tremendous help from others, including Aron Warner, Susan Rogers, and Ken Pearce, who provided essential help getting the project started. As we wrote, our reviewers, Ed Gavin, Kate LaBore, Chris Rock, and Doug Cooper, worked long, hard hours helping us refine our work.

Our editorial staff at Morgan Kaufmann, particularly Belinda Breyer, Mona Buehler, Diane Cerra, and Cheri Palmer have paid for our book's quality with eternal vigilance. It's been a privilege to work with them.

For the second edition, Tim Cox and Richard Camp have been endlessly patient and supportive.

Finally, of course, we wish to thank our family and friends for their relentless support and the time that we've taken away from them to put into this book.

Special Acknowledgment

Thanks especially to Stephan Osterburg, our friend and colleague, for contributing a complete and well-documented character setup for the examples in Chapter 19. These character setup examples contribute enormously to the value of the book for those interested in character applications.

Mark R. Wilkins
Chris Kazmier
2/2005

1

Maya Under the Hood

In this chapter you will learn

- That, to Maya, your scene is nothing more than a collection of nodes and connections, which together compose the *dependency graph*.
- What a *dependency graph node* is and how it relates to what you see in the 3D viewer.
- That the Channel Box and Attribute Editor windows are the Maya interface's most commonly used tools to manipulate the attributes of dependency graph nodes.
- That certain nodes, but not all, are part of the *transform hierarchy*, which establishes spatial relationships among objects.
- How to use the Outliner, the Hypergraph, and the Connection Editor to examine how nodes fit into the dependency graph and the transform hierarchy.
- How common tasks, such as creating objects, setting animation keyframes, and modeling NURBS surfaces, change the dependency graph.
- That Maya's graphic user interface, including menus, toolbars, the timeline, and so on, are built and can be modified with MEL.

Why Look Under the Hood?

One reason some animators find MEL scripting tricky to learn is that it requires an understanding of many details of how the pieces of a scene work together, details that the Maya user interface works hard to hide. This chapter opens up many of those details and relates them to what a Maya animator sees in the interface when working without scripting.

1

Knowing how a Maya scene fits together is important, even when you work entirely without MEL scripting. Thus, if you're an experienced Maya animator, you will already know much of what this chapter describes. However, keeping track of your Maya scene's components and how they fit together becomes critical when developing MEL scripts because, unlike the user interface, MEL forces you to work frequently with your Maya scene at this lower level, doing much less to hide its complexity from you.

The Dependency Graph, Attributes, and Connections

Internally, every part of a scene, whether it is 3D geometry, animation, an expression relationship, a light, a texture, or the arguments that were used to create an object with history, is represented as one or more *nodes,* or, more completely, *dependency graph* or *DG* nodes. Each node has a set of *attributes,* each of which stores a characteristic of the thing the node represents. All of these nodes together with all of their connections are called the dependency graph or the *scene graph* (Figure 1.1).

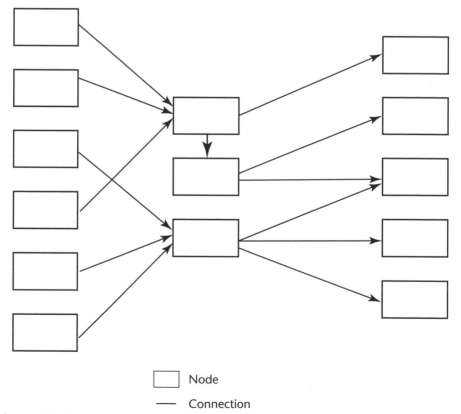

Figure 1.1 The dependency graph.

One useful source of information about DG nodes is Maya's *Node and Attribute Reference,* which is available from the Help menu. This document describes most, if not all, of the nodes that are built into Maya, along with their attributes and what function they serve in a scene.

Attributes themselves have characteristics that control how you can manipulate them. Attributes may be *locked,* which prevents them from being changed. They can be marked *keyable,* which permits you to animate them by setting keyframes, or *nonkeyable,* in which case you can't.

Also, each attribute has a *data type,* which specifies what kind of information the attribute can store. In Maya, attributes can store

- *Integer* numbers (with no fractional part).
- *Floating-point* numbers (with a fractional part).
- *Strings,* which can be a combination of text and numbers.
- *Boolean* values, which are on/off or true/false values.
- *Enumerated* values, which store a value selected from a list of choices defined when the attribute is created.
- Also, some attributes store collections of data of the above types, including *arrays, vectors,* and *matrices.*

One important use of MEL is to create and connect DG nodes that create a particular result when your scene is played back. At first, a good way to learn how nodes and connections work to create animation is to animate by hand, then to examine the nodes and connections that Maya has created while you have done so. Later, as we get further into the MEL language, you will learn how to build networks of nodes and attribute connections with scripts. Seeing what Maya does when you animate without scripting can serve as an important source for ideas about how to script complex tasks.

The *Channel Box,* part of the standard Maya layout, displays the one or more nodes (in this instance `directionalLight1` and `directionalLight Shape1`) that make up the selected object (Figure 1.2).

The Channel Box displays only those attributes that are keyable, because those are the attributes that are most frequently edited while you work. Editing other attributes is usually done through the *Attribute Editor* (Figure 1.3). Even the Attribute Editor, though, does not display every attribute. Certain attributes can be manipulated only through MEL scripts and expressions.

The Attribute Editor displays the selected node's attributes as a series of groups that can be expanded by clicking on the arrow button to their left. In the example shown in Figure 1.3, Directional Light Attributes is one such group. Also, connected nodes appear as tabs at the top of the Attribute Editor to allow you easy access to other nodes related to the one you are editing.

The Attribute Editor allows you to add your own attributes as well, using the choices on the Attributes menu. How custom attributes can be useful in expressions and MEL is discussed in later chapters.

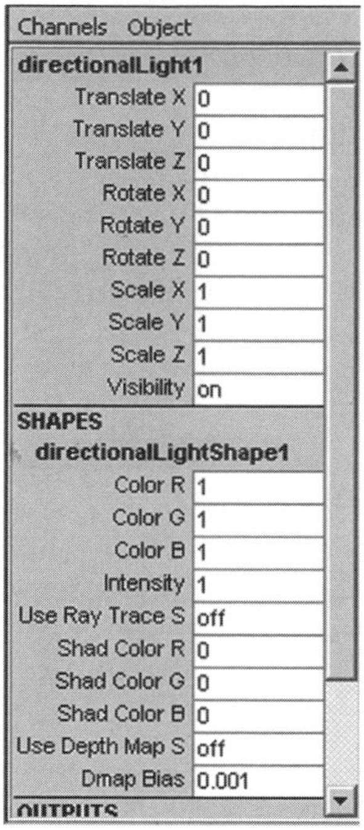

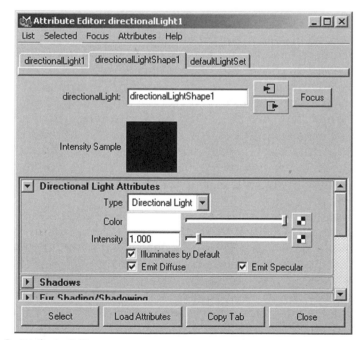

Figure 1.2 The Channel Box.

Figure 1.3 Attribute Editor.

A final important characteristic of attributes is that they can be *connected* to each other. Connecting two attributes forces the value of one attribute to remain the same as the value of another attribute. These connections are directional, meaning, for example, that if you connect one attribute to another you can change the first attribute all you like and the second will follow, but the second attribute cannot be changed because its value is being driven by the connection with the first. You can set up connections between nodes with the *Connection Editor* (Figure 1.4).

This characteristic of connection is what gives the dependency graph its name. It's a "graph" because that's a term for a network of connected nodes, and "dependency" refers to the way that each connected node depends on the values of the nodes that connect to it. Nodes whose attributes' values connect to the current node are *upstream* nodes, and nodes that depend on the current node are *downstream* nodes. The idea of a scene graph like Maya's dependency graph is common in computer animation systems; 3D Studio Max and Softimage, for example, each use scene graph structures.

The most useful tool for seeing interconnections between multiple nodes is the Hypergraph window (Figure 1.5), which you can reach by choosing Window > Hypergraph . . . from the main menu. With the Hypergraph you

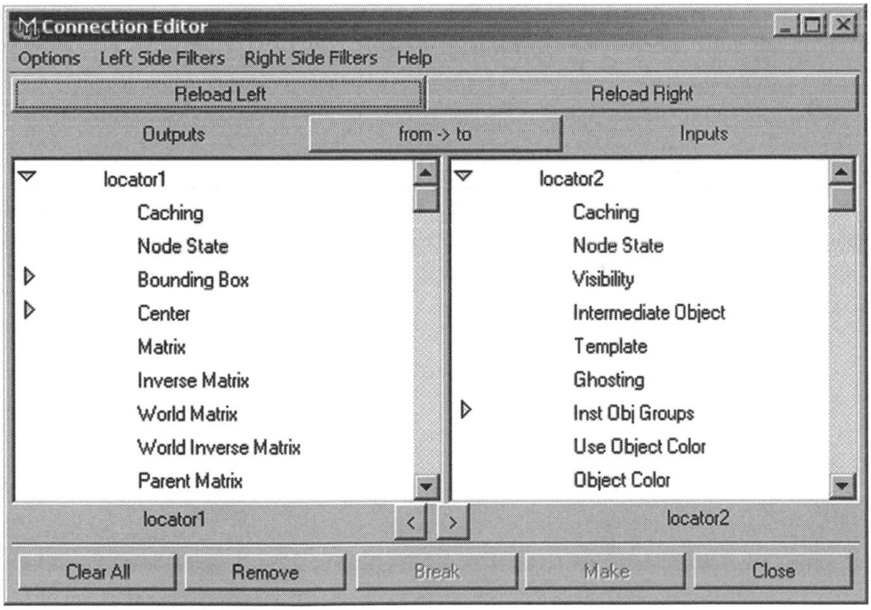

Figure 1.4 Connection Editor.

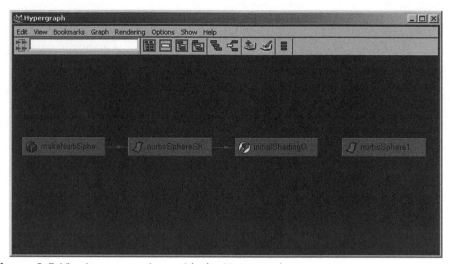

Figure 1.5 Viewing connections with the Hypergraph.

can see the connections that have been made to the selected node by selecting the node and choosing Graph > Up and Downstream Connections from the window's menus.

Note that it is not possible to view the entire scene in Up and Downstream Connections mode. Because there can be so many nodes and connections in even a relatively simple scene, this view in the Hypergraph displays only the connections that lead to the selected object so that working in the Hypergraph remains manageable. While viewing nodes in this mode, you can move the pointer over the arrows that represent connections to see what attributes are connected.

To see how a simple Maya scene is represented as a dependency graph, let's examine what happens when you animate a bouncing ball. For the sake of simplicity, let's assume the ball is only moving along one axis.

As a first pass at animating this ball (Figure 1.6), you might set three keyframes on the ball's vertical motion at, say, 0 frames, 10 frames, and 20 frames into the animation.

As you work, each action you perform creates nodes and connections behind-the-scenes. First, as seen in Figure 1.7, creating the sphere makes three connected nodes.

Then, setting the animation keyframes creates and connects another node (Figure 1.8), this time an animation curve that drives the `translateY` attribute of `nurbsSphere1`. When you play back the scene, Maya's `time1` node, the scene's clock, tells the animation curve which frame num-

Time = 0   Time = 10   Time = 20

Figure 1.6 Bouncing ball keyframes.

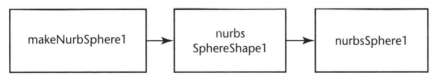

Figure 1.7 Nodes that make up a new sphere.

ber's value to look up. Then, the animation curve sets the `translateY` attribute to the right value. Finally, Maya draws the sphere where you've placed it.

As you can tell, simple operations in Maya, such as making a primitive or animating an attribute, have complex implications under the surface.

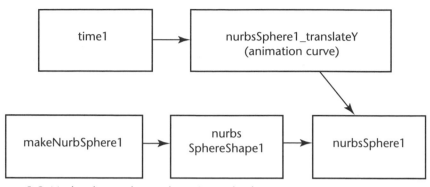

Figure 1.8 Nodes that make up the animated sphere.

One of the strengths of the MEL language is that it can make it easier to set up large networks of nodes to perform a task.

Maya's concept of an expression is more complex than that of a simple connection between attributes, in that an expression can calculate one attribute from another using mathematical operations or almost any other method that you can script in MEL. A connection simply sets one attribute's value to be the same as another's.

How this works is that creating an expression with the Expression Editor or by typing in the Channel Box makes a new node, an expression node. This node contains the expression script and can calculate the expression's output value from its inputs. If you create an expression that calculates an attribute value for node2 from an attribute value in node1, you get the result shown in Figure 1.9. Expressions are discussed much more thoroughly in Chapter 3.

Example 1: Using the Hypergraph to Explore the Dependency Graph

This example demonstrates how to use the Hypergraph to examine how nodes are connected in a scene. First, we'll look at the example, an animated bouncing ball.

Figure 1.9 An expression node and its connections.

1. Make a new scene by choosing File > New Scene from the main menu.
2. Create a sphere by clicking on the Sphere tool or choosing Create > NURBS Primitives > Sphere.
3. Move the sphere up ten units by typing 10 into the Translate Y field in the Channel Box.
4. Click on the 10 in the Translate Y field of the Channel Box. Then, right-click on the field and choose Key Selected from the menu that appears. The Translate Y field should change color.
5. Click on Frame 10 in the timeline to advance the time. The current time marker should move ahead to Frame 10, leaving behind a red mark indicating a keyframe on Frame 0.
6. Type 0 into the Translate Y field; press Enter to commit the change, and set another keyframe using Key Selected.
7. Click on frame 20 to advance the time, and set a Translate Y keyframe with a value of 10.
8. Rewind and play back the animation.
9. Make sure the sphere is selected, and then choose Window > Hypergraph. . . . When the Hypergraph window appears, use Alt + MMB to drag the view so that the selected sphere object is in the center. Note the trapezoidal shape, which indicates that the sphere has been animated.
10. Choose Graph > Up and Downstream Connections from the Hypergraph menu. Now you should be able to see the nodes that make up the sphere as well as several connected nodes, as shown in Figure 1.10.

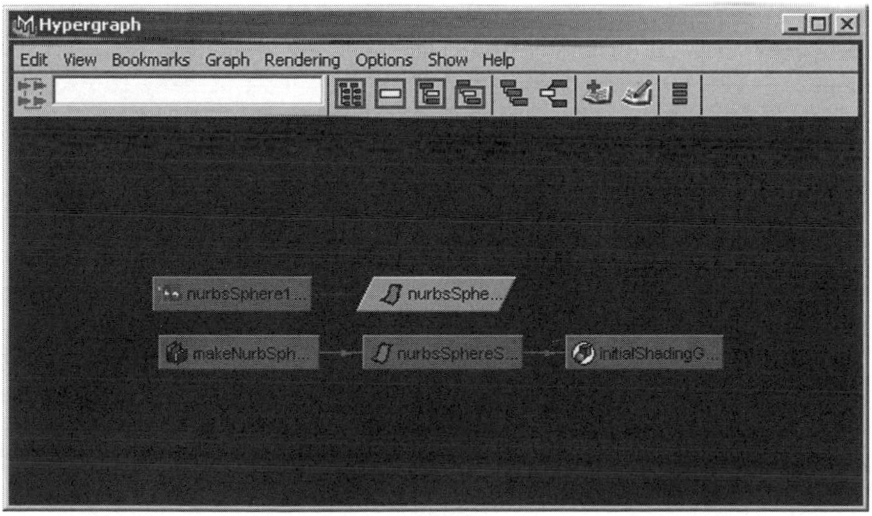

Figure 1.10 Up- and downstream connections for an animated sphere.

In the Hypergraph, you can use the same mouse controls that allow you to move around in perspective and orthographic views. With Alt + LMB + MMB you can zoom in and out, and with Alt + MMB you can track side to side and up and down. Also, as in other views, you can click on a node to select it.

Try moving your pointer over some of the connections. You can see the names of the connected attributes when you do so. If you want to delete a connection, you can click it and press Backspace or Delete. To make a new connection, drag with the middle mouse button from one node to another, and the connection editor will pop up with those nodes already loaded, ready to connect attributes.

The colors of the connections indicate whether the arrow represents connected attributes whose data types are a single numeric value (blue), an array (green), or a more complex type of data (pink) such as a matrix or geometry.

In Figure 1.10, an animation curve called nurbsSphere1_translateY is connected to the trapezoidal nurbsSphere1 node. This node is called a *transform node,* and the related nurbsSphereShape1 is called a *shape node.* The relationship between transform and shape nodes is discussed later in this chapter, but for now it's enough to know that the transform node defines where the ball is in space, and the shape node defines the ball's geometric shape.

Two connections we discussed earlier are not represented in this view in the Hypergraph. First is the connection from the transform node to the shape node, and second is the connection from Maya's scene clock, called *time1,* to the animation curve. Both of these kinds of connections are hidden by default to reduce clutter, because most animation curves are driven by the current time, and most shapes are connected to the similarly named transform.

Now, let's look at a more complex scene. We will create a series of joints that cause a sphere object to bend, and then look at how the resulting nodes are connected.

1. Make a new scene.
2. Tumble your perspective view so that you're facing the XZ plane; create a sphere.
3. Set Scale X for the new sphere to 3.
4. Select the Joint Tool, and make three joints inside your sphere object, and then press Enter to finish.
5. Select the joints and the sphere object, and then choose Skin > Bind Skin > Rigid Bind.
6. Select the middle joint, and choose the Rotate Tool, and then rotate the joint to see that the sphere is bound to the joint (Figure 1.11).
7. Select the sphere and choose Window > Hypergraph from the main menu.

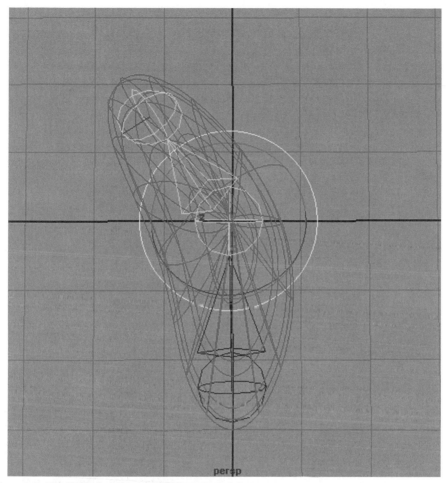

Figure 1.11 Scaled sphere bound to three joints.

8. Choose Graph > Up and Downstream Connections from the Hypergraph's menus.
9. Choose Show > Show Auxillary Nodes.

Results are shown in Figure 1.12

In this example, following the pink connections gives you a general idea of how Maya manipulates the geometry as it calculates how the joints have affected the shape of the sphere. On the far left of Figure 1.12 is the makeNurbSphere1 history node, connected to the old nurbsSphereShape1 node, which has been renamed nurbsSphereShape1Orig and has been hidden. Hidden nodes appear grayed out in the Hypergraph.

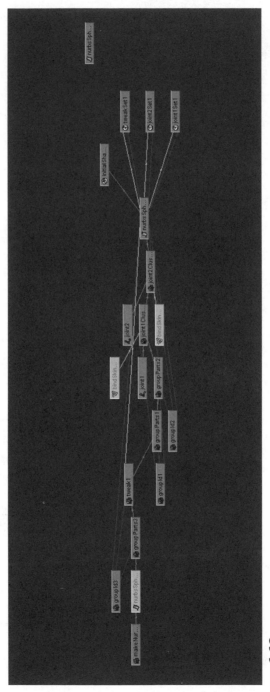

Figure 1.12

Farther to the right, after a number of tweak, group, and joint cluster nodes that Maya sets up automatically when you choose Rigid Bind, is the new `nurbsSphereShape1` node, which contains the deformed geometry. Finally, the Hypergraph contains some hidden cluster handles for the clusters of points that each joint controls and some Set nodes that define the sets of points that each joint influences.

Transform Hierarchy and Parent/Child Relationships

While the dependency graph describes how nodes' attribute values depend on each other, Maya also keeps track of additional geometric relationships among nodes that represent objects in 3D space such as NURBS surfaces, meshes, joints, and locators. These relationships make up a structure called the *transform hierarchy,* or just the *hierarchy.* Maya actually implements the hierarchy as connections between nodes also, but the Hypergraph does not display these connections in the connections viewing modes, in order to keep the graph free of clutter.

The relationships between nodes that make up the transform hierarchy include grouping and parent/child relationships. In a parent/child relationship, the child's position, rotation, and scaling in world space are the effect of its position, rotation, and scaling attributes, added on to the effect of its parent, and so on. To see how this works, here is an example in which we think of nodes called Grandparent, Parent, and Child. Each node's translate X and translate Y attribute values are shown in Figure 1.13.

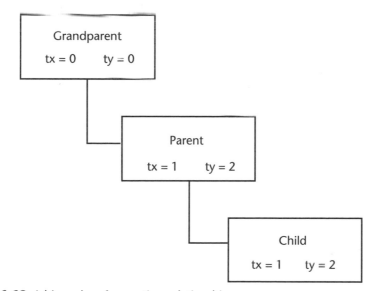

Figure 1.13 A hierarchy of parenting relationships.

Since each child's translation is added to that of its parent, the translate X and translate Y attributes of the node called Parent add on to those of the Grandparent node (which happen to be zero) to put it at an X position of 1 and a Y location of 2 in world space. The node called Child, when its own local translate X and translate Y values are added on, is at a world space location of X = 2 and Y = 4.

From the example in Figure 1.13, you can see some of the rules that govern the geometric relationships represented in the hierarchy. A summary of these rules follows:

■ The values of a node's translation, rotation, and scaling attributes do not describe its position in the entire scene's 3D world, but only describe its position relative to its parent.

■ The translation, rotation, and scaling of a node with respect to the entire scene is the cumulative effect of the node's attributes, and its parent's, and the parent's parent's, and so on.

■ A parent can have multiple children.

There's one more rule, though, that may seem not to make sense:

■ A child can have multiple parents.

The reason this last rule might seem confusing is that if a child hierarchy node has multiple parents, presumably with their own values for translate, rotate, and scale attributes, it would seem that this would mean that the same object (the child object) would be in two different places. In fact, Maya allows you to do exactly that, in its *instancing* feature. When you instance an object or part of a hierarchy, you make a copy that is linked to the original in that a change to either the copy or the original changes both. In the hierarchy, this is represented as one node having two different parents whose attributes place it in two different places.

The above rules also explain why, when you move a parent, the children move as well: moving the parent changes its translation, rotation, and scaling attributes, which affect the children because the parent's attributes are being added on to the children's attributes to find where the children are in global space.

Some nodes that do not have a meaningful location in 3D space, such as constraints or object sets, are in the hierarchy and can have objects parented underneath them. These objects have no effect on the location in space of their child nodes. In calculating where objects appear in global space, Maya treats them as if their children were parented directly to their parents, and moving them in the hierarchy has no effect on how the objects in the scene appear. They are present in the hierarchy just to allow the animator to place them where they can serve as a meaningful reminder of their function.

Examining the Hierarchy

Maya provides a couple of ways to view the hierarchy that can be useful for different purposes. First, the Hypergraph's Scene Hierarchy view is one way to view the hierarchy. You can reach it by choosing Window > Hypergraph . . . from the main menus and then choosing Graph > Scene Hierarchy from the Hypergraph menus.

Note: If the Scene Hierarchy menu item is grayed out, you are probably already viewing in hierarchy mode!

Another common way to view the hierarchy is to open the Outliner window by choosing Window > Outliner. . . . The Outliner makes it easy to collapse parts of the hierarchy that are of less interest and to expand those that are of more interest by clicking on the [+] buttons to expand and the [–] to collapse parts of the tree (Figure 1.14).

Transform and Shape Nodes

At first, it seems that there are many different kinds of nodes that have the basic set of attributes that are needed for a node to make sense in the hierarchy: translation, rotation, scaling, scale pivot point location, rotation pivot point location, and so on.

Actually, most nodes that appear in the Outliner by default are actually a combination of two nodes, a *transform* node whose attributes store all of the information about where an object is in space and how it's scaled, and a *shape* node that stores the object's actual geometric shape and properties of its construction and rendering. Looking back at Figure 1.6, which shows the nodes that are created when you create a NURBS sphere in an empty scene, you'll notice a node called `nurbsSphereShape1` connected to the `nurbsSphere1` that appears in the Outliner. `nurbsSphere1` is a transform node, and `nurbsSphereShape` is a NURBS shape node.

There are many kinds of shape nodes (including NURBS surfaces, meshes, lights, cameras, and locators, among others), but only one kind of transform node. One implication of this is that if you have a MEL script that moves or places one kind of object in space, it's easy to adapt it to work with other kinds of objects.

If you want to see the shape nodes in the Outliner window, you can choose Display > Shapes from the window's menus. If you want to see the shape nodes in the Hypergraph, you can choose Options > Display > Shape Nodes from the Hypergraph window's menus.

Figure 1.14 The same scene in the Outliner and the Hypergraph.

Example 2: Exploring Transform and Shape Nodes, Instancing, and History

This example shows you how an object you can manipulate in the 3D view is built up of nodes in Maya, and how the developers of Maya have implemented common operations, such as instancing and history, as manipulations of the relationships between nodes.

First, create a sphere:

1. Start Maya or choose File > New Scene.
2. Choose Create > NURBS Primitives > Sphere.

A sphere appears, which you can manipulate as a single object. Look in the Channel Box at the top, and you will see the name nurbsSphere1, the object's name. Now, open the Outliner:

3. Choose Window > Outliner. . . .

and you see your nurbsSphere1 object selected.

So far, there are not many indications that the nurbsSphere1 object is particularly complex. Now, though, we'll turn on Shape display in the Outliner window:

4. In the Outliner window, choose Display > Shapes.

Click on the [+] that expands the nurbsSphere1 entry in the outline. Results are shown in Figure 1.15.

Now, what had seemed a single object is revealed to be made up of two nodes. The first, nurbsSphere1, is the sphere's transform node, and the second, nurbsSphereShape1, is the shape node (specifically in this case, a NURBS shape node). Note that when you turn on shape node visibility, the shape node has the NURBS icon, and the transform node that before was represented by the NURBS surface icon acquires the generic transform icon to show you what type of node it is.

Note that when you select the transform node nurbsSphere1, the Channel Box lists the transform node, the shape node, and the history node makeNurbSphere1, while when you select the shape node you only see it and the history node. The Channel Box generally displays related transform and history nodes for easy access to their keyable attributes.

Using the Duplicate command, we can create an instance of the sphere:

1. Select nurbsSphere1 in the outliner if it is not already selected.
2. Choose Edit > Duplicate > ❑.
3. In the Duplicate window, select the Instance button under Geometry Type.
4. Click Apply.
5. Make sure to select Copy under Geometry Type, and then close the window.

Figure 1.15 The nurbsSphere1 transform node and its shape node on Outliner.

Note: If you do not select Copy before closing the window, then all duplicates you make from now on will be instances until you change this setting back again!

At this point, if you look in the Outliner, you will see a second sphere object, nurbsSphere2. So far, so good. Now, expand it by clicking on the [+]. Instead of having its own shape node, the newly instanced sphere shares its shape node with nurbsSphere1 (Figure 1.16). By making one shape node with two transform nodes as parents, Maya allows the same geometry, in essence, to be in two places at once, because the transform node determines an object's location and the shape node defines what it is.

To see what this means in practical terms, move one of your spheres away from the origin and pull some points around:

1. Select nurbsSphere2 in the Outliner and choose the Move tool.
2. Drag one of the arrows to move the sphere away from nurbsSphere1.
3. Click on the Select by Component Type button.
4. Click on one of the vertices of the sphere and drag it around.

You will see that both spheres change shape simultaneously in response to your editing of one sphere. If you're familiar with instancing, this is what you would expect—but if you know that instancing means that two transforms share the same shape, it's obvious why this works.

There is one more node associated with our sphere objects that is not visible in the Outliner.

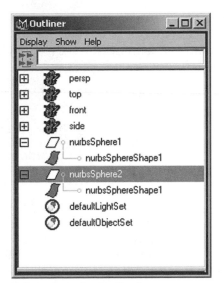

Figure 1.16 Instances of the sphere in the Outliner.

1. Select the shape object, nurbsSphereShape1, in the Outliner.
2. Choose Window > Hypergraph. . . .
3. Choose Graph > Up and Downstream Connections.

Centered in the Hypergraph window is our nurbsSphereShape1 node. To the left is the makeNurbSphere1 node, with an arrow indicating a connection. To the right is the initialShadingGroup node.

When you create an object in Maya, by default it is initially created with *history*. This means that after creation, you can animate or change the parameters (such as sweep angle or number of spans, in the case of a sphere) that were used to build the object. When you select an object and choose Edit > Delete by Type > History, you freeze the current creation parameters in place for that object so that they cannot be modified.

A node such as makeNurbSphere1 is what Maya uses to store history information. Deleting history for one or more objects deletes these history nodes and stores the creation parameters in the shape object to which they are connected. In the Hypergraph, you can select makeNurbSphere1 and examine its parameters, as follows:

1. Right-click on makeNurbSphere1, and choose Attribute Editor . . . from the menu that appears.
2. In the Attribute Editor, you can see all parameters that were used to create the sphere, and you can edit them, if you like.

3. Close the Attribute Editor window.
4. Click on `nurbsSphereShape1` to select it.
5. In the main Maya window, choose Edit > Delete By Type > History, leaving the Hypergraph window open.

In the Hypergraph window, you will notice that the `makeNurbSphere1` history node goes away.

6. Right-click on `nurbsSphereShape1`, and choose Attribute Editor. . . .

Note that the NURBS Surface History section contains the parameters you used to create the sphere, but they cannot be changed or animated.

MEL and Maya's User Interface

Maya's user interface, which includes all buttons and menus around the edge of the work area, is built using MEL. When you pick a menu item, Maya executes a MEL command specific to that menu item. Some of these MEL commands are human-readable scripts that are installed when you install Maya; others are built-in commands that come as part of Maya's executable.

To see the MEL commands being generated by the user interface, open the Script Editor by clicking the Script Editor button next to the timeline or choosing Window > General Editors > Script Editor . . . from the main menu. Choose Script > Echo All Commands from the Script Editor's menu bar. Then, start picking menu items on the main menu bar to see the MEL commands appear in the Script Editor window.

In Chapter 2, we'll look at how to capture these MEL commands that the interface generates to make simple scripts that do more than one task at a time.

What to Remember About How Maya Works Behind the Scenes

■ When you work in the Maya interface, Maya implements what you do as collections of nodes whose attributes are connected to one another to implement the behaviors you've set up in the interface. This structure is called the dependency graph.

■ One use for MEL is to automate the construction of nodes and connections in the dependency graph so that scenes that are complex to build by hand can be built easily.

■ You can use the Hypergraph as a tool to view, establish, and delete connections between nodes with the Upstream, Downstream, and Up and Downstream Connections views.

■ Geometric relationships such as parenting and grouping are implemented in the transform hierarchy.

■ Transform hierarchy relationships can be viewed in the Outliner or the Hypergraph (in the Scene Hierarchy view). These relationships are implemented as connections between attributes, but these connections are not displayed in the Connections views in the Hypergraph for the sake of clarity.

■ Objects that have a position in space are usually implemented as a transform node and a shape node. The one common exception to this is a joint, which is only one node. In the Outliner, you can view shape nodes by choosing Display > Shapes.

■ Another important function of MEL is to build Maya's user interface, including its windows, toolbar buttons, and timeline.

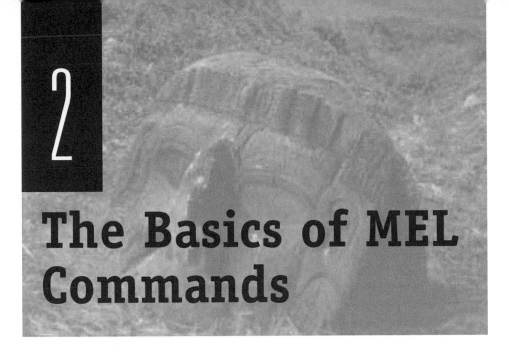

2

The Basics of MEL Commands

In this chapter you will learn

- How to run a MEL command or script and see its result.
- That Maya provides useful tools that let you capture scripts by working in the interface and then using the resulting MEL commands to build shelf buttons.
- How to read MEL commands that you capture from the interface.
- Where to find Maya and MEL information on the Internet.
- How to use MEL scripts that you've found on the Internet.

Can I Use MEL Without Scripting?

Before you sit down to write a MEL script, there are two alternatives that may greatly simplify automating your task, depending on what you are trying to do.

First, in many cases another Maya user may have already developed a script or a plug-in that does what you need. Many Maya users make such tools available on the Internet, and electronic bulletin boards can serve as a place to ask other Maya users for suggestions on how to implement your own solutions.

Second, you can log the MEL commands that correspond to your actions as you work in the interface. Reading the logged commands from the interface can save hours of hunting through the MEL reference documentation to find the particular commands that will do what you already know how to do in Maya's interface.

Resist the temptation to imagine that the commands you log can be used without alteration, though. Once you've learned MEL, you can use these logged commands as inspiration, but you may only cause yourself problems if you use the commands without learning what they do and how they work.

Some keyboards have two keys labeled Enter; others have one labeled Return on the main keyboard and one labeled Enter on the numeric keypad. In the rest of this book, when instructed to "press Enter" you should press the Return or Enter on the main keyboard only, and when instructed to "press Enter on the numeric keypad" you should press Enter on the numeric keypad only.

When you're working in the Script Editor, pressing Return or Enter on the main keyboard takes you to the next line, while pressing Enter on the numeric keypad executes either all the MEL code that's been typed into the Script Editor (if nothing is selected) or whatever MEL code is selected in the Script Editor (if you've dragged over some MEL code to highlight it).

Should you choose to execute the entire contents of the Script Editor by pressing Enter on the numeric keypad without selecting anything, if the contents of the Script Editor execute successfully *it will be deleted!* If you select one or more lines of text in the Script Editor by dragging the mouse over it, when you press Enter that text will remain in the Script Editor. Because of this behavior, many MEL programmers always execute MEL commands by selecting the commands in the Script Editor that they wish to run before pressing Enter, so that they remain in the editor after they've been executed.

Command Line and Command Feedback Line

Maya's *command line* provides a simple and immediate way to run MEL commands. Click in the command line, type a MEL command, and press Enter.

Maya's *command feedback line,* next to the command line, gives you the result from the most recent MEL command or other operation.

Try the following:

1. Choose File > New Scene (and, if you like, save your changes).
2. Click in the command line.
3. Type sphere, and press Enter.

A sphere named nurbsSphere1 should appear, and in the command feedback line you should see

```
Result: nurbsSphere1 makeNurbSphere1
```

The sphere command you just executed gives as its result a list of the nodes that it created. (We'll talk more about results, and how you'll use them in MEL scripts later.) In this command's result, nurbsSphere1 is the name of the sphere's transform node, and makeNurbSphere1 is the sphere's history node. Note that this operation also creates a shape node called `nurbsSphereShape1`, but, in keeping with Maya's practice of hiding the shape nodes from you, the result does not show you the shape node's name.

Command Shell

On Irix and Windows platforms, Maya offers a different version of the command line with which even many experienced Maya users are unfamiliar. By choosing Window > General Editors > Command Shell . . . you can open a window that offers a Maya command line, but retains a convenient history of the commands you type and their results.

1. Choose Window > General Editors > Command Shell. . . .

The command shell window appears.

2. Type `sphere`, and press Enter.

A sphere appears, along with the text indicating the name of the sphere that was created.

3. Press the up-arrow key.

Pressing the up-arrow key takes you back to earlier commands that you have typed. This can be very helpful when you have to apply the same command repeatedly or you have at some point typed a complex command that is close to what you need to type again.

4. Press Enter again.

Another sphere appears.

Script Editor

The *Script Editor* is a much more extensive interface for entering commands and editing scripts than the command shell. Within the Script Editor you can execute commands immediately or develop long scripts that can be saved or executed all at once.

The Script Editor is divided into two parts: the *status message* area on the top and the *command input* area on the bottom. You can type commands and scripts into the command input area, execute them, and see the result in the status message area.

While you work in the interface, the interface also generates MEL commands and their results for what you do. These commands and results appear in the status message area even when the Script Editor window is hidden. Usually, the last line of the status message area is the result that is displayed in the command feedback line when the Script Editor is not open.

Now we will repeat the same example that we have used above for the command line and the command shell:

1. Choose File > New Scene, and click on No to skip saving the old scene.
2. Open the Script Editor by clicking on the script editor button to the right of the command feedback line, or by using Windows > General Editors > Script Editor. . . .
3. Click in the command input area with the white background at the bottom. If you've been working through the previous examples, you should be able to see some of your earlier commands represented in the gray status message area above.
4. Type sphere, and press Enter on the numeric keypad.

Maya now creates a sphere in your scene. Your command, along with its result, appears in the status message area, as follows:

```
sphere;
// Result: nurbsSphere1 makeNurbSphere1 //
```

Note that your command is now deleted from the command input area.

Pressing Enter on the numeric keypad, or holding down Ctrl and pressing Enter or Return on the main keyboard, executes *everything* in the command input area and deletes it from that part of the window.

Often, if you're editing a script and wish to execute a command quickly, or if you have a number of commands that you would like to keep typed into the Script Editor, you may prefer that Maya not delete the commands as you execute them. If you select a command and then press Enter, it will remain in the Script Editor after it is executed. For example:

1. Type sphere.
2. Press Enter on the main keyboard.
3. Type cone.
4. Press Enter.
5. Type cylinder.
6. Press Enter.
7. Double-click on cone to select the whole word, and press Enter on the numeric keypad.

Now, a cone appears, but your commands remain. If you like, you could continue executing those commands by selecting them and pressing Enter on the numeric keypad. You can also select and execute multiple lines of text within the command input area; you're not limited to a single command.

If you find that you like to keep useful commands around in the Script Editor, be careful not to press Enter when you have nothing selected! If you do, Maya will execute everything in the window and empty out the command input area. Using the command line or the command shell for running quick commands can be much less error prone, at the expense of some convenience.

Script Editor Versus Command Shell

Many Maya users always enter MEL commands in the Script Editor rather than the command shell, whether they are writing a script or entering commands to be executed right away. Here are a few advantages to using the Script Editor over the command shell.

- You can keep a repository of useful commands in the Script Editor and execute them repeatedly, or in any order you like.
- The Script Editor allows you to copy and paste parts of commands or other text from the history in the window.
- If a command you've run from the Script Editor strikes you as useful, you can select it and then drag it to a shelf, where it will remain as a button that you can click to run the same command again.

There are also disadvantages to running commands from the Script Editor:

- As pointed out above, because the Script Editor treats the Enter key on the main keyboard differently from the Enter key on the numeric keypad, it can be easy to erase some of your work by mistake.
- If you're editing a complex script in the Script Editor, it can be easier to run one or two commands in the command shell rather than typing those commands into the Script Editor somewhere among your script's code, running them, and then deleting them again.

Script Editor's Messages as MEL Code

One convenient property of the messages that appear in the status message area of the Script Editor is that they are valid MEL commands. Furthermore, as you perform many tasks in Maya, MEL commands that are equivalent to what you do in the interface appear in the status message area. Because these are valid MEL commands, you can do something in the interface, copy a few commands from the status message area in the Script Editor, and then later on run those commands to repeat what you had done earlier.

Looking back at the first Script Editor example, where you typed sphere and pressed Enter on the numeric keypad, you received this result in the status message area:

```
sphere;
// Result: nurbsSphere1 makeNurbSphere1 //
```

Note that Maya has added a semicolon (;) to your command. In a MEL script or an expression, each command must end with a semicolon. If you type a single command into the command input area, you need not place a semicolon at the end. However, if you type more than one command at a time and want to execute them all at once, you must separate them with semicolons. (For example, to make two spheres you could type sphere; sphere and press Enter on the numeric keypad.)

Also, around the result Maya has placed double slashes (//). In a MEL script or an expression, any line that starts with double slashes is ignored. In a script, this is useful to provide notes to yourself about how your script works or how it is to be used. Programmers usually refer to these notes as "comments," and new programmers are often told to "comment their code" by peppering it with notes to remind themselves how their programs work when they return to them later.

The reason Maya presents your commands and results this way in the status message area is so that you can copy the text there into a MEL script to perform those same commands again. The semicolons allow MEL to know where one command ends and another begins, and the slashes allow MEL to know that the result lines are not instructions to Maya to do something, but instead represent information meant for you, the animator, to read.

Leaving the Script Editor open, try the following exercise in the interface.

1. Choose File > New Scene.
2. Make a sphere by choosing Create > NURBS Primitives > Sphere.
3. Click on the Move tool.
4. Move the sphere along the Z axis a few units.
5. Click on the Script Editor's title bar to bring it to the front again. (If the Script Editor window is now covered up by another Maya window, you may have to choose Raise Application Windows from the Windows menu, or you can click on the Script Editor button again to display it.)

Now, the most recent five lines or so in the Script Editor will be similar to the following lines. (Depending on exactly how far you dragged the sphere, your numbers may be slightly different, and the line that starts with sphere will probably wrap around in a different place.)

```
file -f -new;
// Result: ./untitled //
sphere -p 0 0 0 -ax 0 1 0 -ssw 0 -esw 360 -r 1 -d 3 -ut 0
-tol 0.01
-s 8 -nsp 4 -ch 1;
objectMoveCommand;
move -r 0 0 3.001753 ;
```

The lines on the previous page make up a brief MEL script that does what you just did by hand in the interface. Now, try copying those lines of MEL to repeat what you've done, as follows:

1. Select the lines.
2. Choose Edit > Copy in the Script Editor window.
3. Click in the command input area (the white area at the bottom).
4. Choose Edit > Paste in the Script Editor window.
5. Press Enter on the numeric keypad.

Maya will now create a new file, make a sphere, and move it along the Z axis, just as you had done in the interface.

Making a Shelf Button for a MEL Script

You can easily create a button that you can click to repeat a series of MEL commands. Take the following steps:

1. Select the same lines you just executed in the status message area.
2. Hold down the middle mouse button (MMB) and drag the text you've selected up to the shelf.

When the mouse gets over the shelf, it should change to an arrow with a plus (+), indicating that if you let go of the MMB it will add a button for you.

3. Let go of the middle mouse button.

Now you have a new button labeled MEL. If you move the mouse over it, you can see some of the text you dragged to the shelf on the Help Line at the bottom of the screen as a reminder of what it does. (Of course, this text may not be very illuminating, depending on the script!) Clicking on this button would now execute the commands you just dragged onto the shelf.

4. Since this script isn't very useful, use the MMB to drag the new MEL button to the trash can on the far right of the screen.

Away goes your MEL button.

Saving a MEL Script

While placing a MEL script on the shelf is often convenient, most of the time you will want to save your MEL script as a file on disk. Three reasons for this follow:

■ You can share the MEL script with other people. Since shelf buttons are hidden away in your Maya configuration, it's difficult to pass them around to fellow animators.

■ Saving your MEL scripts as files avoids cluttering up your shelf with lots of MEL buttons that you seldom use.

■ Later on, you will find that it is often convenient for one MEL script to run another MEL script. It's easy for one MEL script to run another that is in a file of its own, and difficult for a MEL script to run a script associated with a shelf button.

With the Script Editor open, try this:

1. Select the lines of MEL that create a new file, make a sphere, and move it.
2. From the Script Editor window's menus, choose File > Save Selected. . . .
3. Type `test.mel` as the file name, and click Save.

By default, Maya will save your script in the `scripts` directory under the `maya` directory in your home directory (`My Documents` when running Windows). This is a special location where Maya knows to look for script files.

To run the script, in the Script Editor type

```
source test.mel
```

and press Enter on the numeric keypad. Maya will now run your script.

Note: When working on large MEL scripts (as we'll get into later), it's often best to use an external text editor, such as Notepad or Wordpad (Windows NT), jot (Irix), or TextEdit (Macintosh) to edit and save the file outside of Maya where you can't accidentally delete your code. In later chapters, many of the examples will suggest that you develop your scripts in a separate text editor.

Seductive Dangers of the Status Message Area

It all seems so easy. Work as you normally do, open up the Script Editor, fish around for the MEL commands that Maya has cobbled together for you, and either drag them to a shelf or save them to a file. For some animators, this is all there is to MEL scripting.

Unfortunately, looking in the Status Message Area to see what MEL commands are used to perform some kinds of operations isn't always as simple as the examples we've presented so far. For example, try using Create > Locator from the Maya menus, and watch your Status Message Area for output. You probably noticed that nothing was displayed there at all—then what is the MEL command to create a locator? Rest assured, there is such a MEL command. What is happening is that Maya, in its infinite wisdom, has decided that these MEL commands aren't important to display by default. You can get Maya to display more of the MEL commands it is executing by using the menu item Edit > Show All Commands on the Script Editor window. Check this on, and try performing the

Create > Locator command again. This time, you'll see the following commands appear in the Status Message Area:

```
CreateLocator;
createPrimitive nullObject;
spaceLocator -p 0 0 0;
// Result: locator1 //
editMenuUpdate MayaWindow|mainEditMenu;
autoUpdateAttrEd;
```

If you execute these commands, you'll get not one, not two, but three locators. The reason is that numerous MEL commands print other commands that they execute internally to do their jobs. `CreateLocator`, `createPrimitive nullObject`, and `spaceLocator -p 0 0 0` are each commands that make locators, each at a lower level than the last. Also, the `editMenuUpdate` and `autoUpdateAttrEd` commands are related to updating menus in Maya's user interface and have nothing to do with creating the locator.

Unfortunately, working this way can have troubling side effects, unless you take the time to look at and think through the MEL scripts that Maya generates for you. Even though everything in the status message area is valid MEL code intended to show you what Maya is doing behind the scenes, it is not guaranteed to have the same result as what you did in the interface. In particular, when you enabled Show All Commands, Maya sometimes prints multiple commands in the Status Message Area that do the same thing.

These repeated or extraneous steps are usually related to Maya's user interface updating to reflect what you have done. For example, creating an object usually requires Maya to update the Edit menu to reflect what you may undo, and Maya puts the MEL to perform this update in the status message area. However, whenever you execute a MEL command to create an object, Maya will perform this Edit menu update anyway, so your own script need not include a command to do so.

The solution to this problem is to go step by step through the commands that Maya has printed in the Status Message Area and to determine what they are and what they do. Once you have done this, problems will become obvious.

If you have learned the basics of MEL, you will find it easier to puzzle your way through lists of commands that the Script Editor gives you. Trying each command by itself to see what it does can be a useful approach.

The whatIs Command

The whatIs command can be handy, particularly when you have questions about the commands Maya has printed in the status message area. For example, if you're curious how editMenuUpdate is defined, try typing

```
whatIs editMenuUpdate
```

in the Script Editor and pressing Enter. You will get something like the following result:

```
// Result: Mel procedure found in:
C:/AW/Maya4.0/scripts/startup/buildEditMenu.mel //
```

With the path to the file that contains the MEL script editMenuUpdate, you can hunt down what it is and how it works. Now try

```
whatIs spaceLocator
```

Your result will be

```
// Result: Command //
```

This tells you that spaceLocator is a built-in MEL command and can probably be found in the MEL Command Reference part of the Maya documentation.

Basic Structure of MEL Commands

Some commands include *arguments,* which are generally information the command needs to do its job. Usually, when a Maya command does something to an object or attribute, the object or attribute name will be an argument. For example,

```
select nurbsSphere1;
```

indicates that Maya should select nurbsSphere1 as though you'd clicked on it. In this example, select is the MEL command, and nurbsSphere1 is its argument—the object you want it to select.

Most commands have *flags* as well, which are additional instructions to the command to perform its task in a certain way. For example, one of our ways to create a locator is

```
spaceLocator -p 0 0 0;
```

The flag -p indicates that you want to provide a point in space where the locator should be created, and the numbers 0 0 0 are the X, Y, and Z locations for that point; they are the arguments for the flag. Flags do not have to have arguments, though; to get a list of all the objects that are selected, you can type

```
ls -sl
```

which tells the `ls` command (short for `list`) to list the objects in the selection (for which `-sl` is a shortened form). Usually, flags have a short and long form that mean the same thing; in this instance, it would also be correct to type

```
ls -selection
```

Many commands in MEL that are intended to make nodes have three standard flags: `-c`, `-q`, and `-e`. `-c` stands for "create" and usually tells the command to create an object. `-q` stands for "query" and usually tells the command to print out or return to your script a characteristic of the object. `-e` stands for "edit" and usually tells the command to change an existing object. In later chapters, we will look at how these flags are used in greater detail.

Where to Find Information About Maya and MEL on the Internet

There are several forums on the Internet that offer Maya users the opportunity to exchange scripts and plug-ins, discuss how to approach problems, and give each other assistance. Here are a few places to start.

As you discover what these sites have to offer, keep in mind that many such sites rely on the contributions of their readers to be most useful. If you come up with something clever or something that may benefit someone else, consider sharing the product of your effort in one of these forums.

Also, many sites like these offer community bulletin boards or discussion forums that allow people to post questions or ideas for others' response. If this is your first time participating in such forums, it can be a good idea to read the discussion for a while before contributing or asking a question. Often, such forums have a clearly defined scope of what is an appropriate topic for discussion, and reading for a while before asking a question can give you a sense of what you can expect to learn from a given forum.

Web Sites

www.melscripting.com
At melscripting.com you can find the scripts and scene files from this book, as well as errata and other updates.

forums.melscripting.com
The melscripting.com forums offer a place on the web to share MEL scripts and expressions, seek help from experts around the world on Maya development, and assist others with their projects.

www.highend3d.com/maya/
Highend3D is far and away the most comprehensive Web site for Maya
users. It also includes valuable information for users of Softimage,
Softimage XSI, Alias Studio, and the Renderman and Jig renderers. Also, at
Highend2D, *www.highend2d.com,* you can find similar resources for Shake
and Combustion users.

In the Maya section of Highend3D are hundreds of MEL scripts, plug-
ins, Maya tutorials, discussion forums, sign-up information for mailing
lists, mailing list archives, and other resources. Much of the serious Internet
discussion of Maya has shifted to Highend3D.

www.cgtalk.com
This is a broad-based web forum that specializes in helping students
improve their 2D and 3D computer graphics skills. Many applications have
discussion forums on the cgtalk.com website, and Maya's is among the
most popular.

www.aliaswavefront.com
This site is Alias|Wavefront's official Web site. In addition to information
on Alias|Wavefront's sales and technical support, this site includes useful
articles that can help you learn Maya, discussion forums, information on
user groups, and other information.

Newsgroups

comp.graphics.apps.alias
You can read USENET newsgroups, such as *comp.graphics.apps.alias,* with
Netscape, Outlook Express, or any of a number of other news readers. As of
this writing, there are no Maya-specific newsgroups, but *comp.graphics.
apps.alias* mostly features Maya discussions.

How to Use MEL Scripts Found on the Internet

Usually, once you've downloaded a MEL script, you will have a file whose
name ends with a .mel extension. To start with, look in your home directory for a directory called maya. (In Windows, look for a folder called My
Documents, and a directory called maya underneath that.) Inside the maya
directory is a directory called scripts. Place your script inside this folder.

Scripts can be installed other places, and the list of those places is
known as Maya's *script path*. For more on script paths, see Chapter 15.

If there's no documentation with your new MEL script to tell you how
to use it, try opening the MEL file itself in a text editor. Often, programmers will place a description of how to use a script at the top of the script

itself. If neither of these approaches yields anything useful, try simply typing the name of the MEL file (without .mel) in the Script Editor and typing Enter. Maya will often find the script and execute it on its own when you do this.

Finally, if none of the above works, you may have to type (assuming your file is called blah.mel)

```
source blah.mel
```

This will execute whatever MEL commands are in the .mel file that you have downloaded.

As you should with all software you download from the Internet, consider the trustworthiness of the source before blindly executing MEL scripts. A MEL script could alter your operating environment, change your open scenes, alter scenes on disk in undesirable ways, and more, either intentionally or unintentionally.

What to Remember About How to Use MEL Without Writing Scripts

- If you want to see what commands you've executed or learn whether your commands are generating errors, look in the Status Message Area of the Script Editor window.
- The Script Editor and the command line provide convenient places to try commands before you put them in your MEL scripts.
- Using Show All Commands will tell you the MEL commands that correspond to what you are doing in the Maya user interface by hand, but you should read and understand the generated commands before using them in your own scripts.
- MEL commands are made up of a command name, flags, and arguments, all of which together specify what the command is to do. The command name (generally) specifies what the command is to do; the arguments specify to what the command should do it, and the flags and their arguments specify how it should be done.
- You can install script files downloaded from the Internet in your own Maya scripts directory, or in other directories that may be listed in the Maya script path.

3

Using Expressions

In this chapter you will learn

- How to create an expression.
- How expressions work.
- When to use an expression.
- How to use expressions to create relationships between attributes.
- Techniques of scaling and offsetting numerical attributes with expressions.
- Using a custom attribute to control the behavior of other attributes.

What Is an Expression?

In Maya, an expression is a script that calculates values for one or more attributes in your scene. There are two types of expressions: *particle expressions,* which control per-particle attributes in a particle object, and *object attribute expressions*, which control per-object attributes.

Although on the surface these two kinds of expressions look quite similar, they are created and used very differently. In this chapter, we focus on object attribute expressions, which are most commonly used to set up animation controls (although they have many other uses). In Chapter 4, we discuss particle expressions, which are necessary only when creating particle-based effects.

Let's create a simple object attribute expression:

1. Open Maya.
2. Create a sphere by choosing Create > NURBS Primitives > Sphere.
3. In the Channel Box on the right side of the screen, click once in the Translate X field to select its value of 0.

4. From the Channels menu, choose Expressions. . . .
5. Now you'll see Maya's Expression Editor. The Expression Editor is a tool that lets you edit the expressions that drive the attributes of a given object.
6. In the large text field near the bottom of the Expression Editor labeled Expression:, type

```
nurbsSphere1.translateX = time;
```

7. Click the Create button at the bottom of the editor.
8. Finally, close the Expression Editor by clicking the Close button.

Now, rewind the animation, and click the play button next to the timeline. You'll see your new sphere traveling along the X axis at a rate of one unit in X each second.

How Does an Expression Work?

Let's look at the expression we have created to animate the sphere:

```
nurbsSphere1.translateX = time;
```

As in the scripts discussed in Chapter 2, expressions consist of a series of instructions for Maya to perform different tasks. Each instruction, called a *statement,* ends with a semicolon (;) character. In the case of an expression, as opposed to other MEL scripts, the statements must ultimately result in assigning new values to one or more attributes.

The above expression contains only one statement, which most programmers would read aloud as "nurbs-sphere-one dot translate-x equals time," which is the way an algebra student might read it. However, an equals sign in computer programming does not mean the same thing as an equals sign in arithmetic or algebra. In this instance, the expression takes the value of the current time on the timeline, in seconds, and changes the nurbsSphere1.translateX attribute to match that value. This makes the sphere move along its local X axis.

Equals Sign: Equality and Assignment

An expression exists, ultimately, to assign values to attributes, which one does with the equals sign (=). In arithmetic and algebra, the equals sign is used to represent mathematical equality. When algebra students write "X = 4," they mean that they have decided that the symbol X represents the number 4 throughout the entire computation, and can't ever change.

In a programming language such as Maya's expression language or MEL, though, variables such as object attribute names in an expression are not names for unchangeable values the way they are in algebra. Instead, they serve as containers for values that the programmer can change repeatedly as the script or program executes.

In our example expression, then, the equals sign is used to represent an operation called *assignment,* where a value is calculated from one variable (on the right-hand side of the equals sign) and placed into another (on the left-hand side of the equals sign), replacing whatever may already be stored there. The expression finds the value of the expression node's "time" attribute, which Maya connects by default to the current time on the timeline, measured in seconds. Then, it assigns that value to the variable whose name is on the left-hand side, in this case the attribute called `nurbsSphere1.translateX`.

What can go on the right-hand side of an assignment and what can go on the left-hand side are very different. For example, in an expression it would be acceptable to write

```
nurbsSphere1.translateX = 4;
```

but it would be a mistake to write

```
4 = nurbsSphere1.translateX;
```

because the idea of an assignment is to change the value of a container on the left-hand side to match the value of the right-hand side, and the value 4 is not a container whose value can change.

The equals sign can also be used in what a programmer calls a test or a conditional. In a conditional, a program compares two values to determine whether they are equal or have some other relationship, and optionally, may do something based on the result. Although some programming languages (such as BASIC) use the same equals sign to represent conditional tests and assignment, in Maya expressions and in MEL, the test to see whether two values are the same is written with two equals signs (==) to ensure that you don't confuse the conditional with an instruction that Maya should assign a value to a variable.

An example of a conditional test of equality in MEL is

```
if (3 == 4) print "Hello!";
```

In this instance, Maya checks to see whether 3 and 4 are the same (and of course they are not), and if they were it would output the text `Hello!` to the status line. Since they are not the same, this MEL command does nothing. If the conditional is changed to read `if (4 == 4)`, then this command would print the text `Hello!` There are, of course, other kinds of conditionals to test whether numbers are greater than each other, less than each other, and so on.

All of these uses for the = symbol can be employed in expressions and MEL scripts, but since expressions exist to assign values to attributes, every expression must have at least one assignment.

How Maya Implements Expressions

Once you've worked through the expression example, note that the nurbsSphere1.translateX attribute in the Channel Box has now changed color. The new color for the attribute is the same color that the attribute would turn if you were to set a keyframe, as we did in our animated sphere example in Chapter 1. This color, which can vary depending on your user interface settings, indicates that another node, in this case an expression node, is connected to that attribute.

Internally, Maya represents expressions very similarly to the animation curves that you create when setting keys: each is a node that knows how to create a value for an attribute from other information about the state of the scene, such as the current time on the timeline (in the case of an animation curve or our example expression) or the value of another attribute (if you'd created an expression that calculated one attribute from another's value).

Making sure that the animated sphere is still selected, try opening the Hypergraph and looking at the sphere's up and downstream connections.

As seen in Figure 3.1, the Hypergraph reveals a new node to which the sphere is connected, called expression1. This node contains the expression we've just created, and the connections shown in the Hypergraph reflect that it is taking information about the scene's time on the timeline (which is maintained by the time1 node, automatically created by Maya when you make a new scene) and placing it into attributes of the nurbsSphere1 transform node. If your default units are not set to centimeters in your prefer-

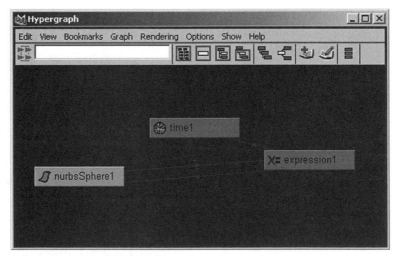

Figure 3.1 An expression node.

ences, there will also be a unit conversion node between the expression and the sphere.

When you create an expression, Maya examines the expression that you have typed to determine how your new expression node needs to be connected to other nodes in the scene to do its job. If you were to type an expression that required Maya to connect the new node to an attribute that could not be animated, such as a locked attribute, you would get an error when you tried to create the expression. In this sense, connections between expressions and other nodes follow the same rules as all other connections in Maya.

Is Maya's Expression Language the Same as MEL?

Although they are substantially the same, Maya's expression language and MEL are not identical. The most significant difference is that Maya's expression language permits you to get the value of an object's attribute just by putting the attribute's name on the right-hand side of an assignment, and it permits you to set the value of an attribute just by putting the attribute's name on the left-hand side of an assignment. In MEL, as opposed to the expression language, you must use the command `getAttr` to fetch the value of an attribute and assign it to a variable, and you must use `setAttr` to assign a value to an attribute. How to use these commands is discussed in Chapter 5, but for the moment it's enough to know that they are a way to get and set the value of object attributes from within a MEL script without using an = assignment.

Maya's expression language and MEL are often confused because they are nearly, but not quite, the same. It's possible to put any valid MEL command into an expression, but since most MEL commands change the scene graph, and because expressions execute when Maya is calculating the state of the existing scene graph, it can be very easy to create expressions that run slowly or produce bizarre results by trying to create or delete nodes, or by getting or setting attributes using getAttr or setAttr rather than the built-in shortcut of just using the name in an assignment.

In the expression example above, note that creating the expression made an expression node that was connected in the scene graph to the attribute the expression was changing. Maya only knows to do this when you get and set attributes by assigning them directly rather than by using `getAttr` and `setAttr`. In fact, Maya's setting up such connections helps your scene evaluate faster because Maya can figure out when it is not necessary to run your expression to evaluate the scene.

As a result, while you must use `getAttr` and `setAttr` to access attribute values in MEL, in expressions it is best to avoid them unless you have no other choice. MEL does allow assignments, for which you use the equals sign as in expressions, but only variables (containers for values whose names, in MEL, begin with $) can be used on the left-hand side of assignments, not attributes.

When (and When Not) to Use an Expression

Using expressions is one of a few ways Maya allows you to drive the value of one attribute with the values of one or more other attributes. Here are some advantages of expressions over other techniques:

■ Expressions are best when you need an arbitrarily complex mathematical relationship between the attribute that the expression drives and the driving attribute. For example, you could use an expression to calculate an object's X position based on the cube root of the object's Y position.

■ Expressions allow relationships between attributes that can change over time or are decided differently depending on the object's environment. For example, an expression could use one rule to set an object's color when the object's Y position is negative, and a different rule when it is zero or positive.

■ Expressions, like all MEL scripts, permit you to add comments to clarify your intent as you develop them.

However, they also have disadvantages:

■ Expressions can be difficult to read and understand by people who didn't write them (and even, sometimes, by people who did). Also, how a scene with many expressions works can be difficult to figure out if the expressions rely on each other's behavior to do their work.

■ Compared to other alternative ways of getting to the same result, expressions are usually slow.

If you want to use one attribute to control several others, using *driven keys* can be a viable alternative, and it will be much faster.

If you are trying to establish a spatial relationship between one object and another, consider whether you can achieve your result by using *constraints*. Sometimes combinations of constraints can achieve a much more complex result than a single constraint alone.

If you simply wish to link two attributes' values together, rather than create an expression that assigns one attribute to another, open the Connection Editor and connect the attributes. (However, if you want to drive an attribute that must be an integer number with a floating-point attribute, an expression will enable you to do so, while the Connection Editor will not.)

Finally, if you're making a simple expression that, for example, adds or multiplies a couple of attributes, consider using a *utility* node instead of an expression. Utility nodes can be much faster and achieve the same result. You can create utility nodes in the Hypershade Editor.

Defining Relationships Between Attributes

The first step to using an expression to build a relationship between two attributes is to find a way to represent the relationship mathematically. Maya permits all kinds of mathematical relationships in expressions, but two of the most common (and simplest) are *scaling* and *offsetting* one attribute to create the value for another.

For example, suppose you wish to create a sphere with an attribute called revolutions. When the revolutions attribute is animated from 0 to 1, the sphere rotates through one full rotation around the Y axis.

Since the typical way to rotate a sphere through a full rotation around the Y axis is to animate the sphere's rotateY attribute from 0 to 360, the revolutions attribute needs to be multiplied, or scaled, by 360. Then, the rotateY attribute needs to be set to this value. In an expression, this relationship would be written as

```
mysphere.rotateY = mysphere.revolutions * 360;
```

(Note that multiplication is represented by the * symbol.)

To see how this scaling works in practice, take the following steps:

1. Make a new Maya scene.
2. Create a new NURBS sphere using Create > NURBS Primitives > Sphere.
3. Rename the sphere to mysphere.
4. With the sphere selected, open the Attribute Editor using Window > Attribute Editor.
5. Choose Attributes > Add Attributes . . . from the Attribute Editor window's menus.
6. Type revolutions in the location for the attribute's name; make sure the chosen data type is float, and click OK.

Now, in the Channel Box, you should see a new attribute for mysphere called revolutions.

7. Click once in the Rotate Y attribute in the Channel Box to select it.
8. Open the Expression Editor by choosing Expressions . . . from the Channels menu in the Channel Box.
9. Type the following expression into the Expression Editor:

```
mysphere.rotateY = mysphere.revolutions * 360;
```

10. Click the Create button; then click Close to close the Expression Editor.

Now, try typing some numbers into the Revolutions field in the Channel Box. If you type 0..5 and press Enter, you'll see that the Rotate Y attribute changes to 180. If you type 1, Rotate Y will become 360.

Scaling an attribute to find a value for another is useful when you want the value of your controlling attribute to have a meaning that's different from the attribute that it controls. In this case, by setting one keyframe for the revolutions attribute at zero and another at 25, you could animate a sphere through 25 rotations. Keying the Rotate Y attribute directly to animate 25 rotations would require setting one key at zero and another at 9000, which is far less intuitive.

Instead of multiplying, you can scale an attribute by dividing by a constant as well. Instead of the * symbol, use / for division.

Another technique for relating one attribute to another is *offsetting* the controlling attribute, or adding or subtracting a constant value. For example, suppose that you want to have two spheres called mysphere and mysphere2, with the rotation around Y of mysphere2 lagging behind the rotation of mysphere1 by 45 degrees. The expression to relate the two would be

```
mysphere2.rotateY = mysphere.rotateY - 45;
```

Of course, you can combine scaling and offsetting to produce a more complex result:

```
mysphere2.rotateY = (mysphere.revolutions * 360) - 45;
```

Try using steps similar to the first example to experiment with some of these combinations.

What Is Operator Precedence?

Because mathematical expressions can be ambiguous, Maya follows a set of *operator precedence* rules to determine the order in which math operations happen.

Here's an example of this ambiguity: if you write out the expression 2 + 3 * 4, you might imagine that Maya could evaluate the expression from left to right, first computing 2 + 3 (which is 5) and then multiplying that result by 4 to get 20.

However, if you open the Script Editor in Maya and type

```
print (2 + 3 * 4);
```

and then press Enter on the numeric keypad, you'll see that the value it prints is 14. What Maya is doing is evaluating the multiplication operation first, and then addition, because multiplication has priority over addition. Thus, Maya first computes 3 * 4 (to get 12), and then adds 2 to get 14.

You can force addition to happen first by putting it in parentheses. The following print statement, for example, will print the value 20:

```
print ((2 + 3) * 4);
```

The extra set of parentheses around 2 + 3 indicates that Maya should execute the enclosed operations first.

Listed below are many of the mathematical operators in Maya, ranked from highest precedence to lowest. If two operators are on the same line in this list, they're executed in the order they appear, from left to right. Otherwise, the operators that are higher on the list get executed first.

```
( ) [ ]
! ++ —
* / % ^
+ −
< <= > >=
== !=
&&
? :
− += −= *= /=
```

When in doubt, you can always force a particular order of operations with parentheses.

Walkthrough of Maya's Expression Language

Once you have defined a relationship between attributes that you want to use an expression to establish, you need to represent that relationship in Maya's expression language. The examples presented thus far include only the most rudimentary scripts, but expression scripts can be far more complex.

Almost all techniques that you will learn by programming in Maya's expression language can be used in MEL scripts as well, and most of these ideas are covered in more depth in later chapters. This walkthrough will present those features of the language that are most useful in expressions, but you should keep in mind that just about any feature of MEL can be used in an expression.

A well-organized expression script consists of three parts:

- Definitions of *variables* (containers for intermediate results in the script).
- Computation of attribute values.
- Assignments of values to the attributes that the expression has computed.

In the first part of an expression script, we define *variables*, or containers for intermediate results that we'll compute along the way to the attribute values that we want our expression to set. The real work is done in the second part of an expression script. In the computation section, an expression uses attribute values and variables' contents to calculate the values of attributes we want the expression to control.

Finally, these values are assigned to the attributes in the third part. Many expressions may dispense with one of these parts or condense two or all three into one, but by thinking of expressions in terms of this structure, it can be easier to figure out where to begin. Here is an example expression:

```
float $xval = time;
float $yval;

$yval = sin($xval);

translateX = $xval;
translateY = $yval;
```

In the next three sections, we examine how the parts of this expression work together.

Definitions of Variables

The first part of a typical expression script is a list of *variable definitions*. Variables are containers for the information that a script has to store along the way while it is working toward its result. Each variable has a unique name as well as a type of information that it can store (e.g., an integer number, floating-point value, or string of characters). Defining them makes Maya aware that it will, further into your script, need to have a place to store the variable's value, and to declare what kind of information will be stored in it.

In many languages, including Maya's expression language and MEL, you can create variables on the fly, as you need them in your script. Some other languages require that you define all of your variable names at the beginning of the script.

While Maya does not require you to define all of the variables up front, it is a good idea to do so anyway. Defining variables at the beginning of your script makes hunting down a variable definition easier, and this helps you organize how you're storing intermediate results in your script by making it easier to keep your names for variables consistent.

In a Maya expression language or MEL script, defining a variable is simply a matter of putting a data type and variable name on a line by itself. Variable names are made up of a dollar sign ($) followed by a combination of letters, numbers, and underscores. The use of the $ prefix to denote variables is common in many programming languages and helps to ensure that the variable is not confused with the name of a command (or in the case of Maya expressions, an attribute).

For example, to define a variable called $rotation_value that holds a floating-point number, you would add the following line to your script:

```
float $rotation_value;
```

Note that the dollar sign ($) is mandatory in variable names. Also, like all statements in a script, this one ends with a semicolon.

To assign a value to your new variable, you use the equals sign (=) just as we did in our expression examples above:

```
$rotation_value = 4.0;
```

Now, to use `$rotation_value` in a computation, just place it into a mathematical expression, such as

```
$rotation_value = $rotation_value * 2;
```

Remember that the equals sign does not mean what it does in algebra, but instead is an instruction to assign the value on the right to the container on the left. So, if `$rotation_value` started out at a value of 4.0, after executing that statement it would be multiplied by two (yielding 8.0,) and its value would be assigned back to the `$rotation_value` variable. With this statement, all we have done is double the value in `$rotation_value`.

Variables may also contain integer numbers, or numbers with no fractional part, such as 1, 2, 3, and so on. When you need to count something in your script, it is usually better to use an integer variable than a float variable, because you'll often be using the value of your counter in ways for which only integers are suitable. Define an integer (`int`) variable like this as follows:

```
int $number_of_spheres;
```

If you like, you can assign a value to a variable at the time you define it. Usually, this is a good idea; you can either assign it whatever would be its natural starting value (i.e., zero, if you're counting something) or you can assign it a value that is clearly nonsense (e.g., –9999) so that when your script is running, you have an easy way to check whether you're trying to use the variable before you've put something useful into it. To assign a variable at the time you define it, just do this:

```
int $num_oranges = 4;
```

In addition to float and int variables, there are also *string* variables, which contain a series of characters strung together (hence the name). Also, there are *vector* variables, which will be discussed in much more detail in Chapter 4.

To assign a value to a string variable, just put the value of the variable in double quotes:

```
string $my_name = "Mark Wilkins";
```

Strings are useful in that you can print them out to the status line, execute them as commands, and concatenate them together to make larger strings. To concatenate strings (which adds them end to end in the order you specify), you use the plus sign (+). Note that Maya remembers the types of your variables, and that operators such as (+) behave differently when operating on strings (by concatenating them) versus integers or floats (which are

added together). For example, the following script has the same result as
the one-liner above:

```
string $first_name = "Mark"
string $last_name = "Wilkins"
string $my_name = $first_name + " " + $last_name;
```

Note that the space between the two names has to be added explicitly, as
space counts as its own character. If the script had just added $first_name
+ $last_name, the result would have been MarkWilkins.

You can add a line break to a string by placing the characters \n into the
string definition. Thus, if you assign the string "testing \n 1 2 3" to a
variable and then print it, you'll see

```
Testing
1 2 3
```

in the Status Message Area.

Maya gets touchy (as do most programming languages) when you
define a variable as one type and then try to redefine it later as another.
Maya prevents you from doing so, and your script quits with an error if
you try.

In all of our expression examples to control the sphere we had created
above, we never needed to place a $ in front of our attribute names. In
expressions, the $ helps Maya distinguish between variables (which have a
$ at the beginning of their names) and object attributes (which do not).

The final detail to remember about variables is that each variable has a
scope, or a limit placed on what part of your script can see and use the variable you've defined. In the examples we are looking at now, a variable
defined in one script can be used anywhere within that script, but will not
be available to a different script. In Chapter 10, we discuss a language feature called *procedures* that lets you break your script up into smaller, easier-
to-comprehend chunks. Procedures generally cannot share each other's
variables either, although it is also possible to explicitly make variables
global so that all scripts and procedures anywhere inside of Maya can see
them.

In our example expression script, the lines

```
float $xval = time;
float $yval;
```

make up the variable definition part. In this script, we're creating containers for two numbers, named $xval and $yval. $xval will start out with the
current time on the timeline, measured in seconds. (Note that the timeline,
by default, displays the current frame number. At 24 frames per second,
that number divided by 24 is the value of time.)

Strictly speaking, time is neither a variable nor a MEL command. In fact,
it's a predefined attribute of the expression node that is created when you

add this expression to an object, and it's connected by default to the `time1` node that is created in every new scene.

Computing the Values of Attributes

Part two of our example script consists of the calculations necessary to find the values of attributes that we want our expression to control:

```
$yval = sin($xval);
```

Since `$xval` already contains the value that we want to set for the node's `translateX` attribute, we only have to calculate `$yval`. So, in this case, we calculate the sine of the value of `$xval` and assign it to `$yval`. Thus, as `$xval` increases, `$yval` will move back and forth between 1 and −1.

To find a comprehensive list of operations useful for calculating attribute values, look at the section in *Using Maya: Expressions* called "Arithmetic, Logic, and Relational Operators." Also, the "Functions" section contains many useful operations, including sine.

Assigning Computed Values

Finally, once the values of the attributes that our expression controls have been calculated, we need to set the attributes' values. This is the one task that is handled differently in expressions than it is in other MEL scripts. In an expression script, one sets the value of an attribute just by assigning the value to the name of the attribute:

```
translateX = $xval;
translateY = $yval;
```

In MEL scripts that are not expressions, you can't assign values to attributes this way. Instead, you would use a command called `setAttr`, for Set Attribute. Setting attributes in a MEL script might look like this:

```
setAttr nurbsSphere1.translateX $xval;
sctAttr nurbsSphere1.translateY $yval;
```

Also, in a nonexpression MEL script, you cannot just assign the value of an attribute to a variable, as we did in our example (where we assigned time to `$xval`). Instead, if you are writing a MEL script that is not an expression, you must use the command `getAttr` to get the value of an attribute:

```
$xval = `getAttr expression1.time`;
```

Note that when a MEL command is designed to come back with a value, in this case the value of the attribute `expression1.time`, you need to put the command in backquotes (`` ` ``) and put the quoted command on the right-hand side of an assignment. By doing this, you store the value that the command returns to your script in whatever variable is on the left-hand side of the assignment.

Although Maya will let you use `getAttr` and `setAttr` in your expression scripts, your scene will play back faster if you directly read and assign attributes whenever possible. It's best to save the `getAttr` and `setAttr` commands for nonexpression MEL scripts that don't let you directly assign or read the values of attributes.

Example 1: Eyes

Normally, a person's pupils will dilate and constrict together, and both eyes will orient themselves toward the object of a person's attention. When, in real life, a person's pupils constrict or dilate without regard to each other, or a person's eyes wander independently, it is usually a sign of a neurological disorder. Viewers bring these same expectations to characters, but in animation an occasional violation of these rules can provoke a laugh or help communicate a character's inner monologue.

If all you want is to point a character's eyes at the object of his or her attention, creating a locator for what the character is looking at and using an aim constraint on each eye does the job nicely without using any expressions. However, applying expressions in a slightly more complex setup can greatly ease the tasks of the animator in certain circumstances. Here is one such approach.

■ Two locators could be constrained to two target objects, and a custom attribute could indicate which locator the character looks at. To look back and forth between the target objects, just animate the attribute.

■ Another attribute could indicate whether a character's eyes can move in an uncoordinated way. If this attribute is 0, both eyes would move together in the way we expect. If it's not zero, they could move independently.

■ Another custom attribute could permit each pupil to dilate and constrict independently of the other if it's set to a nonzero value; otherwise, the two pupils' behavior would be linked.

In this example, we look at how to set up a pair of eyes that can look back and forth between two different objects. To figure out how to approach a character setup application involving expressions, as with any scripting application, it's a good idea to think through how you might animate the behavior by hand, make a list of the attributes and objects you will need to create to automate that behavior, and finally write an expression only after completing your analysis. For this problem, we will take that approach.

Analyzing the Problem

First, let's look at how to achieve as much as we can without expressions at all. Then, we can determine how much of the problem would benefit from using expressions, and, if necessary, either apply expressions to what we have built or start over using what we have learned.

Each eye, at its simplest, is a sphere, aimed at whatever target object we want the eye to look at. Maya's aim constraints allow you to establish multiple target objects, each with a *weight,* an attribute with values between 0 and 1 that establish how much influence each object has over the aiming of the constrained object. So, to animate a pair of eyes looking between objects, you might start by setting up two target objects for each eye's aim constraint and animating their weights.

1. Create a sphere by choosing Create > NURBS Primitives > Sphere.
2. With the sphere selected, click in the `translateX` Channel Box and type –3 to move the sphere to three units in the negative X direction.
3. Create another sphere and set its `translateX` to 3.
4. Now that you have two spheres to serve as eyes, create a locator at which the eyes should point, using the Create > Locator menu item.
5. Rename the locator `target1`, and set its `translateY` to 10.
6. Shift-click on the first sphere you created to select it while leaving the locator selected.
7. Make sure that you're looking at the Animation menu set;then choose Constrain > Aim ❒ to open the Aim option box.
8. Set the three values of the Aim vector to 0, 1, and 0, respectively.
9. Click Add/Remove to add the constraint.

At this point, your first sphere should point at the locator. Move the locator around to make sure that you're getting the behavior you would expect.

10. Now, select the locator and then shift-click on the other sphere to select it. Choose Constrain > Aim to use the same aim settings that you used for the first sphere.

Again, move the locator around to make sure you're getting the result you expect. At this point, both eyes should point at the locator. To help you see the sphere's rotations while you're moving the locator, you may wish to display the scene in wireframe mode (Figure 3.2), or use the Shading > Shade Options > Wireframe on shaded view option.

Now we'll create a second locator and add it as a new target object for each of the spheres.

1. Create a new locator using Create > Locator.
2. Give the locator the name `target2`.

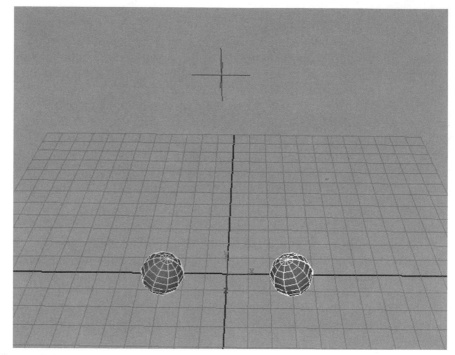

Figure 3.2 Eyes constrained to aim at a locator.

3. Select `target2` and the first sphere, and then choose Constrain > Aim.
4. Now, select `target2` and the second sphere, and choose Constrain > Aim again.

Move both locators around a little bit. Now, it appears that both eyes are responding to an average of the positions of both locators (Figure 3.3).

5. To see why this is the case, pick the first sphere, and open up the Attribute Editor; then choose the tab at the top labeled `nurbsSphere1_ aimConstraint1`. Open the Extra Attributes tab at the bottom.

Here you'll see two attributes labeled `Target1 W0` and `Target2 W1`. Each of these is the relative degree of influence of each locator over the direction that the eyeball is aimed.

6. Set the `Target2 W1` weight to 0; then press Enter or click in another box to make the change take hold.
7. Leaving the Attribute Editor window open, click on the other sphere. The Attribute Editor should show you the attributes for `nurbsSphere2_ aimConstraint1`. Change its `Target2 W1` attribute to 0 as well.
8. Now that you've set the `Target2` weights to 0, close the Attribute Editor, and move both locators around to see what you've done.

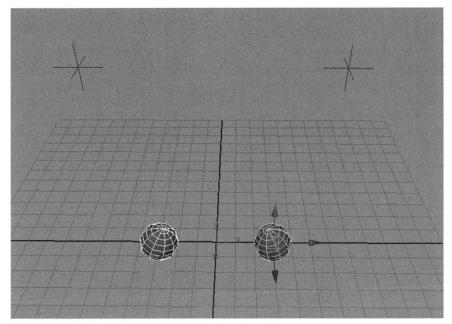

Figure 3.3 Eyes aimed at the average of two locations.

When you move the target1 locator around, the eyes will follow. Moving target2 around does nothing because its weights are set to 0 for both eyes. (Be sure to keep this scene open or save it, as you will need it when we add expressions to the eyes.)

Now that you've gotten this far, by manipulating the weights you can achieve the following results:

- By setting both target1 weights to 1 and both target2 weights to 0, you can make both eyes look at target1.
- By animating the weights of target1 and target2 in sync for both eyes, you can make the eyes look back and forth between the target locators.
- By setting the weights of target1 and target2 independently for each eye, you could make each eye follow its own locator.

As you can imagine, animating the target weights to get the result you want may not be simple, because making a smooth transition from looking between objects to uncoordinated eye movement and back again might be tricky.

Let's add a parent locator to the eyes. This gives us an easy way to move both eyes in space, plus it provides us with a convenient node to which we can add controls that will control both eyes' movement:

1. Create a new locator using Create > Locator and name it eyes.
2. Select the first sphere, then the eyes locator, and choose Edit > Parent.
3. Do the same with the second sphere.

Now, try moving the eyes locator around. Both eyeballs still point at target1, but since the eyes locator is their parent, they move with it.

Planning the Eyes' Animation Controls

At this point, we should make a list of what controls we'd like to have for our eyes.

■ First, we'll make an attribute on the eyes locator called target. When target is 1, both eyes will point at target1, and when target is 2, both eyes will point at target2.
■ Second, we'll make an attribute on the eyes locator called coordination. When coordination is 0, each eye will point at its own locator, without regard to the setting of the target attribute, and when it's set to 1, both eyes will point at the same locator, determined by the target attribute.

One way to get started working out how to implement two controls like this is to plan out what result we'd like with the controls set at different extremes.

■ If eyes.target is 1 and eyes.coordination is 1, we want the target weights fortarget1 to be 1 for both spheres and for target2 to be 0 for both spheres. (In this case, both spheres will "look" at target1.)
■ If eyes.target is 2 and eyes.coordination is 1, we want the target weights for target1 to be 0 for both spheres and the target weights for target2 to be 1 for both spheres.
■ If eyes.target is between 1 and 2 and eyes.coordination is 1, we want the target weights for target1 and target2 to be between 0 and 1 for both spheres so that they tend to point at target1 if the value is near 1 and at target2 if the value is 2. (Thus, animating between 1 and 2 and back again will make the eyes look back and forth.)
■ If eyes.coordination is 0, we want the first sphere to look at target1 and the second sphere to look at target2.
■ If eyes.coordination is between 0 and 1, we'd like to have a state that's intermediate between each eye being fully independent and both eyes following the target.

Writing the Expression

Let's start by figuring out how to control both eyes based on a target variable, assuming that coordination is always 1, meaning the eyes always move together. First, we'll just walk through snippets of code that will make up our expression—don't bother to type these into the Script Editor or Expression Editor window, as they're just intended to illustrate how the parts of our expression work.

First, we'll need variables that will contain our desired weights for each sphere and each target:

```
float $eye1_coord_target1_weight;
float $eye1_coord_target2_weight;
float $eye2_coord_target1_weight;
float $eye2_coord_target2_weight;
```

Although long variable names like this can seem cumbersome, naming variables in such a way that you can remember what they mean goes a long way toward helping others understand your expression. It will also help you to understand your own expressions when you have to revisit them a few months (or even a few days) later. Generally, programming to save typing is a bad idea.

Since a weight of 0 means that a target has no influence and a weight of 1 means that our target has full influence, our weight for target2 for both eyes should be equal to eyes.target − 1. That way, when eyes.target is 2, the target weight for target2 will be 1, and when eyes.target is 1, the target weight for target2 will be 0.

Writing this as a couple of variable assignments, we get the following code. Remember that lines that begin with // are *comments*, explanatory text that exists solely to make your script more readable. You can alter, shorten, or delete these comments when you're experimenting with this expression right now, but keep in mind that such comments are tremendously useful in remembering what you intended when you return months later to code which you have forgotten you wrote.

```
// Drive the target2 weights from the eyes.target attribute
// such that we're fully weighted for target2 when eyes.target
// is equal to 2, and target2's weight is 0 when eyes.target
// is equal to 1

$eye1_coord_target2_weight = eyes.target - 1;
$eye2_coord_target2_weight = eyes.target - 1;
```

The weights for target1 now should be equal to 1 minus the weight of target2. The reason for this is that when target2's weight is 0, we want the eyes to look at target1 only, and when target2's weight is 1, we want the eyes to look at target2 only. When both weights are 0.5, the eyes will look halfway between both locators.

```
// Drive target1's weights by the inverse of target2's weights

$eye1_coord_target1_weight = 1 - $eye1_coord_target2_weight;
$eye2_coord_target1_weight = 1 - $eye2_coord_target2_weight;
```

Converting a value that varies from 0 to 1 into its opposite counterpart from 1 to 0 using the mathematical formula, 1 − value, is called an *inversion*. You'll find that you use this type of formula quite a bit when writing expressions.

Usually, it's a good idea to build and test each piece of our expression before adding more complexity, such as the influence of the coordination attribute. Unraveling where we have made a mistake when we build a complicated structure and things don't work right away is often more difficult than testing each piece and tacking on more when we trust what we have done so far.

To put what we have thus far into an expression, we will need to identify the names for the attributes for the target weights. The easiest way to do this follows:

1. Open the scene in which you were working earlier, or return to your Maya session.
2. Select one of the spheres. You should see a few attributes of its aim constraint in the Channel Box, including the two target weights.
3. In the Channel Box, select Channels > Channel Names > Long. These are the names you should use in your MEL scripts. (You can also use short names, but the long names are more readable and will be more self-evident to your script's readers.)

Now that you know the attribute names, the attribute assignment is easy to write.

```
// Make the weight assignments to the aimConstraint node
   attributes
nurbsSphere1_aimConstraint1.target1W0 =
   $eye1_coord_target1_weight;
nurbsSphere2_aimConstraint1.target1W0 =
   $eye2_coord_target1_weight;
nurbsSphere1_aimConstraint1.target2W1 =
   $eye1_coord_target2_weight;
nurbsSphere2_aimConstraint1.target2W1 =
   $eye2_coord_target2_weight;
```

Now we have the full expression.

```
float $eye1_coord_target1_weight;
float $eye1_coord_target2_weight;

float $eye2_coord_target1_weight;
float $eye2_coord_target2_weight;

// Drive the target2 weights from the eyes.target attribute
// such that we're fully weighted for target2 when eyes.target
```

```
// is equal to 2, and target2's weight is 0 when ey
// is equal to 1

$eye1_coord_target2_weight = eyes.target - 1;
$eye2_coord_target2_weight = eyes.target - 1;

// Drive target1's weights by the inverse of target2's we...

$eye1_coord_target1_weight = 1 - $eye1_coord_target2_weight;
$eye2_coord_target1_weight = 1 - $eye2_coord_target2_weight;

// Make the weight assignments to the aimConstraint node
   attributes

nurbsSphere1_aimConstraint1.target1W0 =
   $eye1_coord_target1_weight;
nurbsSphere2_aimConstraint1.target1W0 =
   $eye2_coord_target1_weight;
nurbsSphere1_aimConstraint1.target2W1 =
   $eye1_coord_target2_weight;
nurbsSphere2_aimConstraint1.target2W1 =
   $eye2_coord_target2_weight;
```

At this point, we need to create our attribute called `target` for the eyes node:

1. Select the eyes locator.
2. Open the Attribute Editor.
3. Choose Attributes > Add Attribute . . . in the Attribute Editor.
4. Set the name to target, the data type to float, attribute type to scalar, minimum to 1, max to 2, and default to 1.
5. Click Add, then close the Add Attribute and Attribute Editor windows.

In the Channel Box you should see your new attribute, `target`.

6. Now, right-click the target Channel Box, and choose Expressions. . . .
7. Enter the expression above, and press Create. Note that if there are any typos or mistakes in your expression, an error message will appear in the Command Feedback Line. You know that your expression has been successfully created when you see `// Result: expression1` in the Command Feedback Line, and the Create button on the Expression Editor window changes to Edit.
8. Move your `target1` and `target2` locators to two different locations.
9. Drag the time slider on the timeline to 0; set a keyframe for target at 1; drag the time slider all the way to the right, and set a keyframe at 2.
10. Play back your animation! (Note that this will look pretty weird if your locators are close to the eyes.)

Now our eyes track one of two locators, chosen by animating the `target` attribute on the eyes node.

To add the `coordination` attribute, we'll need to figure out how it will affect the target weights for each eye. When `coordination` is set to 0, we want `nurbsSphere1` to point only at `target1`, and `nurbsSphere2` to point only at `target2`. If we create variables to contain the weights for the uncoordinated case, they might look something like the following code:

```
float $eye1_uncoord_target1_weight = 1;
float $eye1_uncoord_target2_weight = 0;
float $eye2_uncoord_target1_weight = 0;
float $eye2_uncoord_target2_weight = 1;
```

By setting the weights like this, the first eye will point at `target1`; and the second will point at `target2`.

At this point, we need to figure out how to use our coordination attribute to blend the coordinated settings with the uncoordinated if the coordination attribute is between 0 and 1. To blend two values A and B according to a percentage P between 0 and 1, you use an equation that looks like this:

```
<Result> = (P * A) + ((1 - P) * B)
```

The `(P * A)` part of the equation calculates the fraction of A that we want in our blended result, while `(1 - P) * B` calculates the fraction of B that we want. If P is 0.3, or 30%, then our result will be 30% A and 70% B, or $(1 - 30\%) * B$.

Now we'll change our attribute assignments to average the weights for each case, weighted by the value of the coordination attribute.

```
nurbsSphere1_aimConstraint1.target1W0 =
(eyes.coordination * $eye1_coord_target1_weight) +
((1 - eyes.coordination) * $eye1_uncoord_target1_weight);

nurbsSphere2_aimConstraint1.target1W0 =
(eyes.coordination * $eye2_coord_target1_weight) +
((1 - eyes.coordination) * $eye2_uncoord_target1_weight);

nurbsSphere1_aimConstraint1.target2W1 =
(eyes.coordination * $eye1_coord_target2_weight) +
((1 - eyes.coordination) * $eye1_uncoord_target2_weight);

nurbsSphere2_aimConstraint1.target2W1 =
(eyes.coordination * $eye2_coord_target2_weight) +
((1 - eyes.coordination) * $eye2_uncoord_target2_weight);
```

When `eyes.coordination` is 0, these expressions use the uncoordinated target weight. When `eyes.coordination` is 1, these expressions use the coordinated target weight. In between, say at 0.5, our weights become a weighted average.

Take the following steps to install this expression.

1. Select the eyes locator; open the Attribute Editor, and add an attribute called `coordination` just like our `target` attribute above. This time, though, the minimum should be 0, the maximum 1, and the default 1.

2. Open the Expression Editor; choose By Expression Name on the Selection Filter menu, and pick the expression we've just created called `expression1`. Replace the previous expression with the following one, reflecting our changes.

```
// These variables are the weights for when the coordination
// attribute is set to 1

float $eye1_coord_target1_weight;
float $eye1_coord_target2_weight;

float $eye2_coord_target1_weight;
float $eye2_coord_target2_weight;

// When coordination is set to 0, eye1 always points to
   target1
// and eye2 points to target2

float $eye1_uncoord_target1_weight = 1;
float $eye1_uncoord_target2_weight = 0;

float $eye2_uncoord_target1_weight = 0;
float $eye2_uncoord_target2_weight = 1;

// Drive the target2 weights for the fully coordinated case
// using the eyes.target attribute, such that we're fully
   weighted
// for target2 when eyes.target is equal to 2, and target2's
// weight is 0 when eyes.target is equal to 1

$eye1_coord_target2_weight = eyes.target - 1;
$eye2_coord_target2_weight = eyes.target - 1;

$eye1_coord_target1_weight = 1 - $eye1_coord_target2_weight;
$eye2_coord_target1_weight = 1 - $eye2_coord_target2_weight;

// Now, blend the coordinated and uncoordinated weights

nurbsSphere1_aimConstraint1.target1W0 =
(eyes.coordination * $eye1_coord_target1_weight) +
((1 - eyes.coordination) * $eye1_uncoord_target1_weight);

nurbsSphere2_aimConstraint1.target1W0 =
(eyes.coordination * $eye2_coord_target1_weight) +
((1 - eyes.coordination) * $eye2_uncoord_target1_weight);
```

```
nurbsSphere1_aimConstraint1.target2W1 =
(eyes.coordination * $eye1_coord_target2_weight) +
((1 - eyes.coordination) * $eye1_uncoord_target2_weight);

nurbsSphere2_aimConstraint1.target2W1 =
(eyes.coordination * $eye2_coord_target2_weight) +
((1 - eyes.coordination) * $eye2_uncoord_target2_weight);
```

Now try some settings for coordination. You'll see that as you vary it from 0 to 1 the eyes will go from being uncoordinated (each pointing at its own target locator) to coordinated (pointing at the target locator selected with the target attribute).

What to Remember About Using Expressions

■ Always think about how you can use a constraint instead of an expression for as much behavior as possible. Constraints are more likely to behave well in unusual cases that you may not have thought of, and they will recalculate faster.

■ Think through what custom attributes you will need to create, what data you will need to store while your expression is calculating, and come up with names for variables to contain that data. Then, plan out how to do the actual calculation, and finally work out what attributes you plan to change and how. You should never write an expression without knowing what information you'll need before doing your calculation, what attributes you're changing, and how to calculate those attributes' values.

■ Whenever possible, use long attribute names, especially when someone else will be reading your expression.

■ Remember to avoid using getAttr and setAttr, because in expressions they are less efficient than reading from or assigning to attributes directly. (The reason for this is that Maya can avoid recalculating your expression if it knows that its inputs haven't changed, but it only knows this if you use attribute names directly rather than getAttr and setAttr.)

■ Remember that when writing MEL scripts that are not expressions, you can't read or assign attributes directly. You must use getAttr and setAttr.

4

Controlling Particles with Expressions

In this chapter you will learn

- The difference between per-object and per-particle attributes.
- What a vector is.
- How to create and manipulate vector variables.
- The difference between ordinary and particle expressions.
- Why to use ordinary expressions rather than particle expressions when you can.
- How ordinary expressions can be used to control particles.
- How to control particles with a particle expression.
- Useful hints for efficiently using particle expressions.
- How to think through a more complex particle expression application.

Two Kinds of Particle Object Attributes: Per Object and Per Particle

Certain particle object attributes are shared by all of the particles in the object. For example, if you create a particle object and animate the particle object's Translate X parameter, all of the object's particles will move together in X.

Particle objects also have a number of attributes for which separate values are maintained per particle. For example, while all of the particles in a particle object share common Translate X, Y, and Z parameters, each particle in the object has a unique location, which is stored in a per-particle attribute called "position." The position attribute, like several other per-particle attributes, is a *vector,* or a triplet of numbers that are bound together and manipulated as a group. The most common per-particle attributes to control with expressions are vectors, such as position, velocity, and acceleration.

All About Vectors

Because vector arithmetic is so common in particle expressions, it's useful to know what various vector arithmetic operations mean from a practical standpoint. In Maya, a vector is a group of three numbers that are bound together in a single attribute or variable. Vectors can represent X, Y, and Z distances, velocities, or accelerations in space; they can represent the red, green, and blue values that make up a color; or they can represent any triplet of numbers that makes sense to store together.

Creating a Vector Variable

In either an expression or a MEL script, you can create a new vector variable the same way you create any other variable, as follows:

```
vector $myvec;
```

Once you've created such a variable, to assign it a value you can either take its value from another vector variable, as in

```
$myvec = $myvec2;
```

or you can assign each of the three values contained in the vector literally, as in

```
$myvec = << 1, 2, 3 >>;
```

Usually you'll want to think of a vector as being a set of X, Y, and Z values that represent a direction and a distance in space.

Manipulating Vector Components

It is also possible to break a vector up into its component parts if you want to do arithmetic on each component of a vector separately. If you have a vector variable called $myvec, for example, Maya allows you to refer to the value of each of its component parts as $myvec.x, $myvec.y, and $myvec.z. Note, though, that while you can use the vector component notation in a mathematical expression, you can't assign a value to a single component using the following notation:

```
vector $myvec = <<0, 1, 2>>;
$test = $myvec.z; // sets $test to 2
print ($myvec.y); // prints 1
$myvec.x = 3; // syntax error!
```

Instead of writing

```
$myvec.x = 3;
```

which results in a syntax error, you can write

```
$myvec = << 3, $myvec.y, $myvec.z >>;
```

The above notation leaves the Y and Z components of $myvec alone while setting the X component to 3.

Adding and Subtracting Vectors

Vectors can be mathematically manipulated as a unit. For example, vectors can be added and subtracted, as follows:

```
vector $myvec = << 1, 2, 3 >>;
vector $myvec2 = << 3, 4, 5 >>;
vector $myvec3 = $myvec + $myvec2;
// this sets $myvec3 to << 4, 6, 8 >>
```

Note that adding two vectors adds each of the three components simultaneously. As shown in Figure 4.1 , if the vectors represent X, Y, and Z distances in space, adding vectors like this tells you what position in space you can reach by following the first vector's direction and distance and then the second.

If two vectors represent positions in space, subtracting them gives you a direction and the distance you must travel to get from one point to another. In this example (Figure 4.2), the direction and distance between <<2, 2, 0>> and <<1, 2, 0>> is <<-1, 0, 0>>.

Other Useful Vector Operations

Six other mathematical operations on vectors frequently come in handy: unit, mag, angle, cross, dot, and rot.

unit   The unit operation takes a vector that represents a direction and distance in space, and it gives a vector that points in the same direction but has a length of 1. For example,

```
vector $myvec = << 0, 0, 3 >>;
vector $myvec2 = unit($myvec); // sets $myvec2 to << 0, 0, 1 >>
```

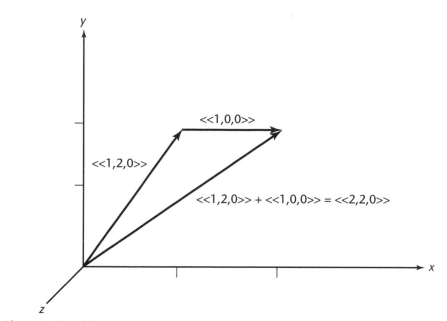

Figure 4.1 Adding vectors.

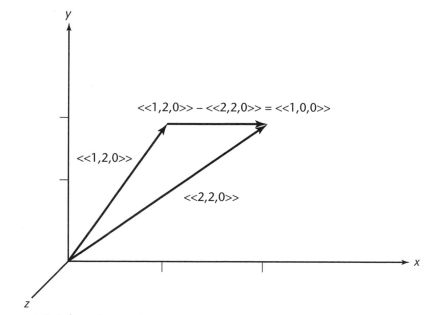

Figure 4.2 Subtracting vectors.

This is useful when you want a vector of a specific length that points in the same direction as another vector that is already defined. For example, if you want a vector that is eight units in length and points in the same direction as $myvec, here is how you can do it:

```
vector $myvec_eight = 8 * unit($myvec);
```

mag The mag operation, short for magnitude, gives you the length of a vector. Given the vectors in the example above,

```
float $myvec_length = mag($myvec);
                                // sets $myvec_length to 3
float $myvec_eight_length = mag ($myvec_eight);
                                // sets $myvec_eight_length to 8
```

angle The angle operation gives you the angle between two vectors (Figure 4.3). The angle is returned in radians, so if you want degrees you will have to multiply by (180 / pi), as shown in the following example code.

```
vector $xvec = << 1, 0, 0 >>; // points in the X direction
vector $yvec = << 0, 1, 0 >>; // points in the Y direction
float $xy_angle = angle ($xvec, $yvec); // 1.570796 radians

$pi = 3.141593;
float $xy_angle_degrees = $xy_angle * 180 / $pi;
// 90   degrees
```

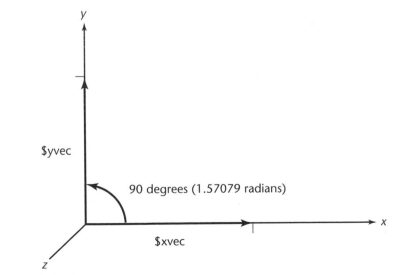

Figure 4.3 Angle.

cross   The cross operation gives you the cross product of two vectors. The cross product is a third vector that is *normal* (meaning perpendicular) to both of the vectors given to cross as arguments, seen in the following code:

```
vector $xvec = << 1, 0, 0 >>;
vector $yvec = << 0, 1, 0 >>;
vector $zvec = cross ($xvec, $yvec); // will be << 0, 0, 1 >>
```

The length of the cross product vector depends on the lengths of the input vectors and the angle between them. If you give cross two perpendicular vectors of length 1 (making each a *unit vector*) then the result will be a unit vector perpendicular to the first two. In general, though, the cross product's length (Figure 4.4) is given by

```
mag ($vector1) * mag ($vector2) * sin (angle ($vector1,
    $vector2))
```

Often, it's convenient to use unit(cross($vector1, $vector2)) to get a unit vector that is perpendicular to $vector1 and $vector2. Note, though, that if both vectors are parallel, then the resulting vector will be << 0, 0, 0 >>.

dot   The dot operation

```
dot ($vector1, $vector2)
```

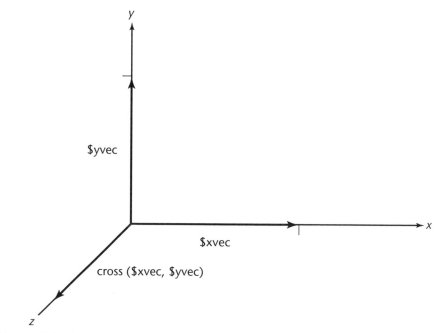

Figure 4.4 Cross product.

is the same as

```
mag ($vector1) * mag($vector2) * cos (angle($vector1, $vector2))
```

Thus, for two perpendicular vectors, the dot product is always 0, and for parallel vectors, it is always the product of the two vectors' lengths. If you want to test whether two vectors are parallel or perpendicular, you can look at the value of

```
dot (unit ($vector1), unit($vector2))
```

If the value of the above expression is 0, the vectors are perpendicular; if the value is 1, they are parallel. If the value is in between 0 and 1, then it is neither perpendicular nor parallel.

rot   The rot operation, for rotate, is the most complex of these. It rotates one vector by a certain angle around an axis defined by another vector (Figure 4.5). For example, if you wanted to rotate the vector

```
vector $myvec = << 0, 1, 1 >>;
```

20 degrees around the Z axis, you could do the following:

```
$pi = 3.141593;
$twenty_degrees = 20 * $pi / 180; // Convert to radians!!
```

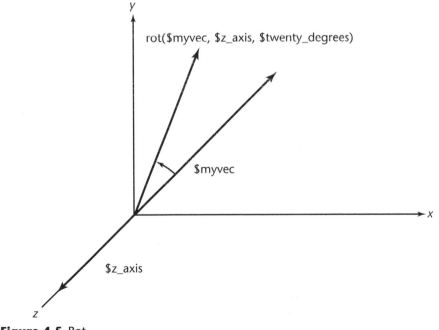

Figure 4.5 Rot.

```
vector $myvec = << 0, 1, 1 >>;
vector $z_axis = << 0, 0, 1 >>;
vector $rot_vec = rot ($myvec, $z_axis, $twenty_degrees);
```

Remember to always use angles in radians with the rot operation.

Two Kinds of Expressions: Ordinary and Particle

Ordinary expressions control per-object attributes. For particle objects, these expressions are just like those we've examined in Chapter 3.

Particle expressions affect per-particle attributes and are executed differently from ordinary expressions. For every frame, a *runtime* particle expression is executed once for each particle, which means that operations that seem quick when used in an ordinary expression can slow your scene's evaluation to a crawl in a particle expression. Also, you can choose to execute a *creation* particle expression once on the frame when each particle is created.

Since you'll often use dynamics to control particle motion, you can elect to have your expressions for a given particle object execute before or after the dynamics engine calculates particle behavior. Executing before the dynamics engine gives you a chance to alter particle positions, velocities, or accelerations, while still allowing the engine to have some effect. Executing after the dynamics engine allows your expressions to completely override the engine's calculated particle motion.

Using Ordinary Expressions to Control Particle Behavior

In many instances, a particle behavior that is difficult to create without using expressions can be created by using ordinary expressions to control the behavior of fields that drive the particle motion. This approach is much faster than using particle expressions to achieve the same behavior.

Deciding between using ordinary expressions to control a field's behavior and using particle expressions usually comes down to the question of whether each particle must have its own individual behavior or whether the particles share a single collective behavior. However, even when each particle seems to be behaving independently of the others, there are often ways to achieve the same result by setting, for example, different goals and goal weights for the particles or by defining volumes of influence for a number of fields.

Example 1: Ordinary Expressions and a Newton Field

This section presents an example of an ordinary expression being used to control particle behavior that might seem like a candidate for a particle expression. Suppose you want a group of particles to orbit a center point.

The center point will move through space, pulling the particles along, until it crosses an invisible barrier (say, when the center point gets to Z = −5) at which point the particles will fly off in all directions.

A Newton field is the natural choice for the object the particles will orbit, and it might seem like a good idea to use a particle expression to add an outward acceleration when the moving Newton field crosses Z = −5. A simpler approach, though, is to make the Newton field's magnitude negative at that point, which will force the particles to fly outward.

First, create some particles orbiting a center point:

1. Choose File > New Scene.
2. Choose the Particle tool, place 10 or 20 particles, and press Enter to create them.
3. Change the Particle Render Type to spheres in the Channel Box (Figure 4.6).
4. Switch into Component selection mode.
5. Drag a selection rectangle around all the particles.

Open the Component Editor (Figure 4.7) by choosing Window > General Editors > Component Editor . . .

6. Select the Velocity Y cells for all the particles, making sure the time slider is at 0.
7. Type 1.0 into the box, setting all of their initial Y velocities to 1.
8. Close the Component Editor.
9. Switch back to Object selection mode.

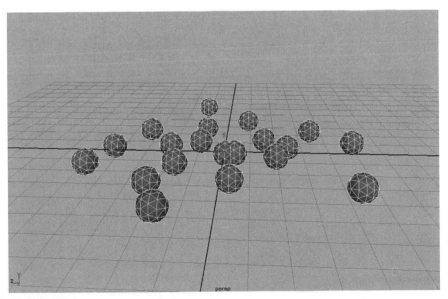

Figure 4.6 Spheres.

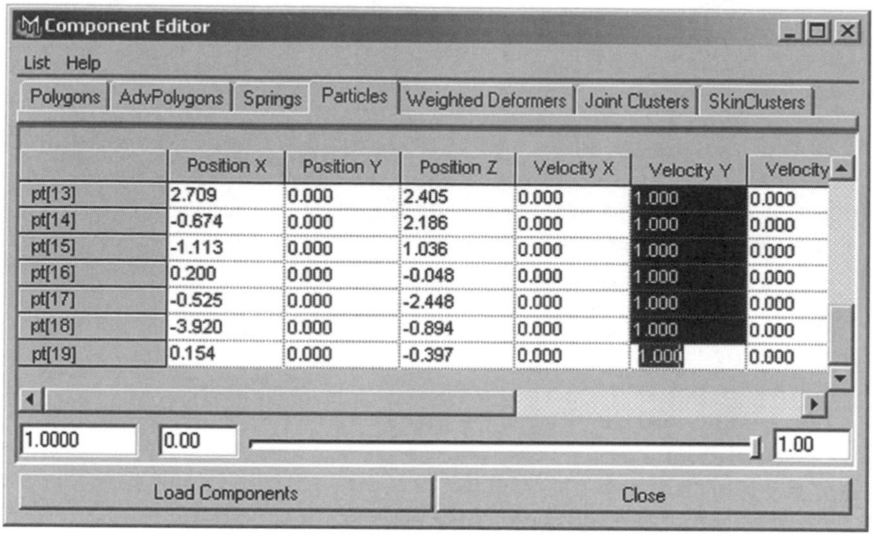

Figure 4.7 Component Editor.

10. With the particle object selected, create a Newton field by selecting Fields > Newton.
11. Play the resulting animation to watch the spheres orbit the field's center (Figure 4.8).

Now, animate the center point.

1. Drag the time slider to 0.
2. Select the Translation X, Y, and Z entries in the Channel Box; then right-click, and choose Key selected.
3. Drag the time slider to a point a couple hundred frames later.
4. Move the Newton field using the Move tool. Make sure that you move the Newton field to a location where the Z value is less than −5, perhaps −6 or so.
5. Select the Translation X, Y, and Z entries in the Channel Box, and then right-click and choose Key selected (Figure 4.9).
6. Rewind and play the resulting animation. Note that the spheres follow the Newton field yet still orbit around it.

Finally, add the repulsion expression.

1. Select the Newton field.
2. Select, then right-click on the Magnitude field in the Channel Box to open the Expression Editor (Figure 4.10).
3. Enter the following expression:

```
if (tz > −5) {

    magnitude = 5.0;
```

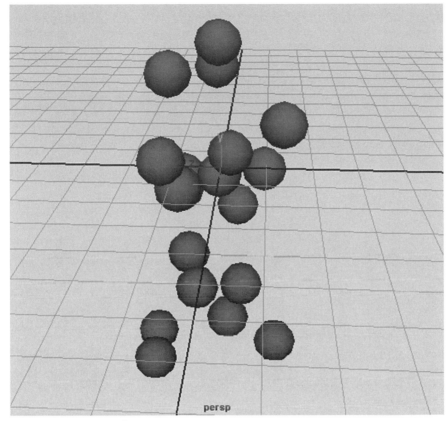

Figure 4.8 Orbiting spheres.

```
} else {
   magnitude = -35.0;
}
```

4. Click Create.
5. Close the Expression Editor, rewind, and play back the animation (Figure 4.11).

How this expression works   The above expression is an example of testing the value of one attribute to control the behavior of another. The phrase if (tz > -5) indicates that the expression should have two different effects, depending on whether the Translate Z parameter is greater than -5. If it is, the Newton field attracts the particles with a strength of 5.0; if it is not, the Newton field repels them with a strength of 35.0.

As Maya plays back the scene, on each frame it evaluates the Newton field's Translate Z parameter and decides whether, for that frame, the

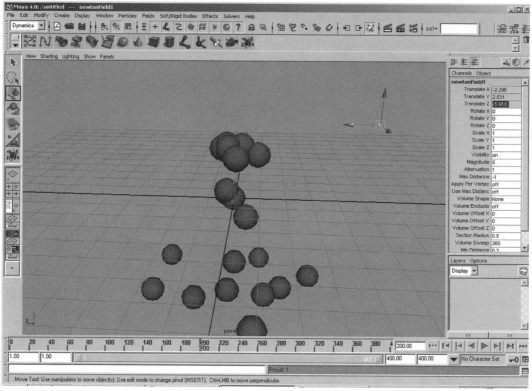

Figure 4.9 Animating the center point.

Newton field has a magnitude of 5.0 or −35.0. What this means is that if the Newton field travels back to a Translate Z value greater than −5, the Newton field will attract the particles again.

When to Use a Particle Expression

Use a particle expression when one of the following conditions applies:

- You want to apply different forces to each particle, making it difficult to use fields.
- You have a well-defined mathematical model for your particles' behavior.
- You want to apply complex decision making to each particle's behavior independently of the others in the particle object.

Since Maya 3.0, if you want a per-particle attribute to change over time, it has been easy to create this behavior with a ramp texture. Before undertaking a complex project with particle expressions, you may wish to have a look at the section entitled "Setting Particle Attributes with a Ramp Texture" in the *Maya: Dynamics* manual.

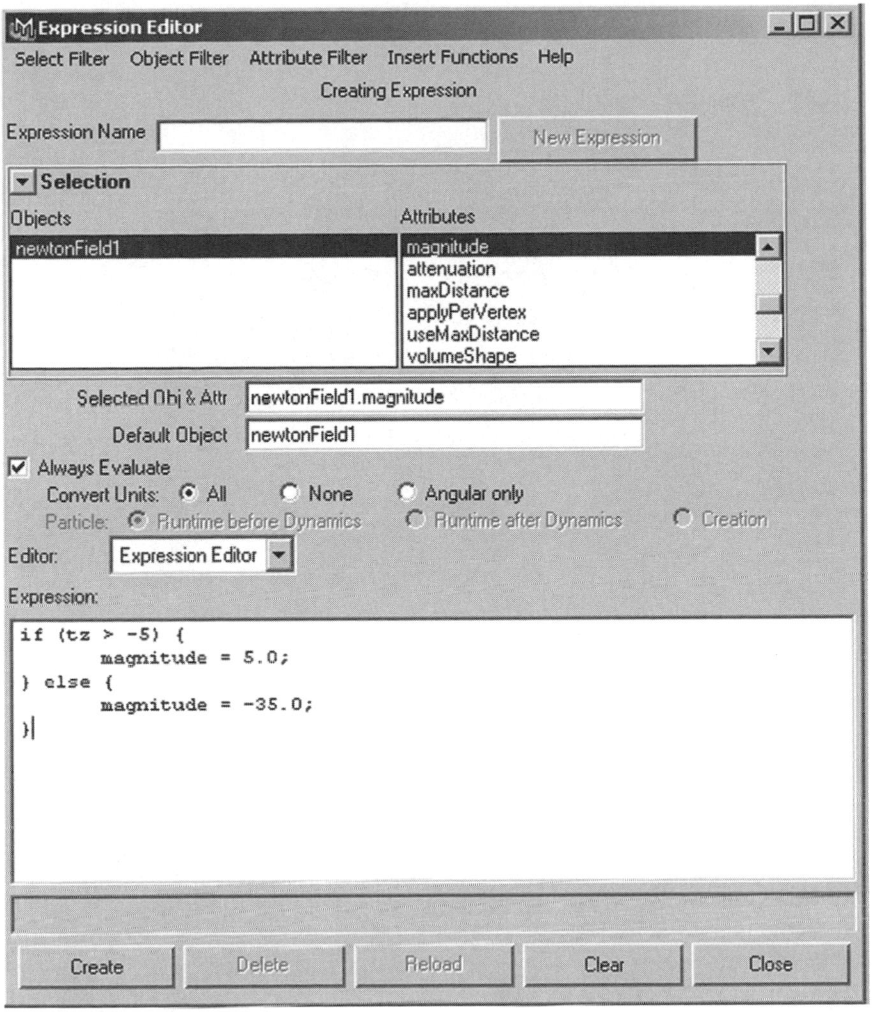

Figure 4.10 Expression Editor.

Example 2: A Simple Particle Expression

Despite the slower performance of particle expressions, certain problems are most easily solved with them. In this example, we use a particle expression to constrain the particles emitted by an Omni emitter to a surface that we define mathematically.

First, create an emitter.

1. Choose File > New Scene.
2. Select the Dynamics menu set.
3. Choose Particles > Create Emitter ❏.

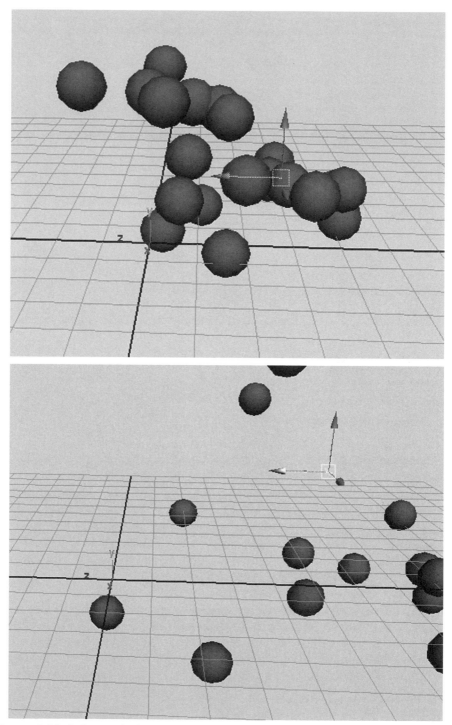

Figure 4.11 Before and after the z = −5 "barrier."

4. In the options box, choose Omni as the emitter type. Leave all other settings unchanged.
5. Click Create.
6. Rewind and play the animation until some particles appear.

At this point, you should see a cloud of particles being emitted in all directions, unaffected by dynamics (Figure 4.12).

The function to which we'll constrain the particles is $Y = X^2 + Z^2$. The particles will be free to move in X and Z but will be forced to remain on that surface in Y, a paraboloid.

Create the expression.

1. Select the particle object by dragging across the emitted particles in Object selection mode.
2. Hold down the right mouse button and select particle1 . . . to open the Attribute Editor (Figure 4.13).
3. Scroll down until you see Per Particle (Array) Attributes and, if necessary, open the tab (Figure 4.14).

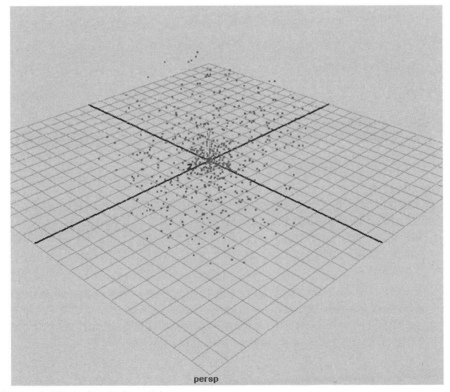

Figure 4.12 A cloud of particles.

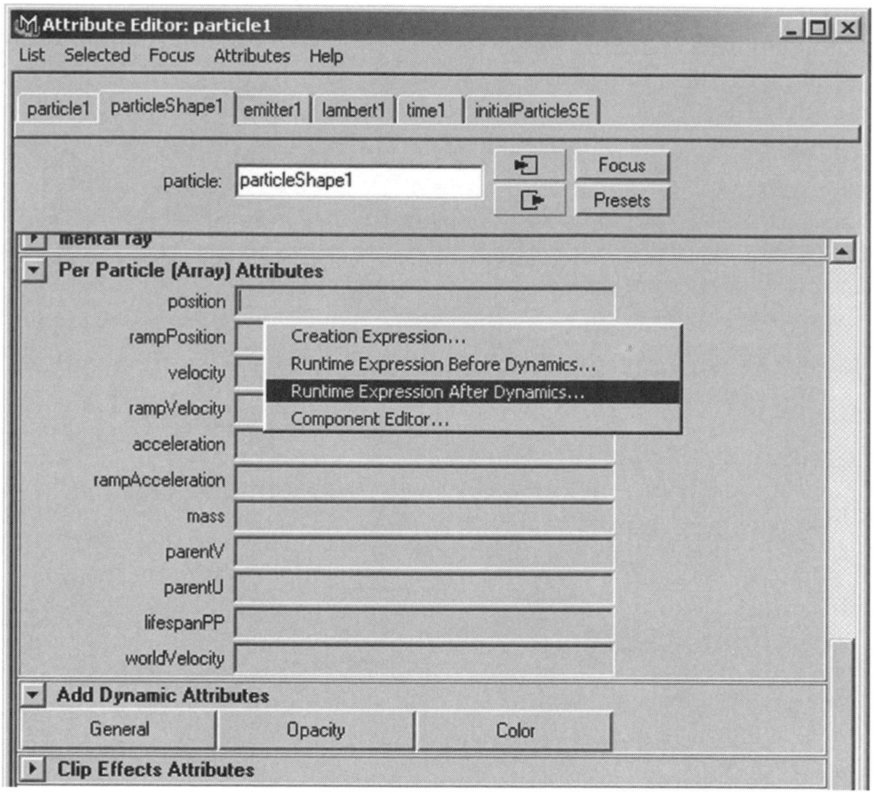

Figure 4.13 Expressions after dynamics control for particleShape1.

At this point, you'll see a list of per-particle attributes with which you can associate either creation or runtime expressions. In fact, this display is slightly misleading. First, there are many more per-particle attributes that you can control with expressions than are listed. Second, each particle object really has only one creation and one runtime particle expression, but it can calculate and set as many per-particle attributes as necessary. Depending on the expression you enter, the display in the Attribute Editor will change to reflect which per-particle attributes you're controlling with your expression.

4. Right-click on the empty box next to position, and choose Runtime Expression after Dynamics (also Figure 4.13).
5. At this point, you will be confronted with the Expression Editor. Enter the following expression and click Create.

```
vector $pos = position;
float $posY = ($pos.x)*($pos.x) +($pos.z)*($pos.z);
position = <<$pos.x, $posY, $pos.z>>;
```

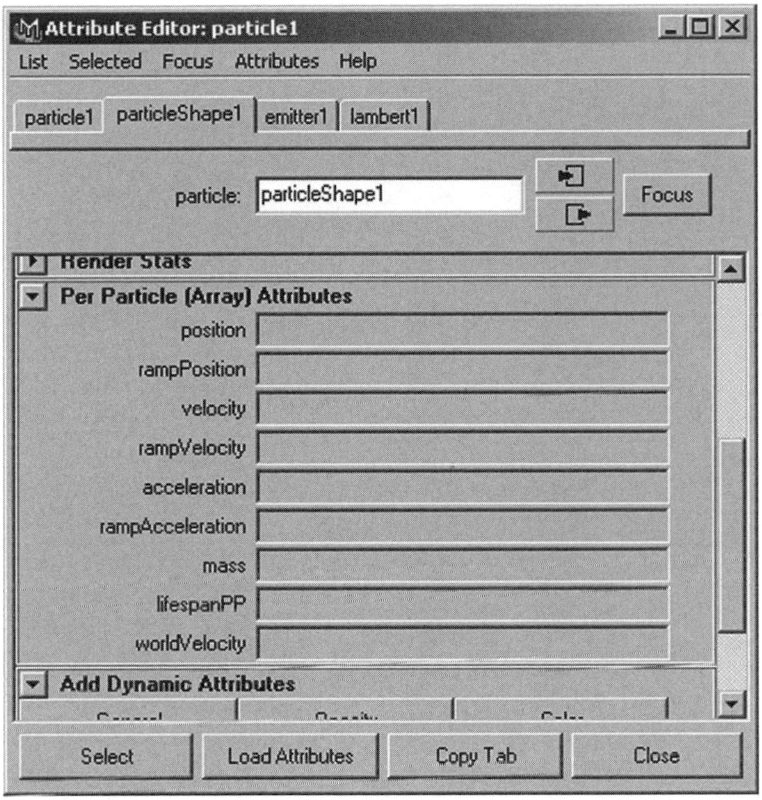

Figure 4.14 Per-particle attributes.

6. Right-click on the box next to position, and choose Runtime expression . . . again.

Remember, runtime expressions are only executed on the frames *after* the first frame that a particle exists. Because we want our constraint to apply to all particles, even on the first frame, we need to place the same expression in the particle object's Creation expression.

7. Select the entire expression, and press Ctrl-C to copy it.
8. Click on the button labeled Creation in the Expression Editor to switch to the creation expression.
9. Press Ctrl-V to paste the expression, and then click Create.

Instantly, you should see your particles snap to the shape of a paraboloid (Figure 4.15).

If we hadn't put our constraint into the creation expression in addition to the runtime expression, particles would not have stayed on the surface during the first frame that they exist. If you're creating more than one

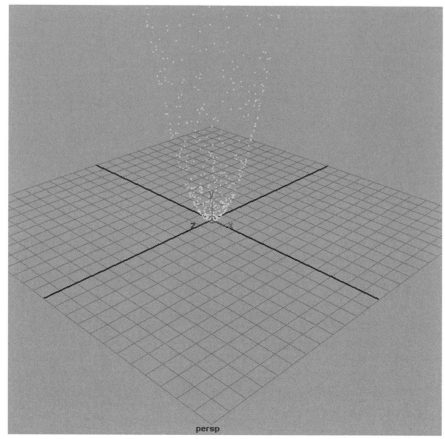

Figure 4.15 Paraboloid of particles.

particle per frame, this means that you would have a small cloud of flickering particles around the emitter.

How This Expression Works

Because there are certain limitations on how we can directly manipulate attributes (such as a particle's position), the first line

```
vector $pos = position;
```

creates a vector variable called $pos and sets its value to the current particle's position. While it is not possible to get the X value of a particle's position by writing position.x, it is possible to get the X value of the $pos variable by writing $pos.x, and we use that in the next line:

```
float $posY = ($pos.x)*($pos.x) +($pos.z)*($pos.z);
```

In the above line, we create a new floating-point variable called $posY. Note that this is *not* the same as $pos.y, which would be the Y value for the position of the particle that we just copied into our vector. Our new Y position is calculated by multiplying the position's X and Z components by themselves and then adding them.

Finally, we assemble the position vector again from our two components that we are leaving alone, $pos.x and $pos.z, and the one component for which we have set a value, $posY:

```
position = <<$pos.x, $posY, $pos.z>>;
```

Choosing the Runtime Expressions After Dynamics option is important for the above expression to work properly. Without this option, expressions execute first. This means that when an expression examines the value of the particle's position or velocity, it sees the value those attributes had on the previous frame. Then, after the expression has had its opportunity to change the per-particle attributes, the dynamics engine applies the effect of forces created by fields and goals.

Using the Runtime Expressions After Dynamics option, as we did, makes the dynamics engine run first. Then, when we examine position, we see the position established for the particle by the dynamics engine on *this* frame, and any changes we make establish the final value for the particle's position.

If you zoom in on the bottom of the paraboloid of particles as the animation is running, you will see that there is a small cloud of particles below the emitter. Turning up the emitter's emission rate to 10,000 or so can make this problem easier to see (Figure 4.16).

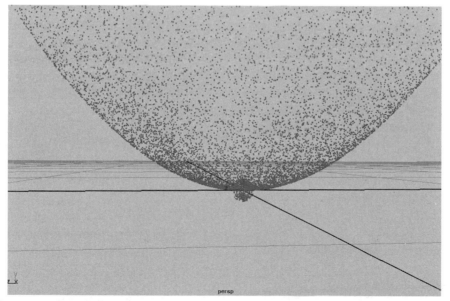

Figure 4.16 A glitch.

Often, once you have a basic particle behavior implemented with a particle expression, it's necessary to fix small glitches like this. These glitches are often caused by the dynamics engine; in this instance, the problem is that the initial velocity of the particles takes a frame to die down in the dynamics engine's calculations. We can solve this problem by setting the initial velocity in Y to zero so that the particles are not moved away from the surface, as follows:

1. Open the Expression Editor for the particle's creation expression as you have before.
2. Add the following lines:

```
vector $vel = velocity;
velocity = <<$vel.x, 0, $vel.z>>;
```

3. Make the same change to the runtime expression as well.

Now rewind and play—you'll see that the cloud of particles below the emitter is gone.

A Few Hints for Efficient Particle Expressions

■ If your expression manipulates position or velocity directly, you can get strange behaviors that result from a confused dynamics engine, as in Example 2. If you can, use Runtime Expressions After Dynamics and manipulate acceleration—then the dynamics engine will ensure that the positions and velocities stay continuous. Manipulating per-particle goal weights is also safe.

■ When possible, only access per-particle attributes and variables in your particle expressions. If you use the values of per-object attributes in your particle expressions, then every particle can force large parts of the scene to be reevaluated, which slows the particle simulation down.

■ Avoid using particle expressions entirely if a per-object expression will do what you need. The speed benefit is enormous.

Often, the problem-solving process you use to develop a working particle expression will send you down paths that don't lead to the results you want. Example 3 shows how you can start with a slow, quick-and-dirty implementation and improve on it repeatedly to achieve a result that is useful in production.

Example 3: Helical Particles Around a Curve

In this example, we look at a more challenging particle expression application: making particles travel in a precise helix around an arbitrary NURBS curve.

An important first step in developing an approach to solving a complex problem using expressions or MEL is to try to come up with the most complete possible list of solutions. Usually, there are several ways to solve a problem in Maya, but only one or two efficient ways, and since particle expressions can be extremely slow to execute, you must keep efficiency in mind when developing a particle application.

Brainstorming Possible Solutions

The following list, almost certainly not comprehensive, suggests ways to approach creating a helix of particles that wind around a curve. Some may not be practical, but it's worthwhile to write them out in any case.

- Using the Curve Flow feature under Maya's Dynamics menu to force the particles to move along a motion path. This requires creating a helical secondary curve around the original curve.
- Using the curve as a goal object and animating the goal offset to force a helical motion around the goal object.
- Developing a particle expression that manipulates position directly based on the particle's age.

At first, it may seem that using curve flow or animating goal offsets might be mathematically simpler than using a direct particle expression for position. Animating goal offsets, though, requires calculating the direction and distance of the offset away from the curve, which is probably just as complicated as directly calculating a particle's position based on its age.

Using curve flow requires making a helical curve that wraps around the original curve. Not only does this raise the same mathematical questions as the other two approaches, it also relies on the Curve Flow feature, which can be very slow when it operates on a complex curve path with many control vertices (CVs).

Thus, directly manipulating the particle position with a particle expression is probably the easiest approach.

A First Attempt at the Particle Expression

1. Start by creating a curve and an emitter (Figure 4.17). Since we will be setting the particle's position directly in our expression, it probably does not matter where the emitter is located. Make sure that the curve has at least one *inflection point,* a point where it goes from convex to concave or vice versa.
2. If necessary, rename the emitter `emitter1` and the curve `curve1` before proceeding.
3. Set your timeline to run from frame 1 to frame 400.
4. Play the animation until particles appear; then drag over them to select the particle object.

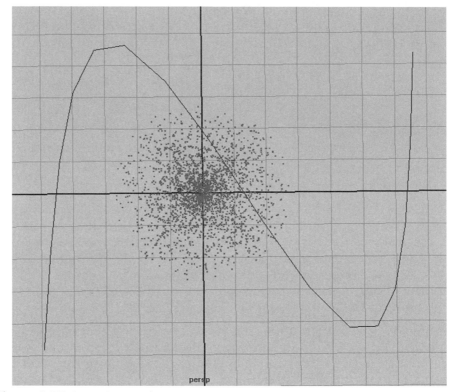

Figure 4.17 An emitter and a curve.

5. Hold down the right mouse button on the particle object, and choose particle1 . . . from the menu to open the Attribute Editor.
6. Scroll down to the Per Particle (Array) Attributes tab, and then right-click on position. Choose Runtime Expression after Dynamics . . . from the menu.
7. Enter the following expression:

```
float $scaleOffset = 0.2;

float $pos[] = `pointOnCurve -pr (age) -p curve1`;
float $tan[] = `pointOnCurve -pr (age) -nt curve1`;
float $norm[] = `pointOnCurve -pr (age) -nn curve1`;

vector $posvec = <<$pos[0], $pos[1], $pos[2]>>;
vector $tanvec = <<$tan[0], $tan[1], $tan[2]>>;
vector $normvec = <<$norm[0], $norm[1], $norm[2]>>;

vector $norm2vec = cross($tanvec, $normvec);
```

```
position = $posvec + ($scaleOffset * $normvec * cos(age*20)) +
                ($scaleOffset * $norm2vec * sin(age*20));
```

8. Click Create.

Now rewind and play back the resulting animation (Figure 4.18). Depending on the curve that you created, you may see a few glitches in the particle motion. Ignore them for now.

How this expression works   The first line,

```
float $scaleOffset = 0.2;
```

defines a floating-point variable that we leave unchanged throughout the expression. This variable defines how far the helix is from the original curve, as we'll see later on. Changing this value will move the helix of particles closer to the curve or farther away.

Immediately following the definition of $scaleOffset are three statements that execute the MEL function called pointOnCurve to get information about curve1. Let's examine the first of these for a moment.

```
float $pos[] = `pointOnCurve -pr (age) -p curve1`;
```

This statement resembles many of our previous definitions of variables, except that $pos is declared with square brackets ❏. These brackets establish that $pos is a variable that will contain an *array*, or a series of values. This is necessary because the pointOnCurve MEL command creates an array that contains its result. We'll see how to access the contents of an array later on in the expression.

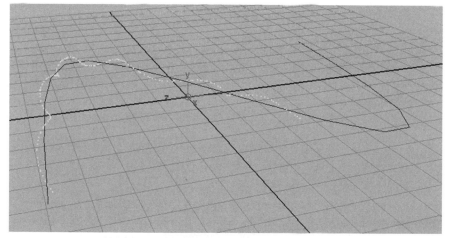

Figure 4.18 A first helix.

The parameters of a curve, just like the U and V parameters on a NURBS surface or mesh, define a particular point on the curve. This script uses the particle's age to find the location on the curve whose parameter has the same value as the particle's age. As a particle gets older, then each time we call pointOnCurve for that particle, it returns a position farther down the curve.

The backticks `` ` `` surround a MEL command that creates a result that we want to capture in a variable. In this case, the pointOnCurve command examines curve1 and returns with values that describe its geometry at a particular point. -pr (age) tells the command to look at the point along the curve that is defined by the parameter corresponding to this particular particle's age (which the "age" particle attribute contains, measured in seconds), and -p tells the command to return the position of the point on the curve. Finally, the curve1 at the end indicates which curve to examine.

You can see which options a particular command can accept by looking at its page in the MEL Command Reference, available from Maya's Help menu. In Chapter 5, we'll look at MEL commands in more detail.

Since this MEL command finds a position in three-dimensional space along the curve, the pointOnCurve command generates a result that has three components, X, Y, and Z. Unlike the particle attributes we've seen, such as position and velocity, pointOnCurve returns these values not in the form of a vector but as an array, which is a list of values (in this instance) in X, Y, and Z order.

Next, we use the pointOnCurve command to extract more information about our curve at the point corresponding to the particle's age, as follows:

```
float $tan[] = `pointOnCurve -pr (age) -nt curve1`;
float $norm[] = `pointOnCurve -pr (age) -nn curve1`;
```

The first pointOnCurve command uses the -nt parameter, which returns the *normalized tangent* on the curve. The X, Y, and Z values that are returned define both a direction and a distance. Requesting a "normalized" tangent ensures that the distance is 1; this saves us some effort, as otherwise we'd have to use the unit vector function to normalize the tangent by hand.

The second command uses the -nn parameter to get the *normalized normal* of the curve. The normal to a curve defines a perpendicular direction to the curve that points in the convex direction of the curve's curvature. Asking for it to be normalized, again, ensures that the normal has a length of 1.

Since we wish to calculate a position for the point, and the position perparticle attribute is a vector, we must now convert the three arrays $pos[], $tan[], and $norm[] to vectors:

```
vector $posvec = <<$pos[0], $pos[1], $pos[2]>>;
vector $tanvec = <<$tan[0], $tan[1], $tan[2]>>;
vector $normvec = <<$norm[0], $norm[1], $norm[2]>>;
```

Now we have three vectors: a position along the curve, a tangent vector pointing along the curve at that point, and a normal vector pointing outward from the curve at that point.

To get the helical motion, we first place the particle at the position on the curve corresponding to the particle's age. Then, we move the particle away from the curve along the normal by an amount that varies with a function that oscillates, either sine or cosine. Thus, as the particle travels down the curve, it will oscillate back and forth along the normal. Finally, we'll apply another oscillation along the vector that is perpendicular to the normal we were given and the tangent vector.

Since this vector is also a normal to the curve, we'll call it $norm2vec. We can find it using the cross operator described above. Since the existing tangent and the normal vectors both have lengths of 1 and are perpendicular to each other, the cross operator will give us a vector that's perpendicular to both with a length of 1 as well:

```
vector $norm2vec = cross($tanvec, $normvec);
```

Finally, we construct the expression for position according to our plan:

```
position = $posvec + ($scaleOffset * $normvec * cos(age*20)) +
                     ($scaleOffset * $norm2vec * sin(age*20));
```

This expression first places the particle at a particular point on the curve ($posvec), and then moves it a distance of ($scaleOffset * cos(age * 20)) along $normvec. $scaleOffset defines how far the particle will move away from the curve in that direction, and cos(age * 20) oscillates between –1 to 1. Changing the value by which we multiply the particle's age (in this case, 20) changes how fast the particle oscillates.

Finally, the expression moves the particle ($scaleOffset * sin(age*20)) along $norm2vec. By oscillating with a cosine curve in one direction and a sine curve in the perpendicular direction, we get circular motion around the curve.

Refining the Solution

The above expression works fairly well to make the particles move in a helix around the curve, and for some applications it might be just fine. However, it has a couple of problems.

First, rewind and run the simulation until the helix of particles has passed the inflection point in the curve. Then, move in close with the camera (Figure 4.19).

At the inflection point, you can see that the particles jump discontinuously from one side of the curve to the other.

Next, examine the volume immediately around the emitter. A few of the particles seem to be clustered there, rather than at the appropriate point on the curve (Figure 4.20).

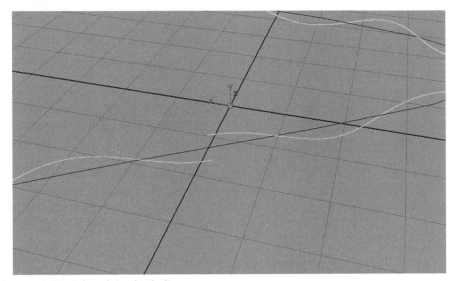

Figure 4.19 A break in the helix.

Since we're determining where to put each particle based on its age, it would be helpful to see the ages of each particle in the cluster around the emitter. The Numeric particle render type gives us an easy way to do this, as follows:

1. Make sure you have the particle object selected, and set the Particle Render Type in the Channel Box to Numeric.
2. Once again, open the Attribute Editor by right-clicking on the particle object and selecting particle1 . . . from the menu that appears.
3. Open the Render Attributes tab if necessary (Figure 4.21). It should be the second tab above the Per Particle (Array) Attributes tab.
4. Click the Add Attributes For [Current Render Type] button.
5. At this point, a couple of new attributes should appear, including Attribute Name. In the Attribute Name field, type age and press Enter (Figure 4.22).
6. Close the Attribute Editor window.

Upon examining the cluster of points around the emitter, we can see that their ages are all less than 1/24, which means they are all in their first frame of existence (Figure 4.23). (If you've let the simulation run far enough that particles reach the end of the curve, you will also see a number of particles exactly at 0, 0, 0.)

The points clustered around the emitter whose ages are less than one frame duration are in the wrong place because, once again, we've assumed that setting a runtime expression will place them correctly on their first

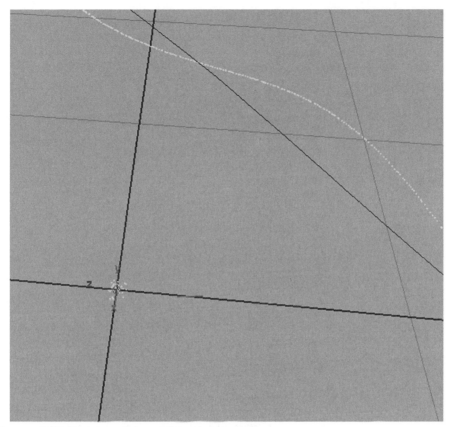

Figure 4.20 Errant particles at the origin.

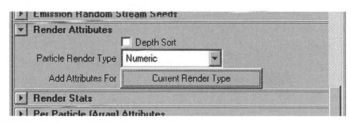

Figure 4.21 The Render Attributes tab.

frame of existence. Fixing this problem requires setting the same expression for both the runtime and creation expressions.

To clean up the particles that are old enough to have reached the end of the curve, setting the particle lifetime parameter appropriately will prevent their ending up at the origin. Solving the problem of the particles'

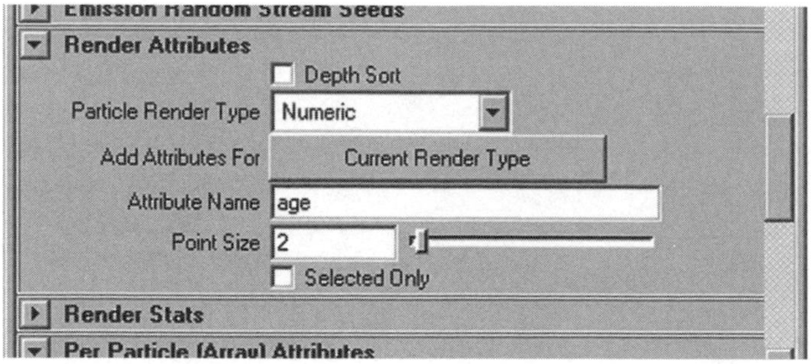

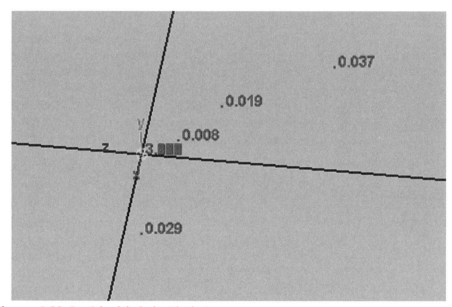

Figure 4.22 Adding the age attribute.

Figure 4.23 Particles labeled with their ages.

discontinuous jump at the inflection point, though, is trickier. The under-lying cause is that using the pointOnCurve function to find a curve's nor-mal gives a result that always points toward the *convex* side of the curve. Unfortunately, at an inflection point, such a normal flips by 180 degrees to point toward the new convex side. Figure 4.24 shows a view looking down the axis of the helix to see the 180-degree jump.

Fixing this problem requires a different approach to choosing a normal to the curve. Start over with a new scene to look at, such an approach, as follows:

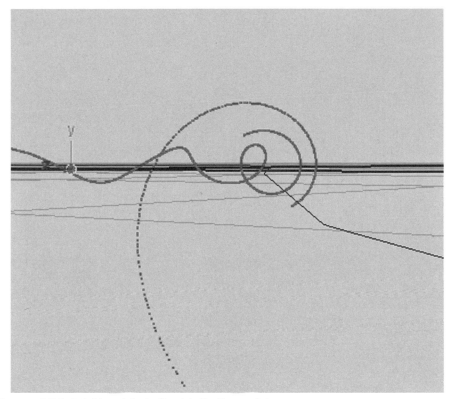

Figure 4.24 Axial break in helix at inflection point.

1. Choose New Scene, and select No when asked whether you want to save.
2. Create a new curve called `curve1` with at least one inflection point.
3. Make sure `curve1` is selected, and then open the Script Editor and type the following:

```
offsetCurve -d 0.1 -n curve1guide
```

4. Press Enter.

Figure 4.25 shows the result of the above expression. Note the second curve running along your `curve1`.

What the `offsetCurve` command has done is produce another curve called `curve1guide` that is a constant distance from the original curve, always in the same direction. The `-d 0.1` parameter specifies that the curve should be 0.1 units from the original. If you see glitches at points where the original curve bends sharply, making the distance smaller should clean them up.

By using `pointOnCurve` to find the point on `curve1` that matches a given parameter, and by using `pointOnCurve` again to find the matching point on

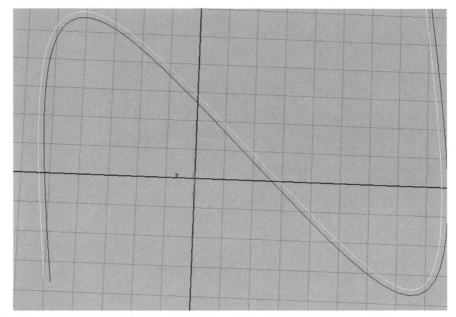

Figure 4.25 Result of offsetCurve command.

curve1guide, we can use the difference of those two points to find a direction that will be our normal. Unlike the normal we get by calling pointOnCurve with the -nn parameter, this normal will always change continuously as the particles travel along curve1.

Finally, there is one other change we can make to our expression that should not change its result but will make it run much faster. Remember that if there is a node that exists to calculate a particular value and also a MEL command for the same purpose, in many cases using the node will be faster.

One of the options for pointOnCurve is -ch on (for "construction history on"). What this does is create a node of type pointOnCurveInfo that has attributes for its inputs and outputs. By creating such a node once for each curve and by using setAttr to set the parameter and getAttr to get the value, the expression will execute much faster. Why? Because the MEL command pointOnCurve creates and destroys one such node every time it runs, which is once per particle per frame. By eliminating this creation and destruction of nodes, the expression will run much faster.

1. In the Script Editor, type the following and press Enter:

```
pointOnCurve -ch on -pr 0 curve1;
pointOnCurve -ch on -pr 0 curve1guide;
```

You'll notice that each command responds with a result like

```
// Result: pointOnCurveInfo1
```

This is the name of the `pointOnCurveInfo` node that the command created.

2. Create a new emitter called `emitter1`.
3. Select the particle object; use the Runtime Expressions After Dynamics option, and lauch the Expression Editor. Now enter the following position expression as both the runtime and creation expressions for the particle object:

```
float $scaleOffset = 0.2;

setAttr pointOnCurveInfo1.parameter (age);
setAttr pointOnCurveInfo2.parameter (age);

float $pos[] = `getAttr pointOnCurveInfo1.position`;
float $tan[] = `getAttr pointOnCurveInfo1.normalizedTangent`;
float $normEnd[] = `getAttr pointOnCurveInfo2.position`;
float $norm[];

$norm[0] = $normEnd[0] -$pos[0];
$norm[1] = $normEnd[1] -$pos[1];
$norm[2] = $normEnd[2] -$pos[2];

vector $posvec = <<$pos[0], $pos[1], $pos[2]>>;
vector $tanvec = <<$tan[0], $tan[1], $tan[2]>>;
vector $normvec = unit(<<$norm[0], $norm[1], $norm[2]>>);
vector $norm2vec = cross($tanvec, $normvec);

position = $posvec +($scaleOffset * $normvec * cos(age*20)) +
                    ($scaleOffset * $norm2vec * sin(age*20));
```

4. Find the maximum parameter of your curve by selecting `curve1`, opening the Attribute Editor, and looking at the Min Max Value boxes under the shape node's NURBS Curve History tab. The Max Value is what you want to set as the particle life span, because it's the age at which a particle will hit the curve's maximum value (Figure 4.26).
5. Select the particle object; change the Lifespan Mode to `Constant` in the Channel Box, and set Lifespan (*not* Lifespan Random) to the curve parameter's maximum value (Figure 4.27).
6. Rewind and play back the animation. As shown in Figure 4.28, you'll see that the first few particles are almost, but not quite, in the right place.

As it turns out, this is due to the particles' initial speed being 1, not 0. Select the emitter, and set Speed to 0 in the Channel Box.

7. Rewind and play back the animation again. The speed is much improved, and the glitches we noted above are gone.

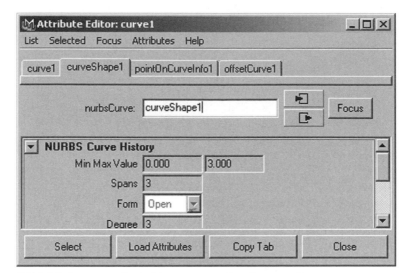

Figure 4.26 Minimum and maximum parameters for curve1.

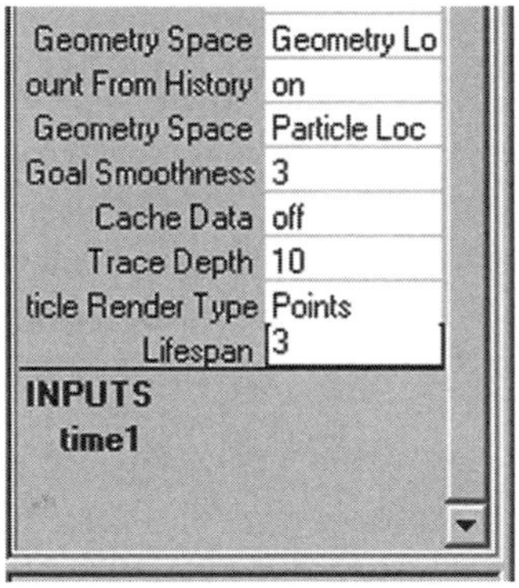

Figure 4.27 Setting Lifespan value.

8. Finally, save your scene; select the particle object; make sure the Dynamics menu set is selected, and choose Solvers > Create Particle Disk Cache. The time slider will run through the entire time range, and when finished you should be able to scrub the time slider and play forward and backward.

Note that in this example we've deliberately violated one of the particle expression tips mentioned earlier—that it's often best to avoid accessing per-object attributes in a particle expression. In this instance, because our particles were calculating their position using a complex geometric relationship to a curve object, there was little choice. Also important to

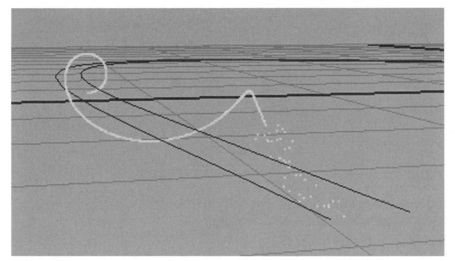

Figure 4.28 A glitch resulting from a nonzero initial velocity.

note is that using the `pointOnCurveInfo` MEL command, as with many MEL commands one might wish to use in an expression, not only broke this rule but quietly created and destroyed nodes behind the scenes.

What to Remember About Particle Expressions in Maya

■ Avoid using particle expressions if you can use a clever system of fields instead. Your system will always be faster without particle expressions.

■ Develop a simple implementation first, and then work toward the more complex, rather than trying to anticipate every problem up front. Don't be afraid to tear down what you've done and build it again differently; all good programmers do this.

■ Execution speed is a priority with particle expressions in a way that it is not with ordinary expressions, because particle expressions may execute thousands of times per frame.

■ Use MEL commands with caution when you develop particle expressions, as they may be creating or destroying nodes, or they might force recalculation of part or all of the scene dependency graph, once for each particle on each frame. This can be quite slow.

■ When it's possible to use a node for a calculation, in some cases it may be faster than the equivalent MEL command. To be sure, you may have to try both approaches.

■ Always remember that the creation expression runs on the first frame a particle exists, and the runtime expression does not run until the second frame. If you want something to happen on every frame of a particle's life, you must make both a creation and a runtime expression.

■ If you are calculating your particle's position or velocity in an expression, you must pay extra care to how your expression interacts with dynamics. In the previous example, selecting Expressions After Dynamics and setting the speed to 0 were necessary to ensure that the motion was what we wanted.

■ Pay careful attention to your particle's lifetime, and make sure that you get rid of particles that live too long for your expression to make sense.

■ Use the Numeric particle render type to debug your particle expressions. Any per-particle attribute can be used with the Numeric render type.

■ Once the particle motion is what you want, use the Create Particle Disk Cache command to speed up your particle's playback by saving to disk the particle's locations and attributes.

5

Problem Solving with MEL Scripting

In this chapter you will learn

- How MEL scripting fits into Maya as a whole.
- That MEL scripts function mainly to build or modify Maya scenes.
- What steps are necessary to plan a MEL script.
- How to create a simple user interface in MEL.
- How to create nodes in MEL.
- How to add, set, and get custom attributes in MEL.
- How to add connections between nodes in MEL.
- How to create expression nodes in MEL.

MEL's Role in Maya: Building Scenes

Throughout the examples in the last few chapters, we've explored how expression scripting fits into the process of building a Maya scene. We've also examined the differences between expression scripting and writing MEL scripts. Expressions are meant to be placed within a scene as DG nodes, taking in the value of one or more attributes and feeding values into one or more other attributes. Expressions are evaluated every time Maya needs to do so when recalculating a scene, such as when you change the time on the timeline.

MEL scripts, though, usually stand apart from scenes. Their execution is triggered by, say, choosing a menu item or clicking on a shelf button. It is possible to embed a MEL script in a scene using a *script node*, a feature that is often used, for example, to establish a script that will execute when the scene is opened, or to ensure that a necessary MEL script is available when you send a scene to someone else who does not share your environment.

However, most MEL scripts ultimately serve one purpose: *to automate building complex Maya scenes.*

What do we mean by building Maya scenes? Mostly, we mean exactly what you do in the interface: making nodes, making attributes, connecting nodes together, and creating expressions, all of which work together to produce your animation when you play the scene back or render it.

A typical MEL script does at least one, possibly several, of the following:

■ Presents an interface to the Maya user that allows the script to collect information about what the user wants the script to do. This interface might be a window with buttons and text boxes, or it might just be a standard set of arguments that the user must type on the Maya command line.

■ Creates nodes in the scene that will have a particular useful effect when evaluated.

■ Creates custom attributes for nodes that it has created to store information that is necessary for the task at hand.

■ Connects attributes between nodes to establish relationships between the newly created nodes and whatever might have already been in the scene.

■ Creates and connects expression script nodes that will process attributes when Maya evaluates the scene during playback or rendering.

As an example of how MEL scripts can be useful, building the expression-driven eye system in Chapter 3 required extensive work in the interface to get to the point where our expressions were relevant. Before putting the expression in place, we needed to create several constraints, locators, and custom attributes. Certainly, this would not be too onerous if we were only to set up eyes for one character, but when presented with 15 or 20 characters, we'd certainly go hunting for a shortcut.

That shortcut could be to build a MEL script. The interface might simply amount to clicking a button on a shelf. The script could make spheres for the eyes, create the constraints (including constraint nodes and their necessary connections), create locators, make the necessary custom attributes, and finally attach expressions to drive the constraints' weights. A more sophisticated script might take on the problem of integrating the eyes into a character setup, including naming the nodes suitably for the character and establishing parenting relationships.

Another typical example of a MEL application would be to automate setting up the particle expressions in Chapter 4. A Maya user could create a curve, select it, and choose a menu item or click a shelf button to do all the remaining work to put our spiral particle system in place.

Sometimes, a MEL script might simply consist of collections of behind-the-scenes tools meant to be used by other MEL scripts that make certain kinds of user interfaces easier, or that implement calculations that might be useful in many different circumstances. Most of the time, the MEL scripts that use these tools will do part of the job of building scenes. Your expressions might use such utilities as well, but it's a good idea to remain cautious, so that you don't unintentionally thwart the efficiency of your scene by using utilities that weren't designed to work well within expressions (e.g., utilities that use the `getAttr` and `setAttr` commands).

Strategies for Planning MEL Applications

A MEL *application* is the entire collection of scripts that are necessary to do something useful. Generally, there are four common phases to the process of writing a MEL application, or in fact any computer program:

- Planning what you want the application to do.
- Planning how you want the application to work.
- Building the application.
- Testing.

Planning what you want a script, menu item, or shelf button to do is sometimes the most difficult part of the process. Does it do only one task, or can users choose between a few related tasks? Are there important decisions the user must make about how he wants the task to be done? Are you going to set requirements in stone such as requiring users to name the objects in their scene in certain ways, for example, or are you going to try to accommodate variation? Can you rely on using the script in the context of a much larger, well-defined production environment (such as most animation studios try to maintain), or is it something you want to stand alone so that you can distribute it?

The questions that you need to answer before writing your script can seem endless. Many programmers faced with building something large fall into one of two traps: either they try to pin everything down and constantly delay building anything, or they forge ahead with too little planning and build a huge system that does not end up doing the job.

In the programmer's world, all kinds of methodologies have been developed to try to help software developers find their way through these questions. Fortunately, most MEL scripts don't ever get to be large enough to warrant a formal software engineering approach. However, there are a few principles that can make planning easier.

- *Do it by hand first.* If your script builds a number of nodes and connects their attributes to set up an effect, first try getting it to work in the interface, and take notes. With your notes on what you've done, you have a head start on scripting it.
- *Make and follow useful rules.* If you're developing scripts that you intend to use for your own animation, for example, establish conventional ways of naming nodes in your characters, or establish a few

standard ways that your scripts' user interfaces will work. By establishing conventions, you save time by avoiding repetitive questions about, for example, how your naming should work.

- *Hack something together and throw it away.* Most of the time it's terrifying to throw something away that almost does the job. However, first attempts often are better for learning how to do something a second time than they are at doing what they are intended to do. If you plan to whip up a prototype as quickly as you can and expect to throw it away and use what you have learned to start over, you will often end up with a much better-designed script.

- *Listen to your critics.* If you are a student on a team or working in a production environment, chances are you won't be the only one using your script. Get people to try prototypes and tell you where you have gone wrong. Most of the time, if people don't like what you have built, they will do things their own way, so it's worth it to build something they like.

- *Leave time for testing.* Very few scripts work perfectly the first time, or every time. Make sure that you have a first pass finished a little bit before you absolutely, positively need your scripts; then take the extra time to make sure they do what you think they do.

- *Underpromise and overdeliver.* If you work with others, particularly in a hectic production environment, it's easy for your offhand guesses about time and features to end up built rigidly into everyone's plans before you have started to write a line of code. Making the unpredictability of development clear to everyone up front can make the inevitable glitches more tolerable, and when you can deliver more than you promised, you will earn users' (and producers') trust.

Once you have a clear idea of what you want to create and how your problem breaks down into the basic steps of getting information from the user, making nodes, adding attributes, connecting attributes, and adding expressions, it's time to start building a MEL script. In this chapter, we look at the basics of each of these steps, and in Chapters 6 through 18 we will build on these basics with the tools for storing data, calculating, making decisions, and building user interfaces that make MEL a full-featured programming language.

The Simplest User Interface

The *user interface* to your script is simply a definition for how the people using your script will interact with Maya when they use it.

MEL provides powerful tools for creating intricate user interfaces; these tools will be discussed in much more detail in Chapters 12 to 14. However, the most basic approach, one favored in most of the tools present in Maya as it ships, consists of selecting an object and choosing a menu item or button to do something to it.

We've already seen, in Chapter 2, how to create a shelf button for a MEL script. A shelf button triggers our MEL script when the user clicks on it. What we're missing, then, is a way to determine what is selected at the time our script runs.

Most MEL commands that work with objects in a scene need only the name of the selected object (which means the name of the transform node if it's a 3D object like a NURBS surface or the name of the DG node if it's some other type of object). So, if you're writing a script that does something to the selected objects, the first task you want your script to perform is to get a list of the names of all the selected objects so that you can operate on them.

MEL provides a command for this called ls, which is short for "list." The ls command can be used to search through your scene to find all of the objects that share certain properties. For example, ls can give your script a list of all of the geometry in your scene, or all the textures. The ls command can also tell you the *types* of the objects you have asked it to list, such as nurbsSurface, mesh, expression, and so on.

To find all of the objects that are selected, use the ls command with the flag -selection, as follows:

```
ls -selection;
```

Try making a few objects, selecting them, and then running this command in the Script Editor window. You will see something like this:

```
ls -selection;
// Result: nurbsSphere1 nurbsSphere2 //
```

From Chapter 4 on particle expressions, you will recall that you can capture the result of a MEL command in a variable by using backticks. So, to get an array of strings that contains the names of the selected objects, you could type

```
string $selectionList[] = `ls -selection`;
```

Like most flags for MEL commands, the -selection flag has a short form, -sl. So, more often, you will see something like this:

```
string $selectionList[] = `ls -sl`;
```

If you had run this command with nurbsSphere1 and nurbsSphere2 selected, then the array element $selectionList[0] would contain the string nurbsSphere1 and the array element $selectionList[1] would contain nurbsSphere2.

See Chapter 9 for a description of how to perform the same operation on many objects in the selection. In the example presented later in this chapter, we look at how to operate on a single selected object.

Creating, Editing, and Querying Nodes in MEL

Many common types of objects in Maya have built-in Maya commands that create, edit, and retrieve information from, or *query,* them. For example, creating a NURBS sphere object, including its shape and transform nodes, is as easy as executing the `sphere` command. Arguments to the command let you pick a name for the object (which then will be incorporated both into its shape and transform nodes) and select many other starting values for a sphere's attributes.

Finding MEL commands that are designed to create a specific node type can sometimes be as simple as searching the online Maya documentation or hunting through the command listing in the online MEL Command Reference, available from the main Maya documentation page. The MEL Command Reference provides information on the arguments for each command, a brief description of what the command does, and examples.

When a MEL command is used to create an object, that MEL command is said to be used in *create mode*. Create mode is usually the *default* for a MEL command, meaning that if you don't explicitly specify that you want to edit or query an object, Maya assumes that you wish to create one when you use its associated command. If you execute the command

```
sphere;
```

you'll see that a new NURBS sphere object appears.

Many of the same MEL commands that can be used to create nodes can also be used to edit their attribute values. This is referred to as using the MEL command in *edit mode*. Now that you have created a sphere, try this command:

```
sphere -edit -radius 3 nurbsSphere1;
```

You'll see that your new sphere has grown to three units in diameter. Of course, you could simply have typed

```
sphere -radius 3;
```

to begin with. Note that not every attribute of a sphere has command-line arguments available in the `sphere` command. If you want to examine or change attributes that do not have arguments available (and you can tell whether such an argument is available by looking on the MEL Command Reference page for the command), you should use `getAttr` and `setAttr`.

Query mode allows you to retrieve the values of those attributes that have command-line arguments. For example, typing

```
sphere -query -radius nurbsSphere1;
```

will tell you the radius of your sphere.

Note: The MEL Command Reference pages indicate which arguments may be used with query and edit modes. Unfortunately, this information is not always complete; specifically, many arguments (such as radius) can be used in create mode but are marked as being useful only in query and edit modes. If you would like to use a particular argument in any of the modes, try it before searching for a different way to accomplish your result.

Adding, Setting, and Getting Values of Attributes in MEL

In Chapters 3 and 4, you have already seen how to add your own custom attributes using the Add Attribute menu item. When you are building a network of nodes to accomplish a task in your MEL script, you will often want your script to do this task automatically. In MEL, you can make a new custom attribute with the `addAttr` command. To add a custom attribute called "bounciness" to `nurbsSphere1`, you could use

```
addAttr -attributeType "float" -longName "bounciness"
        -defaultValue 2 nurbsSphere1;
```

or the shorter form,

```
addAttr -at "float" -ln "bounciness" -dv 2 nurbsSphere1;
```

The arguments to the `addAttr` command, described on its page in the MEL Command Reference, allow you to set minimum and maximum values for the attribute, specify properties such as keyability, and make use of all other features of attributes to which you would have access through the Add Attribute window if you were adding the attribute by hand.

Note that once you have added this attribute to `nurbsSphere1`, you can open the Attribute Editor and see the new attribute name and value under the Extra Attributes tab. Make sure you look at the attributes for the `nurbsSphere1` transform node and not the `nurbsSphereShape1` shape node. Had you wished to add the attribute to the shape node, you could have specified its name explicitly.

As discussed in Chapters 3 and 4, setting the value of an attribute within a MEL script is different from setting its value within an expression. In expressions, you are allowed to assign values to attributes as though they were variables. In fact, doing so makes your expression more efficient because Maya converts those assignments into connections between your expression node and other nodes in your scene, which allows Maya to figure out when it can avoid recalculating your expression. (Note, though, that you can only use this technique to assign particle attributes in particle expressions and object attributes in object expressions, which is why we had to use `setAttr` in our particle expression example to change object attributes.)

In a MEL script, however, assigning values to attributes the way you would in an expression is forbidden. For example, if you type

```
nurbsSphere1.bounciness = 5;
```

in the Script Editor, which follows MEL rules rather than expression rules, you'll get these errors:

```
// Error: nurbsSphere1.bounciness = 5; //
// Error: Invalid use of Maya object
"nurbsSphere1.bounciness". //
```

To set the value of bounciness to 5, use setAttr instead:

```
setAttr nurbsSphere1.bounciness 5;
```

Once again, while you must use setAttr in MEL scripts when you want to set an attribute's value, it's best not to use it in an expression unless you must.

Getting the value of an attribute in a MEL script is also different from doing so in an expression. To do so in a MEL script, use the getAttr command. If you type

```
getAttr nurbsSphere1.bounciness;
```

you will see that Maya gives you its value as a result. To put this into a variable in a MEL script, you would want to do something like

```
float $bounceval = `getAttr nurbsSphere1.bounciness`;
```

This statement creates a new variable called $bounceval and places the result of the getAttr command in the variable.

Connecting Attributes in MEL

In MEL, you can connect two nodes' attributes with the connectAttr command. As in the Connection Editor, the attributes must be of the same data type to connect them.

In Maya, make a new scene, and create two NURBS spheres. Move them apart; then type this command in the Script Editor window:

```
connectAttr nurbsSphere1.translateX nurbsSphere2.translateY;
```

Next, move nurbsSphere1 in the X direction to see what happens. When you move nurbsSphere1 in X, nurbsSphere2 moves along the Y axis.

Maya also offers functions such as isConnected, listConnections, and connectionInfo to allow your script to learn more about the state of connections to or from a given attribute or object. For example, your script can find out whether `nurbsSphere1.translateX` and `nurbsSphere2.translateY` are already connected by placing the result of `isConnected` into an integer variable:

```
int $tx_ty_connected = `isConnected nurbsSphere1.translateX
                       nurbsSphere2.translateY`;
```

(Note that when Maya must return a value from a command that indicates truth or falsehood, the command will return an integer value of 0 or 1, 0 being false and 1 being true. For more on this, see Chapter 9.)

Finally, to disconnect the two attributes, use `disconnectAttr`:

```
disconnectAttr nurbsSphere1.translateX nurbsSphere2.translateY;
```

Creating and Connecting Expression Nodes in MEL

Creating an expression node in MEL is simple in theory, but often more complex in practice. Suppose that instead of connecting the `translateX` attribute of `nurbsSphere1` directly to `nurbsSphere2.translateY`, you wanted `nurbsSphere2.translateY` to be the square of `nurbsSphere1.translateX`.

In the Maya interface, you would right-click on one of the attributes, open the Expression Editor, and type

```
nurbsSphere2.translateY = pow(nurbsSphere1.translateX, 2);
```

(How did we find the `pow` function, used to calculate the powers of a number? This function and many others are enumerated in the "Functions" section of *Using Maya: Expressions,* in the Maya documentation.)

However, if you are using MEL to build many nodes, attributes, connections, and expressions, you would prefer to be able to automate installing such an expression. In this instance, it's quite simple. (Note that if you installed the previous expression by hand, you will have to find the expression node in the Hypergraph and delete it before this will work.) Type the following in the Script Editor and execute it:

```
expression -string "nurbsSphere2.ty = pow(nurbsSphere1.tx, 2)";
```

This command creates and installs an expression containing the given string. Simple enough. However, certain circumstances are tricky.

- Keeping long, multiple-line expressions readable in the context of a MEL script that installs them can be a challenge. The example in this chapter shows one way to improve readability, but it's not a perfect solution.
- When double quotes are required in an expression, you run the risk of confusing both yourself and Maya. The quotes that must be included in the expression (rather than indicating the beginning and

the end of the expression string) must be preceded by a backslash (i.e., \") to indicate that they are to be treated as part of the expression.

In addition to the expression command, there is a dynExpression command that installs particle expressions and works similarly. We use dynExpression in the example below.

Example 1: Using MEL to Automate Setup for Spiral Particles

Not only did the spiral particles example from Chapter 4 require tricky coding, it is also setup intensive. For each curve that you wish to treat with a particle helix, you must create a guide curve, create an emitter, create some custom attributes, and install an expression. If you had to do this for dozens or hundreds of curves, your sanity would not survive for long.

Now that we have an idea of how to accomplish the basic scene-building functions of MEL scripts, (examining the selection, creating nodes, creating and examining attributes, connecting attributes, and installing expressions), we can create a script that will automate the process.

As we discussed earlier in the chapter, the first step is to settle on a user interface for your script. In this instance, the ideal interface is for the script to be activated by a shelf button that applies a helix of particles to a selected curve. The steps for activating the script would be

- Create a curve.
- Make sure the curve is selected.
- Click the shelf button.

Now we have to plan how the MEL script will do the work. Since the curve will already be selected when the MEL script starts to run, the following steps constitute our plan. Some of these steps are clear from the example we did by hand in Chapter 4, and some of them you might have had to discover by trial and error were you scripting this yourself. Once again, though, a good rule of thumb is to do it by hand before attempting to freeze your approach into a MEL script.

1. Put the list of selected objects into an array variable.
2. Read the first object name from the array, and assume that's our curve. (A more robust script would check to make sure that the first selected object is a curve. For the moment, we will let Maya do that for us.)
3. Choose how far away the guide curve is from the original curve.
4. Make a guide curve using the offsetCurve MEL command that we used in Chapter 4.

5. Determine where the emitter should be located, and how it should be oriented. Then make the emitter.
6. Create the particle object.
7. Add an attribute to the particle object for the speed that the particles move down the curve.
8. Add an attribute to the particle object that determines the radius of the helix.
9. Connect the emitter and the particle object so that the particles are emitted by the emitter. (Note that normally these two actions are done for you when you create an emitter in the interface.)
10. Parent the emitter and the guide curve to the original curve. (Don't parent the particle object, or else your particle expression may have an odd result.)
11. Create `pointOnCurveInfo` nodes for the guide curve and the main curve.
12. Create a string variable that includes the expression code for the spiral particles example in Chapter 4.
13. Finally, use `dynExpression` to add runtime and creation expressions for the particles.

Finally, once we have planned an interface and figured out how our approach is going to work, we write the script. Don't be intimidated by this script; everything in it has been discussed before. If parts of it seem hard to follow, go back to some of the earlier examples that discuss in more detail how each piece works. Also, keep in mind that there are many possible solutions in MEL to every problem. Keep thinking about how you might improve the script as you read it.

1. Start with an empty Script Editor.
2. Enter the following script; select it, and choose Save Selected to Shelf. . . from the File menu in the Script Editor window.
3. When prompted, give it a name like `spiralParticles`. A button will appear on the shelf that will run the script when clicked. (If typing this script all at once is too much of a chore, look for it in the additional materials available for download at *www.melscripting.com*.)

```
// First, examine the selection so that we can see what curve we're
// working on

string $selection_list[] = `ls -sl`;

// Assume first item selected is our curve (if we want to get fancy
// later we can add a check to verify that it is a curve)

string $curveSelected = $selection_list[0];

float $startOffset = 0.1;
```

```
float $speed = (1.0 / 24.0);

offsetCurve -d $startOffset -n ($curveSelected +"guide");

float $startPoint[] = `pointOnCurve -pr 0 -p $curveSelected`;

float $startTangent[] = `pointOnCurve -pr 0 -nt $curveSelected`;

float $startGuide[] = `pointOnCurve -pr 0 -p ($curveSelected + "guide")`;

float $startNormal[];

$startNormal[0] = $startGuide[0] – $startPoint[0];

$startNormal[1] = $startGuide[1] – $startPoint[1];

$startNormal[2] = $startGuide[2] – $startPoint[2];
emitter -pos $startGuide[0]
     $startGuide[1] $startGuide[2]
        -dx $startTangent[0] -dy $startTangent[1] -dz
           $startTangent[2]

        -n ($curveSelected +"emitter") -spd 0.0

        -type dir;

particle -n ($curveSelected + "particles");

setAttr ($curveSelected +"particlesShape.expressions AfterDynamics")
        true;

select -r ($curveSelected +"particlesShape");

addAttr -ln "speed" -at "float";

setAttr ($curveSelected +"particlesShape.speed") $speed;

addAttr -ln "scaleOffset" -at "float";

setAttr ($curveSelected +"particlesShape.scaleOffset") $startOffset;

connectDynamic -em ($curveSelected +"emitter")
                  ($curveSelected +"particles");

parent ($curveSelected +"emitter") $curveSelected;

string $mainCurveInfoNode = "pointOnCurve -ch on -pr 0
                              $curveSelected";

string $guideCurveInfoNode = `pointOnCurve -ch on -pr 0
                              ($curveSelected +"guide")`;

// Here's where we embed expression code in a string

string $exprString =
```

```
"float $curve_param = " + $curveSelected + "particlesShape.age * "
                    + $curveSelected + "particlesShape.speed;\n" +

"setAttr " + $mainCurveInfoNode + ".parameter $curve_param;\n" +
"setAttr " + $guideCurveInfoNode + ".parameter $curve_param;\n" +

"float $pos[] = `getAttr " + $mainCurveInfoNode + ".position`;\n" +
"float $tan[] = `getAttr " + $mainCurveInfoNode +
                ".normalizedTangent`;\n" +
"float $normEnd[] = `getAttr " + $guideCurveInfoNode +
                ".position`;\n" +

"float $norm[];\n" +
"$norm[0] = $normEnd[0] - $pos[0];\n" +
"$norm[1] = $normEnd[1] - $pos[1];\n" +
"$norm[2] = $normEnd[2] - $pos[2];\n" +

"vector $posvec = <<$pos[0], $pos[1], $pos[2]>>;\n" +
"vector $tanvec = <<$tan[0], $tan[1], $tan[2]>>;\n" +
"vector $normvec = unit(<<$norm[0], $norm[1], $norm[2]>>);\n" +
"vector $norm2vec = cross($tanvec, $normvec);\n" +

$curveSelected + "particlesShape.position = $posvec +\n" +

"(" + $curveSelected + "particlesShape.scaleOffset * $normvec *
    cos(" + $curveSelected + "particlesShape.age*20)) + \n" +

"(" + $curveSelected +
    "particlesShape.scaleOffset * $norm2vec * sin(" +
    $curveSelected + "particlesShape.age*20));\n";

// Attach expression to the particle object

dynExpression -rad -s $exprString ($curveSelected + "particles");

dynExpression -c -s $exprString ($curveSelected + "particles");
```

4. Now, create a few curves. Then, select them one by one, clicking the new `spiralParticles` button for each.
5. Play back your scene to get the effect in all its glory.

How It Works

First, our script gets the current selection:

```
string $selection_list[] = `ls -sl`;
```

Remember that this creates an array called `$selection_list` that contains all of the selected objects. The first selected object's name is in `$selection_list[0]`, the second in `$selection_list[1]`, and so on.

The next line pulls the first selected object out of the array. A more sophisticated approach could repeat all the rest of the steps once for every selected object, which would let you install the particle system for multiple curves at once.

```
string $curveSelected = $selection_list[0];
```

Now we have our selected curve's name in $curveSelected. In the discussion of string variables in Chapter 3, we looked at how to concatenate shorter strings into longer ones—this will be essential for our script, because we will build various node names from the name of the selected curve by adding, say, "particles" or "emitter" on the end of it. Also, we will be able to build the names of our curve's attributes by adding, say, .tx to the end of its name.

Our next two lines consist of a couple of the variables that define the trajectory of the particles. We have grouped these variable definitions together, but the $speed variable could be defined later on.

```
float $startOffset = 0.1;
float $speed = (1.0 / 24.0);
```

$startOffset contains the distance in units that our guide curve will be from the original curve named in $curveSelected. $speed contains the number of units along the curve that our particles will move in a frame, at least to start. We use 1/24 because we often like to run animations at 24 fps, and one unit per second is a reasonable rate of speed for the effect.

Now that we have basic parameters defined for our particles, it's time to make the guide curve. Note that we are doing this before completing the definition of our variables. However, since we need this guide curve to be able to initialize some of our variables defined after this, it's reasonable to put the offsetCurve command here.

```
offsetCurve -d $startOffset -n ($curveSelected + "guide");
```

In this command, we are building the name of the new guide curve by adding the string guide onto the end of the selected curve. For example, if our selected curve were curve1, our guide curve would be curve1guide.

We want to place the new emitter at the point where we want the particles to start, which should be a distance of the value of $startOffset away from the selected curve. $startPoint will be the beginning of the selected curve in X, Y, and Z. $startTangent will be the X, Y, and Z values for the normalized tangent direction of the selected curve. $startGuide is the location in X, Y, and Z of the start of the guide curve, and $startNormal is the distance and direction in X, Y, and Z of the guide curve's starting point as seen from the start of the selected curve.

```
float $startPoint[] = `pointOnCurve -pr 0 -p $curveSelected`;

float $startTangent[] = `pointOnCurve -pr 0 -nt
                         $curveSelected`;

float $startGuide[] = `pointOnCurve -pr 0 -p
                       ($curveSelected +"guide")`;

float $startNormal[];

$startNormal[0] = $startGuide[0] - $startPoint[0];

$startNormal[1] = $startGuide[1] - $startPoint[1];

$startNormal[2] = $startGuide[2] - $startPoint[2];
```

Now that we've defined variables for the starting point, a tangent, and a normal for our selected curve, and we've stored them away, we can create an emitter at our desired starting point.

```
emitter -pos $startGuide[0]
   $startGuide[1] $startGuide[2]
     -dx $startTangent[0] -dy $startTangent[1]
                         -dz $startTangent[2]

   -n ($curveSelected + "emitter") -spd 0.0

   -type dir;
```

With the -pos flag, we create our emitter at the start of the guide curve. The -dx, -dy, and -dz flags tell emitter what direction to emit, in this instance along the tangent of the selected curve. Our emitter is named $curveSelected with emitter tacked on the end, and our emitter speed is 0 (to prevent strange dynamic behavior on the first frame after emission). Finally, -type dir tells the emitter command that our emitter should be directional.

Now, we create the particle object:

```
particle -n ($curveSelected +"particles");

setAttr ($curveSelected +
        "particlesShape.expressionsAfterDynamics")
   true;
```

The particle command makes the particle object, named appropriately. Then, we set the value of the expressionsAfterDynamics flag to true. This setAttr command relies on a few Maya behaviors to work. First, assuming our curve is called, say, curve1, it relies on the fact that the particle command creates not only a transform node called curve1particles but also a related shape node called curve1particlesShape. Also, it expects this shape node to have an `expressionsAfterDynamics` attribute. This attribute is set to `true` so that our expression gets last crack at positioning the particles. (Recall that in Chapter 4 we did this by hand.)

Next we select our *<curve name>*`particlesShape` node. Because we're adding a couple of attributes in a row to that node, we can select the node once and use several `addAttr` commands without specifying the name of the node to which we want to add the attributes. If you call `addAttr` without a node name to which to add attributes, Maya assumes you want to add the attribute to the selection.

The `select` command with the `-r` flag tells Maya to "replace" the current selection with the node whose name is given to the command. This doesn't modify the nodes themselves; it just changes the selection so that only the named node is selected.

```
select -r ($curveSelected + "particlesShape");
```

The next four lines use `addAttr` to create `speed` and `scaleOffset` attributes for our `particleShape` node, using `setAttr` to assign them initial values that we've computed above.

```
addAttr -ln "speed" -at "float";

setAttr ($curveSelected + "particlesShape.speed") $speed;

addAttr -ln "scaleOffset" -at "float";

setAttr ($curveSelected + "particlesShape.scaleOffset")
        $startOffset;
```

Now that we have created and set up the emitter and the particles, we need to connect them so that the emitter knows what particle object it's emitting. The `connectDynamic` function does this. The `-em` flag indicates the name of the emitter, and the remaining argument is the name of the particle object.

```
connectDynamic -em ($curveSelected + "emitter")
               ($curveSelected + "particles");
```

Next, we parent the emitter to our main curve using the `parent` command.

```
parent ($curveSelected + "emitter") $curveSelected;
```

In Chapter 4, we used the `pointOnCurve` command with the `-ch on` flag to make `pointOnCurveInfo` nodes for our main and guide curves. In our MEL script, we'll do the same, but this time we will assign the return value to a string variable. Since these commands return the name of the object they create, we now have the name of those objects for our expression.

```
string $mainCurveInfoNode = `pointOnCurve -ch on -pr 0
                           $curveSelected`;

string $guideCurveInfoNode = `pointOnCurve -ch on -pr 0
                            ($curveSelected + "guide")`;
```

Finally, we build our expression string. This string ends up containing an expression substantially identical to the expression that we created at the end of Chapter 4, but this time we have to painstakingly assemble it line by line, inserting the names of nodes that we've created along the way. Remember that the parts within double quotes are included in the expression unmodified, while the variables that are outside double quotes have their values placed in the expression.

Since we are using the age of each particle times its speed in multiple places to find out how far along the curve's parameter we are, the script has also been slightly modified to calculate that value and place it in the variable $curve_param. This helps make the expression more readable.

Also, note that we end lines in our expression string with \n. If we didn't do this, our entire expression would be on a single line, which would make it unreadable if we wanted to examine it with the Expression Editor later on. It would still work, though. Remember that using the + sign between a series of strings places them end to end in one large string.

```
string $exprString =

    "float $curve_param = " + $curveSelected + "particlesShape.age * " +
        $curveSelected + "particlesShape.speed;\n" +

    "setAttr " + $mainCurveInfoNode + ".parameter $curve_param;\n" +
    "setAttr " + $guideCurveInfoNode + ".parameter $curve_param;\n" +

    "float $pos[] = `getAttr " + $mainCurveInfoNode + ".position`;\n" +
    "float $tan[] = `getAttr " + $mainCurveInfoNode +
                    ".normalizedTangent`;\n" +
    "float $normEnd[] = `getAttr " + $guideCurveInfoNode +
                    ".position`;\n" +

    "float $norm[];\n" +
    "$norm[0] = $normEnd[0] - $pos[0];\n" +
    "$norm[1] = $normEnd[1] - $pos[1];\n" +
    "$norm[2] = $normEnd[2] - $pos[2];\n" +

    "vector $posvec = <<$pos[0], $pos[1], $pos[2]>>;\n" +
    "vector $tanvec = <<$tan[0], $tan[1], $tan[2]>>;\n" +
    "vector $normvec = unit(<<$norm[0], $norm[1], $norm[2]>>);\n" +
    "vector $norm2vec = cross($tanvec, $normvec);\n" +
```

```
$curveSelected + "particlesShape.position = $posvec + \n" +

"(" + $curveSelected +
    "particlesShape.scaleOffset * $normvec *
    cos(" + $curveSelected + "particlesShape.age*20)) + \n" +
"(" + $curveSelected
    "particlesShape.scaleOffset * $norm2vec * sin(" +
    $curveSelected + "particlesShape.age*20));\n";
```

Finally, our MEL script uses `dynExpression -rad` to make a runtime expression after dynamics and `dynExpression -c` to make a creation expression. These expressions, of course, are added to the particle's node.

```
dynExpression -rad -s $exprString ($curveSelected +
                                    "particles");

dynExpression -c -s $exprString ($curveSelected +
                                  "particles");
```

As we dig further into the MEL language, we will find opportunities to make this script clearer and more concise. For example, much of our expression could be encapsulated in a MEL procedure that would make building the expression string simpler and more readable without sacrificing performance. In many instances, though, building MEL or expression scripts as strings within other MEL scripts is a regrettable necessity.

What to Remember About Writing MEL Scripts

- MEL's strength is creating tools that help you build scenes: creating nodes, adding and setting attributes, making connections, and adding expressions.
- Always determine what your script should look like to the user, and then determine how you think it should work; then build it, and finally test it.
- Do it by hand first: MEL is mostly just shorthand for time-consuming operations in the interface. If you know how to accomplish your script's goal by hand, you are halfway there.
- Make and follow useful rules. Our example started all the node names it created with the name of our selected curve, which allowed us to run the script on multiple curves. Creating a naming rule helped multiple resulting networks of nodes coexist.
- Hack something together, and throw it away. When developing the spiral particles example script, we created five or six different versions, each time learning better how to get where we were going. Don't be afraid to throw away work if you can build something better in the time you have.

- Listen to your critics. Sometimes a fresh pair of eyes can see the answers you have been missing.
- Leave time for testing. Untested code usually doesn't work. Don't gamble on being the exception.
- Underpromise and overdeliver. When working with others, it's easy to assume everything will always go smoothly, because it's what your coworkers want to hear. Usually, though, things go wrong, so set expectations realistically, and be prepared.

6

Variables and Data Types

In this chapter you will learn

- How to declare variables and why it sometimes is not necessary.
- What global and local variables are and how are they used.
- How to choose between global variables, attributes, and option variables for storing data that must persist.
- Which MEL commands can be used to read and set environment variables.
- Why Maya distinguishes between different types of data in the MEL language.
- What the different data types available in MEL are.
- How to perform basic operations on data of each type.
- How and why to convert data from one type to another.
- The differences between integer and floating-point operations, and how they can surprise you.
- The differences between arrays and vectors.

In the examples in Chapters 3 through 5, we talked about and used variables as temporary places to store information that our scripts need to keep around for later use. In Chapter 3, we talked about how Maya classifies the kinds of data that you store in them, and what you can do with that data. In this chapter, we focus on variables themselves and how they work when you're storing data for different purposes.

Declaring Variables (and Not Declaring Them)

Declaring a variable, as we have seen in previous examples, explicitly tells Maya what kind of data you are planning to store in it. For example, to declare an integer a, you can add

```
int $a;
```

to the beginning of your script, or you can type it in the Script Editor. After that, every time you try to put numeric data into $a, it will either be converted to an integer (if possible), or you will get an error telling you that Maya could not convert the data.

Declaring variables this way, although a good idea, is optional. If you simply put something into a variable without declaring it, Maya will look at the data type of what you are putting into the variable and establish, once and forever, that that variable contains that data type. For example, try typing the following into the Script Editor:

```
$t = 54;
$t = { 1, 2, 3 };
```

(As we'll see below in the discussion of arrays, putting a list of numbers in curly brackets {} makes Maya regard them as the elements of an array.) When we try to run these two commands, Maya gives us the following error:

```
// Error: Cannot cast data of type int[] to int //
```

("Type casting" or "casting" data is Maya's process of trying to convert data from one type to another.) Because we told Maya to put the value 54 in $t without declaring $t first as any particular type, Maya looked at the value 54 and decided that we meant $t to be an integer variable.

Then, when we try to put an array into $t, since Maya does not have a way of converting an array to an integer (which it must do, since $t is an integer variable), we get an error message. This kind of error message can be particularly frustrating because often, in a long script, you may be unable to remember where you used $t before, or what kind of variable it was.

Even more frustrating can be tracking down problems caused by data getting converted automatically behind your back. Try running the following code in the Script Editor:

```
$my_variable = 5;
$my_variable = 5.25;

print ($my_variable + "\n");
```

The result it prints is the number 5, not 5.25!! What happened is that when you put an integer value into $my_variable, $my_variable became an integer for the rest of your script (or in this case, since you ran the command in the Script Editor window, for the rest of your Maya session). Then, when you put 5.25 into $my_variable on the next line, Maya's automatic conversion of floating-point numbers to integer numbers kicks in and slices off the fractional part of the number.

Try these statements instead:

```
$my_variable_2 = 5.0;
$my_variable_2 = 5.25;

print ($my_variable_2 + "\n");
```

This time, you get the expected result, 5.25. In this case, because you put 5.0 (which, to Maya, is clearly a floating-point number because it has digits after the decimal place) into $my_variable_2, Maya locked it in as a floating-point variable. Then, Maya doesn't touch the value of 5.25 when you assign it to $my_variable_2; it just places it in the variable.

Declaring the variable can help. Compare the next example to the $my_variable example above.

```
float $my_variable_3;

$my_variable_3 = 5;
$my_variable_3 = 5.25;

print ($my_variable_3 + "\n");
```

Because you have explicitly stated that $my_variable_3 contains floating-point data, Maya realizes that it has to convert the integer 5 to a floating-point 5.0, and honors the data type that you have declared.

Declaring variables like this will not prevent Maya from converting data types from one to the other on the fly, so you can't always rely on it to catch mistakes when you forget what type of data a variable contains or how you were using a particular variable. However, declaring your variables does give you some control over how Maya's data conversions take place, and it also provides a visual reminder in your script that you are storing a particular type of data in a particular variable.

Local and Global Variables

Once you declare a variable, you can use it in the procedure where you defined it, or if you declared it outside a procedure in a MEL file, you can use it anywhere in that MEL file. If you declare a variable in the Script Editor, you can continue using it in the Script Editor until you quit Maya.

For example, try the following code:

```
proc declare_aaa () {
    int $aaa = 10;
}

print ($aaa);
```

You'll get the error

```
// Error: "$aaa" is an undeclared variable. //
```

Variables declared in one procedure normally can't be seen outside that procedure, and vice versa. Where a variable can be used is called its "scope." As in the following code segment, if you declare a variable outside any procedure in a MEL file or in the Script Editor, you will see that that variable can only be used outside a procedure.

```
int $bbb = 34;

proc print_bbb() {
    print ($bbb);
}

print_bbb();
```

Still, you get a similar error:

```
// Error: "$bbb" is an undeclared variable. //
```

This behavior is what makes it possible to use scripts that you have downloaded from the Internet or borrowed from a friend. You don't have to worry about the variables that their procedure or MEL file declares and uses conflicting with yours, because they are, so to speak, playing in their own variable sandbox. Variables that can only be used in the procedure or script in which they are declared are called "local variables."

Sometimes, though, you'd like to have a place to put information that multiple procedures (or multiple scripts) can share. If it makes sense, you can make a custom attribute for a node in your scene. However, Maya provides an end run around the variable-scoping mechanism called the "global variable."

Global variables are declared and used just like local variables, except that you declare them with the word "global" in front of the data type. Let's look at one of our examples that didn't work as we had hoped.

```
int $bbb = 34;

proc print_bbb() {
print ($bbb);
}

print_bbb();
```

To make $bbb a global variable, first we have to declare it to be global. Note that you have to do this when the variable is defined the first time—it won't work if it's already been defined as local. Let's call our new global variable $bbb_2. Try running the following code in the Script Editor:

```
global int $bbb_2 = 34;
proc print_bbb_2() {
    print ($bbb_2);
}

print_bbb_2();
```

Oops! It still doesn't work!

As it turns out, declaring a variable as global once is not enough. In fact, you have to declare a global variable in every script or procedure where it's used. Also, all the declarations must be consistent regarding data type; otherwise, you will get an error that you're trying to redefine a variable (which is forbidden).

Because variables outside our procedure can't be seen by the code inside the procedure (they are out of the procedure's scope), we need to declare the variable both outside and inside the procedure. Try running the following code:

```
global int $bbb_2 = 34;

proc print_bbb_2() {
    global int $bbb_2;
    print ($bbb_2);
}

print_bbb_2();
```

Now the procedure can find the variable $bbb_2, because it's been declared to be global both outside the procedure (where its value is set) and inside the procedure (where it's printed out).

Maya requires you to redeclare global variables in every scope that they are used. If you don't, you can run into troubles like this:

```
global int $my_int = 25;
proc assign_four() {
    $my_int = 4; // puts the value 4 into $my_int
}
assign_four();
print($my_int);
```

Oops again! Now, our script has printed the value 25, despite the fact that we ran our procedure to set $my_int to 4. What happened here is that we did not bring the global $my_int variable into the procedure with a declaration such as

```
global int $my_int;
```

Because we have not made $my_int available in the procedure, when we assign 4 to $my_int, Maya quietly makes a *new local variable* called $my_int that springs into being when the procedure gives it a value of 4, and ceases to exist one line later when the procedure ends! Then, when we print the value in $my_int, since the print statement sees the global version (the one declared outside the procedure), it prints 25 instead of 4.

The solution is to make sure the procedure can see the global variable, as in the following example:

```
global int $my_int = 25;

proc assign_four() {
   global int $my_int;
   $my_int = 4; // Puts the value 4 into $my_int
}
assign_four();

print($my_int);
```

At this point, you may be thinking that perhaps *everything* should be made global. Three reasons for avoiding this strategy follow.

■ First, because forgetting to declare a global variable can sometimes mean that you're modifying the wrong data, as seen in our examples, it's usually safer to use local variables because they don't have that problem.
■ Second, by using local variables and always passing values into procedures using arguments and out of procedures using return values, you can glance at any procedure and know exactly what it's changing. If it uses a global variable, the procedure could potentially change that global variable by mistake if you introduce a bug into your script—these kinds of problems can be very hard to find.
■ Third, many MEL scripts and functions will have similarly named variables. In most cases, the scripts and functions will not intend to share this information with all the others, and in fact rely on the fact that they, and only they, know how to modify their variables.

Global Variables, Attributes, and Option Variables

Both global variables and node attributes are available to any script that runs in your scene, so you can use either one for storing information that you want to persist throughout a single script or multiple scripts. One major difference between the two is that a node's attributes are saved as part of the Maya scene when the scene is saved. Global variables do not persist between Maya sessions. Also, as we've seen, node attributes get duplicated when their nodes get duplicated; attributes can be connected to other attributes, and attributes can be easily edited in the Channel Box or Attribute Editor without using a script.

You can create another type of variable that exists across Maya sessions called an *option variable*. The MEL command optionVar allows you to create and edit option variables, which are stored in each user's preferences, not with the scene. Note that if two different users use the script or open the scene, their option variables will not be the same. For more information, check the MEL Command Reference documentation for optionVar.

Environment Variables

Environment variables are not really a Maya feature, but rather a feature of the operating system. These variables are not guaranteed to work the same under Windows, Mac OS, Irix, or Linux.

Environment variables are typically used when you're writing scripts outside of Maya and wish to communicate information to your Maya session. How to use environment variables is outside the scope of this book, but to get started, have a look at the getenv and putenv commands in the MEL command reference.

MEL Statements and Type Checking

MEL divides data into a number of named types. By keeping track of the type of data on which a script or node operates, Maya can sometimes discern when a developer has made an unintentional mistake by attempting to operate on the data in a way that makes no sense.

MEL commands, as seen in a number of examples, are lines of MEL code that instruct Maya to do something useful to a node or an attribute. MEL commands are always either built into Maya or implemented as part of a *plug-in,* a loadable chunk of software developed outside of Maya in a programming language such as C++.

Procedures, which are discussed in more detail in Chapter 10, are a way of grouping a set of operations in a MEL script or expression that perform a common function. Procedures define sets of data that need to be given to the procedure by the scripts that start, or *call,* them, as well as operations to perform on that data. The advantages of using procedures in a MEL script are that it can help make the structure of your script more transparent to someone else, and that it makes reusing useful code easier.

Functions can be either built into Maya, or they can be a special type of procedure. Functions look much like procedures, except that instead of simply performing a series of operations in MEL, functions pass chunks of data back to the scripts that call them. These chunks of data are called *return values.*

Finally, *operators* are symbols such as + and − that define operations on one or more values. For example, 3 + 3 uses the + operator to add 3 and 3 to make 6.

Most MEL commands, procedures, functions, and operators require one or more chunks of data on which to operate, which as we have seen are called the operation's *arguments,* although some operations can do something useful without being given data. The data must be meaningful for the operation. For example, to Maya, 3 * 3 is meaningful, while "ham" * "sausage" is not, because the * operator describes an operation that only applies to numbers.

As you use MEL scripts, Maya checks to ensure that the data you hand to commands, procedures, functions, and operators are the appropriate data types for each. If Maya knows how to convert one type to another, it will, but when you try to apply an operation of any of these four kinds to a data type that is not consistent with that operation and cannot be converted, MEL cancels your script's execution and gives you an error in the Script Editor window.

The rest of this chapter describes the data types in Maya and MEL, some of the operations each supports, and when to make use of each. Some operations (such as the + operator) can be used with several data types, while others (such as the mag() function, used with vectors) only work with one data type. Usually, MEL commands, procedures, and functions offer you the chance to look up appropriate data types, either in their code or their documentation. Unfortunately, though, sometimes the only way to know whether a given operation will work with a given data type is to try it.

Simple and Aggregate Data Types

Like most programming languages, Maya defines a handful of data types that are basic units of information, called *simple* data types, and it permits building larger structures out of them, often called *aggregate* data types.

There are only three simple data types in MEL: *integers, floating-point numbers,* and *strings.* (If you have programming experience, you may be familiar with languages such as C and Pascal, in which strings are aggregate data types made up of smaller units called characters. MEL does not have a separate data type for a single character—instead, a single character is just a short string.)

Aggregate data types in MEL are *vectors, arrays,* and *matrices.* Vectors are lists of three floating-point numbers (no more, and no fewer) that can be manipulated mathematically in certain ways, while an array is a list of any other data type, including vectors, but which usually cannot be mathematically manipulated as a whole. A matrix is an array of arrays with a predetermined maximum number of elements within it.

Integers

Definition Integer variables and attributes have no fractional parts, and must be one of the counting numbers (1, 2, 3, 4, etc.), zero, or the negative of a counting number (−1, −2, −3, −4, etc.).

How to declare an integer variable   Declaring an integer variable should be familiar from the previous scripting examples:

```
int $i;
int $i = 3;
```

Integer arithmetic operations   The standard arithmetic operators +, −, *, and / can be used to add, subtract, multiply, and divide integers. Also, like in algebra, you can use parentheses to group computations that should be done first. One thing to keep in mind is that operations between two integers always yield another integer. Particularly in the case of division, this can yield unexpected results.

Open the Script Editor; type the following, and press Enter:

```
print (3 + 4);
```

You will get the result you would expect, 7. The next line,

```
print (3 - 4);
```

also gives you the expected result, −1.

Multiplication also gives you what you'd expect:

```
print (3 * 4);
```

yields 12. However, division may not be so intuitive. For instance, the result for

```
print (3 / 4);
```

is 0, even though 3 divided by 4 is 3/4 (0.75).

Integer division, because it must produce an integer result, *always throws away any remainder, or fractional part of the result*. This can present a problem if you have two integer variables and wish to find their ratio, including the fractional part. The solution is to convert one of the numbers to a floating-point number before dividing. You do this with the float() function. (Names of functions and procedures are often written with parentheses after them as a reminder that their arguments are enclosed in parentheses when they're used, and to distinguish them from MEL commands.)

To convert an integer to a floating-point number, then, you can do something like

```
print (float(3));
```

At this point, the result, 3, does not tell you that you've converted the 3 to a floating-point number. In Maya, a floating-point number whose fractional part is 0, when printed, looks just like an integer because Maya does not print a decimal point or a trailing zero. However, you can see the difference between 3 and float(3) with

```
print (float(3) / 4);
```

Now your result is 0.75, not the result of 0 that you got when you divided integers. *When you divide two numbers, if both are integers, you get an integer result with the remainder thrown away. If one or both are floating-point numbers, you get a floating-point number including the fractional part (the remainder).*

Suppose, though, that you want to find the remainder of your division of two integers. Assume integer variables $a and $b, as follows:

```
int $a = 14;
int $b = 3;
```

Taking advantage of parentheses, you could do something like

```
print ($a – ($b * ($a / $b)));
```

This statement yields the correct result, 2, but you'll have trouble figuring out what it does or why you did it later on. Fortunately, there is a built-in operator that will find the remainder for you:

```
print ($a % $b);
```

The percent symbol (%) is called the *modulus* operator, and it gives you the remainder of the integer division of, in this case, $a divided by $b. In algebra, this is often written *a* mod *b*.

Combining arithmetic and assignments   When you want to apply an arithmetic operation to a variable and put the result back into the variable, you can use the +=, –=, *=, /=, and %= operators. In other words,

```
$x = $x + 4;
```

is the same as

```
$x += 4;
```

Similarly,

```
$y = $y % 3;
```

is the same as

```
$y %= 3;
```

Incrementing and decrementing integer variables Also, you can increment and decrement variables with the operators ++ and —. You need not type

```
$x = $x + 1;
```

Instead, you can type

```
$x++;
```

Decrementing is just as easy:

```
$y = $y - 1;
```

is the same as

```
$y--;
```

Most floating-point operations (described below) can be applied to integers as well, but you get a floating-point result, suggesting that Maya automatically converts the integer to floating point for you.

Integer comparisons As discussed in Chapter 9 on control structures, sometimes it's useful to compare two integers to see which is larger or which is smaller. You can do this with comparison operators. Try some of the following examples:

```
print (5 > 6); // greater than
print (5 < 6); // less than
print (5 >= 6); // greater than or equal to
print (5 <= 6); // less than or equal to
print (5 == 6); // equals
```

Note that each of the above comparisons produces a result of 1 or 0. A result of 1 means that the comparison is true, and the result of 0 means that the comparison is false.

Boolean (true–false) operations MEL comparison operators represent true with an integer value of 1 and false with an integer value of 0. Often, your scripts will need to look at the results of multiple comparisons in combination to determine what to do. You can combine the results of multiple comparison operations with the not (!), and (&&), and or (||) operators:

- *not (!)* The not operator returns a value of 0 when it operates on any nonzero number, and it returns a value of 1 if it operates on a number that is zero.

  ```
  print (! 0); // prints 1
  print (! 1); // prints 0
  ```

- *and (&&)* The and operator returns 1 if it operates on two integers that are nonzero (meaning true), and it returns 0 if either one of the numbers on which it's operating is 0.

  ```
  print (0 && 0); // prints 0
  print (1 && 0); // prints 0
  print (0 && 1); // prints 0
  print (1 && 1); // prints 1
  ```

- *or (||)* The or operator returns 1 if either of its two operands are nonzero (meaning true), but if they're both 0, it returns 0.

```
print (0 ÍÍ 0); // prints 0
print (1 || 0); // prints 1
print (0 || 1); // prints 1
print (1 || 1); // prints 1
```

■ *Combinations* You can use the three Boolean operators in combination with each other as well. For instance,

```
print (! (0 && (1 || 0) ) ); // prints 1
```

Floating-Point Numbers

Definition   Floating-point variables and attributes, often called *float* variables because of how they are declared, are numbers that can be positive or negative real numbers (such as 1.2 or −5.4), and optionally with a scientific-notation exponent (i.e., 1.0E3 to represent 1000).

How to declare an integer variable   Declaring a float variable is much like declaring an int variable. For example,

```
float $m;
float $m = 3.2;
```

Useful floating-point operations   All of the same arithmetic operations that apply to integers can be used with floating-point variables as well, including %, which still represents the remainder of the division operation. Arithmetic operations that combine two floating-point numbers in MEL always yield a floating-point number. As noted in the section on integers, if you combine an integer with a floating-point number in a mathematical operation, you will get a floating-point result.

There are additional floating-point functions that frequently come in handy, a few of which we've already seen. For example, if you have float variables $m and $n, as in

```
float $f = 36.0;
float $n = 3.2;
```

some of the floating-point operations that you can perform include

```
sqrt($f) // square root of $f
pow($f, $n) // $f to the power of $n
log($f) // log base e of $f
log10($f) // log base 10 of $f
abs($f) // absolute value
sin($f) // sine of $f
cos($f) // cosine of $f
tan($f) // tangent of $f
```

A comprehensive list of all the arithmetic functions available in Maya is available in *Learning Maya: Expressions,* Chapter 6.

Cautionary note about floating-point comparisons   Often, when doing floating-point arithmetic in your scripts, you may be tempted to use the == operator to check to see whether two floating-point numbers are equal. Most of the time, though, this is a bad idea. The reason is that floating-point math, for various reasons, is a very close approximation but is not entirely precise on a computer.

Performing a series of mathematical operations on a floating-point number and then checking to see if they are equal with the == operator can sometimes tell your script that they are not equal when in fact, mathematically, they should be. This is the result of *roundoff error,* in which the computer cannot keep enough fractional digits around to perform the computation precisely.

Consequently, it is usually a good idea, if you must check floating-point numbers for equality, to see if they are greater or less than the comparison number by a certain amount. This keeps your comparison from being absolutely exact, but it ensures that roundoff error will not cause your script to fail. An example of using greater than and less than operators follows.

```
float $a = 5.0;
float $b = 4.9999999999;
float $slop = 0.0001;
print ($a == $b); // returns 0
print ( ($a > ($b - $slop) ) && ($a < ($b + $slop) ) );
   // returns 1
```

Conversions Between Integers and Floating-Point Numbers

In general, as stated above, combining integer numbers with floating-point numbers in an arithmetic expression yields a floating-point result, while combining integers with integers yields integers, and combining floating-point with floating-point yields floating-point numbers.

When you use a number explicitly in a script (e.g, by using the number 3 instead of a variable), if the number includes a fractional part or a scientific-notation exponent, Maya will treat it as a floating-point number; otherwise, Maya will treat it as an integer. Examples of integers are

```
1
3
-4
0
```

while examples of floating-point numbers are

```
3.0
2.5
-3.4
1E-12
```

This rule, along with the above rule, is why 2 * 3.0 yields a floating-point 6, not an integer 6.

If you want to convert a floating-point number to an integer, you can use the int() function. For example,

```
print(int (3.7));
```

yields 3. Note that converting an integer in this way *always rounds down*, and if you want to implement other rounding behavior, you will have to program it yourself. You can also use the ceil($f) or floor($f) functions, which return the next highest or lowest integer to $f, respectively.

You can convert an integer to floating-point using the float() function. For example:

```
print(float(7)/2);
```

yields 3.5, unlike the 3 that print(7/2) gives you.

Chapter 9 in *Using Maya: MEL* describes all the automatic data type conversions that MEL does for you, along with the rules for how they are performed. Keeping these rules in mind can reduce the possibility that you will be unpleasantly surprised by an unexpected data type conversion affecting your script's arithmetic.

Vectors

Definition   In Maya, a *vector* is a group of three floating-point numbers that are bound together in a single attribute or variable, and that can be operated on as a unit. Chapter 4 contains an introduction to the concept of vectors and their use.

How to declare a vector variable   Vectors are declared much like integers and floating-point numbers, as in

```
vector $vector1;
```

To assign a value to a vector at the point where you declare it, you can surround the list of three numbers with << and >> to establish that they are bound together as a vector. For example,

```
vector $testvector_2 = << 3, 4, 5 >>;
```

Working with vectors   To perform a calculation on one of the three components of a vector, you can use *$vectorname.x*, *$vectorname.y*, *$vectorname.z*, as follows:

```
$a = $testvector_2.y + 2; // sets $a to 6
```

However, you cannot assign a value to one component of a vector using the same notation:

```
$testvector_2.z = 4; // This gives you an error!
```

Instead, to assign one value of a vector, you must assign the whole vector and use the component notation to leave the components that you do *not* want to affect alone.

```
$testvector_2 = << $testvector_2.x, $testvector_2.y, 4 >>;
// This fixes the error.
```

The basic arithmetic operations, +, −, *, /, and %, can be used with vectors just as they are used with integers and floating-point numbers. The computation of these operations' results is described below.

When you add two vectors, each element gets added to the corresponding element. Thus,

$$<< a, b, c >> + << d, e, f >> = << (a + d), (b + e), (c + f) >>$$

When you subtract two vectors, each element gets subtracted from the corresponding element.

$$<< a, b, c >> - << d, e, f >> = << (a - d), (b - e), (c - f) >>$$

When you multiply two vectors, each corresponding element gets multiplied *and then the results are added to produce a single, floating-point value.*

$$<< a, b, c >> * << d, e, f >> = (a * d) + (b * e) + (c * f)$$

Finally, when you divide or apply the modulus operator (%) to two vectors, the corresponding elements get divided.

$$<< a, b, c >> / << d, e, f >> = << (a / d), (b / e), (c / f) >>$$
$$<< a, b, c >> \% << d, e, f >> = << (a \% d), (b \% e), (c \% f) >>$$

Combining vectors and floats in expressionsVectors and floating-point numbers can be combined in expressions. When you operate on a vector and a floating-point number, you will apply the same operation to all the elements of the vector. For example,

```
vector $a_vec = <<1, 2, 3>>;
print ($a_vec + 3); // returns 4 5 6
print ($a_vec * 4); // returns 4 8 12
```

In particular, multiplying vectors by floating-point numbers is often a useful way to scale a vector that you are interpreting as a direction and distance in 3D.

Other common vector operations   The common vector operations such as magnitude, cross product, dot product, normalize, and dotProduct, are implemented with the functions `mag()`, `cross()`, `dot()`, `unit()`, and `dotProduct()`. Also, the `rot()` function can be used to rotate a vector around the origin, and the `angle()` function can be used to find the angle between two vectors. These functions are defined in more detail in Chapter 4, and they are also documented in *Using Maya: Expressions,* Chapter 6.

Strings

Definition   A string is a chunk of text that can either be empty or contain a series of characters. Strings can be used to store names of objects, text to be printed, characters that the user has typed, MEL or expression code, or any other text that your program needs to manipulate.

How to declare a string variable   Declare a string variable like any other variable, as follows:

```
string $my_str;
```

To give a string a value when you declare it, put the text that it should contain in double quotes when you assign the string its initial value, as in

```
string $gettysburg = "fourscore and seven years...";
```

Obviously, most of the arithmetic operations that have been meaningful for integers, floating-point numbers, and vectors are not meaningful for strings (although if the string contains a number, Maya's tendency to automatically convert data types may kick in and do something useful depending on the context). However, you can concatenate two strings (stringing one after another) using the + operator.

```
$string1 = "Testing 1";
print ($string1 + "testing 2"); // this prints Testing
1testing 2
```

Strings can contain useful characters other than the normal alphabetic and numeric characters. For example, if you tried running the above print statement twice, you'd find that it printed `Testing1testing2Testing1test-ing2`, instead of placing its output on two separate lines. By explicitly putting a *newline* character (\n) in the string, you can fix this.

```
print ($string1 + "testing 2\n");
// this prints Testing1testing2 with a newline
```

If you want to put double quotes in the middle of a string, you can precede them with a backslash as well.

```
print ("Here are some double quotes: \" \n");
```

Note that the double quotes that are immediately preceded by the backslash (\) print out, while the pair at the end of the line serves to tell Maya where your string ends. And, as before, \n represents the newline character.

The backslash followed by another character is called an "escaped character." By placing a \ in front of a character, you are causing it to escape from its normal interpretation, and be interpreted in a special way. In the case of \", you're causing it to store a literal " inside the string, instead of indicating the end of the string. For \n, you're causing the n to be interpreted as a special character (newline), which means start the next line.

You may also wish to compare strings. To do this, use the == operator, just as we did before with integers.

```
print ("testing" == "testing"); // returns 1, for true
```

There are also other operations you can perform on strings. For example, you can break a string up into words or other meaningful parts using the tokenize MEL command. The tokenize command accepts a string and an array variable (described below), and it breaks the string into words (meaning each chunk of text separated by whitespace, meaning spaces, tabs, or newlines), and places each part into the elements of an array:

```
string $myarray[];
tokenize "This is a test" $myarray;
print $myarray[3]; // prints "test"
```

If you want to split the string up using something other than whitespace as the separator, you can specify your own, as in

```
string $myarray2[];
tokenize "This is a test" "t" $myarray2;
print $myarray2[1]; // prints "es"
```

The above example printed es because element 0 of the array became his is a and element 1 became es, with the t characters used as separators.

The MEL scripting example from Chapter 5 demonstrates using strings to allow a MEL script to build an expression node. That example is a good place to start for thinking about how you can use strings in MEL beyond printing text in the Script Editor.

Arrays

Definition Arrays are an aggregate data type that allow you to collect a list of values in a single variable. The individual values in the list can be integers, floating-point numbers, strings, or vectors. All values stored within a single array must of be of the same type.

Maya's documentation refers to all data types that can be included in arrays as *scalar*. In mathematics, vectors are not scalar, but in this regard Maya's usage differs from the mathematical terminology.

How to declare an array Here are some examples. The array declaration states the type of the data in the array and the name of the array, and it ends with a pair of square brackets ([]) to indicate that you are declaring an array and not an individual value.

```
string $s[];
int $a[];
float $f[];
```

You can also initialize an array at the time you define it, just as you can other variables, although like other variables you need not initialize the array right away if it doesn't make sense to do so. Surround the values that you want to place in the array with curly brackets ({}), and separate them with commas.

```
string $str_list[] = {"this", "is", "a", "string", "array"};
int $int_list[] = {1, 2, 3, 4};
float $lots_o_floats[] = {1.3, 1.5, 34, -23, 1E-29};
```

To make your array declaration more readable, you can also break up your array declaration in several lines.

```
string $str_list2[] = {"this",
                       "is",
                       "a",
                       "string",
                       "array"};
```

You may also explicitly give the size of the array with a number inside of the square brackets. If you do not specify a number, you're implicitly defining it to be as large as necessary to hold the values that you are initializing it to. What you *cannot* do is declare an array while assigning only one of its elements.

```
int $u[4] = 3; // THIS WILL NOT WORK!
```

In this example, You can do one of two things. You can declare the array first and then assign a value to the fifth element (which, remember, is the element numbered four, because element numbering starts at 0),

```
int $u[];
$u[4] = 3;
```

which will set the fifth element to 3, and all previously unset elements to 0. Or you can declare the array with all the elements 0 through 4 defined, as in

```
int $u2[] = {0, 0, 0, 0, 3};
```

Working with array contents Each item in an array is called an array element. Each array element has a unique number, called its index. The first element in an array has an index of 0; the second has an index of 1, and so on. You can refer to an element of an array using the array name followed by the element's index in square brackets.

```
print($str_list2[2]);
$a[1] = 4;
float $add_it_up = $lots_o_floats[3] + 32.4;
```

What makes arrays even more powerful (and you'll see more examples of this in Chapter 9 on control structures) is that you can use another variable to indicate which element of an array to use in a calculation. For example,

```
int $i = 2;
float $testing = $lots_o_floats[$i] * 2;
```

Array size property and its implications   Arrays have an inherent property called size, which refers to the number of elements in the array. To find the size of an array, you can use the size() function:

```
print (size($str_list2));
```

Assuming that this array is the one we've defined above, the result is 5, because it has five elements. Note that the maximum meaningful index for the array is the size minus 1, because the indexes begin counting at 0.

If you want an array to have more elements, you can add them just by assigning values to them. Try running the following commands, and see what results you get. (Note that we are adding newlines to each print statement to make the results more readable.)

```
int $growing_array[] = {0, 1, 2};
print (size($growing_array) + "\n");
$growing_array[5] = 45;
print (size($growing_array) + "\n");
```

By adding a sixth array element (because its index is 5 and index numbering starts at 0, it's the sixth element), new elements have been created in the fourth and fifth positions in the array as well. These as yet uninitialized elements are given a default value of 0 if the array type is integer or float, <<0,0,0>> if it's a vector type, or the empty string "" if it's a string type.

This has serious implications for how you use arrays in your scripts. If, for example, you were to create an array $i_am_too_long and assign a value to $i_am_too_long[999999], Maya would set aside memory to hold *1 million* array elements, even though you wanted to store only one number. Although Maya manages memory differently in different situations, it is reasonable to presume that that memory will remain set aside until you quit Maya, which can slow down whatever you're doing.

If you need to use an extremely large array in your script, it can be a good idea to clean up at the end with the MEL `clear` command. The command

```
clear $i_am_too_long;
```

will free any memory that the array is using so that Maya can use it for other purposes.

Choosing Between Arrays and Vectors

Arrays and vectors are both useful ways of binding together a group of related values. In many instances, one Maya built-in function will want you to represent a direction and a distance in 3D space as an array with three elements, while another may require you to use a vector. In Maya 5 and earlier, there is no automatic conversion from arrays to vectors or vice versa, so you will need to do this yourself if it is necessary. The particle expression example in Chapter 4 demonstrates how to do this. In Maya 6 and later, you can convert an array of three floats to a vector and vice versa by assigning one to the other.

As a general rule, vectors are found more often in particle expressions, while manipulations that are related to object transforms are more likely to require an array under similar conditions. This correlation is a result of Maya's historical development and does not really reflect a meaningful difference between the data that you are manipulating. However, this is not a hard-and-fast rule, and for your own scripts you should pick whichever type makes your tasks easiest.

What to Remember About Variables and Data Types in MEL

- Variables don't have to be declared explicitly, but if they are, you can be more certain that they will behave as you expect.
- Global variables provide an easy way for multiple scripts to share a chunk of data. However, scripts that use many global variables can be difficult to debug because you can't just look at procedure and function declarations to determine what variables your procedures and functions might change.
- Data that should persist past the execution of your script can be stored in global variables (best if your other scripts need to use the data); object attributes (best if you want to store the data with the scene); option variables (best if you want the data to be stored per user like a preference setting would be); and environment variables (best if you need to pass information to shell scripts that you're executing from within Maya on a Linux, Irix, or OS X system).
- MEL distinguishes between data types so that it can catch certain obvious errors in your scripts, particularly when calling functions

and procedures that you have written. Much of the time, though, it will do its best to convert data in a way that is consistent with what you expect.

■ Because Maya's automatic data conversions sometimes may do the unexpected, convert your own data from one type to another by hand when you can.

■ Integers are used both for the counting numbers and for true–false (Boolean) values.

■ Comparing two floating-point numbers is usually more reliable if you check to see if one is within a reasonable range of the other rather than testing for exact equality, especially if you're manipulating them heavily before comparing them.

■ Strings are not just useful for printing text. You will often want to consider using strings for building MEL commands, expressions, or commands to be executed outside of Maya.

■ Arrays grow as needed, and this can be a problem if you mistakenly assign a value to an array element with an enormous index. You can use the `clear` command to fix this.

7

Using MEL Commands

In this chapter you will learn

- What a MEL command is.
- How to find the right MEL command.
- What query, create, and edit modes are.
- How MEL commands can be executed in a script.
- That, when possible, you should avoid using MEL commands in expressions.

What Is a MEL Command?

Not every MEL statement is a MEL command. MEL commands are operations that manipulate your Maya scene that are either built in to Maya or provided by plug-ins. Like functions (both built-in functions and those that are implemented in MEL), MEL commands can return data values to your script. Like procedures written in MEL, MEL commands can alter your scene in useful ways.

However, most MEL commands differ from built-in functions and operators that are solely meant to manipulate data that you've stored in variables. Most MEL commands alter or collect information from the scene graph, and are thus most useful when building systems of nodes rather than in expressions. Generally, MEL commands are used in MEL scripts, and avoided when writing expressions.

Where to Find the MEL Command You Need

As discussed in Chapter 2, finding the MEL command to perform a task that you know how to do in the interface can be made easier using the Echo All Commands feature in the Script Editor.

Ask an experienced MEL programmer   Sometimes, of course, this is easier said than done, but when the option is available, it's usually the shortest route. In fact, by using Internet newsgroups and the mailing lists and message boards at *www.highend3d.com,* you may well have access to extremely experienced MEL programmers who can help you with the simplest and the most difficult challenges.

Read related scripts from the Internet or elsewhere   If you can find a script that does something close to what you need, you can often find ideas for MEL commands to use by reading through it. After all, there are only a limited number of commands for manipulating NURBS surfaces. This approach is also good for seeing how other programmers attack problems.

Read the documentation   Another essential resource for finding MEL commands to perform useful tasks is to search the MEL Command Reference in the online Maya documentation. By searching through either the MEL Command Reference's alphabetical command listing or the Maya documentation index, for example, you can sift through all the commands that help you manipulate, say, curves.

Unfortunately, searching through the documentation can be time consuming, particularly if you are not sure what you're looking for, but at times it's the only option. When you choose Help > MEL Command Reference . . . from the menu in Maya, you see a list of Maya commands sorted alphabetically (Figure 7.1).

Clicking on any of these MEL commands will open a page of documentation that gives you a brief description of what the command does, a list of arguments you can use, and examples.

Structure of a MEL Command

A MEL command consists of a command's name, a series of *flags*, which generally communicate how the command is to be carried out, and usually one or more *arguments*, which are frequently, though not always, the names of nodes or attributes on which the command should operate. Once again, we'll use the sphere command as an example.

```
Sphere -radius 10.0 -sweep 180
```

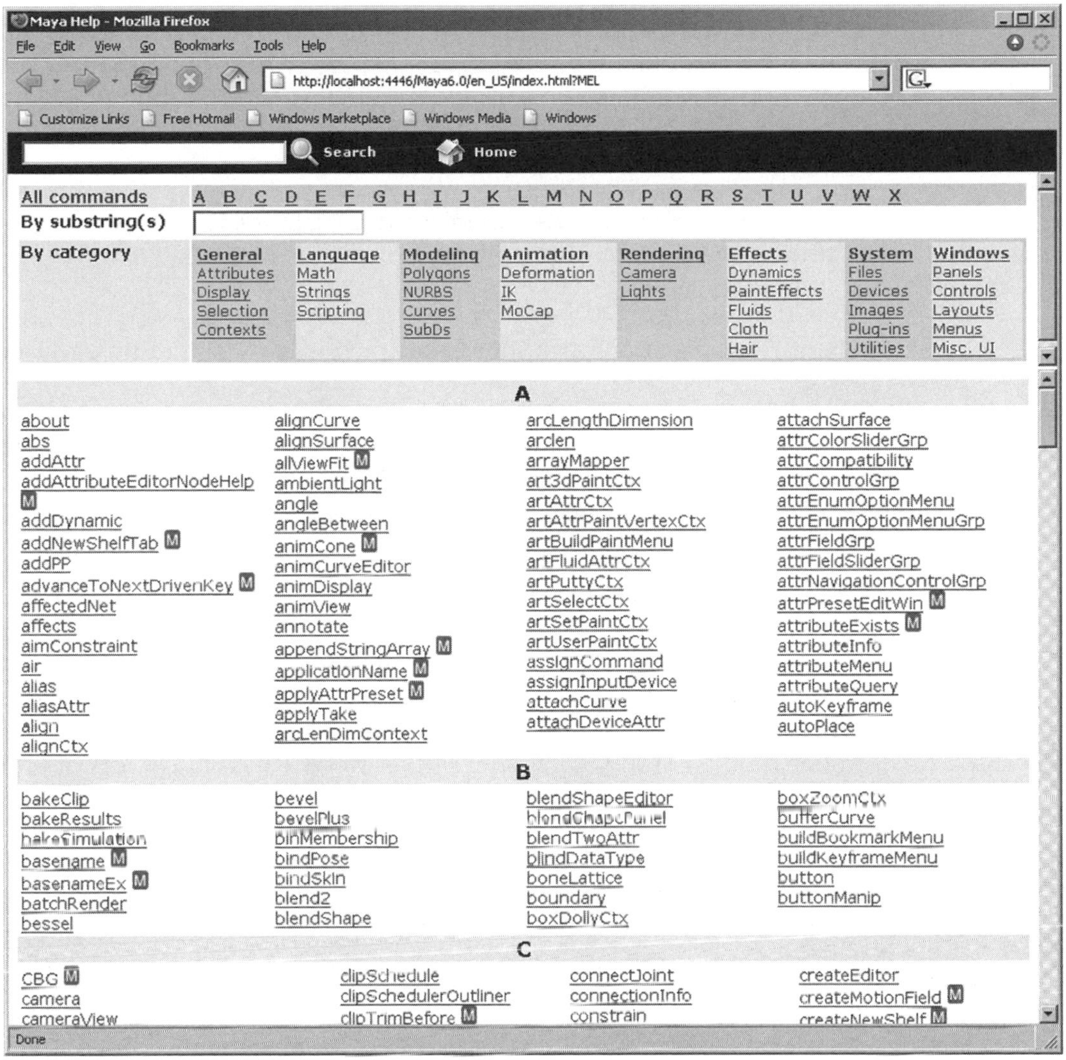

Figure 7.1 MEL Command Reference.

In this example, sphere is the command name, -radius 10.0 is a flag to indicate the sphere's radius, and -sweep 180 is a flag to indicate that we only want to create half a sphere.

Many MEL commands can be run in one of three ways, in *create mode,* in *query mode,* and in *edit mode*. Create mode is selected with a -c flag or with no flag at all, query mode with a -q flag, and edit mode with a -e flag. When none of these flags are used, the command usually defaults to create mode.

Query, Create, and Edit Modes

Running our example command, sphere, in create mode, which is the default, makes a sphere for us. Running the sphere command in query mode, as in

```
sphere -q -radius nurbsSphere1
```

returns an attribute of the sphere, in this instance its radius.
Running the command in edit mode, as in

```
sphere -e -radius 15 nurbsSphere1
```

changes an existing attribute of the sphere, again the radius, to a new value.

Usually, there's a way to query or edit the objects in question with the getAttr or setAttr commands, respectively. However, using the query or edit modes with familiar MEL commands can be a direct way to get the information your script needs from your scene.

Other Command Flags

Most command flags have a short version and a long version. In the MEL Command Reference, the sphere command's radius flag is listed as -r/radius, telling you that you can either use -radius in your command or the shorter form, -r. Usually, the longer form will make your script easier to understand by others, but using the shorter form can save lots of typing and make otherwise long commands reasonable.

The MEL Command Reference lists each flag, indicates the data type for the flag's arguments, notes whether the flag can be used in query or edit mode (important because some flags can only be used in create mode), and describes what the flag does.

> **Note:** Not every valid mode for every flag is listed in the MEL Command Reference. If in doubt, try it.

Command Arguments

The command arguments usually indicate on what object, if any, the command is to operate. Sometimes, though, such as with commands like move, the arguments can be other data, such as, in this case, distances in X, Y, and Z.

The sphere command from our examples only takes arguments in query and edit mode, to indicate on which object they operate.

Using MEL Commands in MEL Scripts

Using MEL Commands as Statements

In a MEL script, of course, you can use a MEL command as a statement on a line by itself. Even if the MEL command provides a return value (as most do) you can throw it away if you don't wish to store it for future use in your script. For example, this MEL script creates a cone, moves it 10 units in X, and deselects it:

```
cone -name testing;
move 10 0 0 testing;
select -cl;
```

The cone command returns the names of both the transform node that it creates, called, in this case, testing, and the name of the history node that describes how the cone is built, called makeNurbsCone1. However, because we're using the cone command on its own line in the MEL script, we've chosen to throw that information away.

Using Backticks

When you do wish to store the return value of a command, you can enclose the command in backticks (` ` `) on the right-hand side of an assignment. For example,

```
string $coneNodeNames[] = `cone -name testing2`;
```

Now $coneNodeNames[0] will contain the name of the cone's transform node, and $coneNodeNames[1] will contain the name of the cone's history node.

MEL commands can also be called as if they were functions, with each flag on the command line treated as though it were an argument. For example, the above assignment could be written like this:

```
string $coneNodeNames[] = cone(`-name`, `testing2`);
```

However, this usage is rarely used, in part because it's more difficult to read for commands with many arguments.

> **Tip:** It's often good practice to use the return value of any MEL commands that you execute for creating or renaming nodes in the scene, instead of relying on the name you specified to be correct. For example, assume you write a script that creates a new cone and moves it 10 units in X:

```
cone -name Cone;
move 10 0 0 Cone;
```

What would have happened if an object called Cone had already existed in the scene when the user ran your script? When your script tried to make a new object with the same name, Maya would automatically rename it to Cone2, and the cone command would return that new name. Then your move command would actually move the Cone object that the user already had in his or her scene, not the new one that had been created by your script. If you don't check the return value of the command you use to create an object, it may have a different name than you expected, and you can lose track of that object in your script.

Using eval

Although it is not often necessary, the eval command can be the most powerful way to run MEL commands within a MEL script. The eval command takes a string as an argument and returns whatever the MEL command contained in the string returns. For example,

```
string $spherecommand = `sphere`;
string $nodenames[] = eval($spherecommand);
```

creates a sphere, placing the sphere command's return values into the $nodenames array.

The reason that the eval command can be so versatile is that your MEL script can construct commands to execute as needed. Your script can assemble a command in a string and then execute it using eval. Here's a simple example:

```
string $theCommand = "";

for ($x = 0; $x < 5; $x++)
{
   int $whichShape = rand(2.0);
                                 // This picks a random number between
                                 // 0 and 2 and that will round
                                 // down to either 0 or 1

   switch ($whichShape)

   {
      case 0:
         $theCommand += " sphere;";
         break;
      case 1:
         $theCommand += " cone;";
         break;
   }

}
```

```
print ("Now we're going to execute " + $theCommand);
eval($theCommand);
```

Although we could have placed a `sphere` or `cone` command in the `switch` statement, this approach allows us to print the precise command string that our script executes.

Avoid Using MEL Commands in Expressions

As discussed in Chapters 3 and 4, using MEL commands is not recommended in expressions. Maya does support using MEL commands in expressions when necessary, as we've seen, but doing so often forces Maya to recalculate the entire scene graph to allow the MEL command to execute.

If you avoid using MEL commands in an expression, Maya can take advantage of internal optimizations that keep your expressions running much faster. Often, when you are tempted to use a MEL command in a script to calculate some aspect of the geometry in the scene, there is a related utility node that you can create in advance and access in your expression to get the same result. In some instances, however, this is not the case. As in the spiral particles example from Chapter 4, it can be difficult to avoid using a MEL command in an expression.

What to Remember About Using MEL Commands

- MEL commands can be Maya's basic built-in operations, or they can be implemented in plug-ins, and they can be used in MEL scripts or typed into the Script Editor.
- When you're trying to find a particular MEL command to perform a task, often the best approach is to ask someone who knows, and failing that to look for similar scripts on the Internet. The online Maya documentation also provides tools for searching and looking up Maya features and information about how to access them from MEL commands.
- MEL commands can often be called in create, query, and edit modes. These modes allow you to either make new objects or read the state of existing objects with the same MEL commands.
- Flags provide instructions to MEL commands that tell them how to do what they do, and arguments provide what the MEL command should operate on.
- There are three ways to run a MEL command in a script: either alone, as its own statement, if you don't care about the return value; in backticks if you want to store the return value in a variable; or using `eval` if you want to build a command in a string and execute that.

Cases where you need to use `eval` are rare, but it can be a powerful approach when you need to build MEL commands on the fly in your scripts.

■ MEL commands are not recommended in expressions because they may force recalculation of the Maya scene graph that would otherwise not be necessary, and they can slow down playback and rendering of your scene.

8

Manipulating Nodes in MEL

In this chapter you will learn

- How your MEL scripts can find nodes in your scene by name.
- How to manage the selection list.
- Choices for ways to create nodes in your MEL scripts.
- Finding parents and children of nodes in the transform hierarchy.
- Finding information about node connections.
- About Maya's node types and the DG Node Reference.

As we discussed in Chapter 5, MEL scripts often serve to help build structures of nodes in your scenes. Chapter 5 discussed the basics of creating nodes, connecting their attributes, setting attribute values with getAttr and setAttr, and creating expressions in your MEL scripts. In this chapter, we discuss in more detail how your scripts can manipulate and create nodes.

Using ls Command to Find Nodes by Name or Other Properties

The ls command, as seen in many of our examples, is Maya's general tool for getting the names of nodes in your scene that satisfy certain characteristics.

Finding Objects with a Particular Name or Partial Name

Finding the objects in your scene whose names contain a particular string is a powerful way to take advantage of the naming conventions that you've set up. For example, assume that your characters are always set up with nodes named *<character name>_<node name>*. For example, your worm character *bill* might have a top-level transform node called `bill` and nodes underneath named

- `bill_joint1`
- `bill_joint2`
- `bill_joint3`
- `bill_skin`
- `bill_eye_l`
- `bill_eye_r`

You can use `ls` to find all of these nodes by combining the name string that they all have in common, `bill_`, with a *wildcard*, which is a special character that matches any set of characters in a particular place in the object's name. For example, if your scene includes the above nodes,

```
string $bill_nodes[] = `ls ("bill_*")`;
```

might return

```
// Result: bill_eye_l bill_eye_r bill_joint1 bill_joint2
bill_joint3 bill_jointShape1 bill_jointShape2 bill_skin
bill_skin|bill_skinShape //
```

For the `ls` command, the character * can be used as a wildcard that matches any set of characters. Also, the wildcard will match if there are no characters where the * is.

Often, you may not know when you're writing your script what string you will need to search for. In this case, you can assemble the wildcard string in your script. For example, if you had a variable called `$character_name` that contained your character's name, you could do this:

```
string $character_nodes[] = `ls ($character_name + "_*")`;
```

Remember that if you only need objects of a certain type in your list of names, you can combine this approach with the `ls` command options described in the Finding Objects of a Particular Type section below.

Depending on your naming conventions, you might want to only find nodes that contain a particular string, such as `joint`. In that case, you can use multiple wildcard characters in your search, as follows:

```
string $joint_list[] = `ls *joint*`;
```

Getting Names of Selected Objects

In our examples in previous chapters, we've seen how to get a list of selected objects:

```
string $selection[] = `ls -sl`;
```

Of course, if you only care about selections that contain a particular name, you can combine the selection flag with a name string:

```
string $selected_joints[] = `ls -sl "*joint*"`;
```

Getting One or More Objects' Types

To list the object types for the objects that ls lists, use the -showType flag.

```
string $bill_skin_listing[] = `ls -showType "bill_skin"`;
// Result: bill_skin transform //
```

Note that the results alternate: first a node name, then a type name, then a node name, then a type name, and so on. So, in this instance, $bill_skin_listing[0] is the node name, and $bill_skin_listing[1is the type of the node whose name is in $bill_skin_listing[0]. If ls were to list more nodes, the names would be in elements numbered 2, 4, 6, and so on, while the types would be in 3, 5, 7, and so on. Note also that our listing for bill_skin indicates that the node is of type transform. To get the underlying object type, in this case a nurbsSurface, you must make sure to list the shape node.

Finding Objects of a Particular Type

Using the -type flag allows you to find all the nodes of a particular type. For example, to find all shape objects of type nurbsSurface, you would use the -type flag:

```
string $nurbs_surface_list[] = `ls -type nurbsSurface`;
```

The strings that you give the -type flag are the same as the strings returned by -showType. So, if you're not sure what type a particular object is, select it and type

```
ls -sl -showType
```

to find its type. Then, you can include the correct -type flag in your code. The ls command is probably the easiest way to check the type of a node interactively, but if you want to check the type of a node in a MEL script, you can use the objectType command.

The ls command also offers a number of flags that let you locate certain types of objects. For example, -transforms allows you to find transform nodes, -shapes finds shape nodes, -lights finds light nodes, and so on. For a complete list, look at the documentation on ls in the MEL Command Reference.

Finding List of Objects Under a Certain Node in Transform Hierarchy

If you have the name of a top node in a hierarchy, you can get a list of all nodes beneath it in the hierarchy using the -dag flag (dag stands for directed acyclic graph). Maya's scene hierarchy (as visible in the Outliner) is a form of a directed acyclic graph, so when you ask for all the DAG objects, you're asking to list everything below the specified object in the hierarchy. If all nodes in the character `bill` were parented under a top node called `bill`, this command would list all nodes in the character, as follows:

```
string $bill_nodes[] = `ls -dag bill`;

// Result: bill bill_joint1 bill_jointShape1 bill_skin
bill_skin|bill_skinShape bill_joint3 bill_eye_1 bill_joint2
bill_jointShape2 bill_eye_r //
```

Of course, you can get type names with the -showType flag, or filter for particular types of objects with the -type flag or other filtering flags.

Listing Full Path Names

With `ls` you can find the fully qualified path to an object with the -long flag. Also, if a particular shape node is instanced, you can find all the paths to that shape node using the -allPaths flag.

```
string $full_bill_skin_path[] = `ls -long bill_skin`;
// Result: |bill| bill_joint1|bill_skin //
```

Using Select Command to Manage Object Selection

Once you have the names of objects you wish to manipulate, you often will need to select them, as many MEL commands and many procedures you write for your own use will assume that they need to operate on the selection.

Clearing the Selection

Many scripts start off by getting a list of what the user has selected. Since many commands require that objects be selected to tell the command on what to operate, often you'll want to consider clearing the selection immediately after using the `ls -sl` command to get the selection list. Clear the selection with this command:

```
select -cl;
```

Once you've run this, nothing is selected. This command is equivalent to clicking on empty space in the Maya interface to deselect everything.

Selecting a List of Objects

To deselect anything that may already be selected and select a new list of objects at the same time, you can pass one or more object names in an array to the `select` command.

If the array `string $bill_nodes[]` defined above had contained all the nodes in the character `bill`, you could select these nodes with the command

```
select $bill_nodes;
```

Note that since you're referring to the entire array you do not need the brackets or an array index.

The order in which you give the object names to be selected matters; many commands treat the first or last selection differently from the rest. Because of this, you may wish to select a certain object from your array first and then add to the selection later.

The `select` command does the same thing as clicking on an object with the Select tool in the Maya interface, or dragging a selection rectangle across several objects.

Adding to an Existing Selection

You can add to the existing selection with the `-add` and `-af` flags for the select command. `-add` adds the objects in the array you give the select command as though they had been selected last, at the end of the selection list. `-addFirst` adds the objects in the array you give the select command as though they had been selected first, at the beginning of the selection list.

```
select -add "bill_joint1";
select -addFirst $joint_list;
```

Adding to an existing selection with the `-add` flag is equivalent to shift-clicking on a new object with the Select tool to add to the selection.

Removing Objects from an Existing Selection

You can use the `-d` flag for select to deselect one or more objects, removing them from the current selection.

```
select -d "bill_eye_l";
```

This is equivalent to shift-clicking on one or more already selected nodes with the Select tool in the interface.

Selecting All Nodes in a Scene

Finally, to select all nodes in the scene (which is probably a rare thing to do), you can use the `-all` flag:

```
select -all;
```

Creating Nodes in a Maya Scene

Using Commands Specific to a Node Type

Many common nodes can be created directly with MEL commands that exist for the purpose. Usually, these commands return the name of the created object and its construction history node, if appropriate. Some of these commands for geometry objects are

- `sphere`
- `cone`
- `torus`
- `nurbsPlane`
- `nurbsCube`

Many of these commands take a flag `-ch` (or `-constructionHistory`), which indicates whether to keep a construction history node in your scene.

```
sphere -ch on; // Retains a construction history node in the scene
sphere -ch off; // Does not retain a construction history node
```

Using Utility Commands that Support the -ch on Flag

Some utility MEL commands that get information from the scene operate by creating a utility node, reading its result, and destroying it. One example of this that we saw in Chapter 4 on particle expressions is the `pointOnCurve` command.

Some of these commands, including `pointOnCurve`, support creating a utility node that is automatically hooked up by the command. To do this, pass the command the `-ch on` flag, as in

```
string $nodeName = `pointOnCurve -ch on curve1`;
```

Usually, as we saw in Chapter 4, keeping the utility node in the scene is *much* faster than making repeated calls to the relevant MEL command. Look at the command's entry in the MEL Command Reference to see whether it supports the `-ch` flag.

Using the createNode Command

When none of the other options is available for creating a particular node, you can use the `createNode` command to make one. This command has relatively few options. You must give it an argument indicating what type of node to create, and optionally you can name the node with a `-n` flag and indicate a parent node with the `-p` flag. For example, the following code segment creates a transform called `locTransform` with a locator *shape* named `loc1`:

```
createNode transform -n locTransform;
createNode locator -n loc1 -p locTransform;

// Result: loc5 //
```

Of course, when you use createNode to make nodes, you must set all of the attributes using getAttr and setAttr rather than relying on a convenient utility function like those mentioned above to take care of that work for you.

Finding a Node's Parents and Children

To find the parents and children of a given node, use the listRelatives command. listRelatives takes as an argument the name of the node whose relatives you want to see. Also, you can specify whether you want to see the node's children (with the -c flag), parents (with the -p flag), child shape nodes (with the -s flag), or all of the node's descendants (meaning all of the node's children and their children and so on) with the -allDescendants flag.

The listRelatives command returns an array of strings containing the relevant node names. To see how listRelatives works, try these commands:

```
sphere -name firstSphere;
sphere -name secondSphere;
parent secondSphere firstSphere;
```

Now, try using listRelatives to show parents and children of these nodes:

```
string $firstSphereChildren[] = `listRelatives -c firstSphere`;
   // Result: firstSphereShape secondSphere //

string $secondSphereParents[] = `listRelatives
                                -p secondSphere`;
// Result: firstSphere //

string $firstSphereShape[] = `listRelatives -s firstSphere`;
   // Result: firstSphereShape //

string $firstSphereDescendants[] = `listRelatives
                                -ad firstSphere`;
// Result: firstSphereShape secondSphereShape secondSphere //
```

Using listRelatives, array variables, and a for-in loop to walk through the elements in the array, your MEL script can do the same thing to all the parents, all the children, or the shape node associated with a given node name.

Finding Information on Node Connections

In Chapter 5, we saw how to connect nodes with the connectAttr command. MEL provides three commands that can give you useful information about existing connections between nodes, which can be used to decide whether to make a new connection or to help your script determine how a node is being used in your scene. These commands are listConnections, connectionInfo, and isConnected.

Using listConnections

The listConnections command takes as its argument either an object name or an object attribute name. To try listConnections, execute these commands to set up two spheres with an aim constraint between them:

```
sphere -n mysphere1;
sphere -n mysphere2;
select mysphere1 mysphere2;
string $myConstraintNode[] = `aimConstraint`;
```

To see a list of all of the connected attributes of the aimConstraint node that results (whose name is in $myConstraintNode[0]), use listConnections on theaimConstraint node with the -c on and -p on options; -s on tells listConnections to list the object connected on the source side of the connection, while -p on indicates that the command should list the attribute names, not just the object name that's connected (which is the default behavior).

```
listConnections -c on -p on $myConstraintNode[0];

// Result: mysphere2_aimConstraint1.constraintRotateX
mysphere2.rotateX mysphere2_aimConstraint1.constraintRotateY
mysphere2.rotateY mysphere2_aimConstraint1.constraintRotateZ
   etc.
```

Using connectionInfo

The connectionInfo command allows you to test whether a particular attribute is a source or a destination for a connection, and if it is, to determine to what it's connected. For example, if you have worked through the listConnections example, try these commands:

```
connectionInfo -isSource
mysphere2_aimConstraint1.constraintRotateX;
// Result: 1 //
```

```
connectionInfo -isDestination
mysphere2_aimConstraint1.constraintRotateX;
// Result: 0 //
```

```
connectionInfo -destinationFromSource
mysphere2_aimConstraint1.constraintRotateX;
// Result: mysphere2.rotateX //
```

`connectionInfo` can also tell you whether a particular attribute is locked:

```
connectionInfo -isLocked
mysphere2_aimConstraint1.constraintRotateX;
// Result: 0 //
```

`connectionInfo` returns a Boolean, string, or string array depending on the arguments it's given. For more information on the `connectionInfo` command, see the MEL Command Reference.

Using isConnected

The `isConnected` function allows you to test whether two attributes are connected. You must know the names of the attributes at *both* ends of the connection for which you are testing. If you only want to see whether a particular node is connected to anything at all, use the `connectionInfo` command with `-isSource` or `-isDestination`.

In our example, `mysphere2_aimConstraint1.constraintRotateX` is connected to `mysphere2.rotateX`. We can test for this connection as follows:

```
isConnected mysphere2_aimConstraint1.constraintRotateX
   mysphere2.rotateX;
// Result: 1 //
```

This statement returns a value of 1 (true) because a connection exists from `mysphere2_aimConstraint1.constraintRotateX` to `mysphere2.rotateX`. The next statement,

```
isConnected mysphere2.rotateX
   mysphere2_aimConstraint1.constraintRotateX
// Result: 0 //
```

returns a value of 0 (false) because the connection does not go the other direction.

About Maya's Node Types and the Node and Attribute Reference

If you know how to create a particular node type in the interface, the easiest way to find what type to use when creating the same node with the createNode command in a MEL script is to make such a node, select it, and use the ls -sl -showType command to show you the type of string to use in the createNode command.

In many cases, though, you either need to find an unusual node type suited to your purpose or look up the purpose of its attributes. The Maya documentation includes a reference document called the DG Node Reference that lists useful attributes of most types of nodes supported in Maya. You can get to the HTML version of the DG Node Reference from the Help menu while you are in Maya.

What to Remember About Managing Nodes in MEL

- In general, start with the ls command when trying to find a way to list the nodes that satisfy certain requirements. ls can help you find nodes given even a partial name and nodes of certain types or with certain relationships in the hierarchy, and it can help you get a list of nodes in the current selection.
- Use the select command to change or manage which nodes are selected. You can add or remove individual nodes from the current selection, clear the selection, or replace the selection with a new list of selected nodes.
- listRelatives gives you information about a node's parents, children, or related shape nodes in the transform hierarchy. Using listRelatives, you can get a list of node names that you can then loop over to walk through the tree of nodes in the transform hierarchy.
- listConnections, connectionInfo, and isConnected help you determine how nodes and their attributes are connected. You can get lists of connections and operate on the entire set of information (with listConnections) or test particular attributes to see whether they are connected to anything (with connectionInfo -isSource or -isDestination) or to a particular thing (with isConnected).

9

Controlling the Flow of Execution

In this chapter you will learn

- What it means to control the flow of execution.
- How conditional operations work.
- How if/then/else statements work.
- How switch statements work.
- How tests work.
- About loops, including for, for-in, and while loops.

Controlling the Flow of Script Execution

Most of the scripts discussed this far have run from beginning to end. However, many useful scripts either need to do something repeatedly or do certain things only if certain preconditions are satisfied. When a part of your script should only be run if certain conditions have been met, you can use a feature of MEL called a *conditional operation* to allow your script to decide whether to run that code.

When a part of your script should run repeatedly, you use a feature of MEL called a *loop operation* to decide how many times to repeat that part of your script, how each time through should differ from the previous iteration, and when to stop.

Figure 9.1 shows how a conditional operation works. You split off a section of the code using an *if-else statement* or a *switch statement,* and enclose the code in curly brackets. The if-else statement or the switch incorporates a *test,* which is usually an assertion about data in your script. If whatever state of your data you're testing is true, the block of code set off in curly brackets executes, and if the test is false, it does not.

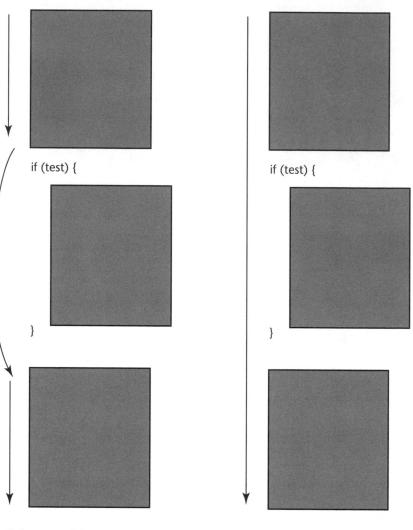

if (test) {

}

if (test) {

}

If the test is false, execution
skips over the block of code
in the if statement

If the test is true, the block
of code in the if statement
is executed.

Figure 9.1 How a conditional operation works.

A loop operation, on the other hand, specifies that a block of code can be skipped over, executed once, or executed many times, depending on the circumstances. As an example, Figure 9.2 shows how the flow of execution works for a *for-in* loop, which we discuss in detail later.

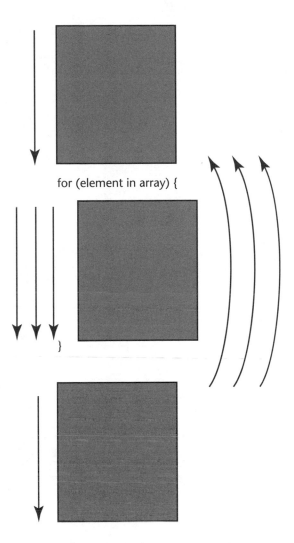

for (element in array) {

}

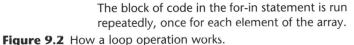

The block of code in the for-in statement is run
repeatedly, once for each element of the array.

Figure 9.2 How a loop operation works.

Basic Conditional Operations: if-else and switch

As illustrated in Figure 9.3, the purpose of a conditional operation is to let
your script decide whether to execute a block of code depending on the
result of a test that you apply to your data. There are two common types of
conditionals in Maya: the *if-else* statement and the *switch* statement.

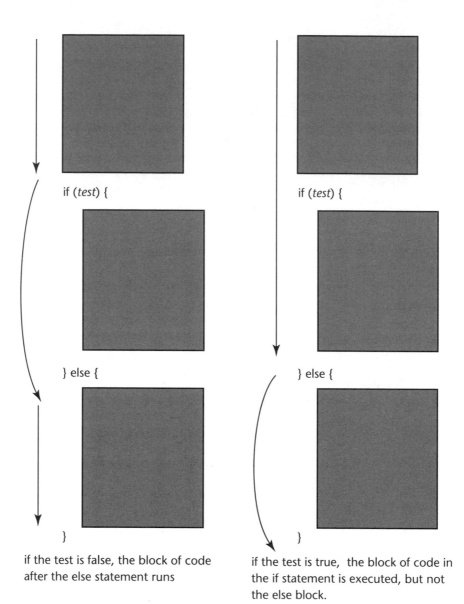

if the test is false, the block of code
after the else statement runs

if the test is true, the block of code in
the if statement is executed, but not
the else block.

Figure 9.3 An if-else statement's execution.

If-else statements are useful when your script needs to decide whether
to execute a particular block of code based on a true or false test. They're
called if-then-else statements because you can tell Maya to execute a particular block of code *if* a particular test is true, or *else* another block of code
if it is not (Figure 9.3).

You can have several layers of tests, so if one test fails you can move on to a second or a third test, each of which can have its own blocks of code. We will look at examples of all of these situations.

Switch statements look at the value of a variable they are given and search through a list of possible values. Each possible value for the variable has a block of code that will be run if the variable has that value. Like a switch that can be turned into many positions, each potential value of the variable selects a different way for your code to run (Figure 9.4).

If-else Statements

If-else statements are useful when you want your script to decide whether to execute a block of code. The following example checks the value of a variable, $number, to see whether it's less than 25, using the *less than* test (<). If it is, the print statement puts a message in the Script Editor to tell you so. If it is not, the print statement gets skipped over.

```
int $number = 14;
if ($number < 25)
{
    print ($number +" is less than twenty-five.\n");
}
```

Type the above example into the Script Editor window, and press Enter on the numeric keypad to run it. You will see that the message appears, as 14 is in fact less than 25. Now, let's look at how the same test works when $number is set to a value greater than 25:

```
int $number = 27;
if ($number < 25)
{
    print ($number +" is less than twenty-five.\n");
}
```

(If you want to run this example easily, the best thing to do is copy and paste the earlier code you had typed out of the status message area by selecting it, choosing Copy from the Edit menu, clicking in the script editing area, and choosing Paste from the Edit menu. Then you can edit it and run it again.) Run the example, and you'll see that nothing happens. Because the condition you're testing (whether your variable $number is less than 25) is false, the code inside the if statement gets skipped over.

Now, suppose that you want to print out a message whether or not the number is less than 25:

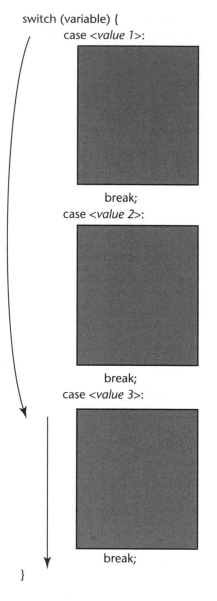

In this instance, the variable in the switch statement
has a value that matches the third case's value (value 3)
Thus, only the third block of code runs.

Figure 9.4 Flow of execution for a switch statement.

```
int $number = 27;
if ($number < 25)
{
    print ($number +"is less than twenty-five.\n");
}
else
{
    print ($number +"is greater than or equal to twenty-five.\n");
}
```

When you add an else block to your if statement, you provide an alternate block of code that Maya is to execute if the original test is not true. In this case, the else block is what gets executed, because 27 is greater than 25.

If you like, you can continue to add additional tests to try if the first one fails by changing the else block to an else if, as follows:

```
int $number = 25;
if ($number < 25)
{
    print ($number +"is less than twenty-five.\n");
}
else if ($number == 25)
{
    print ($number +"equals twenty-five.\n");
}
```

The above test checks to see whether $number is less than 25. If it's not, it then goes ahead to check whether $number is the same as 25. If that's not true either, it does nothing.

You can continue to add on more else if blocks if you like. Each one will run only if all the previous tests are false. Finally, at the end, you can add an else block to run if nothing else has, as follows:

```
int $number = 27;
if ($number < 23)
{
    print ($number +"is less than twenty-three.\n");
}
else if ($number < 25)
{
    print ($number +"is less than twenty-five.\n");
}
else if ($number == 25)
{
    print ($number +"is equal to twenty-five.\n");
}
```

```
else
{
   print ($number +" is greater than twenty-five.\n");
}
```

In the above example, when the first test (is 27 less than 23?) comes up false (because 27 is not less than 23), the first block of code in curly brackets—the print statement that says that $number is less than 23—gets skipped over. Then, the next test checks whether it's less than 25. That is false also, which causes Maya to skip over the next block of code, and so forth. Finally, at the end, none of the rest have run, so the final else block is run, and the script prints out that 27 is greater than 25.

Note that as we are writing the code that runs for each of these tests, we are adding spaces so that they are indented to the right. Maya does not require this; you could just as easily type:

```
if ($number < 23) { print ($number +" is less than twenty-three.\n"); }
```

However, by indenting the code inside the if-else blocks, it makes more clear which code will or will not be run after Maya checks each test, both to yourself and others.

Indenting like this becomes even more useful when you start putting if statements within if statements, which is a perfectly valid (and often necessary) thing to do:

```
if ($number > 10)
{
   print ("It's more than ten!\n");
   if ($number > 20)
   {
      print ("What's more, it's more than 20 also!\n");
   }
}
```

In this example, we placed another if statement inside the block of code that the first if statement decides whether to execute. Unlike the if-else if statements we saw before, where the second test would take place only if the first one failed, in this case we'll get to the innermost print statement only if $number is *both* greater than 10 and greater than 20.

This, though, does not make sense:

```
if ($number > 10)
{
   print ("It's more than ten!\n");
   if ($number < 10)
```

```
    {
        print ("Oops, sorry, now it's less than 10!\n");
    }
}
```

In this case, Maya will *never* get to the innermost print statement. The reason is that unless `$number` is more than 10, Maya never gets as far as checking whether `$number` is less than 10. If `$number` is more than 10, the proposition that `$number` can be less than 10 will never be true, so the innermost print statement will never run.

Indenting the code in `if` statements helps us find this problem because it serves as a visual reminder to ourselves what has and has not already been tested. Look at the next two (identical, from Maya's standpoint) examples, and decide which is easier to follow:

```
if ($number < 30)
{
if ($number < 20)
{
print ("It's less than 20!\n");
if ($number == 13)
{
print ("It's 13!\n");
}
}
print ("Hmm, I think it's between 20 and 30?\n");
}
```

Here's the indented version:

```
if ($number < 30)
{
    if ($number < 20)
    {
        print ("It's less than 20!\n");
        if ($number == 13)
        {
            print ("It's 13!\n");
        }
    }
    print ("Hmm, I think it's between 20 and 30?\n");
}
```

As you can see, it's much easier in the second version to tell exactly which chunk of code is run when which tests are satisfied. Maya does not need this cue, but most programmers find code much easier to read if it's indented. Note that programmers who have been around a while get very passionate about how to indent their code, precisely because the computer doesn't care.

Conditional Tests

In an if-else statement, you use a *conditional test operator* to indicate what condition you want to have satisfied before running the code in the if part of the statement. In the examples above, you saw the > operator (used for checking whether the item on the left of the operator is greater than the item on the right), the < operator (used for checking whether the item on the left is less than that on the right), and == (used for checking whether the two are equal to each other).

In fact, you can use any variable in the test for an if-else statement, as long as Maya knows how to convert it to an integer. When Maya encounters a conditional test operator, such as (3 == 4) or (2 > 7), it evaluates it to determine whether or not it's true. If it's true, it evaluates to a value of 1, and if it's false, it evaluates to a value of 0.

For example, try printing the results of some of these tests:

```
print (2 == 4);
print (3 > 2);
print (4.5 < 4.7);
```

When an if-else statement is evaluated, if the conditional test is 0, the code in the if block does not run, and if it's anything other than zero, it does. In addition to using the conditional test operators, you can use any integer as a test for the if statement. For example, try typing the following into your Script Editor window, and see what happens when you press Enter:

```
int $test = 23;

if ($test)
{
    print "I'm not zero!\n";
}
```

It prints the message. Now, try this:

```
$test = 0;

if ($test)
{
    print "I'm not zero!\n";
}
```

Because conditional tests and integers are so deeply intertwined, in Chapter 6 we discuss these conditional test operators and more in the section on integers.

One other useful set of operations you can use in if-then statements are *Boolean operators*. These allow you to check whether something is *not* true (using the ! operator); whether both of two tests are true (using the &&, or *and*, operator); and whether one or the other of two tests are true (using the ||, or *or*, operator).

The *not* operator   For example, you would read the test ! (3 < 4) as "Not three is less than four." When you use the not operator, the if block executes when the test *is* zero and does not when the test is anything else. For example,

```
$test = 0;

if (! $test)
{
    print "I'm zero!\n";
}
```

The *and* operator   If you want to see whether both of two tests are true, use the *and* operator, &&, as in

```
if ((3 < 4) && (3 < 5))
{
    print "Both are true\n";
}
```

The *or* operator   The *or* operator is true if *either* or both of the two tests are true:

```
if ((3 < 4) || (3 > 5))
{
    print "Either or both are true!\n";
}
```

The above tests and operators are the most commonly used, but for a more comprehensive look at conditional tests, see the section on integers in Chapter 6.

Switch Statements

The switch statement is designed for the situation where you have a single variable that can have several specific values for which you want your script to do different things. For example, suppose you have an integer variable $number that can be 1, 2, 3, or something else:

```
switch ($number)
{
```

```
   case 1:
      print "It's one!\n";
      break;

   case 2:
      print "It's two!\n";
      break;

   case 3:
      print "It's three!\n";
      break;

   default:
      print "I don't know what it is!\n";
      break;
}
```

This `switch` statement picks a block of code depending on each possible choice for $number. If it's 1, it runs the first block (labeled `case 1`); if it's 2, it runs the second (labeled `case 2`), and if it's 3, it runs the third (labeled `case 3`). If $number is something other than 1, 2, or 3, such as –27, the `switch` statement runs the case labeled `default`, if there is one, or does nothing if there isn't.

Unlike `if-else` statements, `switch` statements, as you can see in the above example, do not use curly brackets to delineate where blocks of code start and end. Instead, each block of code that the `switch` statement chooses between starts with a `case` label (or the `default` label) and continues running until it hits a `break` statement.

A common mistake with `switch` statements is to leave the `break` statements out. For example,

```
switch ($number)
{
   case 1:
      print "It's one!\n";

   case 2:
      print "It's two!\n";
      break;

   case 3:
      print "It's three!\n";
      break;

   default:
      print "I don't know what it is!\n";
      break;
}
```

In this `switch` statement, we've left the `break` statement out of `case 1`. Try creating a variable `$number` equal to 1 and running this `switch` statement to see what happens.

The result is that, if `$number` is 1, the `switch` statement prints out "It's one!" and then, in quick succession, "It's two!" Because a `switch` statement relies on the `break` statement to know where each block of code ends, and because there is no `break` statement at the end of `case 1`, it goes ahead and executes `case 2` as well. This behavior can sometimes be useful. Usually, though, it is done by accidental omission, and it can take hours or days to debug.

Loops

Loops are structures that allow your script to execute a chunk of code repeatedly. The types of loops MEL supports are `while` loops, `for-in` loops, and `for` loops.

- While loops allow you to repeat a chunk of code until some condition is satisfied.
- For-in loops are designed to let you repeat a section of code once for each element in an array variable, automatically stopping when there are no more elements in the array.
- For loops are designed to let you repeat a section of code, incrementing or decrementing a variable each time, until some condition that you specify is satisfied. Changing the value in a variable each time through the loop lets you repeat the same operation on different data each time through.

While Loops

The `while` loop is the simplest type of loop, only a short step from conditional statements like `if-else`. A `while` loop works just like an `if` statement, except that it repeatedly executes the code inside the loop until the condition is satisfied. Also, unlike an `if` statement, a `while` loop cannot have an `else` part.

For example, here's a simple `while` loop:

```
int $test_int = 3;

while ($test_int < 100)
{
    $test_int = $test_int * 3;
    print ("$test_int is equal to" + $test_int + "\n");
}
```

When there is no more code in the `while` loop, the test (in this case `$test < 100`) is checked one more time, and if it's still true it's run one more time.

Each time through the loop, $test gets larger, until finally it is larger than 100, and the block does not execute again.

The danger of while loops is that it's easy to make mistakes that cause them to run forever. For example, if you run the following while loop, it would run until you kill Maya. *(Don't do this unless you've saved your work!)*

```
$test_int = 3;

while ($test_int < 100)
{
    $test_int = $test_int / 3;
    print ("$test_int is equal to " + $test_int + "\n");
}
```

Because $test_int never gets to be larger than 100, the above loop runs until you kill Maya (using Ctrl-Alt-Delete in Windows, Cmd-Option-Esc on the Macintosh, or Ctrl-C in the shell window where you started Maya under Linux or Irix).

So, when you write a while loop into your script, it's always a good idea to *make sure that the loop will eventually terminate on its own.*

For-in Loops

The for-in loop is useful when you have to do something to each element in an array. For example, make three spheres and select all three of them. Then type

```
ls -sl
```

in the Script Editor, and press Enter on the numeric keypad.

The ls -sl command lists all of the selected objects, giving back the result in an array. So, if you want to perform an operation on each selected object, you can use the ls -sl command to get a list of all of the selected objects and a for-in loop to operate on them, as follows:

```
string $selectedList[] = `ls -sl`;
string $currentObject;

for ($currentObject in $selectedList)
{
    print ("You've selected " + $currentObject + "\n");
}
```

The code in the for-in loop runs once for each object in the $selectedList array, putting that array entry into the $currentObject variable.

You don't need to worry as much about for-in loops running forever as you do with while loops, as they will only run once for each entry in the array. However, if you add elements to an array in the middle of your loop, you may run into trouble. Usually, it's a good idea not to do so.

For Loops

The for loop is the most useful type of loop and is only a little more complex than the for-in loop. The for loop is intended to be useful when you want to have a variable, usually a counter, that you want to start at a particular value and change each time the loop runs. Then, each time through the loop a test will be run that decides whether to run through the loop one more time.

At the start of the for loop is the for statement, which usually looks something like this:

```
for ($counter = 1; $counter < 100; $counter++)
{
    < code >
}
```

There are three MEL statements inside the parentheses in a for statement, separated by semicolons. The first (in this example, $counter = 1) is called the *initializer*. This statement is run once at the beginning of the loop, usually to set a value for a variable that will increase or change value as the loop is run. The second statement (in this example $counter < 100) is called the *test*. Like in the while loop, the test indicates whether the loop should continue running the code inside. The third statement (in this example $counter++) is called the *increment statement*. Every time through the loop, *after* the code in the loop executes, and *before* the test for the next time through the loop, the increment statement is run.

In our example above, the loop will run 99 times. The reason for this is that the first time through the loop $counter is set to 1, and the test is run to see if the loop will execute. Since 1 is less than 100, it will.

The code in the loop executes, and at the end the increment statement is run. Since $counter++ tells Maya to add 1 to $counter, $counter becomes 2, and the test is then run again, to see whether the code inside will be executed. Since 2 is less than 100, it will. Later on, after the loop has run many more times, $counter is finally up to 98. Once the loop executes, $counter++ increments the loop to 99, and the test is run one more time. Since 99 is less than 100, it runs. Finally, at the end, $counter++ increments the $counter variable to 100. Now when the test is run, 100 is not less than 100, so the loop does not run again. Since $counter was 1 on the first time through the loop, and 99 the last time, the loop has run 99 times.

If you wanted to run the loop 100 times instead, you could take one of two approaches. Many programmers initialize the $counter variable to 0 the first time through, as follows:

```
for ($counter = 0; $counter < 100; $counter++)
{
    < code >
}
```

Another approach is to test for the counter being less than or equal to 100:

```
for ($counter = 1; $counter <= 100; $counter++)
{
   < code >
}
```

Note that these two approaches are not exactly the same. In the first one, the counter runs from 0 to 99, and in the second it runs from 1 to 100. Depending on what you are doing, one or the other may be more appropriate.

To try a for loop, type the following code segment into the Script Editor, and press Enter on the numeric keypad:

```
int $counter;

for ($counter = 0; $counter < 100; $counter++)
{
   print ($counter + "\n");
}
```

Now, watch while the counter counts from 0 to 99!

What to Remember About Controlling the Flow of Execution in MEL

- ■ If-else statements are useful when you need to decide whether to execute one part of your script or another.
- ■ A switch statement is useful when a variable may have one of a number of values and you want to choose a block of statements to run based on its value.
- ■ A while loop makes sense when you want to run a loop as many times as it takes for some condition to be satisfied.
- ■ A for-in loop is useful when you want to run the loop once for every element in an array, particularly when you wish to work your way through a selection list obtained with the ls -sl command.
- ■ A for loop is best when you want to execute a portion of your script a certain number of times, counting as you go.

10

Procedures and Functions

In this chapter you will learn

- A useful strategy for breaking up a large problem into smaller pieces called *top-down design*.
- How MEL features for breaking up your scripts into small chunks of code can help implement the top-down strategy.
- The differences between a procedure and a function.
- How you define a procedure or a function.
- How procedures and functions support a top-down approach.
- What is a procedure's *scope* and how you can use global procedures to make scripts available anywhere in your code.
- About procedures and functions calling themselves, an approach called *recursion*.

Top-Down Design

When designing a script to solve a complicated problem, it's rarely a good idea to try to write the entire script, beginning to end, in one sitting. Since programming in MEL is simply creating a set of instructions that tell Maya to do a series of actions, one by one, a substantial piece of the challenge is figuring out what the script should do in the first place.

Although there are other strategies, the simplest, most common, and easiest-to-apply approach to developing software, including MEL scripts, is called *top-down design*. The top-down approach requires that you first work out a statement of what problem you're trying to solve with your program, then a statement of the basic steps that your program has to take to yield a solution.

Once you have started with a "top level" statement of the problem you're trying to solve, you move one step into sorting out the detail of solving it by breaking it up into component steps. Then, repeatedly break each step that you have identified into smaller steps. If you're doing this along the way to writing a MEL script, sooner or later the smaller and smaller scale refinements of your design will lead the way to each line of code in your script.

It can help to think of the process of figuring out the steps to solve a problem as being distinct from writing the code to implement them. To see how the top-down approach works, let's first look at an example that has nothing to do with Maya, or even programming.

Example 1: A Trip to the Grocery Store

Suppose that you are cooking dinner and have just placed your food in the oven when you realize that you're missing carrots. Your 16-year-old cousin, freshly awarded his driver's license, is over to visit, and dying to drive around town at every opportunity. Meanwhile, you can't leave the food in the oven unattended. A broad statement of your problem is this: finish preparing the meal. Immediately, two approaches occur to you. The first follows:

- Get the still-frozen food out of the oven.
- Choose whether to leave your cousin at home and then go to the store.
- Buy carrots.
- Return home and finish cooking.

The second approach:

- Tell your cousin to go to the store to buy carrots.
- Continue watching the food in the oven while waiting.
- When your cousin returns with the carrots, finish cooking.

Having enumerated two different ways of solving the problem, it's obvious now that you have important decisions to make about your priorities. Are you comfortable leaving your cousin at home? Are you comfortable letting your cousin drive your car? How concerned are you that the carrots be exactly what you had envisioned? Are you in a hurry?

One aspect of top-down problem solving that this example illustrates is that at first it is as much a tool for deciding your priorities and your specifications for solving a problem as it is a mechanism for refining exactly how you will accomplish your goals. More sophisticated alternative approaches to programming more clearly distinguish specification from choosing an implementation, but the top-down approach is a good place to start for most problems.

Let's continue with the example. At this point you have decided that you may be willing to let your cousin drive your car, but only if your insurance is paid up. You can live with the wrong style of carrots, and you would like to please your cousin by giving him a chance to drive your car. Plus, guests are coming, so you would like to hold things up as little as possible.

From your priorities, it's obvious that letting your cousin go is the answer. Now, you're ready to divide each of your highest-level steps to solving the problem into smaller steps.

- Tell your cousin to go to the store to buy carrots
    1. Look in your checkbook for a recent insurance payment.
    2. Explain to your cousin how to get to the store.
    3. Point out your car's quirks so that your cousin doesn't have an accident adjusting the rear-view mirror or the radio.
    4. Give your cousin the keys.

- Continue watching the food in the oven while waiting.
    1. Enjoy a stiff drink to calm your nerves.
    2. Start the minute timer.
    3. Every 10 minutes, check the food.
        a. If the food starts to look well cooked, turn down the oven.
        b. If the food starts to burn, take it out.

- When your cousin returns with the carrots, finish cooking.
    1. Check the car for dings and dents.
    2. Check the carrots to ensure that they're edible.
    3. Peel the carrots.
    4. Pour water into a pot.
    5. Boil the carrots.
    6. Drain the water.
    7. Place the carrots on a plate with the food from the oven and serve.

At this point, it should be obvious that this successive refinement of each step to accomplish a goal could be carried on nearly without limit. Of course, most people don't apply this kind of top-down refinement approach to everyday life, but not because it doesn't work. Instead, most people have internalized how to make all of these decisions on the fly without really thinking about it.

Because programming a computer is rarely truly intuitive, though, when solving that kind of problem, the top-down approach takes on unusual value. By writing down your thoughts about how to solve a problem, you can see in front of you a representation of what you want your script to do. It's easier to keep many details in your head about what may or may not work, and in thinking through each step in more and more detail you will often discover where in your plan your original ideas were too simple or headed in the wrong direction.

Later, we will look at an example of using top-down design in developing a MEL script. First, though, let's look at how the structure of the MEL language supports taking the top-down approach.

What Are Procedures and Functions?

Procedures and *functions* are simple ways to group together a number of MEL statements into a single operation that your script can use again and again. When a script (or another procedure) uses one of these predefined groupings of MEL statements, that script is said to *call* the procedure or function, in the sense that the procedure or function is called upon to do its job.

A function is a special type of procedure that is able to hand a data value back to the script that called it. This value is called the function's *return value*. Functions, then, are procedures that return values to the script that calls them.

Procedures and functions can receive data from the scripts that call them in special variables called *arguments*. Remember that the information you give to a built-in MEL command to tell it how to do its job is given to it as a series of arguments as well. Calling a procedure is written slightly different from calling a MEL command, but they are similar in purpose. Each instructs Maya to perform an operation on a set of data arguments; the difference is that MEL commands are either built into Maya or they are provided by a plug-in, while procedures and some functions are generally written in MEL. (Certain functions, particularly for math operations, are built into Maya as well.)

Procedures and functions serve two useful purposes. The first is to separate out the MEL code that performs each step that you identify when you break your problem up into its components, and the second is to make it easy to reuse the code for operations that you may need to use many times in your scripts. Using procedures and functions in these ways can make your scripts easier to read and easier to understand. First, we'll look at how to define and use procedures and functions, and then we'll look at a simple example.

Scope and Global Procedures

Like variables, procedures in MEL have *scope,* meaning that the conditions of how they're defined determines where they can be used.

As a rule, a procedure defined in the script editor, by hand, is *global,* and like a global variable, it can be used anywhere in any MEL script you run, whether it's in a MEL file in your script path or defined in the script editor by typing it in.

Procedures are often defined by putting them in MEL files in the script path, usually in your maya/scripts directory. (For more information on how to install MEL scripts, see *Chapter 18: Installing MEL Scripts*.) Then, either the procedure is defined when you use the source command to load the MEL file, or the file is sourced automatically if (and only if) certain conditions explained below are met.

When you define a procedure in a MEL file, normally it cannot be used outside that file *even if you source the .mel file!* For example, make a file containing this in your maya/scripts directory, and name it test.mel:

```
proc testing ()
{
    print "it worked!\n";
}
```

Now, in the script editor, execute these commands:

```
source "test.mel";
testing();
```

You'll get an error. Even though Maya found and ran the file test.mel, it could not see the procedure testing contained within it, because that procedure (like a variable defined in a MEL file) is *local* to that MEL file.

Now, exit Maya, and edit that MEL file to contain this:

```
global proc testing ()
{
    print "it worked!\n";
}
```

Run Maya again; then run the commands to source the file, and execute the global procedure. Now, you should get a satisfying message saying that your experiment worked.

Using the global keyword to define the procedure, then, makes it available outside the MEL file in which it's defined.

Now, exit Maya, and edit the MEL file to contain this:

```
global proc test ()
{
    print "it worked!\n";
}
```

This subtle change renames the global procedure to give it the same name as the MEL file (except for the .mel extension). Now, start Maya, and run the procedure *without* sourcing the file:

```
test();
```

The procedure should run without having sourced the file.

Maya is able to automatically source .mel files in your script path if you are calling a global procedure with the same name as the containing file. So, most of the time, you'll create at least one global procedure inside a

.mel file that will serve as that script's *entry point*, or the first code to be executed in the script.

Procedures that you only want to use within other procedures in that MEL file can be defined with `proc` alone, and procedures that you want to expose to the outside world of other MEL files or the script editor should be defined with `global proc`.

Note that sometimes you will install a command (in the form of a procedure you've written) to execute when a user clicks a button in a user interface. This kind of procedure is often called a *button action procedure*. These commands *must* be declared global, even though it looks like you are using them within the same Maya file. The reason is that all you are doing when you declare a command to associate with a button is storing the name of the command for later use. When the button is clicked, Maya, *outside* that MEL file in which you defined the button, runs that command, and if the command is not global, the button will do nothing.

Defining and Using Procedures and Functions

Before you can use a procedure, you have to tell Maya what the procedure does by *defining* the procedure. A function or procedure definition tells Maya the function or procedure's name, what arguments (if any) it needs to do its job, what kind of data will be handed back in a return value (if it's a function), and what MEL statements to execute when Maya encounters a call to a procedure in a script.

Procedure and function names are often written with parentheses () after them. When you define or use a procedure or function, its arguments, if any, go inside the parentheses.

For example, here's a procedure called `print_hello()` that prints the words `"Hello there!"` in the Script Editor window. Try typing the following code into the Script Editor and pressing Enter on the numeric keypad.

```
proc print_hello()

{
    print "Hello there!\n";
}
```

To use a procedure like this in a script once you have defined it, just place its name (with parentheses and arguments, if necessary) on a line by itself in your script. If you have defined `print_hello()` in the Script Editor window, try running it by typing

```
print_hello();
```

and pressing Enter.

Following is a variation of that procedure that can say hello to a user by name. Note that the argument to the procedure provides the name to which it will say hello. Also, remember that you can concatenate strings, or place them end to end, by using the + sign between them. Thus, the print statement in this procedure prints Hello, then the name, and then an exclamation point and newline, represented by \n.

```
proc hello_name(string $name)
{
   print ("Hello " + $name + "!\n");
}

hello_name("Mark");
hello_name("Sarah");
```

The argument definition for $name looks just like a variable definition. In fact, when you define arguments for a procedure or function, you're defining variables that are valid only in that procedure or function. Then, when the script calls the procedure, the values of the arguments are *passed* into the argument variables.

If your procedure has more than one argument, list the arguments with commas between them, as follows:

```
proc hello_two_names(string $name1, string $name2)
{
   print ("Hello " + $name1 + " and " + $name2 + "!\n");
}

hello_two_names("Mark", "Sarah");
```

Note that the arguments to a procedure or function are specified in order. The value for $name1 must always be listed first, and $name2 second, when calling the hello_two_names() procedure.

To define a function, a procedure that returns a value, you define your procedure with a data type for the return value between proc and the name. For example,

```
proc int square (int $num) {
  int $squared_val = $num * $num;

   return $squared_val;
};

print (square(5));
```

First of all, note that the function is defined with the words proc int square. This establishes that the function square will hand back an integer value to the script that calls it. (Remember that functions are just procedures that return values, so we still use the proc keyword to define it.) Then, after calculating the square of the value that's passed in with the argument $num, the function uses a *return* statement to hand back what it has calculated.

When you use a function, rather than simply placing the function on a line by itself, like you would a procedure, you normally will want to do something with the result handed back. You can do this by placing the call to the function (in this case, square(5)) in a place where Maya expects a data value (in this case, the argument to the print command).

Alternatively, you could assign the result of the function to a variable, as in

```
int $sixty_four = square(8);
```

Functions, because they return a data value, can be used anywhere you would use a variable or explicit data values. For example, you could call a procedure with a call to a function as one of its arguments, as in

```
hello_name(square(square(8)));
```

When presented with a statement like this, Maya starts at the innermost function call, square(8), and calculates the result, 64. Then, it calls the next-innermost function call with the return value 64 as its argument: square(square(8)) becomes square(64), which evaluates to 4096. Then, that result is passed to hello_name.

"Wait," you might say, "hello_name requires a string, not an integer, as its argument. Why does this work?" Since Maya knows how to convert (or in programmers' language, "cast") an integer to a string, it does so, and prints

```
Hello 4096!
```

The rebellious reader, at this point, might answer, "I am not a number!"

Example 2: Geometry-Constrained Locators

In this example, we create a script that creates three spheres, each with a locator constrained to its surface with a geometry constraint to keep them on the spheres' surfaces and a normal constraint to keep them oriented perpendicular to the spheres' surfaces.

At the highest level, this script needs to do the following:

■ Make a sphere, moving it away from the origin.
■ Create a constrained locator on the sphere's surface.
■ Repeat the last two steps two more times.

At this point, it's worth thinking for a moment about how this script might be useful in the future. If, for example, all you need are spheres with locators constrained to them, you could combine creating the sphere and creating the constrained locators in one procedure that you could reuse again and again. On the other hand, if you envision constraining the locators to, say, arbitrary NURBS patches, you will want to create a procedure to handle creating and attaching the locators while leaving the creation of the underlying geometry separate.

In this example, we'll take the second approach, described below.

- Create a sphere and store its name somewhere so that we can refer to it later.
  Make a sphere
  Move the sphere away from the origin
- Create and constrain a locator to geometry that has already been created.
  Create a locator, named appropriately.
  Create a geometry constraint for the locator.
  Create an aim constraint for the locator.
- Repeat twice more.

Creating a sphere, as we've seen before, can be done with a single MEL command. Since the sphere command can make a sphere with a name you give it in the -name argument, it's easy to keep the sphere's name handy so that it can be used later on. To create a sphere, placing its name into a variable $mySphere, and then move it five units in the X direction away from the origin, use the following code:

```
string $mySphere = "sphere1";
sphere -name $mySphere;
move 5 0 0;
```

This segment creates and moves a sphere called sphere1—assuming that you do not already have an object called sphere1 in the scene. (Remember that you can look at the return value for the sphere command to see what Maya actually named the object.)

Now, let's turn these three lines of MEL into a procedure that you can give any name and any location for the sphere to end up. This procedure needs to have one argument (a string) for the sphere's name, and three arguments (floating-point numbers) for its X, Y, and Z location values.

```
proc makeSphere(string $sphereName, float $xval, float $yval,
    float $zval)
{
    sphere -name $sphereName;
    move $xval $yval $zval;
}
```

Try typing this procedure definition into the Script Editor and pressing the Enter key on the numeric keypad.

Since all you have done to this point is define a procedure, you haven't yet made a sphere. To do so, you need to call the procedure with a real name and x, y, and z values for the sphere's location. Try making a sphere by calling the procedure, as follows:

```
makeSphere("myNewSphere", 3, 3, 3);
```

A sphere called myNewSphere should appear at the location you selected.

To make and constrain a locator to our new sphere requires a few MEL commands. Remember, the easiest way to find the commands for simple operations like this is to use the Show All Commands feature in the Script Editor while going through the steps by hand in the interface. Also, looking in the Maya documentation index for references to the MEL Command Reference can help you find all the commands that refer to a particular object or concept. With a little practice, you can look through the online list of commands in the MEL Command Reference and find the appropriate command most of the time.

The commands to make and constrain a locator follow:

```
spaceLocator -name "myNewSphereLocator";
geometryConstraint "myNewSphere" "myNewSphereLocator";
aimConstraint "myNewSphere" "myNewSphereLocator";
```

Our procedure to make and constrain a locator to arbitrary geometry should work for any name that we have given the geometry. Also, in this instance we have decided to name the locator <name>Locator, where <name> is the name of the geometry to which the locator is constrained.

If we build our procedure to accept the name of the geometry to which we are constraining as one of its arguments, called, say, $geometryName, we can create the locator's name like this:

```
string $locatorName = ($geometryName + "Locator");
```

So, our procedure to make and constrain the locator looks like the following:

```
proc makeConstrainedLocator (string $geometryName)
{
    string $locatorName = ($geometryName + "Locator");

    spaceLocator -name $locatorName;
    geometryConstraint $geometryName $locatorName;
    aimConstraint $geometryName $locatorName;
}
```

Type the above procedure into the Script Editor, and press Enter on the numeric keypad.

You can use the following procedures to make a few spheres with locators constrained to them:

```
makeSphere ("sphere1", 4, 0, 0);
makeConstrainedLocator("sphere1");
```

```
makeSphere ("sphere2", 0, 4, 0);
makeConstrainedLocator("sphere2");

makeSphere ("sphere3", 0, 0, 4);
makeConstrainedLocator("sphere3");
```

Now, let's look at the entire script, including the procedure definitions.

```
proc makeSphere(string $sphereName, float $xval, float $yval,
    float $zval)
{
  sphere -name $sphereName;
  move $xval $yval $zval;
}

proc makeConstrainedLocator (string $geometryName)
{
  string $locatorName = ($geometryName + "Locator");

  spaceLocator -name $locatorName;
  geometryConstraint $geometryName $locatorName;
  aimConstraint $geometryName $locatorName;
}

makeSphere ("sphere1", 4, 0, 0);
makeConstrainedLocator("sphere1");

makeSphere ("sphere2", 0, 4, 0);
makeConstrainedLocator("sphere2");

makeSphere ("sphere3", 0, 0, 4);
makeConstrainedLocator("sphere3");
```

With the entire script before us, it's obvious that developing procedures to create spheres and locators helps us organize the problem.

- It lets us break down our problem into chunks that are easier to tackle than the whole project at once.
- It makes the main body of our script (the six lines of calls to makeSphere and makeConstrainedLocator at the bottom) easier to read and understand for others who might read the script later.
- It allows us to have only one piece of code to make and constrain a locator, for example, so that if we change how we want to do that task we only need to change it in one place rather than several.

Recursion

A more advanced trick that you can do with procedures is to have a procedure call itself, repeatedly. This is called *recursion,* and it can be particularly useful in some kinds of procedural modeling applications, certain mathematical tasks, and so on.

If you're going to have a procedure call itself repeatedly, you must make sure that your procedure eventually stops doing so; otherwise, Maya will crash or give you an error. If you want to make Maya 4.0 crash, try entering and running the following recursive function that keeps calling itself over and over again until Maya can no longer take it. *(Make sure that you have saved your scene before doing this experiment!)*

```
proc test()
{
    test();
}
```

Once you have defined this procedure that calls itself repeatedly (doing nothing) until Maya crashes, you can run it by typing the following in the Script Editor and executing it with the numeric keypad's Enter button:

```
test();
```

To make sure that a recursive function eventually stops calling itself, it should include a standard for deciding when to go no further. Now, let's go through a more interesting example of recursion to see how it can be useful.

Example 3: Recursive Antenna

Let's use recursion to create an insect antenna using a series of spheres, smaller and smaller, curling in on themselves, until they reach a certain minimum size. Each will be a smaller size and should be rotated a certain angle from the previous sphere (Figure 10.1).

To think through how we'd do this, we can break down the problem as we did before.

1. If this is the first sphere, make a new sphere of, say, radius 1.
2. Duplicate the selected sphere.
3. Parent the new sphere to the first sphere, so that the first sphere is the parent and the second is the child.
4. Scale the child sphere down by a reasonable percentage (like 95%).
5. Move the child sphere along the X axis, in the parent's local space, a distance of 1 + the scaling percentage times the parent sphere's radius. (Since the duplicated sphere shares its center point with the parent, moving it that distance places it so that its edge just grazes the parent's edge.)
6. Rotate the parent by the rotation angle, which will carry the child sphere with it as it rotates.

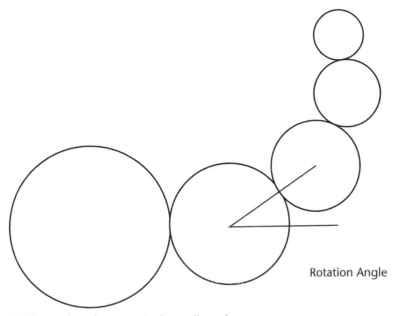

Rotation Angle

Figure 10.1 A series of progressively smaller spheres.

7. Now, repeat at step 2, with the new sphere selected. Since we need to make sure that we stop after we have made enough spheres, let's check the new sphere's radius to make sure that it is larger than, say, 0.1 units.

We could certainly make each of these steps a procedure, if we wanted to, but this amount of work seems about right for a single procedure. How you break a process up into procedures is largely a matter of judgment, and in this case, particularly because these steps need to share so much information, we will make a single procedure from the steps we have laid out.

Each time this procedure calls itself, it will need to pass along the name of the latest sphere that has been created. Also, passing along the latest sphere's radius will be easier than trying to figure it out on the fly. Passing along the rotation angle will mean that any time we call the procedure we can select a different value for it. We'll need to give the function an amount to scale down each new sphere. Finally, since this procedure needs to make a first sphere only the first time it's called, we'll pass in an integer value that will be 0 if our procedure is calling itself and 1 if we're calling it by hand (and thus it should make the first sphere of the series). Our procedure definition, then, looks something like the following code segment:

```
proc makeAntenna(string $parentSphereName, float
            $parentRadius, float $rotAngle, float
            $scale, int $firstSphere)
```

```
{
   < code >
}
```

Next, the code inside the procedure, as we have planned it out, has two parts. First, we need to handle the special case where we are creating the first sphere. Then, we need to do all the work for the smaller child sphere. If we're not making the first sphere in the series, we treat the previous child sphere as the current parent sphere.

If we're making the first sphere in the series, which we can figure out by looking at the value of `$firstSphere`, we should use the `$parentSphereName` variable as its name and `$parentRadius` as its radius. `$rotAngle` is useful later, but is not needed for this process.

Remember that `if` (*<value>*) executes the code that follows in curly brackets if *<value>* is anything but 0, and it doesn't execute it if *<value>* is 0.

Here's the code to create the first sphere:

```
if ($firstSphere)
{
   sphere -name $parentSphereName;
   scale $parentRadius $parentRadius $parentRadius;
}
```

Now, we'll move on to making the next child sphere in the series. On the second and successive calls to the procedure, this will be where it will start to execute, because `$firstSphere` will be 0.

First, we'll select the parent sphere so that we can use the `duplicate` command on it.

The `duplicate` command will make a copy of the selected object, and it returns an array of strings, only the first of which is useful, as it contains the name of the duplicate. We'll capture the name of the duplicated object in an array called `$duplicateName[]`. The first item in the array, `$duplicateName[0]`, contains the name of the new duplicate sphere. Chapter 6 provides more information on defining and using arrays.

```
select -r $parentSphereName;
string $duplicateName[] = `duplicate`;
```

Our duplicate sphere's name is in the array element `$duplicateName[0]`, but a more descriptive name might be `$childSphereName`. Now, we'll create a variable `$childSphere` so that the rest of our script is more readable:

```
string $childSphereName = $duplicateName[0];

select -cl; // Clear out the selection

select $childSphereName $parentSphereName; // select the child,
                                            // then the parent
```

```
parent;

select $childSphereName;
```

Once we have a duplicate sphere, we can scale it down to a size of ($scale * $parentRadius). We'll place this value in $childSize:

```
float $childSize = $scale * $parentRadius;

scale $scale
      $scale
      $scale;
```

Now, we have a duplicate sphere that's a factor of $scale smaller than the original, centered at the same point. At this point, we want to parent the duplicate sphere to the original, and then move it one plus the new sphere's radius along the X axis. Since the move operation is taking place in local space, and since we've scaled the parent sphere, the world space distance of this move will get smaller as the parent sphere gets smaller. This move needs to take place in local space, of course, so that the new position is relative to the original position rather than to the origin.

```
move -localSpace (1 + $scale) 0 0;
```

Finally, we'll rotate the parent by the rotation angle, around the Z axis, as follows:

```
select $parentSphereName;
rotate 0 0 $rotationAngle;
```

Now we're ready to make an even smaller sphere. We need to call our procedure again, but only if our latest child sphere is not too small. After all, we don't want to continue making an infinite number of smaller and smaller spheres.

```
if ($childSize > 0.05)
{
   makeAntenna ($childSphereName, $childSize, $rotAngle,
                $scale, 0);
}
```

Note that the child's name is now the parent's name for the next time through. The child's radius is now the new parent radius; the rotation angle stays the same, and because we don't want to make the first sphere again, we are passing 0 in the $firstSphere parameter.

The entire procedure, just as you would type it in, follows:

```
proc makeAntenna(string $parentSphereName, float $parentRadius,
                 float $rotAngle, float $scale, int
                 $firstSphere)
{
```

```
if ($firstSphere)
{
   sphere -name $parentSphereName;
   scale $parentRadius $parentRadius $parentRadius;
}

select -r $parentSphereName;
string $duplicateName[] = `duplicate`;

string $childSphereName = $duplicateName[0];

select -cl; // Clear out the selection
select $childSphereName $parentSphereName;
                               // Select the child,
                               // then the parent

parent;
select $childSphereName;

float $childSize = $scale * $parentRadius;

scale $scale
      $scale
      $scale;

move -localSpace (1 + $scale) 0 0;

select $parentSphereName;
rotate 0 0 $rotAngle; // Rotate around Z, because we're
                          moving in X

if ($childSize > 0.05)
{
   makeAntenna ($childSphereName, $childSize, $rotAngle,
             $scale, 0);
}
}
```

Once you have typed in the procedure and defined it by pressing Enter on the numeric keyboard, try running it (Figure 10.2). (Be sure to start with a new scene.)

```
makeAntenna("firstSphere", 1, 20, 0.75, 1);
```

What to Remember About Procedures, Functions, and Top-Down Design in MEL

- Taking a top-down approach to developing scripts, in which you break the problem down into successively smaller parts until each part is easy

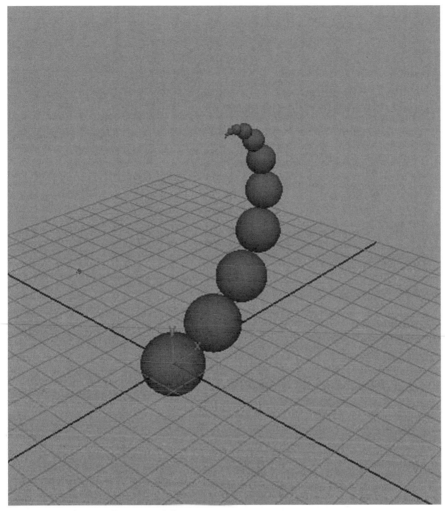

Figure 10.2 The resulting model.

to tackle, helps keep you organized, particularly when your scripts get more and more complex.

■ Procedures and functions help you do two things: first, they help break your script up into manageable pieces that are more readable and easier to fix when things go wrong, and second, they allow you to reuse chunks of code that are meaningful in more than one place in your script.

■ Procedures are commands that do not return a value to the script that calls them, while functions do return a value.

- A procedure's *scope* defines where in a MEL script a procedure can be used. Defining a procedure with the `global` keyword makes it available anywhere in your Maya session, once the enclosing MEL file has been loaded, either automatically or with the `source` command.
- Recursion can allow you to do certain kinds of tasks that are difficult to do otherwise, particularly when you are dealing with deep hierarchies or repetitive tasks where each step depends on the previous one.

11

Naming Nodes, Scripts, and Variables

In this chapter you will learn

- Why naming conventions are important.
- Useful strategies for naming scripts.
- Useful strategies for naming variables.
- Useful strategies for naming nodes.
- How to write scripts that manipulate node names.
- What namespaces are and their purpose.

Why Naming Conventions Are Important

As you develop scripts or create Maya scenes, you have tremendous freedom in naming your nodes, scripts, and variables. When your scenes are simple, often Maya's default node names, for example, are enough to organize your thoughts about what you are manipulating. However, once your scenes are sufficiently complex, you have begun to build up a library of MEL scripts, and you have defined enough variables in a particular script to be at risk of forgetting their function, naming becomes an essential tool for organizing your thoughts.

Good naming conventions are helpful in several ways.

- When you create a node, write a script, or define a variable, you usually have in mind what that node, script, or variable is supposed to do. Names can serve as a reminder later, when you've forgotten.

- Obvious names for nodes, scripts, and variables pop up again and again in different circumstances. A well-organized scheme for naming can ensure that when you install a new script, import more nodes from a different scene, or add to an existing script, you won't have to worry about naming conflicts. Naming conflicts occur when more than one object, variable within a given scope, or MEL function have the same name—Maya does not allow this at any time.
- By having well-organized naming, you can often guess what you have named a particular node, script, or variable, even if you have forgotten.
- Structuring your naming conventions properly can allow you to use utility scripts that rename nodes in your scene in meaningful ways.

Naming Scripts

Script, procedure, and function names, ideally, can communicate a great deal about the script, such as

- What kind of data does the script operate on?
- What does the script do?
- Who wrote the script?

Script, Procedure, and Function Names

You can use any string of characters to name a script, procedure, or function that is made up of *letters, numbers,* or *underscores*. Also, a letter or an underscore character must come first. Thus, the following would be valid names:

```
Myfunction
a_proc_name
a_proc_name2
_myfunction
```

The following would not be valid:

```
1st_function
my$function
```

Identify Data and Purpose

There are two reasons for including information about on what data a script operates and what it does in its name. First, by doing so you can better guess a script's purpose from the name alone. This is essential if you are sharing scripts with others. Even if you're only developing them for your own use, it can be quite useful, as scripts in which you've been immersed for months can seem oddly unfamiliar after you have left them behind for a while.

Second, by including both a script's function and on what it operates in its name, you reduce the risk that you'll want to have multiple scripts with the same name. For example, if you develop a script called `rename` that renames your character's geometry, when you later write a script to rename joints you may wish that you'd named your original script `rename_geom` so that you could name your new script `rename_joint`.

Identifying the Script Developer in the Script Name

Indicating who wrote a script might be just a matter of establishing a standard for putting, say, your company name or your initials in your script's names. For example, Bozz Studios developers might name their `rename` scripts `BOZZ_rename_joint` and `BOZZ_rename_geom`.

First, this kind of convention is valuable if you are going to make the script available via the Internet, say on the *highend3d.com* site. Since the scripts one person or studio develops are likely to work well together, readers of such Web sites come to have preferences for scripts from certain developers whose work fits well into their approach to animation.

Second, this kind of naming convention greatly reduces the chance that a script you download from the Internet will conflict with your naming.

Finally, by following this kind of naming convention when you have multiple developers working together on a team, you can instantly distinguish between scripts that you have created and scripts that have come from outside your team.

Naming Variables

Valid and Invalid Names

Variable names consist of a dollar sign ($) followed by a name that must conform to the same rules described for scripts, procedures, and functions. A variable name must follow the $ with letters, numbers, or underscores, with the first character after the $ being a letter or an underscore. The following are valid variable names:

```
$Myvar
$a_var_name
$a_var_name2
$_myvar
```

These are not valid:

```
$1st_variable
$my|variable
a_bad_variable
```

Identify Data Type and Purpose

Like script names, variable names benefit from indicating data type and purpose. Well-named variables make scripts easier to read. After all, which of the following is easier to understand?

```
select $bozo_left_hand_geom_node_name;
select $blhgnn;
```

Global Variables: Identifying Developer

Because variables that you define in scripts have limited scope, you usually don't have to worry about naming conflicts. However, when you use global variables, naming conflicts are a serious concern.

For example, suppose that you download a series of scripts from the Internet to help you with exporting particle data, and you hope to use these scripts in combination with your existing library of particle-related scripts.

Now, imagine that your scripts and those from the Internet have defined a global variable:

```
global string $particle_node;
```

Because of the way global variables work, your scripts and your new downloads will share this global variable, which will probably break both sets of scripts!

Again, a workable solution (although not the only possible solution) to this problem is to include a studio name or your initials in your global variables' names. Then, the

```
global string $particle_node;
```

definition from your Internet-downloaded scripts will coexist peacefully with your scripts'

```
global string $BOZZ_particle_node;
```

global variable.

Naming Nodes

Valid Names

Node names follow the same rules as procedure and function names. They must consist of letters, numbers, or underscores, and begin with a letter or an underscore.

Transform Paths

Node names are different from script, procedure, and variable names, though, in that a node's name might not be unique in a scene. For example, open a new scene, and try the following steps:

1. Make a new NURBS sphere by clicking on the sphere button.
2. Make a second NURBS sphere by clicking on the sphere button again.
3. Click on the Move tool, and move the second sphere away from the origin.
4. Select both spheres.
5. Parent one sphere to the other.
6. Open the Outliner window by choosing Window > Outliner.
7. Double-click on the name nurbsSphere1, and rename it sphere.
8. Double-click on the name nurbsSphere2, and rename it sphere.

Now, you have two spheres, each named sphere. If you open the Script Editor window and type the command

```
select -r "sphere";
```

you get an error message:

```
// Error: More than one object matches name: sphere //
```

So, a node's name is not necessarily unique, and if it is not unique, you cannot assume that you can use the node's name for common operations like selection, because Maya cannot determine which node you mean.

The answer to this problem is what is sometimes called a *transform path*. The transform paths for the two spheres follow:

- |sphere for the sphere that is parented under the world.
- |sphere|sphere for the sphere that is parented under the other sphere.

In the transform hierarchy, each object has one or more children and one or more parents. (Remember, when an object has multiple parents, it means that object is instanced and can exist in multiple spatial locations in the scene.)

Transform paths tell Maya how to find a particular node in the transform hierarchy. When a node name starts with a *pipe* character (|), such as |sphere, it refers to the node called sphere that is parented to the world. Nodes that are children of other nodes can follow, with a pipe character separating each node name. So, by saying |node1|node2, you're referring to the node called node2 that is parented under the node called node1, which is parented to the world.

If a particular node is unique but has nonunique names below it, you can start the transform path with the unique node name. For example, assume that you had the arrangement of nodes in the Outliner shown in Figure 11.1. The full transform path for the node called sphere at the

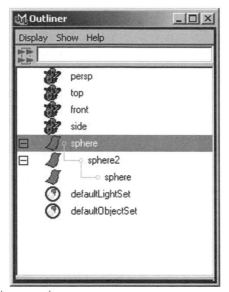

Figure 11.1 |sphere|sphere2|sphere in a hierarchy.

bottom of the hierarchy is |sphere|sphere2|sphere. This path is called the *fully qualified transform path* because it explains in full how to find that node when starting from world space.

However, since sphere2 is uniquely named in the scene, you could refer to the sphere node at the bottom of the hierarchy by the name sphere2|sphere. Since sphere2 is unique, Maya can find it within the scene, and that leaves its child node called sphere unambiguous.

You can use a transform path almost anywhere that you can use a node name in Maya. One important exception is the rename MEL command. A rename call looks like this:

```
rename "|sphere|sphere2|sphere" "mysphere";
```

This rename command changes the name of the sphere node at the bottom of the hierarchy to mysphere without changing where it falls in the hierarchy. You might hope that you could *move* that node to somewhere else in the hierarchy by giving rename a different transform path as a second argument. This does not work, however; rename will only rename a node in place, since moving a node to a new place in the hierarchy is actually re-parenting that node.

Identify Type and Purpose

Node naming presents a slightly different problem than script or variable naming because contents of Maya scenes are not shared so widely as useful scripts or global variables. However, like scripts and variables, it's a good idea to include an indication of the node type for your nodes and the purpose they serve.

The importance of node naming is obvious once your scenes become sufficiently complex. The relationship between `nurbsCylinder23` and `joint14` may be unclear, but once those nodes are named `left_arm_geom` and `left_arm_joint`, their relationship becomes obvious.

Unique Names and Writing Scripts

By keeping node names unique in your scenes, you can avoid potential confusion that can result from relying on transform paths to distinguish between nonunique nodes.

To the extent that your scripts need to walk the node tree in your scene, keep track of nodes by their fully qualified transform paths. Even if you prefer to enforce rules of unique names in your scenes, when you have multiple instances of a node, the node has a single name but multiple transform paths. The alternative, which is often very inconvenient, is deciding not to support instancing in your scripts.

Example 1: Adding a Name Prefix to Objects in a Hierarchy

It is often desirable to add a *prefix* to the names in a transform hierarchy, such as a character name. For example, if a node in character `bill` were named `joint1`, it might be renamed `bill_joint1` so that, for example, you can identify the character to which it belongs when you come across it in the hypergraph.

When you adopt a naming convention like this, it can be convenient to have a script that will add the prefix to all the objects in a character's transform hierarchy.

1. Create a new scene, and then create four spheres.
2. In the Outliner, parent the spheres to each other to create this hierarchy (Figure 11.2).
3. Now, enter the following procedure definition into the Script Editor; select it, and press Enter on the numeric keypad.

```
global proc add_prefix_to_selection(string $prefix){
   string $nodes[] = `ls -sl -dag`;

   for ($current_name in $nodes) {
      rename -ignoreShape $current_name
         ($prefix + "_" + $current_name);
   }
}
```

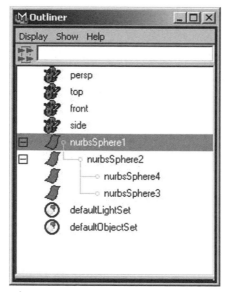

Figure 11.2 A hierarchy.

4. Try the script by selecting *only* the nurbsSphere1 node and typing

   ```
   add_prefix_to_selection("spheres");
   ```

   and then selecting it and pressing Enter on the numeric keypad.
   Now you see that all of the node names in your hierarchy begin with
   spheres_.

How the Script Works

The starting point for writing the script is to make a list of what it needs
to do: first, make a list of all the nodes to rename; and second, rename
each one in order. The usual starting point for making lists of nodes is
the ls command, so re-reading its documentation in the MEL Command
Reference is a good place to start. Also, hunting through the MEL
Command Reference gives us the rename command, which changes node
names. Around these two commands we'll construct a way to rename the
nodes in the hierarchy.

First, we have defined the script as a global procedure, because if we
were to put it into a MEL file we would want it to be accessible outside that
MEL file, such as in the Script Editor. The following single string parameter
contains the prefix that we want to add:

```
global proc add_prefix_to_selection(string $prefix){
```

The first thing our new procedure does is get a list of all of the nodes in the transform hierarchy below the selected node. The ls command offers numerous choices for how to automatically traverse the hierarchy to find lists of nodes, and in this case we use -sl (short for -selection) to tell ls to start with our selection, and -dag (short for -dagObjects) to tell ls to follow all the way down the transform hierarchy to find all the nodes below the selected node.

Try executing the ls -sl -dag command in the Script Editor to see what the result is. You should see a list of each node in the hierarchy below nurbsSphere1. Put the ls command in backticks, and assign the result to an array of strings, as follows:

```
string $nodes[] = `ls -sl -dag`;
```

Now, we use a for-in loop to rename each node in the list that we have stored in the array:

```
for ($current_name in $nodes) {
rename -ignoreShape $current_name
        ($prefix + "_" + $current_name);
}
```

The loop repeats once for every name that the ls command returned, running the MEL rename command to rename the node. The -ignoreShape flag tells rename that when it renames the transform node it should not rename the shape node. This is necessary because both the transform and shape nodes are in the list that ls gave us, and if renaming the transform automatically renamed the shape, then when our loop later tried to rename the shape node, it would fail.

Example 2: Changing Name Prefixes in a Hierarchy

A second useful script changes the name prefix for each node in a hierarchy. Start with our spheres_ hierarchy above, then enter the following script into the Script Editor:

```
global proc change_selection_prefix(string $newprefix){

    string $nodes[] = `ls -sl -dag`;
                            // Find a list of all nodes to
                            // rename

    for ($current_name in $nodes) { // Loop over those nodes

        string $parts_list[]; // This string will contain the
                            // parts of node name separated
                            // by underscores
```

```
        int $num_parts = `tokenize $current_name "_" $parts_list`;
                         // split name
    if ($num_parts > 1) { // Test to make sure that there
                         // is a prefix in the name at all

        string $old_prefix = $parts_list[0];
                         // The old name prefix

        string $no_prefix_name = $parts_list[1];
                         // The first part of
                         // the rest of the
                         // node name

        for ($count = 2; $count < $num_parts; $count++) {
                         // Rebuild the rest
                         // of the name

            $no_prefix_name = ($no_prefix_name + "_"
                         + $parts_list[$count]);
        }

        rename -ignoreShape ($current_name) ($newprefix + "_"
                         + $no_prefix_name);

    }

    }

}
```

Select the top node, and execute the following procedure call:

```
change_selection_prefix("spheresyak");
```

How the Script Works

Renaming the prefixes for a hierarchy is more complex than adding prefixes to existing node names. Since the ls command will not easily give you a node's name without its prefix, you have to find a way to strip it off yourself so that you can create the new name with the new prefix for the rename command.

The solution to this problem is to use the tokenize command. This command takes a string and splits it into parts that are separated by spaces or other special characters.

Suppose that you have a string that contains

```
spheres_test_node_name
```

You can use tokenize to split this string into all the pieces that are separated by the underscore character (_). For example, execute the following commands in the Script Editor:

```
string $resulting_parts[];
tokenize "spheres_test_node_name" "_" $resulting_parts;
```

The result of the tokenize command is 4, which is the number of parts that it found in the string that you gave it in the first argument. Each of these parts is placed into the array $resulting_parts. Run the next print statements to see what they contain:

```
print $resulting_parts[0];
print $resulting_parts[1];
print $resulting_parts[2];
print $resulting_parts[3];
```

The script above, like the previous example, uses ls to get a list of nodes in the hierarchy and a for-in loop to loop through them. Then, with this command, it uses tokenize to split each node name into the underscore-separated parts:

```
int $num_parts = `tokenize $current_name "_" $parts_list`;
                                        // Split name
```

The tokenize command puts the separated parts of the contents of $current_name into the array of strings that we've called $parts_list and returns an integer, which is the number of parts it found.

If $num_parts is 1, then that means that there are no underscores in the name. This is a sure sign that the hierarchy node names lack prefixes. So, we check for that case with an if statement:

```
if ($num_parts > 1) { // Test to make sure that there
                      // is a prefix in the name
```

Once the script determines that tokenize has given us more than one part, we know that the first must be the prefix, and the remaining ones must be the rest of the name. In our example string spheres_test_node name, the first part that tokenize returns (in the array element $parts_list[0]) is spheres; and the second, third, and fourth are test, node, and name, respectively.

To properly rename spheres_test_node_name to, say, otherprefix_test_node_name, we need to reconstruct the rest of the name beyond the prefix. The tokenize command has split the rest of the name into three parts; now our script will put them back together.

Note: If you're familiar, from shell scripting or Perl scripting, with the concept of regular expressions, you may want to look at three MEL commands—match, gmatch, and substitute—that can perform this entire process in one line. However, regular expressions are beyond the scope of this book.

Finding the prefix and reassembling the nonprefix part of the name are accomplished with the following script segment:

```
string $old_prefix = $parts_list[0]; // The old name prefix
string $no_prefix_name = $parts_list[1];
                          // The first part of the rest
                          // of the node name
for ($count = 2; $count < $num_parts; $count++) {
                          // Rebuild the rest
                          // of the name
    $no_prefix_name = ($no_prefix_name + "_"
                 + $parts_list[$count]);
}
```

The prefix, of course, is in $parts_list[0], and the first part of the remainder of the name is in $parts_list[1]. The loop that follows goes through any remaining parts and adds them, separated by underscores, to $no_prefix_name. So, in our example, $no_prefix_name first contains test, then test_node, and then test_node_name.

Finally, our script runs the rename command to change the old name (still stored in $current_name) to the new name (which consists of $newprefix, plus an underscore, plus the assembled $no_prefix_name).

```
rename -ignoreShape ($current_name) ($newprefix + "_"
                 + $no_prefix_name);
```

This script could benefit from additional error checking. For example, you should probably make sure that the new prefix does not itself contain an underscore character. This too can be easily done by calling tokenize with _ as the separator character and then checking how many strings are returned, or by using the match command.

What Are Namespaces?

Namespaces are a feature that was added in recent versions of Maya to better manage names when you import or reference other scenes into the scene on which you're working. Namespaces work something like transform paths in that they separate node names into groups. If you choose to use namespaces to refer to your nodes, you provide a namespace in front of the transform path. For example, all the nodes that are in the namespace called my_namespace: would be called my_namespace:<node name>. Namespaces always end with a colon (:), so that you and Maya can tell the difference between a namespace name and the transform path.

Namespaces can contain other namespaces. When they do, the containing namespace is listed first, and the namespace that it contains is second. For example, you could create a namespace called my_namespace:

`your_namespace:` that consists of a namespace called `your_namespace` that is contained in `my_namespace`.

Just as objects in world space have transform paths that begin with a pipe character (|), objects in the default namespace for a scene have namespace paths that begin with a colon (:). In our example above, the object |sphere|sphere2|sphere, because it's in the default namespace for the scene (where everything you create ends up unless you deliberately change that), can be referred to as :|sphere|sphere2|sphere. The colon at the beginning says that it's in the default namespace, and the pipe that follows says to start at world space for the transform path.

You can set a *current namespace*. When you do, whenever you use a transform path or a node name without specifying a namespace explicitly, Maya will assume that you are referring to the contents of the current namespace. The current namespace starts out the default namespace (:), unless you change it.

When you import or reference another Maya file, you have a choice about whether to use namespaces to separate the objects and expressions in the scene you import or reference. When you open the option box for the import command by choosing File > Import . . . > ☐, you see the choices shown in Figure 11.3.

Note the checkbox labeled Use Namespaces. If you check this box, when you import another Maya file, all the nodes in that file will be placed in a namespace named for the file. For example, if the file to be imported were called test.ma, imported objects would be placed in a namespace called test. (The Create Reference . . . option box also offers a Use Namespaces checkbox.)

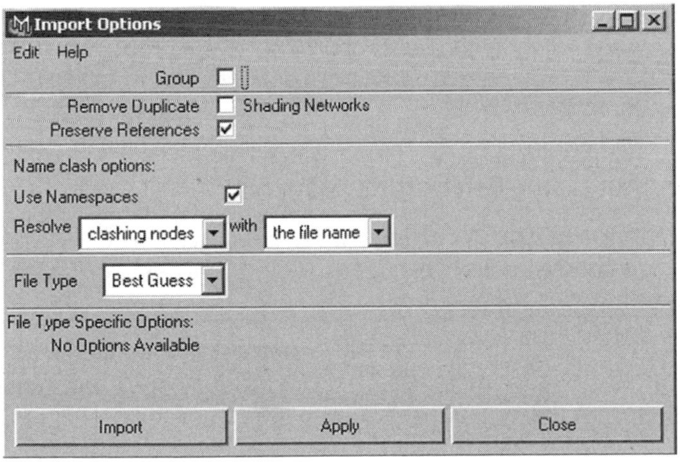

Figure 11.3 Import options.

After this point, every node that you've imported must be referred to using the namespace. For example, if you had imported a sphere called nurbsSphere1, you would manipulate that sphere using the name test: nurbsSphere1.

If you do *not* use namespaces when importing a file, Maya will rename any nodes that conflict with nodes in the existing scene. In our example, those names would be changed to test_<name>.

One pitfall that can be a problem whether or not you are using name-spaces relates to expressions in the scene that you are importing or refer-encing. If your expressions follow the suggestion that you only set or read attributes using the attribute name directly, then you will not experience this problem. However, if your expressions create attributes, change their names, or use the getAttr or setAttr MEL commands, Maya may be unable to figure out how to modify your expression scripts to accommo-date the newly renamed nodes or the use of namespaces in your new scene.

Finding Information About Namespaces

Maya's namespaceInfo command allows you to find useful information about namespaces in your scene in the following ways:

- You can find the current namespace name with the namespaceInfo -currentNamespace command.
- You can find the name of the namespace that contains the current namespace with the namespaceInfo -parent command.
- You can list all of the contents of the current namespace, including other namespaces and all the nodes it contains, with the namespaceInfo -listNamespace command.
- You can get a list of all the namespaces that are contained in a given namespace with the namespaceInfo -listOnlyNamespaces command.
- You can get a list of all the dependency graph nodes contained in the current namespace with the namespaceInfo -listOnlyDependency Nodes command.

Creating, Setting, and Deleting Namespaces

In MEL scripts or at the command line, you can make your own name-spaces, set the current namespace, and delete namespaces with the name-space command.

- namespace -add "blah" creates a namespace called blah contained in the current namespace. Its contents would be referred to as blah:<name> where <name> is the name or transform path of the node.

- `namespace -set ":blah"` tells Maya to set the current namespace to `:blah`. This namespace path begins with a colon in this example because all namespaces with the `namespace -set` command must be fully qualified, meaning they cannot be relative to the current namespace, unlike in the other namespace-related commands.
- `namespace -rm "blah"` tells Maya to remove the namespace called `blah` that is contained in the current namespace.

Strategies for Using Namespaces

One straightforward strategy for using namespaces is to avoid them entirely, except when importing or referencing scenes. Particularly when using referencing, namespaces are useful in that they make perfectly clear from which referenced file a particular node comes.

More complex strategies for use of namespaces are possible, depending on how you like to work, but they probably require developing support scripts to help animators stay within their bounds. For example, you might use namespaces as part of a crowd system to separate the naming of multiple copies of characters in a crowd that share the same setup.

Usually, even when you do not plan to use namespaces, if your scripts can accommodate their use, you can adapt if it becomes necessary or more convenient to use them.

What to Remember About Naming Scripts, Variables, and Nodes

- Having a strategy for naming your scripts, variables, and nodes is essential, particularly if you are working in a team.
- A well-selected script name can communicate where a script comes from, what it does, and possibly what data it can manipulate. By propagating a consistent standard in your organization for script naming, you facilitate sharing scripts, bringing scripts in from the outside, and finding the right script for a task.
- A well-selected variable name can communicate what the variable is used for and what kind of data it contains. Not only do good variable names make your scripts more readable, having a standard for global variable names helps ensure that your scripts can work well with scripts from the outside and with various scripts developed by various people in your organization.
- Choosing a useful scheme for naming nodes can help identify what the node is, even when it appears out of context. Furthermore, developing utility scripts to implement your node-naming conventions can greatly

reduce the amount of time you have to spend ensuring that your nodes are named properly.

■ Namespaces are a way of creating separate naming "worlds" for your nodes to prevent conflicts when mixing nodes from different scenes. Namespaces are probably most useful when importing or referencing objects from another scene. However, it's important to make sure that any but the simplest expressions are well tested in the new scene, as Maya may not be able to automatically update node names that are constructed in a script to include the correct namespace names.

12

Designing MEL User Interfaces

In this chapter you will learn

- What a user interface is.
- What Maya users expect from your script's user interface.
- How to choose how your script will collect needed input from the user.
- When and how to design a dialog box.

What Is a User Interface?

Since 1984, when the graphic look of the Apple Macintosh first brought the concept of the *user interface* before the popular eye, most people who use computers have come to associate the term with the windows and graphics that have become the standard means of interacting with computers. As software developers use the term, though, a program's user interface encompasses all interaction between human and computer. This interaction starts with what users expect to see when they run any program, through the information that users see and how that information is presented and how users contribute input to the running program, and finally results in the program doing something useful.

The best user interfaces are often the simplest and are built with the following aspects of the underlying problem that you're trying to solve in mind:

- How does the user expect to work with an unfamiliar script or program, and what can the program do to accommodate these expectations?
- What information does the script or program need from the user as input, and what information does the user need to see up front to provide that input?

- How can the dialogue of information between the user and the program best be implemented to minimize the user's confusion and maximize convenience?
- When the script or program finishes, what kind of feedback does the user need so that he or she will know that the program has done the right thing?

Answering these questions is often the most difficult part of programming. Fortunately, many MEL scripts do not need complicated user interfaces. Also, since MEL scripts run in the familiar Maya environment, many clear user expectations are already set, and you can use these expectations to make your design task easier.

What Maya Users Expect to See from a MEL Script

There are many ways your scripts can interact with their users, but by drawing as much inspiration as you can from the tools that ship with Maya, you will ensure that your script behaves in a familiar and easy-to-understand way. Rather than try to analyze the entire range of possibilities for what you can implement, we'll focus on a few patterns for designing your scripts' user interfaces that will be familiar and useful for all but the largest applications.

Approach 1: Operate on the Selection

If you look at how Maya's built-in tools work, you'll see that many of the tools, like the Move tool or the Edit > Parent menu operation, work by following a very simple procedure.:

- First, select one or more objects.
- Then click or drag the mouse somewhere (e.g., on one of the Move handles, on a toolbar button, or to a menu item) to make the operation happen.

Some tools and menu items in Maya, such as the Sphere tool, don't even require that anything be selected. Alternatively, if it were appropriate for your task, you could use MEL to build a tool or menu item that would know to do different things if an object were selected or if nothing were selected when the user clicks on the tool or menu item.

A tool or menu item that uses this type of user interface must be able to do its job with no information other than what objects it's supposed to operate on, because it does not ask for anything other than a selection.

Approach 2: Using a Dialog Box

Some menu items and tools have a more sophisticated interaction with the user.

- First, if necessary, select one or more objects.
- Click or drag the mouse to activate a menu item or tool.
- The menu item or tool creates a window to ask for more information. This window, because it allows the script to have a dialogue with the user about how the task is to be performed, is called a dialog box (Figure 12.1).
- When the user clicks a button in the dialog box with a label such as Accept or OK, the dialog box disappears, and the script performs the task.

Many Maya menu items allow you to choose whether to perform their tasks with common settings, or whatever settings you've last chosen, or to open an option box that will let you change all of the command settings if you pick the option icon (□). These option boxes are dialog boxes.

Also, some menu items always create a dialog box. Usually, these menu item names end in an ellipsis (. . .).

Approach 3: The Persistent Dialog Box

The third common approach is for a command to create a dialog box that remains open, even after the task has been executed. Then, by selecting

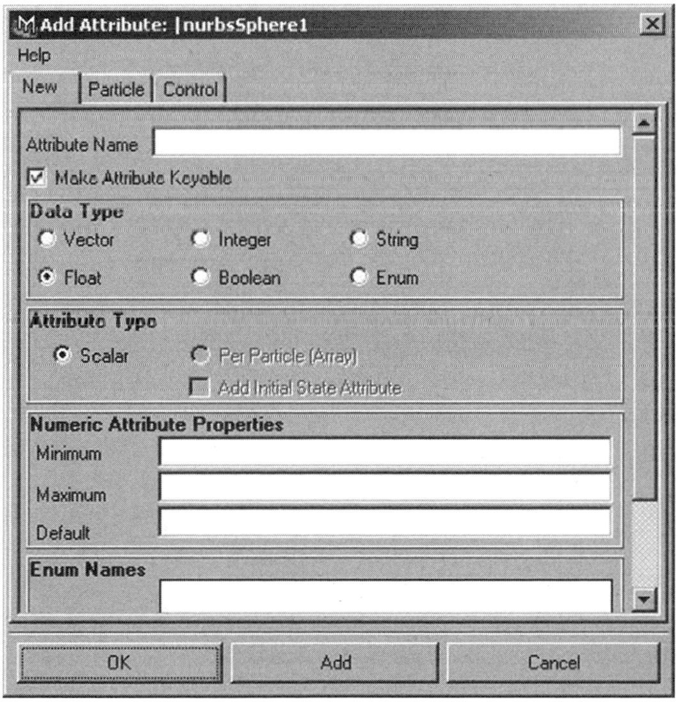

Figure 12.1 A dialog box.

other objects and possibly changing settings, the user can perform the task again and again.

The Add Attribute dialog box pictured in Figure 12.1 works like this. You can enter the characteristics of a new attribute and click Add, and then enter another attribute and click Add again, until you've added all the custom attributes you need.

Approach 4: Something Else

Of course, the three approaches above do not cover the entire range of interfaces that you may want to build. MEL provides some tools for building more complex interfaces, but you're likely to need to move beyond a simple MEL script and build the interface using either an external scripting language or Maya's Application Programming Interface (API) and the C++ language. Both of these approaches are beyond the scope of this book, but you can find more information in the Maya API Reference in Maya's documentation set.

Questions to Answer Before Designing a User Interface

When you're planning to write a MEL script, your first job is to decide how your script will get the information it needs to work. The easiest user interface to build is to write a script that must be run by typing a procedure call into the Script Editor by hand, but even for your own scripts that is usually an unacceptable long-term solution.

Answering the following questions before you proceed will simplify the task greatly:

- Is your script a one-off solution to a problem that can do the job with little user interface at all, such as by being run by hand from the Script Editor?
- Does your script operate on objects? If so, does it make sense for the user to select the objects first before running the script?
- Do you want to activate your script with a shelf button, a menu item, or both?
- Does your script need additional information from the user before it can do its job, or can it collect all the information it needs by looking through the objects in the scene? If so, what information does it need? (This will help you decide what your dialog box will contain.)
- Will the user need to use your script over and over again? If so, consider allowing your dialog box to persist rather than closing it each time your script is run.

With answers to the above questions in hand, you'll be ready to decide what interaction your script should present to the user.

Designing and Testing a User Interface

By taking a systematic approach to building the interface for your script, you can take a much shorter path to a useful interface than you would otherwise. Since building a user interface is often more complicated than building the script it controls, often the best approach is to design and build the interface first, and then move on to the underlying script, as outlined below.

1. Write down the information that your script needs to do its job.
2. Write down what your interface will do to activate your script and draw any dialog boxes it presents. Make sure that you are collecting any information identified in step 1.
3. If your script requires a dialog box or a window, plan how to implement your dialog box in your script. Quickly throw together a MEL script that creates a dialog box that is close to what you want. It is not necessary for the dialog box to do anything at this point.
4. Start showing your mock-up to people who might use your script. Ask what they think the various buttons and switches do and how they would navigate through the task at hand. Be attentive for confusion, and redesign if necessary.
5. Build the underlying scripts that do the work in your Maya scene.
6. Add your finished script to the Maya environment as a shelf button or a menu item.

With this overall approach in mind, you are prepared to tackle the more subtle question of what makes a good user interface for your problem.

Hints for Planning a Good User Interface

Building excellent user interfaces is an art which requires that many factors work well together. However, there are a few guidelines that can help you find a useful design.

Do the repetition for the user When you know, or can reasonably anticipate, that your user is going to want to perform the same operation on multiple objects, build your script to handle operating on multiple objects at once. Alternatively, if you can traverse the directed graph or the transform hierarchy to figure out what the user wants to operate on, consider offering the user that option.

One input window is better than many Rather than bringing up dialog box after dialog box, figure out how to get the information you need from one. If you need the answers to certain questions to decide whether you need the answers to others, plan to activate and deactivate controls in one dialog box based on what your script needs.

Put effort into most-used interfaces   If you are developing a number of dialog boxes for one or more scripts that work together, make sure that you put the bulk of your effort into the dialog boxes that will be most used. Get those dialog boxes in front of others who may use your scripts as early as possible.

Show choices rather than ask questions   For example, rather than prompting your user to type in the name of an object, perhaps your script can list the objects on which it can operate and encourage the user to click on one. Or, in some instances, rather than having the user type a number, a few well-selected choices may help direct the user toward a reasonable choice.

Minimize number of choices presented to the user   It's easy to design a user interface that presents a dizzying array of choices when a few might suffice. Try to avoid doing this. Also, if turning on one feature of your script in a dialog box makes others meaningless, think about implementing your script so that the irrelevant features are disabled when the first is activated. Chapter 14 describes in more detail how to build your dialog boxes to do this.

Build simple tools rather than large systems   Avoid the desire to create grand structures of interrelated scripts that share a common interface and try to do everything. Instead, you'll have an easier development task and probably please your users more by building smaller tools that they can use together in ways that perhaps you have not anticipated.

Structure of a Dialog Box

Dialog boxes consist of a number of *controls* that are bound together in an overall structure called a *layout*. The controls provide the means that the user uses to fill in the dialog box with information the script needs, while the layout determines how those controls will be displayed. In Chapter 14, you will see how controls and layouts are constructed, but for now we will just examine some of the common component parts (Figure 12.2).

Menus in a dialog box work just like menus in the main Maya window. In your dialog boxes, you can create a menu with a number of choices, each of which runs a MEL script.

Tabs are one of the ways that MEL allows you to group controls in a dialog box so that the user can choose to look at only one set at a time.

Frames allow you to group controls into subgroups that belong together, such as the Data Type controls in Figure 12.2. Although it is not shown in this figure, frames can also be collapsible, in which case they

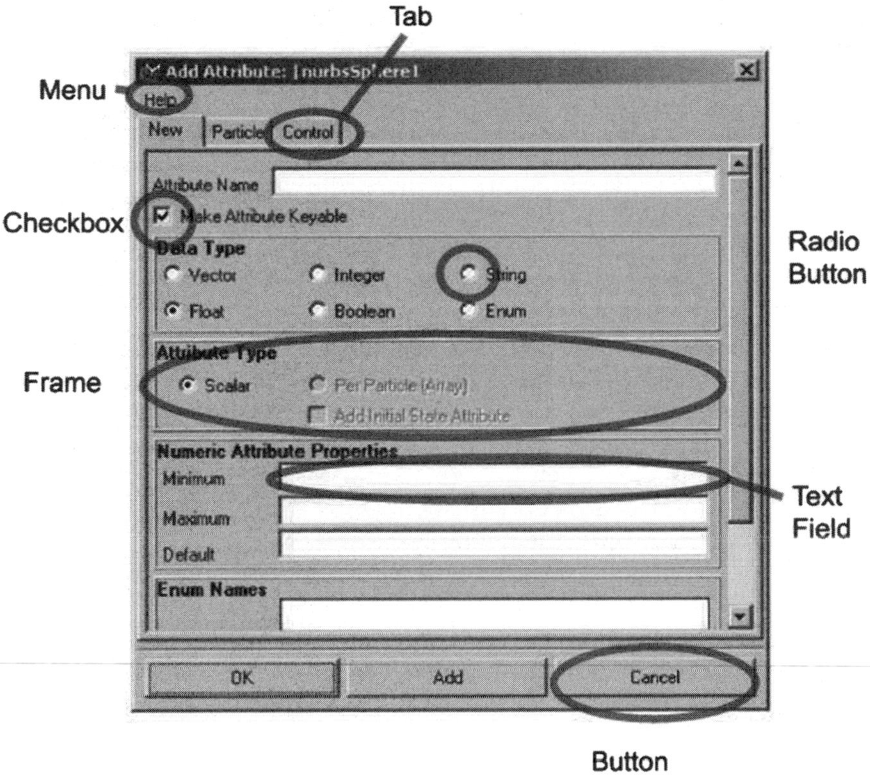

Figure 12.2 Parts of a dialog box.

have a triangular button on the upper left side that hides the frame when clicked.

The most common controls are *checkboxes, radio buttons, text fields, sliders* (not pictured), and *buttons*.

Checkboxes are either checked or unchecked, and they denote a true or false value. Radio buttons come in sets, called *radio button groups,* and like the buttons on a car radio, when one is turned on, all the rest turn off. Text fields provide a place to type text or numbers. Sliders offer a handle that can be dragged left or right to provide a numeric value. (Figure 12.2 does not contain a slider.) Finally, buttons are controls that the user clicks to activate a script, often one that reads the other controls and executes an action.

When designing dialog boxes, remember that you should not only plan how the controls are laid out, but also how they work. Does enabling certain controls disable other controls? Do certain buttons make the dialog box disappear when clicked?

What to Remember About Designing User Interfaces in MEL

- Plan to satisfy user expectations about how tools work in Maya. Make sure that familiar controls work in familiar ways, and make sure that your scripts work like similar tools that ship with Maya.
- Collect the necessary information before you begin. What information does your script need to do its job? How does the user activate your script? Should they select objects before doing so? Do you need to use a dialog box?
- Follow a systematic process of building the user interface first, testing it with other people, answering their thoughts and concerns, and then building the underlying scripts. After all, the MEL commands that create a dialog box may be the most complicated part of your script.
- Remember to plan not just how dialog boxes appear but also how their controls work. After all, you will spend some time scripting that behavior once you have built the dialog box itself.

13

Simple MEL User Interfaces

In this chapter you will learn

- How to create a simple dialog box with one or more buttons to either present a series of options or a warning message to the user.
- How to create a dialog box with a text field and one or more buttons so that the user can enter text for your script.
- How to prompt the user to browse for a file on disk with a file browser dialog box appropriate for your operating system.
- How to use the warning and error commands to provide feedback to the user that will be logged in the Script Editor.
- What regular expressions are.
- How regular expressions work.
- How regular expressions can be used to validate integers, floating-point numbers, and object names that a user has typed into a text field.

Collecting Information from Users

In Chapter 12, we looked at a few standard ways that your script's user expects to interact with your script. Usually, if appropriate, the user will select something, and your script will examine the state of the scene. If your script needs more information (and, of course, it may not), it uses a *dialog box* to prompt the user for that information, either a dialog box that persists so that the user can do your script's task again and again, or one that disappears as soon as the user has provided the information that your script needs. Then, the script runs, doing whatever it's designed to do.

Often, your script may need a small amount of information that does not warrant developing a complex dialog box with many controls. For example, your script may only need the user to provide a single piece of information, such as

- The desired name for an object that your script will create.
- A number that indicates how many times your script should do a repetitive task.
- The path to a file on disk that your script will read or write.
- A yes or no answer to whether the user really wants to continue with something dangerous.

Also, you may want to present a warning or error to the user that does not present a choice, but instead only requires that the user acknowledge it by clicking a button.

Maya provides simple MEL commands to present a message to a user, allow a user to type in a text string or a value, pick a file on disk, or click a button to answer yes or no to a question without designing and building a custom dialog box. Many queries of the user may be implemented with nothing more than these commands.

If you do need to build a custom dialog box to collect more complex information from the user, Chapter 14 will tell you how to do so.

Validating User Input: When and Why

In our examples thus far, the scripts have taken the input they need from the parameters used in the procedure call that executes them. When you declare a script's parameters, you specify the data type (integer, string, float, and so on) that the parameter must be, and when a user types a call to your script in the Script Editor, Maya provides a helpful error message if any of the parameters are the wrong data type.

Maya's built-in checking of the data type and printing an error message is a simple type of *input validation*, in which inputs are checked to make sure that they are meaningful in context. Note that this validation is rudimentary; it will catch a user's attempt to provide the word "hello" in place of a floating-point number, but it will not catch a user's attempt to type the the number 243.4 when only a number between 0.0 and 1.0 makes sense to your script.

Usually, your purpose in creating a dialog box for your script, whether you use one of the simple built-in dialog boxes or a custom dialog box, is to avoid requiring that your user type commands into the Script Editor. If you use a dialog box without validating what the user types, you lose much of the value of Maya's built-in data type checking, because even if Maya does catch the error and prints a useful message because a user has typed something meaningless, it will appear in the Maya status line or the Script Editor, where probably nobody is looking, and your script will quit in the middle with no warning.

The solution to this is to validate all of the user's dialog box input in your script. Types of goals that you should have for this validation are listed below.

- That integers and floats are valid numbers before they are assigned to a numeric variable.
- That strings that need to be typed by hand are valid (e.g., if the user is typing an object name, that the name consists only of letters, numbers, and underscores). Also, that strings that must not be empty are not empty (in other words, that the user has filled in the string with something).
- That numbers are within the ranges, if any, that your script will find meaningful.
- That strings that contain, say, a path to a file or an existing object's name actually point to a real file or object.

When you validate a user's input, your goal is to determine whether the input is valid and your script should proceed to do what it's intended to do, or whether the input is not valid and your script should provide a message explaining the problem.

Thus, every script that creates a dialog box should at least perform the following tasks, in the order given.

- Examine the scene and the selection to determine that the state the scene is in (including what's been selected) makes sense for the script.
- Create one or more dialog boxes, if necessary, that ask the user for input.
- Validate the contents of any parameters that your script may define as well as any variables that have been filled in from the user's dialog box input. This step should check that all the data received makes sense for what your script is to do, and if some of the data are not valid, that the script produces an error message that tells the user how to fix the problem *before* changing the scene.
- If the input data are valid, run the main body of your script.

You will find that much of the time most of your script consists of MEL that collects information from the scene and the user and makes sure that that information is valid. The meat of your script is often simple (and quick to write) in comparison. However, all this work to validate the input pays off in that it ensures that your script is much more likely to tell the user when things are wrong and less likely to leave the scene broken.

In the remainder of this chapter, we first discuss MEL's simple dialog box tools and then provide some approaches to validating common kinds of data. Then, we look at an example of how to build a simple script that satisfies the requirements laid out above.

Asking for Confirmation with confirmDialog

When your script needs to prompt the user for one of a few choices, you can use the `confirmDialog` MEL command to temporarily stop execution of your script and create a small dialog box that prompts the user to pick from a set of buttons.

One of the buttons, called the *Default button,* is specially marked. (Depending on the operating system, it may be marked with a dotted outline, as in Windows or Linux, or a throbbing blue color, as in the Mac OS.) Pressing Enter is the same as clicking the Default button.

Another button can be designated the *Cancel button,* and pressing the Esc key is then the same as clicking the Cancel button. The Cancel button is not specially marked.

When the user clicks on a button, the dialog box goes away, and the `confirmDialog` command returns the name of the button that the user clicked. If the user clicks on the close box instead, rather than any of the buttons, the `confirmDialog` command returns the string `dismiss`. If you prefer, you can specify another string for `confirmDialog` to return.

For example, your script might contain this command:

```
string $returnVal = `confirmDialog
   -title "Identify and Destroy All Termite Species!"
   -message "Are you sure?"
   -button "Yes"
   -button "No"
   -button "I'm not sure"
   -button "Maybe"
   -defaultButton "Yes"
   -cancelButton "I'm not sure"
   -dismissString "Oops"`;
```

When this `confirmDialog` command runs, your script will pause and produce the window shown in Figure 13.1. When the user clicks a button, the script's execution resumes, and the name of the button is placed in the `$returnVal` variable. The Enter key triggers the Yes button, and the Esc key triggers the I'm not sure button. Clicking the close box returns the string `Oops` to the `$returnVal` variable.

Figure 13.1 A window created with `confirmDialog`.

After the script has a return value from the `confirmDialog` command, it can use a `switch` statement or an `if-else` statement to determine what to do based on the user's response.

Another use for `confirmDialog` is as a means of presenting an important message, such as a warning, to the user, as in

```
confirmDialog -title "Warning"
              -message "Everything is about to be deleted"
              -button "OK";
```

Because there is only one button, which dismisses the dialog, the user's response doesn't matter in this instance. Instead, this dialog simply presents a warning, shown in Figure 13.2. Usually, a warning such as this would be better presented with an OK and a Cancel button to allow the user to back out before deleting everything.

Although presenting a warning to the user in this way is useful, you should also use the MEL command `warning` to print the warning string into the Script Editor. That way, if the user looks in the Script Editor to see what happened, a record will be there.

Asking User for Text String with promptDialog

The `promptDialog` command works much like `confirmDialog`, but includes in the dialog box a text field into which the user can enter text. You can use `promptDialog`, for example, to prompt for the name of a new object that your script will create.

Like `confirmDialog`, `promptDialog` returns the name of the button that the user clicks to close the dialog box. To get the text that the user typed, you call `promptDialog` again in *query mode,* which causes it to return the text value.

For example, suppose that your script made a new sphere object, and you want to prompt the user for the desired name of that object. You could create a dialog box like this:

```
string $buttonResponse = `promptDialog -title "Make Sphere"
                                       -message
                                         "Name for your new
                                          sphere?"
```

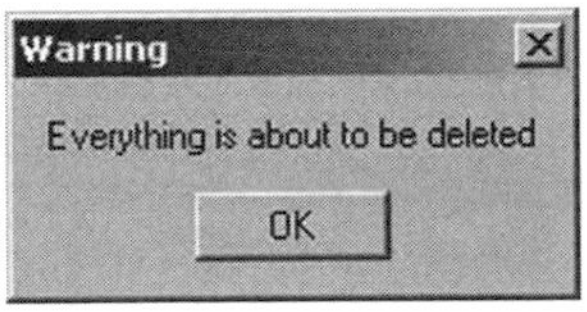

Figure 13.2 Warning created with `confirmDialog`.

```
                                          -button "OK"
                                          -button "Cancel"
                                          -defaultButton "OK"`;
```

```
string $textResponse = `promptDialog -q`;
```

When the `promptDialog` command is called for the first time in create mode (which, if you recall, is the default mode for commands that support create, edit, and query modes), it pauses the script's execution and creates a dialog box that looks like the one shown in Figure 13.3. In the code segment above, once the user enters a string and clicks either OK or Cancel, the button he or she clicked is placed in the `$buttonResponse` variable. The second call to `promptDialog`, in query mode, returns the string that the user typed into the text field. In the code above, this is assigned to the `$textResponse` variable.

By testing the value of `$buttonResponse`, your script can decide what, if anything, to do with the text string the user has entered. If the string is needed (such as if the user clicks OK instead of Cancel), the text string in `$textResponse` can be used as the name for the new sphere object.

The `-title`, `-message`, `-button`, `-defaultButton`, `-cancelButton`, and `-dismissString` flags all work the same for `promptDialog` as they do for `confirmDialog`. Additionally, you can use `-text "string"` so that a text string will appear in the text field when the window opens, or you can use `-scrollableField true` to permit scrolling in the text field if there may be a large amount of text to collect.

Asking User to Pick File or Directory with fileDialog

When you want to create a dialog box that contains a file browser to allow your user to pick a file, you can use the MEL command `fileDialog`. Unlike the `confirmDialog` and `promptDialog` commands, `fileDialog` does not give you a great deal of control over the look of the window. The only available option is the `-directoryMask` flag, which allows you to specify the directory that the user should browse or the types of files that should be seen in the browser. For example,

```
string $filePath = `fileDialog -directoryMask "*.ma"`;
```

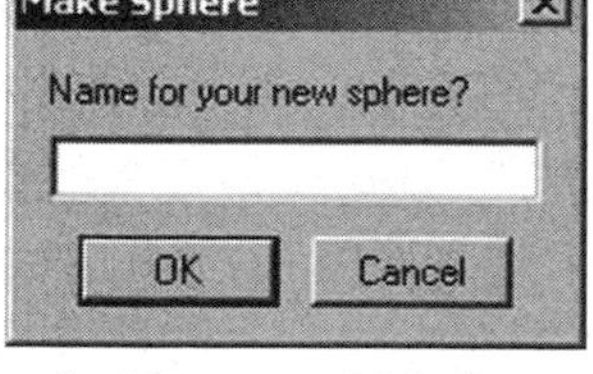

Figure 13.3 Dialog box created with `promptDialog`.

creates a file browser that will only display files ending in .ma, or Maya Ascii files. When the user chooses a file, the file's full path is put into the $filePath variable.

The file browser dialog box that fileDialog creates looks like the standard file browser for whichever operating system you use.

Handling Warnings and Errors with Warning and Error Commands

Your script will often need to generate a warning of an anomalous condition, or to print an error message that indicates that something has gone wrong. The warning command prints a string into the Script Editor window so that there will be a record of the warning there when a user tries to debug what went wrong. The message will also appear on the status line. The warning command works much like the print command. Try typing the following into the Script Editor and executing it:

```
warning "Oops, too many objects";
```

The result is a message on the status line that reads "Oops, too many objects" and one in the Script Editor that reads like this:

```
// Warning: Oops, too many objects //
```

The flag -showLineNumber true will cause a warning to print the file and line number where the warning occurred if it's being run from within a .mel file.

For errors that prevent your script from continuing, you can use the error command, as in

```
error "I've reached the end of my rope";
```

This error command prints the message

```
// Error: I've reached the end of my rope //
```

and then terminates the containing script. When your script executes an error command, the script stops running immediately, so that any clean-up that your script has to do (e.g, undoing a task that's been left half-done because of the error) should be done before running the error command itself.

The -showLineNumber true flag works with the error command just as it does with the warning command, by printing the file name and line number on which the error occurred if the command is run from within a .mel file.

Using Regular Expressions and match to Validate Data

When a user types characters into a dialog box, you may be expecting to get back an integer, a floating-point number, or a name for an object that your script will create. However, Maya will return all of these to your script as a string.

Before proceeding on the assumption that your user has typed what you expect, your script should *validate* the data that it has received from the dialog box to ensure that it's correct. If the validation succeeds, you can be sure that Maya will allow you to use the validated data as you intend without generating an error. If it fails, you can provide a useful message to your user while allowing your script to continue executing.

Many scripting languages, particularly shell scripting and Perl, provide a common means of checking to see whether a string matches a predefined pattern, by using a way of defining patterns called *regular expressions*. You can define patterns that distinguish between numbers, words, or other types of strings.

MEL allows you to check whether a string or part of the string matches a regular expression pattern using the `match` command. By defining patterns that match what you need from your script's input data, you can use the `match` command for validation.

How Regular Expressions Work

A full description of regular expressions and how to use them is beyond the scope of this book. You can use certain "cookbook" regular expressions without being able to write them yourself, and even many programmers find regular expressions confusing because they use special symbols in unfamiliar ways. However, to give you a basic idea of how these cookbook expressions work, we'll look at the structure of regular expressions and some practical expressions that can be used to validate common data types.

A regular expression describes a range of possible strings that match a pattern which the expression describes. When you use the `match` command to compare that regular expression to an actual string, you'll get back the part of the string that matches that pattern.

The simplest regular expressions consist of a sequence of letters or numbers that you would like to find in your string. If the letters or numbers appear in the string, `match` will return only the part of the string that matches. If they do not appear, `match` will return an empty string. Try typing and executing the following statement in the Script Editor:

```
match "blah" "abcdblahhaha"
```

The result is the first sequence of characters in your string that matches the expression ("blah") exactly:

```
// Result: blah //
```

Now, try the `match` command to see what happens when your test string does not contain the word you're looking for:

```
match "blah" "abcdefghi"
```

This command does not return a result because the expression "blah" does not match the string that you are testing, "abcdefghi".

By assigning the return value of match to a variable, you can test to see whether anything matched by testing whether the return value is the same as the empty string, "". Alternatively, you can find out whether your entire test string matched by seeing whether the return value is the same as your test string.

For example, following is a loop that requests that your user type strings again and again until he or she finally types a string that contains the word "blah". (Make sure that you type the string into the text field in the window!)

```
int $keepgoing = 1;

while ($keepgoing) {

    promptDialog -message
    "type a string containing the word blah please!";

    string $typedString = `promptDialog -q`;

    string $matches_blah = `match "blah" $typedString`;

    int $found_match = ! `strcmp "blah" $matches_blah`;
        // Remember, strcmp returns 0 if the strings are equal

    if ($found_match) {
        $keepgoing = 0;
    }
}

print "Found blah!\n";
```

The above loop combines using the match command to test for the word "blah" in the input string with the strcmp command that compares two strings to see if they are the same or different. As the comment in the code notes, strcmp returns 0 if two strings are the same. Since we know that only the string "blah" can match the regular expression pattern "blah", either you will get an empty string back from match (if the word isn't there) or get the word "blah" back (if it is). Thus, we can use strcmp to see whether the word is there.

Regular expressions also provide a variety of means to test for repetition of a particular pattern. By putting a word in parentheses and placing + after it, you will match one or more occurrences of the word, as in

```
match "(blah)+" "abcdblahblahblahefg";
// Result: blahblahblah //
```

Quantifiers are characters that specify matching a certain number of the preceding thing. A few common quantifiers are listed on the next page.

- ■ * means "match zero or more."
- ■ + means "match one or more."
- ■ {2,4} means "match two, three, or four of the preceding thing."
- ■ Some versions of the Maya documentation mention the ? quantifier, which in most implementations of regular expressions means the same as {0,1}, or either 0 or 1 of the preceding thing. This quantifier does not work in versions 3 or 4 of Maya, but may in earlier or later versions. If in doubt, use {0,1} instead.

You can refer to a class of characters that a particular character must match by putting a list of the characters in square brackets. This kind of pattern is called a *character class*. For example, if a letter must be a, b, or c, you can match it with the character class [abc]. If you need a string of letters that must be a, b, or c, you can use a quantifier that says, for example, "one or more letters that are either a, b, or c," as follows:

```
[abc]+
```

Also, you can refer to ranges of letters or numbers by putting a dash in the middle. For example, to match upper-case letters you can use the character class

```
[A-Z]
```

A few other special characters that can appear in regular expressions are the period (.), which matches any character at all; ^, which matches the beginning of a string; and $, which matches the end of a string. Finally, if you need to match a character that has a special meaning in a regular expression, you can precede it with a backslash \.

Validating Integers

Validating integers may not be necessary if you have collected the number from an intFieldGrp dialog box item (described in Chapter 14). However, if you're using the prompt command or reading the integer from a source that's not guaranteed to give you a valid integer number, this validation is necessary.

To ensure that a string is an integer before converting it to an integer variable, you can test it with the following function:

```
global proc int validInteger (string $testString){
    string $matchingPart = `match "^[+\-]{0,1}[0-9]+$"
                           $testString`;

    int $goodMatch = ! `strcmp $matchingPart $testString`;
        // Remember, if the two strings are the same,
          strcmp will return 0
```

```
    return $goodMatch;
}
```

Since the entire string must be made up of numbers, our regular expression "^[+\-]{0,1}[0-9]+$" starts with the beginning of the string (matched with ^), and ends with the end of the string (matched with $). In between, we allow for one of either plus (+) or minus (–) without requiring it (using the quantifier {0,1}), and we require that there be one or more digits between 0 and 9 (matched with [0-9]+).

Then, we use strcmp to make sure that the part of the string we matched is the same as the input string. (Of course, in this example we will either match the entire string or nothing, because our pattern specifies that it must match both the start and the end of the string and everything in between. However, that may not always be the case for every pattern you may want to use.)

Try out the validate function, as follows:

```
validInteger("123s");
// Result: 0 //

validInteger("-125");
// Result: 1 //
```

As you examine more validation functions, they will all return 0 if the string passed is not valid and 1 if it is. Go ahead and try them in the Script Editor to see what they do.

Validating Floating-Point Numbers

Validating floating-point numbers may not be necessary if you have collected the number from a floatFieldGrp dialog box item (described in Chapter 14). However, if you are using the prompt command or reading the floating-point number from a source that's not guaranteed to give you a floating-point number, this validation is necessary.

The regular expression to match floating-point numbers is about as unreadable as they get. A valid floating-point number may, but need not, start with a plus or minus character:

```
+5, -3, +25
```

Then, there may or may not be a decimal point, optionally with some digits following it:

```
23., 245.32
```

After the decimal digits, there may optionally be an exponent, which consists of E, an optional plus or minus, and at least one digit:

```
-23.34E24, 1.0E-34, 3.4E+24
```

Following is the regular expression that matches floating-point numbers. Note the backslashes before the – symbols and the double-backslash required before the decimal point (because the period and – have other regular expression meanings).

```
^[+\-]{0,1}[0-9]+(\\.{0,1}[0-9]*){0,1}(E{0,1}[+\-]{0,1}[0-9]+){0,1}$
```

Whew! Following is the function that uses the regular expression to validate floats:

```
global proc int validFloat (string $testString) {

    string $matchingPart = `match
    "^[+\-]{0,1}[0-9]+(\\.{0,1}[0-9]*){0,1}(E{0,1}[+\-]{0,1}[0-9]+){0,1}$ "
        $testString`;

    int $goodMatch = ! `strcmp $matchingPart $testString`;
        // Remember, if the two strings are the same, strcmp will
            return 0

    return $goodMatch;
}
```

Once you think you understand regular expressions, go over the above example to see why it works.

Validating Object Names (Without Namespaces)

If you want the user to type a valid object name, it must contain only letters, numbers, and underscores, and must begin with a letter. We can use a similar approach to our integer validation function to validate object names.

Our regular expression says that everything from the beginning (^) to the end ($) must be a valid character. There must be at least one letter [a-zA-Z] at the beginning and optionally as many letters, numbers, and underscores as one likes after that ([0-9a-zA-Z]*). Following is the function that validates object names based on these rules:

```
global proc int validObjectName (string $testString) {
    string $matchingPart = `match "^[a-zA-Z][0-9a-zA-Z_]*$"
                            $testString`;

    int $goodMatch = ! `strcmp $matchingPart $testString`;
        // Remember, if the two strings are the same, strcmp
            will return 0

    return $goodMatch;
}
```

Example 1: Simple Dialogs and Input Validation

Assume that you want to create a number of sphere objects in your scene, spaced along the X axis every five units. You would like to provide an interface that will allow the user to type a valid base name for the objects and a number of spheres to make.

This script, which we will call makeSpheres, must perform each of the following tasks:

- Create a simple dialog box to prompt for the base object name, to which it will tack a sequence number for each sphere. (So, if the user types sphere, the objects will be named sphere1, sphere2, sphere3, and so on.)
- Verify that the object name typed is valid, and if not, quit with an error explaining that the name is not valid.
- Create a simple dialog box that prompts for a number of spheres to create.
- Verify that the number of spheres typed is valid, and if not, quit with an error explaining that what was typed is not an integer.
- Make the correct number of spheres, as specified.

To do this, we will use our validObjectName and validInteger scripts, plus promptDialog. The following script is not a complete example of all the error checking you might wish to do, but it illustrates how some of these tools fit together.

```
// Before the script does anything, establish our validation
   procedures
   proc int validObjectName (string $testString) {
      string $matchingPart = `match "^[a-zA-Z][0-9a-zA-Z_]*$"
                                    $testString`;

      int $goodMatch = ! `strcmp $matchingPart $testString`;
         // Remember, if the two strings are the same,
            strcmp will return 0

   return $goodMatch;
}
proc int validInteger (string $testString) {
   string $matchingPart = `match "^[+\-]{0,1}[0-9]+$"
                                 $testString`;

   int $goodMatch = ! `strcmp $matchingPart $testString`;
      // Remember, if the two strings are the same,
         strcmp will return 0

   return $goodMatch;
}
```

```
global proc makeSpheres(string $myBaseName, int $myNumSpheres)
{
   int $count = 0;
   for ($count = 0; $count < $myNumSpheres; $count++) {
      string $thisName = ($myBaseName + ($count + 1));
      sphere -name $thisName;
      move ($count * 5) 0 0;
   }
}


global proc makeSpheresUI()
{

   // First, get the object base name for our spheres

   string $getBaseNameButton = `promptDialog
                    -title "makeSpheres"
                    -message "What base name would you like?"
                    -text "mySphere"`;

   string $baseName = `promptDialog -q`;

   if (! validObjectName($baseName)) {
      // If we get here, the object name isn't valid
      confirmDialog -title "Error"
                    -message "Bad characters in object name!"
                    -button "OK";

      error "Bad characters in object name!";
   }

   // Now, get the number of spheres we'd like to create

   string $getSphereNumButton = `promptDialog
         -title "makeSpheres"
         -message "How many spheres would you like to make?"
         -text "5"`;

   string $numSpheresString = `promptDialog -q`;

   if (! validInteger($numSpheresString)) {
      // If we get here, the object name isn't a valid integer
      confirmDialog -title "Error"
         -message "The number of spheres must be an integer!"
         -button "OK";
      error "The number of spheres must be an integer!";

   }

   // If we didn't validate the integer, this might crash our script
```

```
int $numSpheres = $numSpheresString;

// We need the number of spheres to be positive, so validate for it:

if ($numSpheres <= 0) {
  confirmDialog -title "Error"
          -message "The number of spheres must be positive!"
          -button "OK";

  error "The number of spheres must be positive!";
}

// Once we get here, we can make our spheres

makeSpheres($baseName, $numSpheres);
}
```

To run this script, try running the function makeSpheresUI in the Script Editor:

```
makeSpheresUI();
```

Do your best to trip the script up by typing numbers and object names that you know are not valid.

How It Works

First, our script defines our integer and object name validation scripts as defined above:

```
proc int validObjectName (string $testString) {
  string $matchingPart = `match "^[a-zA-Z][0-9a-zA-Z_]*$"
                        $testString`;

  int $goodMatch = ! `strcmp $matchingPart $testString`;
    // Remember, if the two strings are the same, strcmp will return 0

  return $goodMatch;
}
proc int validInteger (string $testString) {
  string $matchingPart = `match "^[+\-]{0,1}[0-9]+$"
                        $testString`;

  int $goodMatch = ! `strcmp $matchingPart $testString`;
    // Remember, if the two strings are the same, strcmp will return 0

  return $goodMatch;
}
```

These functions are exactly the same as the ones we discussed earlier for this purpose.

Next, we define a global procedure that actually makes the spheres. Note that this procedure, called makeSpheres, creates no user interface at all, but is instead called by a different function (called makeSpheresUI) that creates the interface and validates the input before passing it along to this function. Separating out the user interface into its own function is important since you might want to run the operation in Maya's batch mode, which does not allow you to present a user interface.

```
global proc makeSpheres(string $myBaseName, int $myNumSpheres)
{
    int $count = 0;
    for ($count = 0; $count < $myNumSpheres; $count++) {
        string $thisName = ($myBaseName + ($count + 1));
        sphere -name $thisName;
        move ($count * 5) 0 0;
    }
}
```

Now we begin the function definition formakeSpheresUI:

```
global proc makeSpheresUI()
{
```

Because the makeSpheresUI function gets its input from the user, no parameters need to be defined.

The makeSpheresUI function begins by prompting for the base name for the spheres:

```
string $getBaseNameButton = `promptDialog -title "makeSpheres"
                    -message "What base name would you like?"
                    -text "mySphere"`;

    string $baseName = `promptDialog -q`;
```

Note that the first call to promptDialog creates the dialog box window, while the second call in query mode gets the text that the user has typed and places it into the $baseName variable.

Now we need to validate the base name. The following code snippet checks that the base name is a valid object name and if not creates both an error window for the user and an error in the Script Editor with the error command:

```
if (! validObjectName($baseName)) {
        // If we get here, the object name isn`t valid
        confirmDialog -title "Error"
                    -message "Bad characters in object name!"
                    -button "OK";

    error "Bad characters in object name!";
}
```

We do the same type of thing to prompt for the number of spheres and validate that the response is a valid integer:

```
// Now, get the number of spheres we'd like to create

    string $getSphereNumButton = `promptDialog
        -title "makeSpheres"
        -message "How many spheres would you like to make?"
        -text "5"`;

    string $numSpheresString = `promptDialog -q`;

    if (! validInteger($numSpheresString)) {
        // If we get here, the object name isn't a valid integer
        confirmDialog -title "Error"
            -message "The number of spheres must be an integer!"
            -button "OK";
        error "The number of spheres must be an integer!";
    }

// If we didn't validate the integer, this might crash our script

int $numSpheres = $numSpheresString;
```

Now, even though we have checked to ensure that $numSpheres contains a valid integer, we still need to make sure that it is positive. After all, we don't want our script to try to create a negative number of spheres.

```
// We need the number of spheres to be positive, so validate for it

if ($numSpheres <= 0) {
    confirmDialog -title "Error"
        -message "The number of spheres must be positive!"
        -button "OK";
    error "The number of spheres must be positive!";
}
```

Finally, the makeSpheresUI procedure calls the makeSpheres procedure to do the work of creating the spheres:

```
// Once we get here, we can make our spheres

makeSpheres($baseName, $numSpheres);
```

In production, more error checking might be desirable. For example, checking to make sure that there is not already an object with the name you want to create before you try to create it might be a good idea. Also, checking the return values for commands such as sphere would allow you to detect and recover from errors that would cause this script to fail.

Note that this script's errors are both placed in the Script Editor log and in dialog boxes for the user. By reporting errors and warnings both ways, you can ensure that the user sees your warnings and errors while still retaining a record of the problem for debugging after the fact.

Finally, a script like this, which requires multiple text inputs, is an excellent candidate for a custom dialog box. Chapter 14 discusses custom dialog boxes in more detail.

What to Remember About Simple MEL User Interfaces and Input Validation

- Simple scripts that require only a small amount of confirmation or user input can use `confirmDialog` and `promptDialog` to get input from the user, or `confirmDialog` to present messages in a window.
- When a user types a string into a text field, remember that you must check that it is a valid string for the purpose for which you would like to use it. If a string contains a valid integer, you can assign it to an integer variable, for example, but if it is not valid, your script will crash.
- Regular expressions are useful for validating strings of text. Learn to use regular expressions when you can, but even if they seem daunting, search for useful regular expressions others have created that you can use to validate your data.
- When you need to present the user with multiple text fields or more complex controls, consider creating a custom dialog box rather than using the built-in dialog box types.

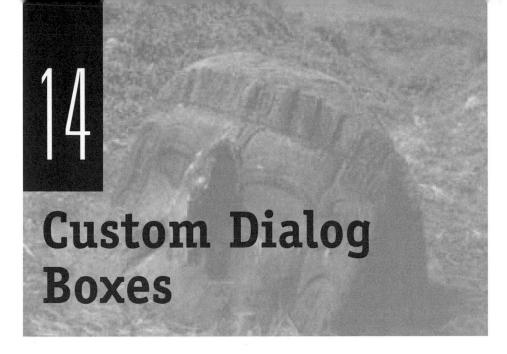

Custom Dialog Boxes

In this chapter you will learn

■ The structure of a script that will create and use a custom dialog box for input.

■ The structure of a custom dialog box window.

■ How to build a custom dialog box.

■ Some basic controls available for your custom dialog box, and how they work.

■ How to connect functions to buttons in your custom dialog box so that the functions execute when the buttons are pressed.

■ How to collect the user's data from the controls in the dialog box.

How to Structure a Script That Uses a Custom Dialog Box for Input

In the example in Chapter 13, we saw that one benefit of creating separate procedures for the user interface and the main substance of your script is that you can choose to run the latter in batch mode. When you create a custom dialog box, you will need to write more procedures to perform at least the actions of some buttons the user can click. By keeping in mind the benefit of separating user interface and input validation from your script's main function, though, you can still keep the implementation of the interface and the main function separate.

A script that creates a custom dialog box implements a number of procedures: an *entry point* procedure that creates the dialog box; one procedure for each button (such as OK or Cancel) that the user can click to dismiss the dialog box or trigger the script's operation; and one or more functions to implement the script's non–user-interface code. Finally, you will need to validate input with input validation functions as discussed previously.

Normally, in your MEL file, you will define each procedure in reverse order of their execution, so that as Maya interprets your MEL file, the later procedures will be defined for the earlier ones to call. These procedures generally run in the following order: entry point procedure, button action procedures, validation functions, and then finally the script implementation. Listed below are the procedures in the order they will run, and what each has to do.

- Entry point procedure
  Build the dialog box, including all of its controls.
  Bind button action procedures to the buttons.
- Button action procedures
  Collect data that the user has entered into the dialog box's controls.
  Validate all the entered data.
  If validation fails, provide an error message, and do nothing.
  If validation succeeds, call the main script implementation procedure.
  If your dialog box is not persistent or you are implementing a Close button, close the dialog box.
- Validation functions
  Accept a string as input, and return a Yes or No as to whether the string's value is acceptable for a particular input to your script.
- Main script implementation procedure
  Perform the main purpose of your script.
  Inputs to this script should be parameters to the procedure and generally *not* global variables, so that it is perfectly clear from the procedure definition how to call the procedure to bypass the user interface, if desired.
  This script should not rely on the user interface at all, so that it can run in batch mode.

There are other ways to structure MEL scripts requiring dialog boxes as part of their user interfaces. However, the above structure makes it easy to change how your script's interface operates without rewriting the underlying script; it makes changes to data requirements easier to implement by providing only one procedure (the validation function) that must change; and it gives you a way to bypass the interface to run your script from another procedure or in batch mode.

Dialog Boxes and Their Contents

Dialog boxes consist of a few standard parts. The dialog box is contained in a *window,* which behaves like all other windows on your computer. Within the window are *layouts* that organize controls in a window, which are different ways of grouping together controls in the window. Finally, the layouts contain *controls, groups,* and *collections,* which offer controls for the user to manipulate. The window can also have menus that work like the menu bar in the main Maya window.

Figure 14.1 shows a dialog box that contains a number of standard window components. This dialog box consists of a containing window, a *menu bar* containing two menus, a few nested *layouts* that help organize controls, and a few *groups* that tie together related controls. Within the radio button group is a collection of radio buttons.

Layouts

Layouts organize other layouts, groups, and controls into rows and columns. Common layouts are `rowLayouts`, `columnLayouts`, and `rowColumnLayouts`, which make simple rows and columns of controls.

The `frameLayout` layout type draws borders around groups of controls, with the option to provide a button that will collapse and expand the controls to hide them and show them. Normally a `frameLayout` will contain a `rowLayout`, `columnLayout`, or `rowColumnLayout`. The collapsible frames in Figure 14.2 are examples of the `frameLayout` layout type.

As shown in Figure 14.3, the `tabLayout` type of layout makes a series of tabs near the top of the window. Each tab can contain a full window's worth of user interface controls, allowing you to group many kinds of controls by task or by purpose.

Layouts are built by issuing a command that indicates that your script is about to define a layout, and then creating the other layouts and controls that the enclosing layout contains.

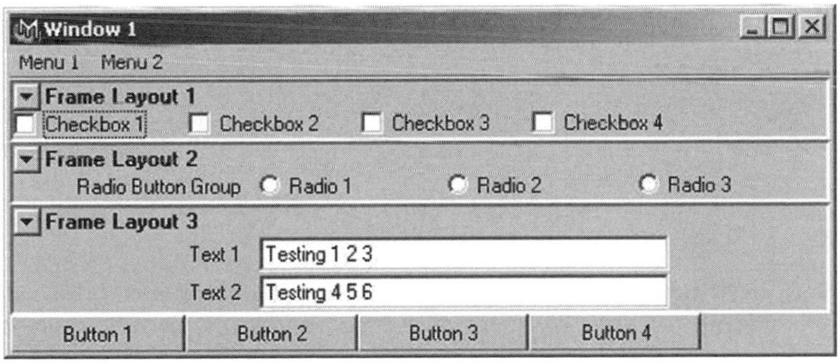

Figure 14.1 Example dialog box.

Figure 14.2 A collapsible `frameLayout` that contains some radio buttons.

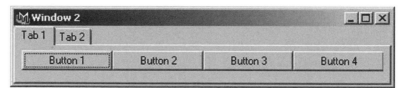

Figure 14.3 Dialog box containing a `tabLayout`.

Groups

Often, you will want to create a few controls that are set up to work together. One example is a text field with its related label that tells the user what to type there. Another is a group of radio buttons, or circular buttons that turn off when another button in the group is clicked to turn it on.

MEL provides common associations of related controls called groups (Figure 14.4). Unlike layouts, MEL allows you to make common types of groups with a single command, rather than having to define each part separately.

Collections

A collection is an object type that MEL provides to make several controls work together. A common use for collections is to make all the rest of a group of radio buttons turn off when one turns on.

Normally, when you make a radio group, the `radioButtonGrp` command makes a collection automatically so that the radio buttons work together without your intervention. One example of a case in which you may want to interact directly with collections occurs when you want to have multiple `radioButtonGrp` objects that work together as a single collection of buttons.

This can be useful because the default `radioButtonGrp` object does not support more than four radio buttons. Although you can build your own group of radio buttons to overcome this limitation, it can be easier to make two `radioButtonGrp` objects and connect them with a single collection.

Controls

Within the layouts, groups, or collections are the controls that the user clicks, types into, or manipulates to enter information once your entry

Figure 14.4 Two kinds of groups: `textFieldGrp` and `radioButtonGrp`.

point script has created the dialog box. When the user clicks on a button to do something useful, the button action procedure associated with that button collects data from the controls in the windows, and then proceeds to validate that data as necessary, and run your main script.

Example 1: Making the Example Dialog Box

The best way to see how these parts work together is to create a dialog box and examine the script you have used to do so. Try entering and running this script, which will create the dialog box in Figure 14.1. Once you have done so, try manipulating some of the controls in the window that appears.

Note: Maya requires that the flag to create a collapsible frameLayout be spelled "collapsable."

```
// Build main window

string $window_name = `window -title "Window 1"
                            -menuBar true
                            -widthHeight 483 203`;

// Everything below this point goes in the window we've just
// made, but it's not displayed until we get to the
// showWindow command below.

// Build menu bar

menu -label "Menu 1";
    menuItem -label "Menu Item 1";
    menuItem -label "Menu Item 2";

menu -label "Menu 2";
    menuItem -label "Menu Item 3";
    menuItem -label "Menu Item 4";

columnLayout;

    frameLayout -collapsable true -label "Frame Layout 1"
                -width 475;

        rowColumnLayout -nc 4;
            checkBox. -label "Checkbox 1";
            checkBox. -label "Checkbox 2";
            checkBox. -label "Checkbox 3";
            checkBox. -label "Checkbox 4";

        setParent ..; // Back up to the frameLayout

    setParent ..; // Back up to the columnLayout
```

```
frameLayout -collapsable true -label "Frame Layout 2"
            -width 475;

    radioButtonGrp -numberOfRadioButtons 3
                   -label "Radio Button Group"
                   -labelArray3 "Radio 1" "Radio 2" "Radio 3"
                                "Radio 4";

setParent ..; // Back up to the columnLayout

frameLayout -collapsable true -label "Frame Layout 3"
            -width 475;

    columnLayout;

        textFieldGrp -label "Text 1" -text "Testing 1 2 3";
        textFieldGrp -label "Text 2" -text "Testing 4 5 6";

    setParent ..; // Back up to the frameLayout

setParent ..; // Back up to the columnLayout

rowColumnLayout -nc 4;

    button -label "Button 1";
    button -label "Button 2";
    button -label "Button 3";
    button -label "Button 4";

// Show the dialog box that we've just built

showWindow $window_name; // Ends the creation of the
                         // rowColumnLayout, the enclosing
                         // columnLayout, and the window
```

Try typing and executing the above script. You will get a window that looks much like the dialog box in Figure 14.1.

How It Works

Before we examine in detail how the script builds the window, let's look at the script's overall structure. Generally, scripts that build dialog boxes in MEL consist of commands that build windows and layouts, and between these commands are other commands that make menus, menu items, and groups.

Once you have created a window or layout, all further layouts and controls you create will go into that window or layout until you end its creation with either a call to showWindow, another window command, or the command setParent... The setParent.. command tells Maya to end creation of the current layout and add further items to the layout or window that contains the layout to which you have been adding most recently. All controls and control groups must go into a layout; they cannot go directly into a window.

In this script, all the commands to build our window are enclosed in a command to `window` that makes the window, and a call to `showWindow` to display it. To create the empty window, try typing just the following two commands, which are from the beginning and end of the above script:

```
string $window_name = `window -title "Window 1"
                              -menuBar true
                              -widthHeight 483 203`;

showWindow $window_name;
```

You need not follow every `window` command with `showWindow`. If you like, you could make a series of windows, which are by default automatically hidden when they are created, with a number of `window` commands, then show one or the other with a call to `showWindow`. However, all of the user interface items created between one call to `window` and the next, or between a call to `window` and a call to `showWindow`, will appear in the most recently defined window.

The following window definition first creates a couple of menus for the menu bar and a couple of items in each one:

```
// Build menu bar

menu -label "Menu 1";
    menuItem -label "Menu Item 1";
    menuItem -label "Menu Item 2";

menu -label "Menu 2";
    menuItem -label "Menu Item 3";
    menuItem -label "Menu Item 4";
```

To create an empty window containing a couple of menus, then, you would place the above menu commands between the `window` command and the `showWindow` command, as follows:

```
string $window_name = `window -title "Window 1"
                              -menuBar true
                              -widthHeight 483 203`;
// Build menu bar

menu -label "Menu 1";
    menuItem -label "Menu Item 1";
    menuItem -label "Menu Item 2";

menu -label "Menu 2";
    menuItem -label "Menu Item 3";
    menuItem -label "Menu Item 4";
showWindow $window_name;
```

The resulting window is shown in Figure 14.5.

Now, to fill the body of the dialog box, we create a layout that will visually organize its contents in an appropriate way:

```
columnLayout;
```

The above command indicates that MEL should start building a column layout, which will organize its contents into a column from top to bottom in the window. Like the `window` command before, the call to `showWindow` at the end of the script ends the creation of this column layout, and everything in between goes into the column layout.

Next, we will add the commands to create the first collapsible frame, which contains four checkboxes. Place these commands between the `columnLayout` command and the call to `showWindow`, as follows:

```
frameLayout -collapsable true -label "Frame Layout 1"
            -width 475;

rowColumnLayout -nc 4;

  checkBox -label "Checkbox 1";
  checkBox -label "Checkbox 2";
  checkBox -label "Checkbox 3";
  checkBox -label "Checkbox 4";
```

Unlike following one call to "window" after another, if you follow a call to one of the layout commands with another, the new layout will be created *inside* the previously created layout. Thus, the `frameLayout` command makes a frame layout inside the column layout we had created earlier, and the `rowColumnLayout` command makes a `rowColumnLayout` inside the `frameLayout`.

Note that we are explicitly specifying a width for the `frameLayout`. Most UI commands allow you to specify a width and height for the control

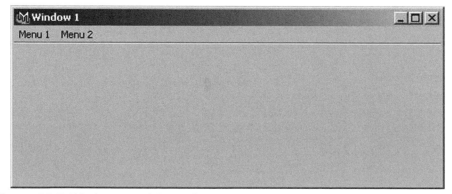

Figure 14.5 Window containing only menus.

in pixels. By specifying width and height, you can often get UI elements to line up nicely in ways they would not otherwise. In this instance, by specifying a fixed width that is appropriate for the size of the containing window, we can line up the right edges of the frame layouts at the window boundary. However, this width flag is not necessary, and if you leave it out, MEL will size the frame layouts to fit the contents.

The `rowColumnLayout` arranges objects into rows and columns. Instead of making a single row or column of user interface objects like `rowLayout` or `columnLayout`, a `rowColumnLayout` fills items into columns until it hits a maximum limit, set with the `-nc` flag; then it wraps around to a new row.

Within the `rowColumnLayout`, the script makes four checkbox objects, labeled as indicated in the `-label` flag. As usual, these objects go into the most recently defined layout.

Now, our script looks like the following. In this version of the script, the `columnLayout`, the `frameLayout` within it, and the `rowColumnLayout` within that are ended by the `showWindow` command.

```
string $window_name = `window -title "Window 1"
                              -menuBar true
                              -widthHeight 483 203`;

// Build menu bar

menu -label "Menu 1";
    menuItem -label "Menu Item 1";
    menuItem -label "Menu Item 2";

menu -label "Menu 2";
    menuItem -label "Menu Item 3";
    menuItem -label "Menu Item 4";

columnLayout;

    frameLayout -collapsable true -label "Frame Layout 1"
                -width 475;

        rowColumnLayout -nc 4;

            checkBox -label "Checkbox 1";
            checkBox -label "Checkbox 2";
            checkBox -label "Checkbox 3";
            checkBox -label "Checkbox 4";

showWindow $window_name;
```

Figure 14.6 shows the window with the first layout built in it.

Once we have finished defining the `rowColumnLayout`, we need to tell MEL that we wish to add new objects to the container that is two levels up in the hierarchy, the `columnLayout`. You can do this with two of the

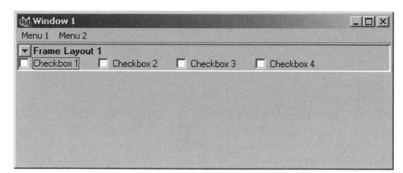

Firuge 14.6 Window containing the first frame.

`setParent  ..` command, each of which tells Maya to add the following layouts and controls to the container that is one level up in the hierarchy:

```
setParent ..; // Back up to the frameLayout
```

```
setParent ..; // Back up to the columnLayout
```

Now, further layout and control commands will make objects within the `columnLayout` object, not the `rowColumnLayout` or the `frameLayout`. These commands, paired up with the original `columnLayout` and `rowColumnLayout` commands, enclose the commands necessary to make the objects that those layouts contain.

The next layout that we will create in the `columnLayout` object is a second `frameLayout`. Like the first one, this `frameLayout` is collapsible.

```
frameLayout -collapsable true -label "Frame Layout 2"
            -width 475;

radioButtonGrp -numberOfRadioButtons 3
               -label "Radio Button Group"
               -labelArray3 "Radio 1" "Radio 2" "Radio 3"
                   "Radio 4";
```

The `radioButtonGrp` command can make one, two, three, or four radio buttons that work together. The `-numberOfRadioButtons` flag tells it how many to make; `-label` indicates what the entire group should be labeled, and `-labelArray3` allows you to list the labels for three individual radio buttons. If, for example, you had four labels to specify for four buttons, you would use the `-labelArray4` argument. There are various ways to specify labels for the `radioButtonGrp` command, all of which are described in detail in the command's entry in the MEL Command Reference.

Following is our full script thus far:

```
string $window_name = `window -title "Window 1"
                              -menuBar true
                              -widthHeight 483 203`;

// Build menu bar

menu -label "Menu 1";
   menuItem -label "Menu Item 1";
   menuItem -label "Menu Item 2";

menu -label "Menu 2";
   menuItem -label "Menu Item 3";
   menuItem -label "Menu Item 4";
columnLayout;

frameLayout -collapsable true -label "Frame Layout 1"
            -width 475;

   rowColumnLayout -nc 4;

       checkBox -label "Checkbox 1";
       checkBox -label "Checkbox 2";
       checkBox -label "Checkbox 3";
       checkBox -label "Checkbox 4";

   setParent ..; // Back up to the frameLayout

setParent ..; // Back up to the columnLayout

frameLayout -collapsable true -label "Frame Layout 2"
            -width 475;

   radioButtonGrp -numberOfRadioButtons 3
                  -label "Radio Button Group"
                  labelArray3 "Radio 1" "Radio 2" "Radio 3"
                              "Radio 4";

showWindow $window_name;
```

Executing the above partial script will give you the window shown in Figure 14.7.

Note that none of the radio buttons in our example is selected until the user clicks on one. Often, you will want a radio button selected when your dialog box first comes up. Had we wanted to do this, we could have used the `-select < number >` flag to select one of the radio buttons. For example, `-select 1` would have selected the first radio button.

Now, we will add the third collapsible `frameLayout`, including a couple of `textFieldGrp` objects by adding the following lines to our script:

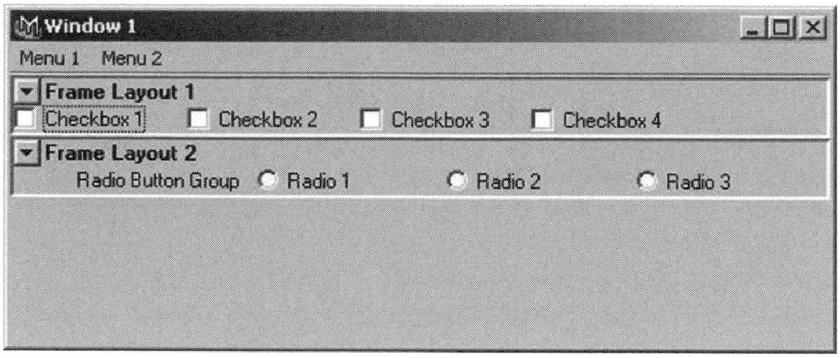

Figure 14.7 Window including first and second frameLayout.

```
setParent ..; // Back up to the columnLayout
frameLayout -collapsable true
            -label "Frame Layout 3" -width 475;
    columnLayout;
        textFieldGrp -label "Text 1" -text "Testing 1 2 3";
        textFieldGrp -label "Text 2" -text "Testing 4 5 6";
```

As before, the setParent .. command is used to put our new frameLayout in the columnLayout that the other two share. Without the setParent .. command, the new frameLayout would appear inside the frameLayout that contains the radio buttons.

Because we want our textFieldGrp objects to be placed above and below one another, we create a columnLayout within the frameLayout. Then, we make our textFieldGrp objects, each of which contains a label and a text field that the user can type into.

Finally, we will add the buttons to the bottom of the window. For the buttons, we will use a rowColumnLayout with a number of columns of four. Since we have only four buttons, we could have used a rowLayout instead, but by using a rowColumnLayout, we ensure that if we add additional buttons they will wrap around to their own row, rather than continuing off to the right side of the window.

```
    setParent ..; // Back up to the frameLayout
setParent ..; // Back up to the columnLayout
rowColumnLayout -nc 4;
    button -label "Button 1";
    button -label "Button 2";
    button -label "Button 3";
    button -label "Button 4";
```

At this point, we have added all the controls in the original window.

Note that the window is not fully functional. Most commands to create layouts or make controls return a name for the control that the command has created, and usually you will need to store those names in string variables for use when you want to read values out of the dialog box after the user has filled in data.

We examine how a dialog box fits into a complete application later in this chapter in Example 2.

Common Types of Controls

Maya supports a large number of different kinds of controls and control groups. A few common kinds are used in just about every dialog box, while others are so esoteric that you may never have a need for them. To see a complete list of controls, look in the MEL Command Reference with commands sorted by function, in the UI: Windowing section under "Controls: Buttons, Sliders, etc."

As a Maya user, you are already familiar with how many of these control types work. For each of these control types, try typing the MEL provided to create a window containing that control, and then interact with the control you have created.

button

Buttons in MEL dialog boxes are the most basic control. Normally, you will associate a command with a button with the -command flag, which tells Maya what command to execute when the button is clicked. This script creates a window that contains one button that creates a sphere in your scene when it's clicked:

```
string $myWindow = `window`;

    rowLayout;

        button -label "Make me a sphere" -command "sphere";

showWindow $myWindow;
```

Figure 14.8 shows the resulting window. Note that your window may be a different size—since we are not specifying a size for the window, Maya

Figure 14.8 A window containing a button.

chooses the size of the window it creates. Try clicking on the button to see Maya execute the sphere command in your scene.

checkBox

A checkBox is a control that, like a button, responds to mouse clicks. However, unlike a button, a checkbox is either on or off. Once you have created a checkBox in a window, you can query it to tell you whether it's on or off.

To make a window containing a checkbox, execute the following script:

```
string $myWindow = `window`;

    rowLayout;

        string $myCheckbox = `checkBox. -label "Truth or Dare:"`;

    showWindow $myWindow;
```

Note that we have placed the name of the new checkbox into the $myCheckbox variable. This MEL code creates the window shown in Figure 14.9.

Now, click the checkbox on or off. Leaving the window open, try this command:

```
checkBox. -q -v $myCheckbox;
```

This command returns a result of 1 if the checkbox is on and a result of 0 if the checkbox is off.

If you like, a checkbox can execute a command when it's switched on, switched off, or both. You specify these commands with the -onCommand flag, the -offCommand flag, and the -changeCommand flag. Try creating the following window and playing with its checkbox:

```
string $myWindow = `window`;

rowLayout;

string $myCheckbox = `checkBox. -label "Sphere"
                                -onCommand "sphere -name \"blah\""
                                -offCommand "delete blah"`;
showWindow $myWindow;
```

When you click this checkbox on, a sphere called blah is created, and when you turn it off, the sphere is deleted.

Figure 14.9 A window containing a checkbox.

floatFieldGrp

Like a `textFieldGrp`, a `floatFieldGrp` provides a text box into which a user can type. However, a `floatFieldGrp` greatly simplifies validation because only a valid floating-point number can be entered into the text box.

To create a window containing a `floatFieldGrp`, try the following script:

```
string $myWindow = `window`;

   rowLayout;

      string $myFloatFieldGrp = `floatFieldGrp -label
                                   "Gimme a number:"`;

showWindow $myWindow;
```

The resulting window looks something like the one shown in Figure 14.10.

Try typing both valid floating-point numbers and invalid strings into the field to see how it behaves. To get the value, leave the window open, and execute the following command in the Script Editor window:

```
floatFieldGrp -q -value $myFloatFieldGrp;
```

This command returns the value in the field.

floatSliderGrp

The `floatSliderGrp` creates a slider that controls a floating-point value. If you like, you can add the `field true` flag to provide an associated field that allows the user to type a floating-point number instead of using the slider, as follows:

```
string $myWindow = `window`;

   rowLayout;

string $myFloatSliderGrp = `floatSliderGrp -min 0
                                           -max 10
                                           -label "Gimme a number:"
                                           -field true`;

showWindow $myWindow;
```

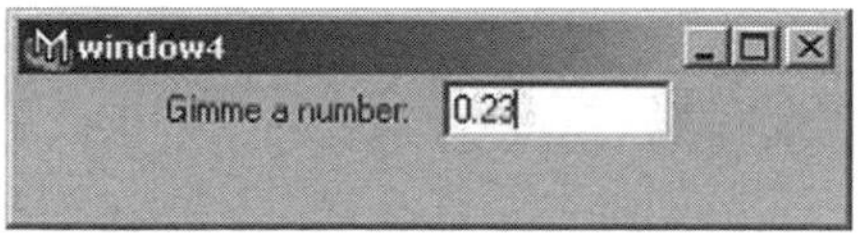

Figure 14.10 Window containing a `floatFieldGrp`.

Note the -min and -max flags that set the minimum and maximum values for the slider. The floatSliderGrp command also supports -fieldMinValue and -fieldMaxValue flags that let you set a separate minimum and maximum for values that can be typed in. (For example, if most of the time values between 0 and 1 are necessary, but sometimes your user will want to override those limits and set the value to 10, by setting the -fieldMaxValue to a number higher than 1, you can enforce the normal limits with the slider but permit a much larger number to be entered in the text field.) The floatSliderGrp window is shown in Figure 4.11.

To get the value from the floatSliderGrp, the command looks much like the one to get the value from a floatFieldGrp:

```
floatSliderGrp -q -value $myFloatSliderGrp;
```

intFieldGrp

An intFieldGrp works and looks just like a floatFieldGrp, except that it requires the entered number to be a valid integer. Like a floatFieldGrp, using the intFieldGrp in your dialog boxes can simplify your scripts by automatically verifying that the number you receive will be a valid integer.

intSliderGrp

An intSliderGrp works and looks just like a floatSliderGrp, except that it requires the entered number to be a valid integer.

textFieldButtonGrp

A textFieldButtonGrp creates a labeled text field with an associated button that can execute a command. This script is a little more complicated than the other examples, but it serves to give you an idea of how a textFieldButtonGrp might be used. This script works by building a string that contains the following command:

```
sphere -name (`textFieldButtonGrp -q
        -text $myTextFieldButtonGrp`)
```

The textFieldButtonGrp -q -text command queries the text in the text field, which is then handed to sphere as the name of the sphere to create.

Then, when the actual textFieldButtonGrp is created, this command is set up to be triggered when the button is clicked, as follows:

Figure 14.11 Window containing a floatSliderGrp.

```
string $myWindow = `window`;

rowLayout;

    string $myTextFieldButtonGrp;

    string $myButtonCommand =
        "sphere -name (`textFieldButtonGrp " +
        "-q -text $myTextFieldButtonGrp`)";

    $myTextFieldButtonGrp = `textFieldButtonGrp
        -label "Sphere name:"
        -text "Sphere"
        -buttonLabel "Make Sphere"
        -buttonCommand $myButtonCommand`;

showWindow $myWindow;
```

Figure 14.12 shows what the resulting window looks like. Try typing a string into the field and clicking Make Sphere to see what happens.

textFieldGrp

A textFieldGrp works just like an intFieldGrp or a floatFieldGrp but without restrictions on what text can be typed in the box. When you use a textFieldGrp for input, remember to validate the text that you retrieve from the text field.

Following is a script that creates a window with a textFieldGrp in it:

```
string $myWindow = `window`;

rowLayout;

$myTextGrp = `textFieldGrp -label "Gimme some text:"
                            -text "OK, text"`;

showWindow $myWindow;
```

Figure 14.13 shows the window that the script creates. Without closing the window, type some of your own text in the field, and use the following command to read it:

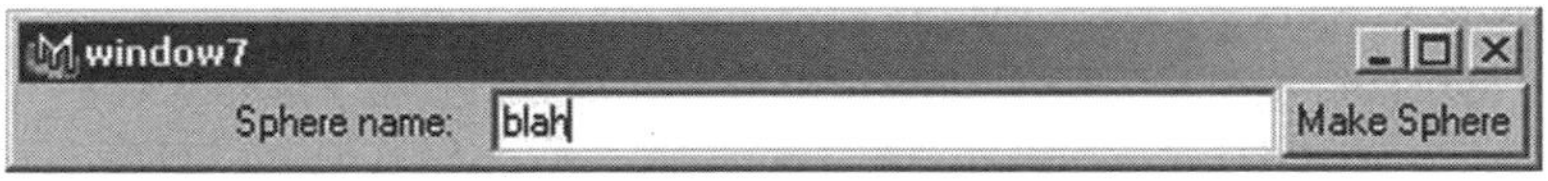

Figure 14.12 Window containing a textFieldButtonGrp.

Figure 14.13 Window containing a textFieldGrp.

```
    textFieldGrp -q -text $myTextGrp;
```

The return value contains the text that has been typed into the window.

radioButtonGrp

The last of the common control types that we will examine is the
`radioButtonGrp`, which we have seen in the example dialog box.

To create a `radioButtonGrp` in a window, try the following script:

```
string $myWindow = `window`;

    rowLayout;

        $myRadioButtonGrp = `radioButtonGrp -numberOfRadioButtons 2
                                            -label "How do you feel?"
                                            -labelArray2 "Good" "Bad"
                                            -select 1`;
    showWindow $myWindow;
```

Note the use of the `-select` flag to make sure that one of the buttons starts
out selected. This script creates the window shown in Figure 14.14.

To read the value of the selected `radioButtonGrp`, before you close the
window, run the following command:

```
    radioButtonGrp -q -select $myRadioButtonGrp;
```

If the first radio button is selected, this command will return 1; if the
second, 2.

As we discussed above, you can create multiple radio button groups that
share one radio button collection, meaning that they work together. When
you click one button in either radio button group, all the rest turn off, as
follows:

```
string $myWindow = `window`;

columnLayout;

$myRadioButtonGrp = `radioButtonGrp -numberOfRadioButtons 2
                                    -label "How do you feel?"
                                    -labelArray2 "Good" "Bad"
                                    -select 1`;
$myRadioButtonGrp2 = `radioButtonGrp -numberOfRadioButtons 2
                                -label ""
```

Figure 14.14 Window containing a `radioButtonGrp`.

```
                                     -labelArray2 "OK" "Don`t Know"
                                     -shareCollection $myRadioButtonGrp`;
          showWindow $myWindow;
```

The above script creates a window with two connected `radioButtonGrp` objects, as shown in Figure 14.15.

To determine which radio button is selected, you need to query *both* `radioButtonGrp` objects. If no buttons in one of the groups are selected, the result is 0. If one of the buttons in a group is selected, then you get a result of 1 or 2, depending on which button it is.

```
radioButtonGrp -q -select $myRadioButtonGrp;
// Result: 0 //
radioButtonGrp -q -select $myRadioButtonGrp2;
// Result: 1 //
```

Note that you do not need to use the `radioButtonGrp` command. Instead, you can create your own radio buttons with the `radioButton` command and a single collection for all of them with the `radioCollection` command. However, for most uses the `radioButtonGrp` command is a simpler approach.

Common Types of Layouts

MEL provides a number of layout types that organize controls within a window. Every window must contain a layout if it will contain any controls.

To see a complete list of the layouts that MEL supports, view the MEL Command Reference by function. In the UI: Windowing page, the section "Layouts: Organizing UI Components" contains a list of the commands that can be used to make layouts.

columnLayout

The `columnLayout` command arranges a number of controls in a window from top to bottom. Try the following script:

```
string $myWindow = `window`;
```

Figure 14.15 Two `radioButtonGrp` objects that share a collection.

```
columnLayout;
    button -label "button";
    button -label "button";
    button -label "button";
    button -label "button";
    button -label "button";
    button -label "button";
showWindow $myWindow;
```

Figure 14.16 shows the window created by this script.

formLayout

The `formLayout` command is a layout type that provides total control over positioning of controls in the layout at the expense of requiring you to do more work to specify how your controls are to be positioned. `formLayout` offers much more control than the other layout types, at the expense of extra complexity. Chapter 15 describes how to use formLayout in detail.

frameLayout

The `frameLayout` command creates a group of controls that have a boundary around them. Try the following script:

```
string $myWindow = `window`;

frameLayout -borderStyle "etchedIn";
    rowColumnLayout -nc 4;
        button -label "button";
        button -label "button";
        button -label "button";
        button -label "button";
```

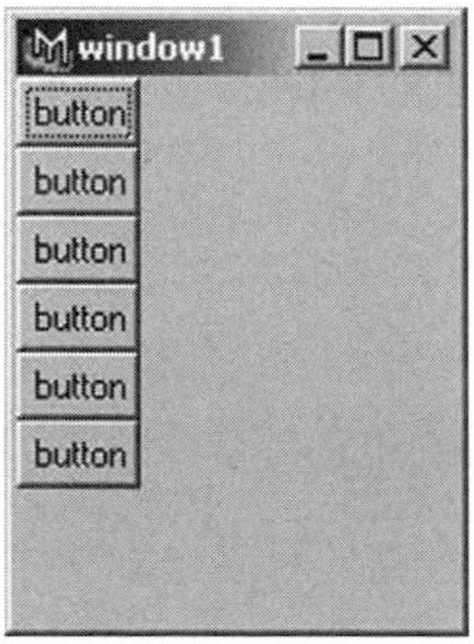

Figure 14.16 Window containing a `columnLayout`.

```
        button -label "button";
        button -label "button";

    showWindow $myWindow;
```

Figure 14.17 shows the window created by this script.

A `frameLayout` should contain a `rowLayout`, `columnLayout`, or `rowColumnLayout` to organize the controls within it. You can set the frame layout's name with `-label`, change the border style, and make the frame collapsible with the `-collapsable` flag.

rowColumnLayout

A `rowColumnLayout` places controls into a row until it hits a maximum number of controls, at which point the controls wrap around to the next row. See the `frameLayout` example for an example of a `rowColumnLayout`.

rowLayout

The `rowLayout` command places controls in a row, left to right, as wide as necessary to hold all of them. Try the following script:

```
    string $myWindow = `window`;

    rowLayout -nc 6;

        button -label "button";
        button -label "button";
        button -label "button";
        button -label "button";
        button -label "button";
        button -label "button";

    showWindow $myWindow;
```

Figure 14.18 shows the resulting window.

Remember to specify the number of columns in a `rowLayout` with an `-nc` or `-numberOfColumns` flag. Without this, the `rowLayout` will only accept one control because it defaults to having only one column.

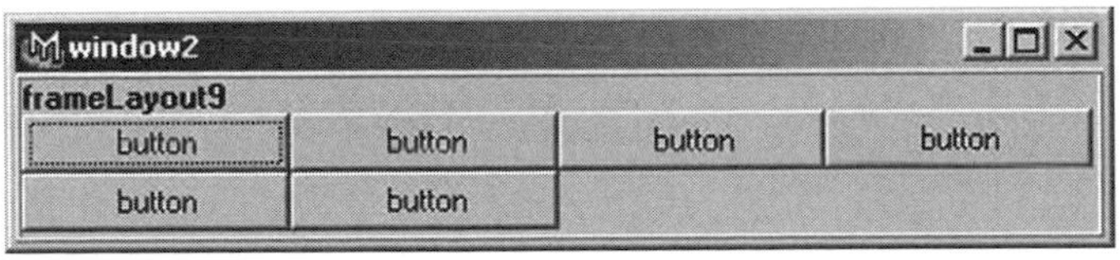

Figure 14.17 Window containing a `frameLayout`.

Example 2: Dialog Box for Making Geometric Primitives

Now that we have seen the building blocks for creating a dialog-box–based user interface, we are ready to build a complete script that uses a dialog box for its interface. We will create a script that allows the user to create a sphere, cone, or cube at a location in space that he or she enters into a dialog box.

Creating the Main Script

As is typical for scripts with a user interface, the simplest part of the script is the main procedure that does the primary task of the script. Following is a procedure that can perform this script's task from the command line:

```
proc makePrimitive(int $type, float $x, float $y, float $z) {
    // makePrimitive takes an integer called $type, which is 1
    // for asphere, 2 for a cone, and 3 for a cube. Also, it
    // accepts X, Y, and Z position values for the location
    // of the object it creates

switch ($type) {
    case 1: sphere;
            break;

    case 2: cone;
            break;

    case 3: polyCube;
            break;
default: error -showLineNumber true "Invalid object type";
         break;
}
// Since the most recently created object is selected, AND since
// if we get here we created a valid object, we can just use the
// move command

move $x $y $z;

}
```

Figure 14.18 Window containing a rowLayout.

Type the following procedure into the Script Editor; select it; press Enter to define it, and then run it:

```
makePrimitive (1, 10, 10, 10); // makes a sphere at (10, 10, 10) in
                               // world space
makePrimitive (2, -3, -3, -3); // makes a cone at (-3, -3, -3)
makePrimitive (8, 0, 0, 0); // yields an error.
```

Building the Dialog Box

Now, we will build a dialog box to call the makePrimitive function. At first, we will build a dialog box that doesn't do anything to make sure we have the look we want, and then finally we will build the button action procedures that enable the dialog box to trigger the makePrimitive function.

Our dialog box should have a descriptive title, such as Create Primitive. Also, there should be three floatFields to accept the x, y, and z positions for the primitive. Finally, there should be three buttons: one of them makes a sphere, one makes a cone, and one makes a cube.

We will build our dialog box to be persistent so that we can make many primitives at once. To close the window, our user will click the Close box.

As it turns out, the floatFieldGrp object can contain multiple float fields. To get three fields, we can call floatFieldGrp with -numberOfFields 3.

We will use a columnLayout to place the floatFieldGrp on top and the buttons on the bottom, and a rowLayout to arrange the buttons left to right. Note that we are putting the name of the floatFieldGrp into a global variable. Since the button action procedures don't have access to this procedure's variables, we need to make this string global so that they can find the field group's names to read the fields' values.

```
global proc makePrimitiveUI() {

// Define a global string for the positionGrp floatFieldGrp name
   global string $positionGroup;

// makePrimitiveUI builds a dialog box for the makePrimitive
// function

string $dialogBoxWindow = `window -title "Create Primitive"
                                  -rtf true`;
   columnLayout;

   $positionGroup = `floatFieldGrp -numberOfFields 3`;

   rowLayout -nc 3;
```

```
            button -label "Sphere";
            button -label "Cone";
            button -label "Cube";

    showWindow $dialogBoxWindow;

    }
```

Try entering the procedure and executing it by typing `makePrimitiveUI()` and pressing Enter.

In the above script, we use the `-rtf true` flag for the `window` command. This flag tells the command to resize to fit the contents of the window so that we don't have to specify the correct size with the width and height commands. The window created by this procedure is shown in Figure 14.19.

Defining the Button Action Procedure

Since all three of the buttons do just about the same thing, we can use one button action procedure for all three. As discussed at the beginning of this chapter, the button action procedure must collect any necessary data from the dialog box, validate it, and then call the main procedure for the script. Since any floating-point number is fine for the X, Y, and Z position values, we need not validate the data from the `floatFieldGrp`.

Following is a function that collects the necessary data from the dialog box. This function needs to know the name of the `floatFieldGrp` that contains the X, Y, and Z position values, and it needs to know which button was clicked. We will number the buttons 1, 2, and 3, so that their values correspond to the object types that our main procedure uses.

```
proc buttonAction (int $whichButton, string
    $floatFieldGrpName) {

    // Get the values of our dialog box's x, y, and z values

    float $xval = `floatFieldGrp -q -value1 $floatFieldGrpName`;
    float $yval = `floatFieldGrp -q -value2 $floatFieldGrpName`;
    float $zval = `floatFieldGrp -q -value3 $floatFieldGrpName`;

    // Call the main procedure

    makePrimitive($whichButton, $xval, $yval, $zval);

    }
```

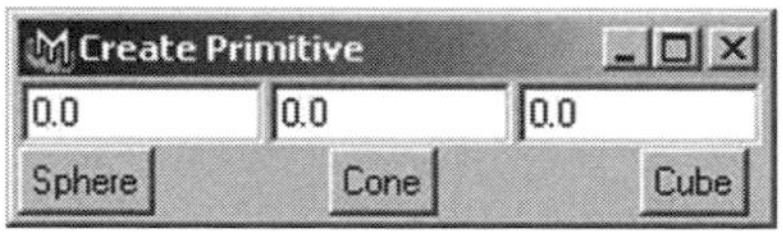

Figure 14.19 Create Primitive dialog box.

Finally, we need to modify the part of our main entry point procedure so that the buttons, when clicked, call the entry point procedure. The code that was

```
button -label "Sphere";
button -label "Cone";
button -label "Cube";
```

now becomes

```
button -label "Sphere" -command "buttonAction(1, $positionGroup)";
button -label "Cone" -command "buttonAction(2, $positionGroup)";
button -label "Cube" -command "buttonAction(3, $positionGroup)";
```

Now that we have made the above changes, the complete script follows:

```
proc makePrimitive(int $type, float $x, float $y, float $z) {
    // makePrimitive takes an integer called $type, which is 1 for a
    // sphere, 2 for a cone, and 3 for a cube. Also, it accepts X, Y,
    // and Z position values for the location of the object it creates

switch ($type) {
case 1: sphere;
        break;

case 2: cone;
        break;

case 3: polyCube;
        break;

default: error -showLineNumber true "Invalid object type";
        break;
}

    // Since the most recently created object is selected, AND since
    // if we get here we created a valid object, we can just use the
    // move command

move $x $y $z;

}

    proc buttonAction (int $whichButton, string $floatFieldGrpName) {

    // Get the values of our dialog box's x, y, and z values

    float $xval = `floatFieldGrp -q -value1 $floatFieldGrpName`;
    float $yval = `floatFieldGrp -q -value2 $floatFieldGrpName`;
    float $zval = `floatFieldGrp -q -value3 $floatFieldGrpName`;
```

```
// Call the main procedure

makePrimitive($whichButton, $xval, $yval, $zval);

}

global proc makePrimitiveUI() {

// Define a global string for the positionGrp floatFieldGrp name
   global string $positionGroup;

// makePrimitiveUI builds a dialog box for the makePrimitive
// function

string $dialogBoxWindow = `window -title "Create Primitive"
                                 -rtf true`;

columnLayout;

$positionGroup = `floatFieldGrp -numberOfFields 3`;

rowLayout -nc 3;

button -label "Sphere" -command "buttonAction(1, $positionGroup)";
button -label "Cone" -command "buttonAction(2, $positionGroup)";
button -label "Cube" -command "buttonAction(3, $positionGroup)";

showWindow $dialogBoxWindow;

}
```

Execute the above script to define these procedures, and then execute the user interface by typing `makePrimitiveUI()`, selecting it, and pressing Enter on the numeric keypad.

Try typing some numbers into the dialog box, pressing buttons, and making cubes, spheres, and cones.

What to Remember About Building Custom Dialog Boxes in MEL

- Plan out the nested layouts that will place controls where you want them to be. If you encounter difficulty creating a complex layout, consider using `formLayout`.
- Remember to separate out your script's main procedure from *any* dependencies on user interface. Then, you can ensure that you can run your main procedure in batch mode, where user interfaces are not available.
- Use control groups rather than making the individual controls yourself when you can. Using Maya's prepackaged control groups will save time and produce useful results with less work.

- Remember to use button action procedures to validate data and produce a useful error message before you call your main script procedure. In this way, you can display a meaningful error in a dialog box. However, in your main script procedure you should not display dialog boxes to ensure that it will run in batch mode.
- Remember that many UI-related commands offer flags not discussed here that control object size and spacing. This can help clean up dialog boxes that are not initially pleasing to the eye. For more detail, look in the MEL Command Reference.
- Remember that you can see a list of all the available controls, layouts, and so on in the UI: Windowing page of the MEL Command Reference when you view by function.

15

Making Advanced Dialog Boxes with formLayout

In this chapter you will learn

- Why formLayout, which is the most complicated layout type in MEL, is also the most powerful.
- How formLayout demands that you think about laying out controls in your dialog box.
- What formLayout can do.
- How you should structure your MEL code to build a dialog box with formLayout.

Why Use formLayout?

Unlike the other types of layout objects, such as rowLayout and columnLayout, formLayout offers the ability to precisely place the controls in a dialog box by specifying exact positions in the dialog for each control. Also, with formLayout, you can define how controls will move or grow as a window is resized by attaching one or more of each control's sides to another control or to the window.

The formLayout object also has the advantage that, because it is used to build most of the Maya user interface, it tends to function more predictably than many of the simpler, but less common, layout types, once you understand the principles behind its operation.

Planning a Dialog Box for formLayout

Dialog boxes built with formLayout can place buttons and controls at precise locations in the dialog window, so for this purpose, it might be sufficient just to draw a picture of what you would like your dialog box to look like on the screen.

However, formLayout adds the additional capability of letting you specify how, or whether, controls will grow or shrink as the user resizes your dialog box window.

For example, suppose you wish to create a dialog box that makes a nurbsSphere object. Two sliders control radius and sweep angle, and the user enters the object's name into a text field. Two buttons, "Create" and "Close," make the sphere or close the window, respectively.

The first step is to draw the dialog box as you would like it to appear when it is first created (Figure 15.1).

If you are using formLayout to create your dialog box, you could easily stop here. If you make the enclosing window non-resizable and specify exact positions for each control in the window, you can achieve exactly this layout.

However, it might be desirable to allow the user to resize the window. Perhaps the user wishes to type a long name into the Name field and would like to read the entire name at once. Maybe the user wants to have more precise control over the Radius or Sweep Angle sliders.

If you want to build a layout for a resizable dialog box, you must decide which objects will change in size and position, and how, when the window changes size. For a resizable window, then, it is useful to draw a diagram that shows how you would like the window drawn at a larger size, and then examine the differences to plan how to build the dialog box using formLayout, as seen in Figure 15.2.

At this point, the design for the resized dialog box has been drawn without regard to any constraints that Maya may place on the placement of controls in the dialog box – this design is simply how we would like the resized dialog box to appear. Now, we will analyze how the spacing has changed to determine how to tell formLayout to place the objects in the dialog box.

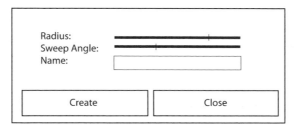

Figure 15.1 A Dialog box design for making a sphere.

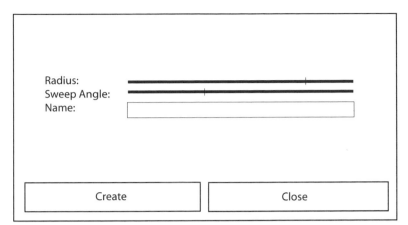

Figure 15.2 The dialog box after resizing the enclosing window.

The Create and Close buttons remain the same height, and they retain similar spacing, both from each other and from the sides and bottom of the window. They have, however, grown wider so that they still fill the window.

The controls in the middle remain the same distance from the left- and right-hand sides, and they have retained the same spacing from each other. However, they have widened from side to side to take advantage of the extra window width, and they have remained centered top-to-bottom in the space between the top of the window and the buttons at the bottom.

As we go on to examine how formLayout places objects within a window (in the section *Using formLayout: Features and Capabilities*), think about how you might use its features to achieve these requirements. In Example 1, we'll follow this design to build a dialog box that grows and shrinks as we've planned.

Using formLayout: Overview

The window layout objects that we've discussed so far, such as columnLayout and rowLayout, have been simple to use to define a window, define a layout object, and create user interface objects like buttons or text fields. When you show the resulting window, the objects you've created (after the layout object) are arranged according to that type of layout's rules.

When you use formLayout to place a window's objects, you must also define how you want each user interface object placed in the window after you have created them. Building a window with formLayout, then, requires these steps:

- Use the window command to make an enclosing window object.
- Make a formLayoutobject that will contain the window's UI objects.
- Create the window's UI objects.
- Use the formLayout command with the -edit flag to tell the formLayout, object by object, how you want the enclosing objects placed.
- Show the window using the showWindow command.

Calling formLayout a second time, after the objects it contains are created, is necessary so that the formLayout can interact with each object as you specify its placement.

To see how a simple formLayout works, enter these commands into the script editor, and execute them by pressing the Enter key on the numeric keypad:

```
string $test_window = `window`;
string $form = `formLayout -numberOfDivisions 100`;
string $button_1 = `button`;

formLayout -edit

          -attachForm $button_1 "top" 25
          -attachForm $button_1 "left" 25
          -attachNone $button_1 "bottom"
          -attachNone $button_1 "right"

$form;

showWindow $test_window;
```

You should see a window that looks like this (Figure 15.3), though the window's size might be different:

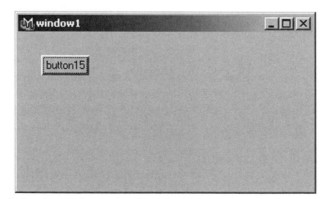

Figure 15.3 A simple window using formLayout.

Try resizing the window you've made. You should see that the button remains fixed in the upper left corner of the window, and the button stays the same size as you resize the window.

How It Works

Initially, making this window follows the same pattern that should be familiar from the simpler layout types presented in earlier chapters:

```
string $test_window = `window`;
string $form = `formLayout -numberOfDivisions 100`;
string $button_1 = `button`;
```

These lines make the window object, create a formLayout object within it, and make a button inside the formLayout.

The -numberOfDivisions flag in the formLayout command tells the formLayout object to divide the window up into that number of horizontal and vertical units. Later, when we specify where to place the objects in the layout, these divisions will be the units used for one of the flags (-attachPosition) to specify a position in the form as a fraction of its width. By setting -numberOfDivisions to 100, each division will be 1% of the form's size.

Once the button object is created in the form, we call formLayout again in edit mode to fix its edges at particular positions in the window:

```
formLayout -edit

            -attachForm $button_1 "top" 25
            -attachForm $button_1 "left" 25
            -attachNone $button_1 "bottom"
            -attachNone $button_1 "right"

    $form;
```

In this step, we specify how the formLayout is to position each side of the button that we created above. The formLayout command accepts several flags that define different rules for placing one of the object's sides, and here we use two of these flags, -attachForm and -attachNone.

The first -attachForm flag, above, tells the formLayout to place the top of the button 25 pixels below the top of the window. The second tells the formLayout to place the left-hand side of the button 25 pixels over from the left-hand side of the enclosing window.

The two -attachNone flags tell the formLayout not to change the width or height of the button as the window is resized, and tell it instead to let the bottom and right edges float in the window.

Note that we've included a rule for placing all four sides of the button (top, left, bottom, and right), even though the bottom and right sides are not attached to anything. While the formLayout may yield acceptable results if you leave out the `-attachNone` rules for sides that are not attached to the form, including these rules explicitly makes your code more readable, and it ensures the correct behavior for those sides of the object.

Finally, the `showWindow` command reveals the window we've built.

Using formLayout: Defining Placement Rules for UI Objects

When you edit a formLayout to define how it is to place each object's edges, you can use one of a number of rules to place that edge in the window. Which rules you use determines not only how the object will be placed initially, but also how the object will behave as you resize it.

-attachForm

`-attachForm` fixes an object's side a specific number of pixels from the corresponding side of the enclosing formLayout object, which usually shares its edges with the window. The `-attachForm` flag takes three additional parameters: the name of the object, which of its sides (top, left, bottom, or right) to place, and a number of pixels from the same edge of the form to place that side of the object.

For example:

```
-attachForm $button_1 "top" 25
```

tells the formLayout to place the top edge of the button whose name is in the string `$button_1` twenty-five pixels below the top of the form.

-attachOppositeForm

`-attachOppositeForm` fixes an object's side a specific number of pixels from the opposite side of the enclosing formLayout object. `-attachOppositeForm` takes similar parameters to `-attachForm`. Here's an example:

```
-attachOppositeForm $button_1 "top" −25
```

This example places the *top* of `$button_1` 25 pixels above the *bottom* of the form. The offset must be negative because positive offsets for the "top" side of an object always move the object *down*, and this rule would place the top side of the object 25 pixels *up* from the bottom. If the offset were 25, the button would be below the bottom of the window, and it would not be visible.

-attachControl

`-attachControl` fixes an object's side a specific number of pixels from the nearest side of another control. This is useful when you want two controls to remain a certain number of pixels apart whenever the window is resized. `-attachControl` takes four parameters: the name of the object to place, which of its sides to place, a number of pixels from the nearest side of another control, and the name of the other control. For example:

```
-attachControl $button_1 "right" 5 $button_2
```

places the right edge of $button_1 five pixels from the *left* edge of $button_2.

-attachOppositeControl

`-attachOppositeControl` fixes an object's side a specific number of pixels from the same side of another control. You could use `-attachOppositeControl` to set a distance between the right sides of two buttons, as in:

```
-attachOppositeControl $button_1 "right" 100 $button_2
```

This would place the right side of $button_1 100 pixels to the left of the right side of $button_2. This time, unlike in the `-attachOppositeForm` example above, we have chosen an offset in the same direction as `-attachControl` would have specified, so we leave the offset positive.

-attachPosition

This flag is useful when you want a user interface object's position to scale as the window is resized, instead of having a fixed distance from an edge. `-attachPosition` fixes an object's side to a location in the window that's determined by a position in the units defined by the `-numberOfDivisions` flag we discussed above. Usually, you'll define the number of divisions to be 100, so the position is specified as a percentage of the window's width.

`-attachPosition` takes four arguments: the name of the control, the name of the side to position, an offset in pixels from the corresponding side of the form, and a position in the units defined by the number of divisions.

The offset value passed to `-attachPosition` allows you to add a number of pixels to the position specified in divisions. An offset of 4 and a position of 50 would place the edge of an object four pixels over from the midpoint of the form. For example:

```
-attachPosition Button "left" 5 50
```

If the number of divisions were set to 100 when the formLayout object was created, this would place the left edge of the button object called Button 50% away from the left side of the form, plus an additional five pixels, as seen in Figure 15.4.

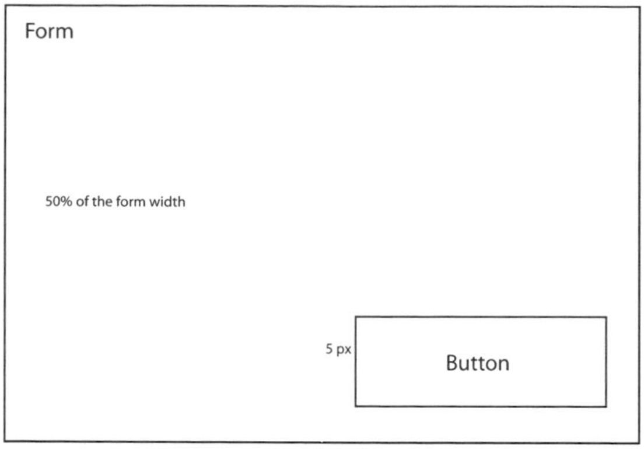

Figure 15.4 `attachPosition` with an offset of five pixels and position 50%.

-attachNone

`-attachNone` takes an object and a side as an argument, and it tells the formLayout object that that side is to move as the window is resized. This causes the object to remain the same size as it started. For example:

```
-attachNone $button_1 "right"
```

tells the formLayout object to follow whatever rule is set for the left side, and to allow the right side to float so that the button remains the same size as the window is resized.

Example: Implementing a Dialog Box with formLayout

Now, we have the tools to implement the dialog box for making spheres. Enter this script into the Script Editor, and run it:

```
string $example_window = `window`;

string $example_form = `formLayout -numberOfDivisions 100`;

string $radius_grp = `floatSliderGrp -label "Radius:"
                                     -field false
                                     -minValue 0.0 -maxValue 10.0
                                     -value 1 -adj 2`;

string $sweep_grp = `floatSliderGrp -label "Sweep Angle:"
                                     -field false
                                     -minValue 0.0 -maxValue 360.0
                                     -value 360.0 -adj 2`;
```

```
string $name_grp = `textFieldGrp -label "Name:"
                                 -text "mySphere"
                                 -adj 2`;

string $create_button = `button -label "Create"`;

string $cancel_button = `button -label "Cancel"`;

formLayout -edit
       -attachPosition $radius_grp "top" 0 40
       -attachForm $radius_grp "left" 10
       -attachNone $radius_grp "bottom"
       -attachForm $radius_grp "right" 30

       -attachControl $sweep_grp "top" 5 $radius_grp
       -attachForm $sweep_grp "left" 10
       -attachNone $sweep_grp "bottom"
       -attachForm $sweep_grp "right" 30

       -attachControl $name_grp "top" 5 $sweep_grp
       -attachForm $name_grp "left" 10
       -attachNone $name_grp "bottom"
       -attachForm $name_grp "right" 30

       -attachForm $create_button "bottom" 5
       -attachPosition $create_button "right" 2 50
       -attachForm $create_button "left" 5
        attachNone $create button "top"

       -attachForm $cancel_button "bottom" 5
       -attachForm $cancel_button "right" 5
       -attachPosition $cancel button "left" 2 50
       -attachNone $cancel_button "top"

   $example_form;

   showWindow $example_window;
```

The resulting dialog box (Figure 15.5) closely resembles the design described above, though it is not yet functional.

Importantly, it retains the desired proportions when resized, as planned.

How It Works

First, the script to create this window defines the window, a formLayout object, and the UI objects that make up the form. Defining a window, a layout, and a series of UI objects for a formLayout object is very similar to doing so for any other type of layout:

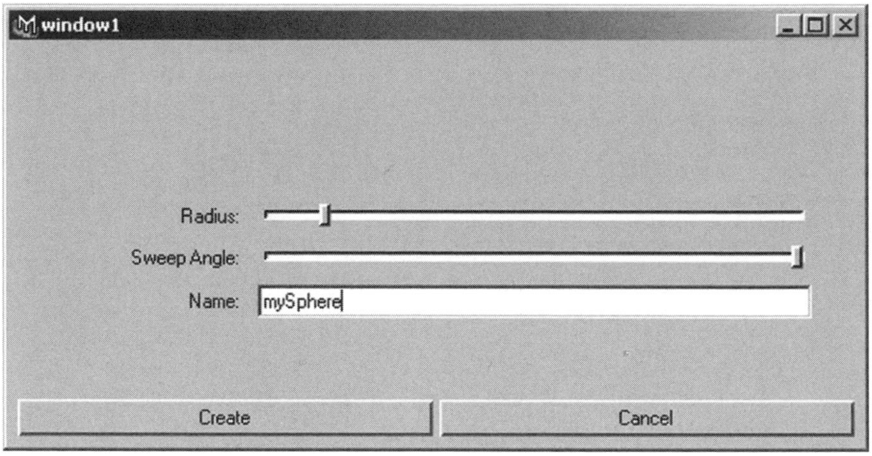

Figure 15.5 Example sphere creation window.

```
string $example_window = `window`;

string $example_form = `formLayout -numberOfDivisions 100`;

string $radius_grp = `floatSliderGrp -label "Radius:"
                                   -field false
                                   -minValue 0.0 -maxValue 10.0
                                   -value 1 -adj 2`;

string $sweep_grp = `floatSliderGrp -label "Sweep Angle:"
                                   -field false
                                   -minValue 0.0 -maxValue 360.0
                                   -value 360.0 -adj 2`;

string $name_grp = `textFieldGrp -label "Name:"
                                -text "mySphere"
                                -adj 2`;

string $create_button = `button -label "Create"`;

string $cancel_button = `button -label "Cancel"`;
```

The floatSliderGrp objects are created with the -adj 2 flag to indicate that the sliders, not the titles of the groups, are to grow and shrink as the enclosing window is resized.

Once we define each object in the window, we call the formLayout command in edit mode to establish where each object will be drawn in relation to the window. At the start of the command are the flags that place the radius slider:

```
formLayout -edit

    -attachPosition $radius_grp "top" 0 40
    -attachForm $radius_grp "left" 10
    -attachNone $radius_grp "bottom"
    -attachForm $radius_grp "right" 30
```

The -attachPosition flag places the top of the radius slider group 40%
down from the top of the window, and it does not add any additional pixels as an offset.

The left and right sides are placed 10 and 30 pixels from the left
and right sides of the window using -attachForm. Note that the left-hand
side appears to be much farther over from the left than 10 pixels. This is a
result of the wide default column width for the title in a slider group, and
it could be fixed with an appropriate argument to floatSliderGrp.

Finally, because we want the bottom of the radius slider group to float
with the control, we use -attachNone to leave that side unattached.

The flags for the sweep angle's slider group are similar, but this time the
top of the control group is fixed by placing it five pixels from the bottom
of the radius slider group with the -attachControl flag:

```
-attachControl $sweep_grp "top" 5 $radius_grp
-attachForm $sweep_grp "left" 10
-attachNone $sweep_grp "bottom"
-attachForm $sweep_grp "right" 30
```

The name text field group looks the same, but it is attached to the bottom
of the sweep angle slider group:

```
-attachControl $name_grp "top" 5 $sweep_grp
 attachForm $name_grp "left" 10
-attachNone $name_grp "bottom"
-attachForm $name_grp "right" 30
```

The two buttons at the bottom are placed a fixed distance from the near
form sides and the bottom edge, with their tops floating and the sides clos-
est to the form's centerline using a 50% position and a two-pixel offset to
establish some space between them:

```
-attachForm $create_button "bottom" 5
-attachPosition $create_button "right" 2 50
-attachForm $create_button "left" 5
-attachNone $create_button "top"

-attachForm $cancel_button "bottom" 5
-attachForm $cancel_button "right" 5
-attachPosition $cancel_button "left" 2 50
-attachNone $cancel_button "top"

$example_form;
```

Finally, the script uses showWindow to display the window:

```
showWindow $example_window;
```

What to Remember About Making Dialog Boxes with formLayout

- If your dialog box window is going to be resizeable, draw it at a couple of different sizes to plan how user interface elements will move as the window changes sizes.
- Creating a formLayout object with a number of divisions of 100 allows you to think of positions in the form as percentages.
- Using formLayout is just like using one of the other layout types, with the additional step of editing the formLayout object after the window has been built to define placement for your user interface elements.
- Use the -attachForm flag when you want to place an object at a particular pixel position in the window.
- Use the -attachControl flag when you want to fix a particular pixel distance between two objects.
- Use the -attachPosition flag when you want an object to scale or float with a window as it resizes.
- Take advantage of features in each UI object's creation command to tell it how to draw itself as well; not every characteristic of position and size is definable by flags to the formLayout command.

16

Making Advanced Dialog Boxes with Web Panels

In this chapter you will learn

- What you need to know before proceeding to make dialog boxes with web panels.
- What web panels are, and why you would choose to use them.
- Where to go for the information you need to learn to author web pages.
- How a dialog box built with web panels works.
- How to plan and build a dialog box using web panels.
- How to create the HTML for your web panel user interface.
- How to launch the dialog box you've created from within a MEL script.
- Ideas for things to try with web-based dialog boxes in Maya.

What You Need to Know Before You Proceed

Making dialog boxes using web panels is a powerful, new feature in Maya 6 that will appeal most to MEL scripters who already know the tools and techniques to build web pages. If you are not familiar with web authoring, you may find it easier to use Maya's built-in user interface commands.

For this chapter, you should know how to make a simple web page using Hypertext Markup Language (HTML), what Uniform Resource Locators (URLs) are and how they are formatted, and how to create dialog boxes in MEL as presented in the last few chapters.

Example 1 later in this chapter will make more sense if you are familiar with JavaScript, a simple language originally implemented by Netscape that allows scripts to be embedded within HTML web pages. Even if you do not know JavaScript, though, it may give you an idea of what learning JavaScript might enable you to do.

If these concepts are not familiar, the section entitled *Learning Web Authoring*, below, suggests some sources for information about how to learn the skills you need.

Note: *You must run Maya 6.0 or later to use the techniques in this chapter, as they rely on features not available in earlier Maya versions.*

What Are Web Panels?

Web panels, a new feature in Maya 6, are a means to embed a live web page in a Maya window, either the main Maya window or one you create with Maya's `window` command. Web pages can contain large amounts of graphic and text information, as well as multiple-page layouts with easily implemented navigation, and clickable links that can trigger commands. Therefore, having access to their capabilities within Maya offers new possibilities for user interfaces that were not possible with Maya's built-in user interface commands, which Alias collectively calls *ELF*, short for *Extension Layer Framework*.

Using web panels to build user interfaces can be very different from using ELF; instead of writing MEL code to create and place each element of your user interface, you can use a range of free or commercial web authoring tools to build a web page that you can test in any browser, or even deliver over the internet.

ELF's technique for building dialog boxes, which we've seen in the previous chapters, consists of a few steps that are usually the same, regardless of what you are implementing:

- Make a window using the `window` command.
- Make a layout, such as a `columnLayout`, `rowLayout`, or `formLayout`, that will contain your dialog's controls.
- Make text, slider, or other controls that allow the user to input parameters for your MEL scripts.
- Make buttons that use button action procedures to collect the user's input and to execute MEL scripts that do something useful.

Building a dialog based on a web panel works like this:

- Create the text or graphics that you want to appear in your user interface.
- Create one or more HTML files that contain the web pages that will comprise your interface. Any HTML is fine in such an interface. Links

that you would like to use to trigger a MEL command will point to a special, Maya-specific URL that begins with `mel://`.

- Write a MEL script that locates the HTML files on your disk; then uses `window,` one of the layout commands, and MEL's `webBrowser` command to open the web page in a Maya window.

There are several advantages to using ELF to build dialogs: The windows you create will look and feel more like Maya windows, getting parameters back from user input is simpler, and launching the dialog is much faster.

There are advantages to building dialog boxes using web panels: The windows you create can be more graphically complex, you can easily create interfaces that communicate large amounts of information as well as perform useful tasks, and you can deliver your interfaces, if you like, from a web server. Also, if you are a skilled web author, you might find web panels to be an easier way to design and implement complex user interfaces.

Note that only Maya's web panel windows can interpret the special URLs that execute MEL commands. You cannot use a web page to control Maya from an external web browser.

Learning Web Authoring

The examples later in this chapter assume different levels of experience with web authoring. The example presented below in the sections called *Creating a Web-Based Dialog Box for Maya* and *Launching a Web-based Dialog Box from MEL* should be suitable for beginners, and *Example: Implementing a Dialog Box with JavaScript* is more appropriate for those with a more advanced knowledge of web authoring, including the JavaScript language.

Learning advanced web authoring can be at least as complex and time-consuming as learning MEL. Fortunately, on the internet you can find a wide range of instructional resources for all skill levels of web authors.

http://www.webmonkey.com/
One site that has plenty of information for beginning and intermediate web authors is webmonkey.com. Look for the how- to library on their front page to get started.

http://www.htmlgoodies.com/
Another highly recommended site is htmlgoodies.com, which is associated with a highly-rated book called *HTML Goodies*, by Joe Burns.

Creating Web Pages for Dummies
This book from the popular For Dummies series offers a simple introduction to web authoring for the absolute beginner.

Both on the web and in bookstores, you'll find many other sources, each recommending different techniques and offering different perspectives. As you develop your web authoring skills, consider exploring other books and web sites on the topic.

How a Dialog Box Built with Web Panels Works

Typically, a dialog box built with web panels will consist of a number of files that work together to present the user interface and do something useful:

- A MEL file provides the procedures that open the web panel in a window and perform the Maya tasks that the web panel will trigger.
- One or more HTML files define the look of the user interface in the web panel.
- Graphics files can serve as illustrations within the user interface, just as they would on a web page.
- Additional files can contain JavaScript, Java applets, or CGI scripts that perform tasks that would be difficult within MEL.

To use such a dialog box, a user might use a MEL command in the script editor, a shelf button, or a menu item to trigger a MEL script that launches the user interface.

This MEL script then builds a `file:` URL that leads to the location on disk of the HTML page that defines the user interface. Then, it makes a window containing a layout and a web panel that is directed to that URL at creation time. Finally, it shows the window, displaying the HTML page.

The HTML page that's displayed can contain links to URLs that consist of `mel://` followed by a MEL command or a call to a global procedure, then another / character. For example, a MEL URL that creates a sphere of radius 5 would look like this:

```
mel://sphere -r 5/
```

So, a link to that URL that creates such a sphere when it is clicked would look like this in the HTML file:

```
<a href="mel://sphere -r 5/">Make a sphere</a>
```

This creates a link with the text "Make a sphere" that, when clicked, executes the MEL command `sphere -r 5`.

Note that this link only can create a sphere in Maya if the web page that contains it has been loaded through a Maya web panel. If you run Maya and then load this page through an external browser, it will have no effect when clicked, and it will probably generate an error message.

Of course, you need not restrict yourself to built-in commands when constructing MEL links in for a web panel interface. If you had defined a global procedure makespheres() in the MEL file that created your window, you might link to a URL like

```
mel://makespheres()/
```

which would call the global makespheres() procedure defined in the related MEL file.

Planning a Dialog Box for Web Panels

As with dialog boxes created entirely within MEL, you should plan what your dialog box will do and how its interface will be arranged before you begin implementing it.

In addition to the questions you would ask yourself when planning any dialog box in MEL, determining answers to the following issues can help when planning your web panel dialog box:

- Do you prefer to use a web page editor like Mozilla Composer or Microsoft FrontPage that can help you format your HTML dialog box? If so, these tools can save a great deal of time achieving the appearance that you want your dialog box to have.
- Will you want to implement forms in your interface so that you can provide switches, controls, and text fields for collecting information from the user that your MEL script then can use to control its actions? If so, you should be prepared to use JavaScript.
- Do you wish to provide navigation controls in your web browser window, such as back, home, and reload buttons? If so, you will probably choose to create these yourself, in MEL, since in the simplest web browser windows these are not provided for you.
- Do you need to create any additional graphics such as icons or image maps that you would like to use in your web panel interface?

What's most important to keep in mind is that web panels provide many of the capabilities of web pages, meaning that you can create advanced interfaces that can present complex information or even tutorials in addition to triggering MEL scripts. The rich features of modern web development tools give you options for interface development that would be impractical when using MEL and ELF by themselves.

Creating a Web-Based Dialog Box for Maya

Maya's web browser panel type is derived from the open-source Mozilla web browser. Most web page features that will work in Mozilla will work in a Maya web panel, and making a web-based dialog box for Maya is like creating any other web page. There are, however, a few limitations with which you should be familiar before you proceed:

- Features that require browser plug-ins might or might not work as expected. On the Macintosh and Windows platforms, common media plug-ins such as Quicktime, Windows Media, and Flash *do* work, but others may not. Before investing significant time in authoring with a format that requires a plug-in, try a simple example first.
- Maya will not permit web pages to open pop-up windows. If a web page tries to open a pop-up, the message "Warning: Maya embedded web browser unable to create more than one window" will appear in your script editor window.
- If you create a web browser panel in your own window, you will not, by default, have navigation buttons unless you create them yourself. See *Example 3* later in this chapter for more information on how to do this.

The simplest possible web-based interface for Maya consists of a list of links that will perform MEL commands. To see an example of this, open Maya and in any panel's menu bar; choose Panels > Panel > Web Browser to make that panel a web browser. Then choose Panels > Tear Off. . . to make a separate web browser window so that you can see the 3D viewer.

By default, the browser's home page is a brief help page on Maya's web browser (Figure 16.1). On this page are a series of clickable links that will execute simple MEL commands. Try clicking on them to see what happens. Each of these links consists of a link to a MEL URL.

To create your own web page that can execute a MEL command, open a text editor such as Notepad (on Windows) or TextEdit (on the Macintosh), and create a file that contains this HTML. Name your file `makesphere.htm`:

```
<HTML>

<HEAD>

<TITLE>My Web Page</TITLE>

</HEAD>

<BODY>

<A HREF="mel://sphere -r 10/">make a sphere</A><P>

<A HREF="http://www.melscripting.com/">melscripting. com</A>

</BODY>

</HTML>
```

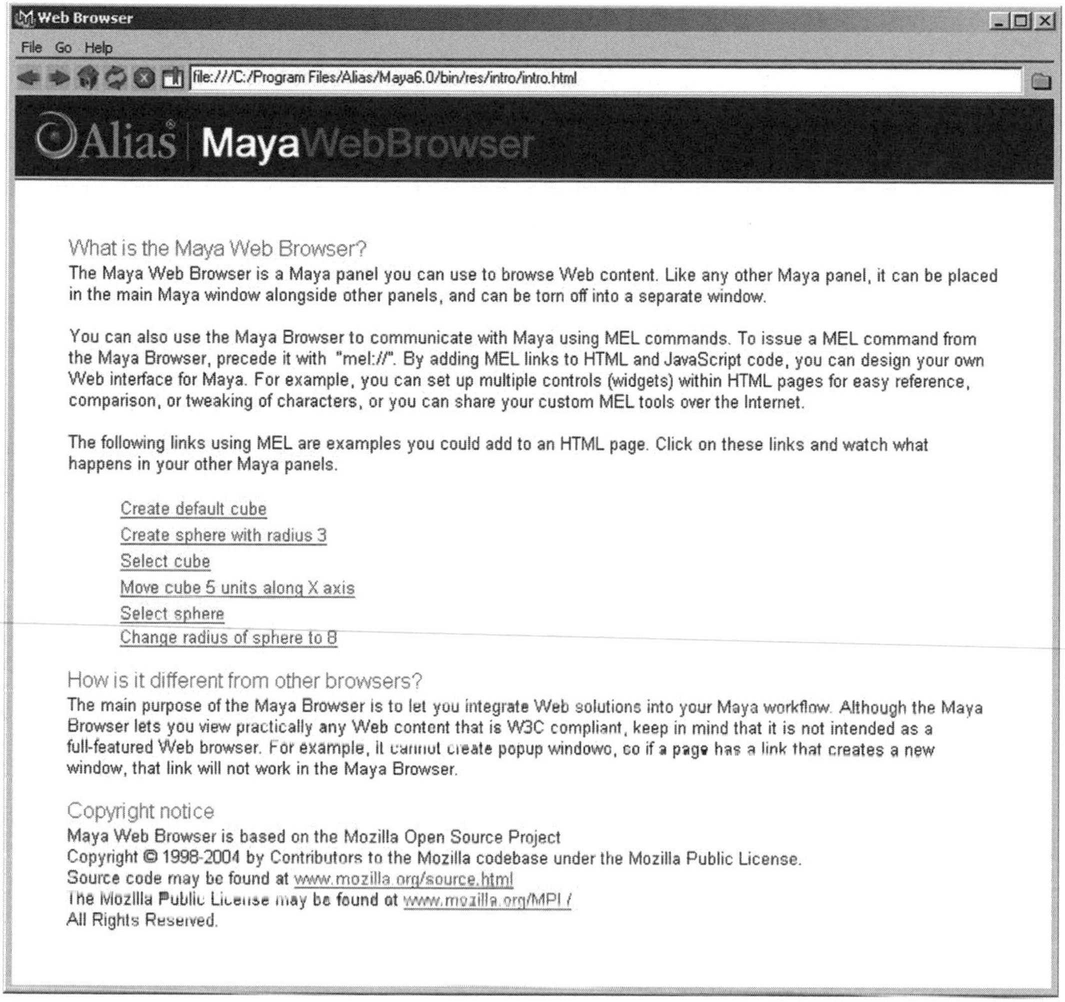

Figure 16.1 Maya's web browser's home page.

(HTML experts will note that this is missing the recommended W3C DOCTYPE tag. Fortunately, it still renders correctly in Maya, so it has been omitted for clarity.)

In the Maya web browser window, at the upper right, click on the File Browse icon, which looks like a file folder. Browse to your `makesphere.htm` file, select it, and click Open.

Once you do this, you will see two links, one titled "make a sphere" and the other titled "melscripting.com." Click on "make a sphere," and a sphere will appear in your 3D viewer. Click on "melscripting.com," and you should see. . . something very familiar. . .

All that a web panel dialog box is, then, is a web page that contains links to one or more `mel:` URLs.

Neither of these examples so far offers a way for the user to provide input to the MEL script. Since Maya's web browser supports JavaScript, though, you can easily collect and act on user input by doing the following:

■ Within the HTML document, use the FORM tag and related tags to build a form within your user interface.

■ In the FORM tag, set the `onSubmit` attribute to call a JavaScript function that will call a MEL procedure you've defined.

■ In the JavaScript function, collect the values of various form elements, and build a MEL command that will pass their values as parameters to the MEL procedure.

■ Finally, assign the MEL URL to the standard JavaScript object attribute `window.location` to load the URL and thus execute the MEL procedure. Since loading a MEL URL doesn't actually change the page in the browser (it just executes a command), your form will remain on the user's screen after the procedure finishes executing.

Some of these steps may seem unfamiliar if you do not know JavaScript. *Example 1* below describes in detail how a simple form implementation works. However, for more advanced techniques, using the resources in *Learning Web Authoring* to learn JavaScript is strongly recommended.

Launching a Web-Based Dialog Box from MEL

Once you have created a web-based dialog box that you can open and run in Maya's web browser by hand, you can simply bookmark the dialog box HTML file and use the bookmark to launch your dialog box. Just click on the web browser's bookmark menu icon, and choose "Bookmark This Page" from the menu that appears(Figure 16.2).

However, if your dialog box is part of a larger application, or if you would like to make your dialog available via a menu item or shelf button, you will need to launch your web-based dialog box from a MEL script.

To do this, you can use the `webBrowser` MEL command to create a web browser in a window in much the same way as you would create a slider or a button. For example, these commands create a web browser in a columnLayout within a new window:

Figure 16.2 The web browser bookmark menu icon.

```
string $myWindow = `window -widthHeight 800 600
myBrowserDialog`;
  columnLayout;
    webBrowser -url "http://www.melscripting.com/";
showWindow;
```

Unlike creating a web browser panel in Maya's main window using the Panels > Panel > Web Browser menu item, the web browser that is created in your new window does not contain browser controls such as the back, forward, or home buttons, or a URL field. Example 1 will look at how you can create these controls yourself.

Launching your own dialog box requires that you replace the URL with a `file:` URL that points to your HTML document. So, a script to launch a particular web-based dialog might look like this. (Do not try to run these commands on your system, as the URL's path is guaranteed to be different for your file.)

```
string $myWindow = `window -widthHeight 800 600
myBrowserDialog`;

columnLayout;

  webBrowser -url ("file:///C:/Documents and Settings/Mark" +

                   " R. Wilkins/My Documents/maya/6.0/" +

                   "scripts/makesphere.htm");

showWindow;
```

One significant problem with this approach to launching a web-based dialog box is that moving the HTML file to a different directory requires changing the script. Unlike running a MEL script that is installed in your script path, launching a web URL in Maya cannot automatically search a list of directories for an HTML file.

The solution is to place the HTML file in your script path alongside a MEL file to launch it, which *can* find its own location. Pick one of the directories in your script path, which you can view using the command

```
getenv("MAYA_SCRIPT_PATH");
```

and place your `makesphere.htm` file in that directory. Then, in that same directory, make a file called `make_web_panel.mel` that contains this MEL code:

```
proc string get_path_url() {

string $path_to_proc = `whatIs make_web_panel`;
string $path_parts[];
string $lead_in = "Mel procedure found in: ";
string $path_url = "file:/";
```

```
int $i;

$path_url = $path_url + substring($path_to_proc,
                                   (size($lead_in) + 1),
                                   size($path_to_proc));

tokenize $path_url "/" $path_parts;

$path_url = "";

for ($i = 0; $i < (size($path_parts) -1); $i++) {

    $path_url = $path_url + $path_parts[$i] + "/";

}

return $path_url;

}

global proc make_web_panel() {
    string $myurl = (get_path_url() + "makesphere.htm");
    print ($myurl + "\n");

string $myWindow = `window -widthHeight 800 600`;
  columnLayout;
    webBrowser -url $myurl;

showWindow $myWindow;

}
```

To make Maya aware of this new script, either quit and relaunch Maya, or run the rehash command in the Script Editor. Then, in the Script Editor, type:

```
make_web_panel();
```

and press Enter to execute the script. Now, you can move this pair of files to any directory in your script path. Type rehash, or relaunch Maya to make Maya aware of the change, and the script will still work.

How It Works

Launching a web browser to display a particular web page somewhere on your disk requires that your script construct an explicit file: URL that contains the full path to that web page's HTML file. The get_path_url procedure, above, returns a string that contains such a file URL for the directory that encloses the MEL file that contains the procedure.

The make_web_panel procedure mirrors the commands we used in the previous section to launch a web panel. The biggest difference is that it calls get_path_url() to find the URL that points to the enclosing directory, and it adds the name of the HTML file on the end to find the HTML file's URL:

```
string $myurl = (get_path_url() + "makesphere.htm");
```

When the code to create the window runs, $myurl will contain something like this:

```
file:/C:/Documents And Settings/Administrator/My
Documents/maya/scripts/makesphere.htm
```

This string (which may vary based on your system) is a valid file: URL to the web page that contains the dialog box we created above, provided that makesphere.htm was placed in the same directory as make_web_panel.mel.

The get_path_url procedure is a tricky MEL script that can be re-used in MEL scripts that launch web-based dialog boxes by replacing the name of the procedure make_web_panel in the whatIs command on the first line with the name of the procedure you use to launch your own dialog box. While it is not necessary to examine get_path_url in detail to create your own web-based dialog boxes, seeing how it works may be of interest as an example of advanced string manipulation.

About get_path_url

This procedure assumes that the web page you wish to launch is located in the same directory as the script that launches it, and it uses Maya's whatIs command to find the path to that directory. To see how this works, try typing this into the script editor and executing it:

```
whatIs make_web_panel
```

If you are running Microsoft Windows and have been following the examples up to this point, you should see something that looks like this (perhaps with different line wrapping):

```
// Result: Script found in: C:/Documents And
Settings/Administrator/My
Documents/maya/scripts/make_web_panel.mel //
```

The return value of whatIs consists of an introductory phrase (in this case "Script found in:") that indicates what type of code a particular MEL construct is, and in what file it can be found. For another example, try typing

```
whatIs whatIs;
```

```
// Result: Command //
```

When you call whatIs from within a MEL script with the name of a procedure, the string that the command returns begins with "Mel procedure found in:" and lists the file in which the procedure is defined.

To find where it has been installed, the procedure `get_path_url`, above, calls `whatIs` with the argument `make_web_panel`, which returns the `"MEL procedure found in: "` phrase followed by a path to the containing file. The resulting string might look something like this, if you are running Windows:

```
Mel procedure found in: C:/Documents And
Settings/Administrator/My
Documents/maya/scripts/make_web_panel.mel
```

If you are running Linux or the Macintosh, the path will be different, but the phrase at the beginning will be the same; and, importantly, all three operating systems will use forward slashes (/) to set off directories in the path from each other.

So, the `get_path_url` procedure uses the following line to get the result of calling `whatIs` on the `make_web_panel` procedure:

```
string $path_to_proc = `whatIs make_web_panel`;
```

Now, to isolate the path to the directory that contains the `make_web_panel.mel` file, it is necessary to strip off the `"Mel procedure found in: "` phrase at the beginning and the `make_web_panel.mel` filename at the end.

The function defines a string called `$lead_in` that contains the introductory phrase returned by `whatIs`:

```
string $lead_in = "Mel procedure found in: ";
```

This string is only defined so that the script can find the number of characters to chop off the front of the result of `whatIs` by calling `size($lead_in)`. This could just as easily be done by counting the characters by hand and just using the number 24 in place of `size($lead_in)`, but doing so would not be nearly as clear to someone who reads the script after it is written.

Maya's `substring` command, which we covered in *Chapter 6 – Variables and Data Types*, can be used to find the portion of the return string that contains the path to the MEL file. Since the first character of the path is at the position numbered `size($lead_in)` + 1, and the last character of the path is at the position `size($path_to_proc)`, this call to substring yields the path portion of the string returned by `whatIs`:

```
substring($path_to_proc, size($lead_in) + 1,
size($path_to_proc));
```

Because constructing a URL that points to this path requires adding the string `"file:/"` to the front, we've done both of these steps at once by defining the variable $path_url like this:

```
$path_url = "file:/";
```

and then, a couple of lines later, adding the result of substring to `$path_url` like this:

```
$path_url = $path_url + substring($path_to_proc,

                    (size($lead_in) + 1),

                    size($path_to_proc));
```

Now, `$path_url` contains a valid file URL, but one that points to the MEL fileIts contents at this point look something like this (but all on one line, of course):

```
file:/C:/Documents And Settings/Administrator/My
Documents/maya/scripts/make_web_panel.mel
```

Instead of the URL pointing to the MEL file that includes the code for these procedures, we want `get_path_url` to contain a URL to the directory that contains that MEL file, requiring that we remove everything after the final forward slash (/) character. To do this, we use the `tokenize` command (as we did in Chapter 11), to split up the string into a list of parts separated by slashes. Then, we put the string back together, leaving off the last part. The string array `$path_parts` will contain the parts of the path separated by slashes:

```
tokenize $path_url "/" $path_parts;
```

Tokenize, as discussed before, places the parts that result from splitting up its first argument (`$path_url`) into the chunks separated by the second argument (`"/"`) into the array indicated by the third argument (`$path_parts`).

Now, we use a `for` loop to build the string again, this time leaving off the last part (Remember: `size($path_parts)` tells our script the number of parts that resulted when we ran `tokenize`, and we need to concatenate all the parts except the last one to rebuild the string without the final filename.)

```
for ($i = 0; $i < (size($path_parts) -1); $i++) {

   $path_url = $path_url + $path_parts[$i] + "/";

}
```

Finally, the return command is used to pass back to the calling procedure the URL that points to the MEL script's enclosing directory:

```
return $path_url;
```

Example 1: Implementing a Dialog Box using JavaScript

While it sometimes may be useful to offer a list of links to static MEL commands on a web page (for example, to run scripts to set up an online tutorial), taking advantage of the real power of building dialog boxes with web techniques requires using JavaScript, a scripting language originally developed by Netscape and today integrated into most web browsers.

With JavaScript, you can build web-based forms that assemble a customized MEL command, passing a user's input to your script. Also, you can implement rollovers and client-side image maps that can enhance the appearance and functionality of your user interfaces.

In the directory where you placed the file makesphere.htm from the previous example, use a text editor to create this HTML file. Name the file makesphereform.htm:

```
<HTML>
<HEAD>

   <TITLE>Make Some Spheres...</TITLE>
   <SCRIPT language="JavaScript">
   function js_makespheres()

   {

     var num_spheres =
         document.makespheres_form.num_spheres.value;
     var max_radius =
         document.makespheres_form.max_radius.value;
     var mel_url = `mel://makespheres(` +
                    num_spheres + `, ` +
                    max_radius + `)/`;
       location = mel_url;

   }

</SCRIPT>
</HEAD>
<BODY>
  <A href="http://www.melscripting.com/">
    go to melscripting.com
</A><P>
<FORM name="makespheres_form"
     onSubmit="js_makespheres(); return false;">
<B>How many spheres do you want to make:<B>

<INPUT type="text" name="num_spheres"
size="30"><P>
<b>Maximum radius: </b>

<INPUT type="text" name="max_radius" size="30"><P>

<INPUT type="submit" value="Make Spheres">

</FORM>
```

```
</BODY>
</HTML>
```

Alongside it, in the same directory, create this file, calling it
make_js_web_panel.mel:

```
proc string get_path_url() {

string $path_to_proc = `whatIs make_js_web_panel`;
string $path_parts[];
string $lead_in = "Mel procedure found in: ";
string $path_url = "file:/";
int $i;

$path_url = $path_url + substring($path_to_proc,
                                  (size($lead_in) + 1),
                                  size($path_to_proc));

tokenize $path_url "/" $path_parts;
$path_url = "";

for ($i = 0; $i < (size($path_parts) - 1); $i++) {

  $path_url = $path_url + $path_parts[$i] + "/";

}

return $path_url;

  }

  global proc makespheres(int $num_spheres, float
    $max_radius) {

  int $i;

    for ($i = 0; $i < $num_spheres; $i++) {

    float $curr_radius = rand(0, $max_radius);
    float $curr_X = rand(-10, 10);
    float $curr_Y = rand(-10, 10);
    float $curr_Z = rand(-10, 10);
    sphere -r $curr_radius -p $curr_X $curr_Y $curr_Z;

  }

}

global proc browserBack() {
  global string $myWebBrowser;
  webBrowser -e -back $myWebBrowser;

  }
```

```
global proc browserForward() {
   global string $myWebBrowser;
   webBrowser -e -forward $myWebBrowser;
}

global proc browserHome() {
   global string $myWebBrowser;
   webBrowser -e -home $myWebBrowser;
}

global proc make_js_web_panel() {
   global string $myWebBrowser;

   string $myurl = (get_path_url() + "makesphereform.htm");
   print ($myurl + "\n");

   window -width 800 -height 632 -title "Make some spheres";

   columnLayout;

   rowLayout -numberOfColumns 3

   -columnWidth3 32 32 32
   -columnAlign 1 "right"
   -columnAttach 1 "both" 0
   -columnAttach 2 "both" 0
   -columnAttach 3 "both" 0;

   iconTextButton -c "browserBack()"
   -image "back.xpm";

   iconTextButton -c "browserForward()"
   -image "forward.xpm";

   iconTextButton -c "browserHome()"
   -image "homepage.xpm";

   setParent ..;
   $myWebBrowser = `webBrowser -url $myurl`;
   showWindow;

}
```

If Maya is not running, launch it; otherwise, execute the command rehash in the Script Editor. Then, execute the command

```
make_js_web_panel()
```

and enter a number of spheres and a maximum radius into the form that appears. Click on the "Make Spheres" button to see the result, shown in Figure 16.3.

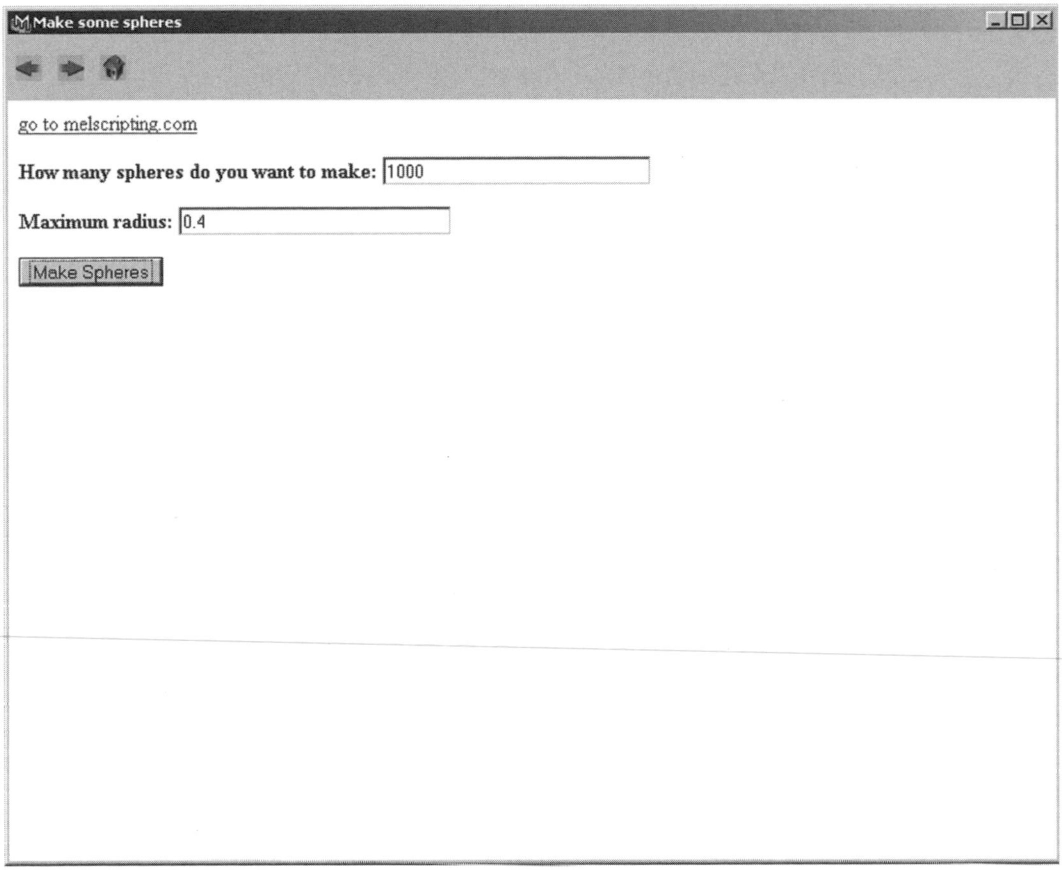

Figure 16.3 The resulting JavaScript-based dialog box.

Note that this web panel adds forward, back, and home buttons; so, if you surf away from the form by clicking on "go to melscripting.com," you can return by clicking the left arrow button to go back.

How It Works

The MEL script that launches the web panel in this example consists of five procedures:

- `get_path_url`, which constructs the file URL that points to the directory containing the web form. This procedure is defined to be local to the MEL file so that it does not conflict with the `get_path_url` procedure in the previous example.
- `makespheres`, which does the work of creating randomly placed spheres with random radii. This procedure takes two arguments: an

integer `num_spheres` that contains the number of spheres to create, and a float called `max_radius` that contains the maximum radius for each sphere. This function is defined to be global so that it can be launched from a MEL URL on the web form.

- `browserBack`, which makes the web panel display the last page viewed before the current page. This function is defined to be global so that it can be used as a button action procedure for the Back button.
- `browserForward`, which makes the web panel display the next page, if the user has already used the back button to navigate to previous pages. This function is defined to be global so that it can be used as a button action procedure for the Forward button.
- `browserHome`, which makes the web panel display the browser's home page, by default a help page that describes how Maya's embedded web browser works. This function is defined to be global so that it can be used as a button action procedure for the Home button.
- `make_js_web_panel`, which builds the window that contains the web browser panel. This function is defined to be global so that it can be called from the script editor, from a menu item, or from a shelf button.

The `get_path_url` procedure is nearly identical to the same function in the first example, but the `whatIs` command that returns the path to the MEL file looks for the path to `make_js_web_panel` instead of the other example's `make_web_panel` procedure.

Here is the `makespheres` procedure that the web form calls:

```
global proc makespheres(int $num_spheres, float $max_radius) {

    int $i;

    for ($i = 0; $i < $num_spheres; $i++) {

        float $curr_radius = rand(0, $max_radius);
        float $curr_X = rand(-10, 10);
        float $curr_Y = rand(-10, 10);
        float $curr_Z = rand(-10, 10);

        sphere -r $curr_radius -p $curr_X $curr_Y $curr_Z;

    }

}
```

This procedure loops `$num_spheres` times. Each time through the loop, it picks a random radius between 0 and `$max_radius`

```
float $curr_radius = rand(0, $max_radius);
```

then it chooses random X, Y, and Z locations between −10 units and 10 units:

```
float $curr_X = rand(-10, 10);
float $curr_Y = rand(-10, 10);
float $curr_Z = rand(-10, 10);
```

Finally, it creates a sphere with radius $curr_radius and the selected X, Y, and Z position:

```
sphere -r $curr_radius -p $curr_X $curr_Y $curr_Z;
```

If you wished to make a web form that controlled a different task, you would replace the makespheres procedure with a different procedure to perform that task.

The browserBack, browserForward, and browserHome procedures are very similar to each other:

```
global proc browserBack() {
    global string $myWebBrowser;

    webBrowser -e -back $myWebBrowser;

}

global proc browserForward() {
    global string $myWebBrowser;

    webBrowser -e -forward $myWebBrowser;

}

global proc browserHome() {
    global string $myWebBrowser;

    webBrowser -e -home $myWebBrowser;

}
```

Each of these procedures defines a global string $myWebBrowser, so that each is able to use the contents of that global variable within its code. Remember that failing to declare a global variable in a procedure before using it makes a new, empty local variable with the same name, which might lead to strange error messages or difficult-to-debug silent failures. This variable will contain the name of the web panel object in our dialog box window.

Each procedure then calls the webBrowser command in edit mode, using one of the flags -back, -forward, or -home to send the web browser back to the previous page, forward to the next page (if the user has already used the back button), and to the home page.

Finally, the make_js_web_panel procedure contains the script that builds the dialog window, including the browser's row of navigation buttons at the top:

```
global proc make_js_web_panel() {
    global string $myWebBrowser;
```

```
      string $myurl = (get_path_url() + "makesphereform.htm");
      print ($myurl + "\n");

      window -width 800 -height 632 -title "Make some spheres";
      columnLayout;
      rowLayout -numberOfColumns 3

            -columnWidth3 32 32 32
            -columnAlign 1 "right"
            -columnAttach 1 "both" 0
            -columnAttach 2 "both" 0
            -columnAttach 3 "both" 0;

      iconTextButton -c "browserBack()"
                -image "back.xpm";
      iconTextButton -c "browserForward()"
                -image "forward.xpm";
      iconTextButton -c "browserHome()"
                -image "homepage.xpm";

      setParent ..;
      $myWebBrowser = `webBrowser -url $myurl`;
      showWindow;

   }
```

First, the procedure defines the global string variable $myWebBrowser, to which it will assign the name of the web browser panel.

```
   global string $myWebBrowser;
```

Second, it calls get_path_url() and concatenates the result with make-sphereform.htm to create the file: URL that points to the web form.

```
   string $myurl = (get_path_url() + "makesphereform.htm");
   print ($myurl + "\n");
```

Then, it creates a window with a columnLayout and a rowLayout within the columnLayout. The columnLayout will arrange the row of buttons and the web panel vertically, while the rowLayout will arrange each button horizontally across the top of the window:

```
   window -width 800 -height 632 -title "Make some spheres";
   columnLayout;
   rowLayout -numberOfColumns 3

            -columnWidth3 32 32 32
            -columnAlign 1 "right"
            -columnAttach 1 "both" 0
            -columnAttach 2 "both" 0
            -columnAttach 3 "both" 0;
```

The rowLayout contains three iconTextButtons which call the browserBack, browserForward, and browserHome procedures. Each also uses the -image flag to choose an icon.

```
iconTextButton -c "browserBack()"
               -image "back.xpm";

iconTextButton -c "browserForward()"
               -image "forward.xpm";

iconTextButton -c "browserHome()"
               -image "homepage.xpm";
```

Since any icon available to the Maya user interface scripts is available to any other script, this procedure uses the names for the icons that are provided for the main web browser panel interface built by Maya when you choose Panels > Panel > Web Browser. Their names can be found by reading the code in the browser related files in Maya's startup scripts directory. You can find the path to this directory by looking at the Maya script path using the getenv("MAYA_SCRIPT_PATH") command.

The procedure then uses the setParent command to ensure that the webBrowser object gets placed in the columnLayout but not the rowLayout:

```
setParent ..;
```

Then, it creates the webBrowser panel (open to the URL of the web form), and places the name of the resulting Maya user interface object in the $myWebBrowser variable.

```
$myWebBrowser = `webBrowser -url $myurl`;
```

Finally, the procedure uses showWindow to display the window:

```
showWindow;

}
```

So far, we've seen that the MEL associated with this web-based dialog box has defined a window in which our web form, including rudimentary browsing controls, will be launched, and it has defined a procedure to implement the underlying function that the dialog box will control.

The HTML file, though, defines the bulk of the user interface for the makespheres procedure. First, the document is wrapped with standard <HTML> and </HTML> tags. Then, the header defines the title of the page plus the necessary JavaScript functions:

```
<HEAD>
<TITLE>Make Some Spheres...</TITLE>
<SCRIPT language="JavaScript">

function js_makespheres()
```

```
{
    var num_spheres =
        document.makespheres_form.num_spheres.value;

    var max_radius =
        document.makespheres_form.max_radius.value;

    var mel_url = 'mel://makespheres(' +num_spheres + ',' +
                    max_radius + ')/';

    location = mel_url;

}
</SCRIPT>
</HEAD>
```

The Submit button for the form calls js_makespheres() to build the MEL command to execute, to construct a URL for it, and to load the URL. First, it loads the values of the two fields on the form, num_spheres and max_radius, into variables with the same names:

```
var num_spheres =
document.makespheres_form.num_spheres.value;

var max_radius =
document.makespheres_form.max_radius.value;
```

Then, it creates a variable called mel_url that contains the appropriate URL for the MEL command to be executed:

```
var mel_url = 'mel://makespheres(' + num_spheres + ', ' +
max_radius + ')/';
```

For example, if num_spheres were 1000 and max_radius were 0.3, this MEL URL would become

```
mel://makespheres(1000, 0.3)/
```

Since makespheres is a global procedure that has been defined in the MEL file that loaded this form, this MEL URL will execute that procedure when it's loaded in the browser.

Finally, assigning the value of the mel_url variable to the default window's location attribute makes the web browser load the new URL. Usually, with a conventional http: or file: URL, this would load a new page, but in the case of a MEL URL, the browser continues to display the existing web page, and it simply instructs Maya to execute the embedded MEL command:

```
location = mel_url;
```

The body of the page is defined in this manner. A <FORM> tag and its counterpart </FORM> surround the controls that make up the form. The onSubmit attribute instructs the form to call js_makespheres() when the submit button is clicked. Also, return false; is necessary to prevent the form from attempting to use the legacy method to build a URL for a server-side CGI script, which it will otherwise try to do.

Two text input fields and a submit button are defined, using the <INPUT> tags, and finally, </FORM> ends the form, and </BODY> ends the page body:

```
<BODY>
<A href="http://www.melscripting.com/">
  go to melscripting.com
</A><P>
<FORM name="makespheres_form"
      onSubmit="js_makespheres(); return false;">
  <B>How many spheres do you want to make:</B>
  <INPUT type="text" name="num_spheres" size="30"><P>
  <b>Maximum radius:</b>
  <INPUT type="text" name="max_radius" size="30"><P>
  <INPUT type="submit" value="Make Spheres">
</FORM>
</BODY>
```

The trailing </HTML> tag completes the page's definition.

```
</HTML>
```

When the make_js_web_panel() MEL procedure is executed, then it calls get_path_url to build the URL to the enclosing directory for the HTML file, it builds a simple web browser window, and it creates a web panel that launches this HTML file. The HTML file defines a form that then uses JavaScript to build and load a MEL URL that instructs Maya to run the makespheres() command.

Using a more complex form to call a MEL procedure with more arguments is as simple as adding additional form objects to the HTML file, adding additional code to the js_makespheres JavaScript function to build a MEL URL that passes more arguments to a MEL procedure like makespheres(), and adding additional code to the MEL procedure it calls to handle the extra arguments.

Ideas for Dialog Boxes Built with Web Panels

The examples of dialog boxes built with web panels that have been presented in this chapter are quite simple, but the ease of building more complex applications in HTML and JavaScript and the ease of delivering these applications over a network can lend itself to solving problems that would be extremely difficult to solve with MEL alone:

- A web-delivered interface to an asset management system could load assets from a database-managed library into Maya and configure them for use with the click of a button.
- A web-based tutorial could describe what is to be done and provide a button that would set up a new Maya scene for the next step of the tutorial.
- A software vendor could develop a complex MEL application, such as a character rigging system, and deliver it to clients in real time over the web.
- A character interface could use Flash animations to provide advanced graphic feedback for the animator using the character.

Maya's web panel feature significantly broadens the range of what experiences a Maya user interface can present, and these ideas only scratch the surface.

What to Remember about Making Dialog Boxes with Web Panels

- Launching a web-based dialog box requires finding a path to the HTML document that contains the web form. One way to do this is to use the whatIs command to find the path to the function that launches the dialog box and break up the results to build a URL.
- You can build a web panel in a Maya window using the webBrowser command.
- Building a webBrowser object in a Maya window does not automatically give you basic navigation buttons. However, calling webBrowser in edit mode with the right flags can perform the functions of the back, forward, and home buttons.
- You can build forms that collect a user's input and call a MEL function using JavaScript. The onSubmit attribute for your form provides a JavaScript function to call, and the JavaScript function should collect the user's input from the form, build the MEL URL, and jump to it. Don't forget to return false in the onSubmit JavaScript so that the browser does not attempt to load a CGI script that doesn't exist.
- Since web-based dialog boxes are just web pages, you can mix controls with useful information, develop graphically and functionally complex user interfaces unimaginable in MEL, and take advantage of sophisticated web authoring tools that can help you build complex user interfaces for your MEL scripts extremely quickly.

17

Improving Performance with Utility Nodes

In this chapter you will learn

- What is a utility node?
- When to consider using a utility node in place of an expression.
- How to create and connect a utility node with your scene.
- What some of the common utility nodes are, and where to look up more information about them.

What Is a Utility Node?

A *utility node* is a dependency graph node that accepts one or more connections as input, performs a useful calculation, and produces an output that you can attach to another node. Utility nodes, like expressions, perform calculations on attributes as Maya evaluates the dependency graph in your scene, and they can often be used in place of simple expressions. Furthermore, utility nodes can be much faster than expressions that perform the same calculation, because Maya does not have to interpret a human-readable expression to evaluate them. However, since a given type of utility node can only perform a single, predefined task, expressions can be much more flexible if their relative slowness is not an issue.

Because utility nodes can be much faster than expressions, Maya users with a strong programming background often will implement certain common calculations as custom utility nodes using Maya's *plug-in* feature. Writing plug-ins requires skill with the C++ programming language and is beyond the scope of this book, but if you find yourself writing expressions that perform complex geometric calculations, you may find that you can combine writing a plug-in with using the techniques presented in this chapter to speed up your Maya scenes or to achieve things that are difficult to do with MEL. However, Maya provides a useful collection of utility nodes that you can use without having to develop plug-ins.

When Should You Consider Using a Utility Node?

While utility nodes can often be used in place of expressions, it can be easier to use expressions in your scene first, and then convert those expressions to utility nodes only when you begin to experience slowness in evaluating your scene.

Expression nodes can perform many operations in a single node. They are easy to read and change through the expression editor, and they automatically connect their own inputs and outputs to other nodes' attributes when you refer to an attribute in the expression. However, expression nodes can be substantially slower than utility nodes for computations that are run many times in evaluating your scene because evaluating the expression's code is slower than executing code that was written in C++ and compiled to create a utility node.

Use utility nodes in custom shading networks.

If you are developing shading networks in Maya to create unusual effects, particularly if you are using a `samplerInfo` node to evaluate points on a surface, calculate a color, and return that color to the object's surface shader, you should always use utility nodes in preference to expressions.

Shading networks that use `samplerInfo` nodes to sample the surface are calculated many times per rendered image. While it is possible to use expressions in such shading networks, the speed penalty of even a single expression node is multiplied hundreds of thousands or millions of times per image.

Because utility nodes are particularly suitable for shading networks, Maya's Hypershade editor provides tabs labeled "General Utilities," "Switch Utilities," and "Particle Utilities" that contain convenient buttons to create utility nodes and connect them with other nodes in your shading networks.

Use utility nodes in place of expressions when many expressions will need to be evaluated in the scene.

Utility nodes can be useful if you are creating a large number of rigged objects for applications like foliage or crowd character rigs. Duplicating tens or hundreds of a character's rig for a crowd, for example, can be inter-actively cumbersome and slow to evaluate. Heavy use of expressions can make this problem much worse. By replacing these expressions with utility nodes, you can improve your scene's performance.

How to Create and Connect a Utility Node

Suppose that you want to create two spheres, connected such that the second sphere's Y-axis position is the first sphere's X-axis position, multiplied by −1.

Creating this connection with an expression is simple:

1. Make a new scene by choosing File > New Scene.
2. Create the first sphere by choosing Create > NURBS Primitives > Sphere.
3. Create the second sphere by repeating Step 2.
4. Using the Outliner, select `nurbsSphere2`.
5. In the Channel Box or Attribute Editor, right-click on the translate Y attribute and choose Create New Expression. . .
6. Enter this expression:

    `ty = −nurbsSphere1.tx;`

7. Click the Create button in the Expression Editor.
8. In the Outliner, select `nurbsSphere1`; choose the move tool, and move the sphere along the X axis. `nurbsSphere2` should move along the Y axis when you do this.

Note that, in this example, creating the expression made all the necessary connections between `nurbsSphere1` and `nurbsSphere2`. To see this, open the Hypergraph with `nurbsSphere1` selected, and click on the Input and Output Connections button (or choose Graph > Input and Output Connections from the menu).

You will see that `nurbsSphere1` has been connected to a new expression1 node, the output of which Maya has connected to `nurbsSphere2` (Figure 17.1).

To create the corresponding connection with a utility node, you must find one or more utility nodes whose functions duplicate the operations in your expression. Some expressions cannot be replaced by utility nodes in this way. In this case, the `multiplyDivide` utility node can produce exactly the same result as the expression, if we use the `multiplyDivide` node to multiply the tx attribute of `nurbsSphere1` by −1.

Unlike an expression, which connects itself, you must create the reverse node and connect it to the sphere's transform nodes by hand.

1. Make a new scene by choosing File > New Scene.
2. Create the first sphere by choosing Create > NURBS Primitives > Sphere.

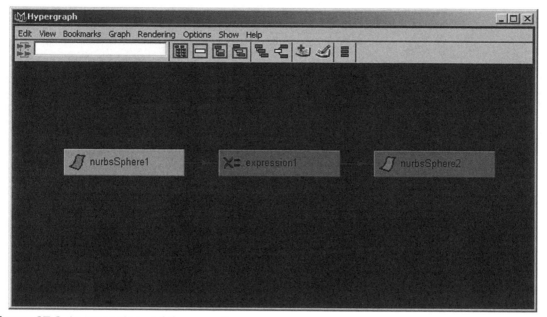

Figure 17.1 An expression node's connections.

3. Create the second sphere by repeating Step 2.
4. In the Script Editor, execute the command

```
createNode multiplyDivide
```

5. At this point, the new reverse node should be selected. Open the Attribute Editor. Under Multiply-Divide Attributes; you'll see two triplets of attributes, labeled Input1 and Input2. Set the first of Input2's attributes (which is called Input2 X, though the attribute editor does not display this) to –1. Also, make sure the Operation pop-up menu is set to Multiply.
6. Open the Connection Editor by choosing Window > General Editors > Connection Editor. . . .
7. Click on the Reload Right button. The multiplyDivide1 node's attributes should appear on the right side of the Connection Editor.
8. Open the Outliner, and choose nurbsSphere1, then click on Reload Left in the Connection Editor.
9. Now, since the Translate X attribute of nurbsSphere1 will drive the motion of the other sphere, open the Translate tab, and click on Translate X on the left side of the Connection Editor.
10. On the right side of the Connection Editor, open the Input tab, and choose Input1 X. (Because the multiplyDivide node is designed to be able to operate on a color or a location in space, it can multiply

or divide up to three pairs of numbers at one time.) This makes the connection between the Translate X attribute of `nurbsSphere1` and the input of the `multiplyDivide1` node.

11. In the Script Editor, execute the command

```
select multiplyDivide1
```

12. In the Connection Editor, click Reload Left to load the `multiplyDivide1` node's outputs on the left side of the editor.
13. Select `nurbsSphere2` in the Outliner, and click Reload Right in the Connection Editor.
14. Connect Output X on the `multiplyDivide1` node to the Translate Y input of `nurbsSphere2`.
15. Try moving `nurbsSphere1` in X, and see what happens.

If you open the Hypergraph and look at `multiplyDivide1`'s input and output connections as before, you will see the connections you made (Figure 17.2).

In this case, the connections look very similar to the equivalent expression's connections. However, you might need to create and connect multiple utility nodes to get the same result as a more complex expression.

When you're experimenting, it can be useful to create and connect nodes using the Connection Editor or the Hypershade window. However,

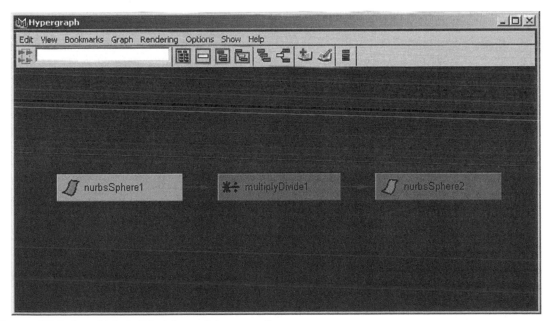

Figure 17.2 A `multiplyDivide` node's connections.

once you know exactly what you wish to connect, you can do the work with a short MEL script:

```
file -force -new;
sphere;
sphere;
createNode multiplyDivide;
setAttr multiplyDivide1.i2x -1;
connectAttr nurbsSphere1.tx multiplyDivide1.i1x;
connectAttr multiplyDivide1.ox nurbsSphere2.ty;
```

While this is not as simple as the expression-based script

```
file -force -new;
sphere;
sphere;
expression -s "nurbsSphere2.ty = -nurbsSphere1.tx";
```

your scene will execute without the overhead of evaluating the expression, a savings that can in many cases (though probably not this example) be significant.

Example 1: Using the plusMinusAverage Node to Find the Midpoint Between Two Locators

Suppose that you wish to use plusMinusAverage to find the midpoint between two locators in world space and place a third locator there:

1. Make a new scene, and create two locators with the default names locator1 and locator2, as well as a plusMinusAverage node by executing these commands in the script editor:

```
file -f -new;
spaceLocator;
spaceLocator;
createNode plusMinusAverage;
```

2. Connect the translate attributes of locator1 and locator2 to plusMinusAverage1's input3D input. Note that because translate is a float3 (or float triplet) attribute, it must be connected to elements of the input3D array:

```
connectAttr locator1.translate plusMinusAverage1.input3D[0];
connectAttr locator2.translate plusMinusAverage1.input3D[1];
```

3. Make a third locator with the default name locator3

```
spaceLocator;
```

4. Connect the `output3D` attribute of `plusMinusAverage1` to the translate attribute for `locator3`:

   `connectAttr plusMinusAverage1.output3D locator3.translate;`

5. Finally, set `plusMinusAverage1`'s operation attribute to 3, to tell it to average (rather than add or subtract) the inputs to set the output:

   `setAttr plusMinusAverage1.operation 3;`

Now, try moving `locator1` and `locator 2` with the move tool. You'll see that `locator3` remains centered between them, because its x, y, and z translation attributes are being set to the averages of `locator1` and `locator2`'s x, y, and z translation attributes.

Common Utility Nodes

Maya's *Node and Attribute Reference* describes each type of utility node in detail, and it is a good place to start if you are trying to develop a network of nodes that achieves some particular result. Here are some of the more common kinds of utility nodes to investigate.

plusMinusAverage

The `plusMinusAverage` node can add, subtract, or average a series of float values, pairs of floats, or triplets of floats.

Single float values are plugged into the elements of an array input called `input1D`; pairs of float values are plugged into the elements of an array input called `input2D`, and triplets of float values are plugged into the elements of an array input called `input3D`.

The operation input specifies whether the node should do nothing, add, subtract, or average the inputs to produce the output value.

multiplyDivide

The `multiplyDivide` node can multiply or divide one, two, or three float values at a time. Inputs and outputs are similar to those of the `plusMinusAverage` node.

vectorProduct

The `vectorProduct` node allows you to multiply vectors and matrices in all the common combinations used in 3D arithmetic, including dot product, cross product, and products between a vector and a matrix and products between a point in space and a matrix.

condition

The condition node allows you to compare two input values and choose an output, based on the relationship (for example, greater than, less than, equal) between the inputs. Note that the `condition` command in MEL is not related to this node.

setRange

The `setRange` node allows you to scale and offset a range of input values into a different range of outputs, for example converting a range of 0 to 1 to a range of 0 to 255. This can be particularly useful when manipulating color values or scaling animation curves.

What to Remember About Improving Performance With Utility Nodes

- That a utility node is a tool for performing certain simple calculations quickly and without coding in Maya's dependency graph, at the cost of having to create and connect the node yourself.
- That when you can replace an expression with a utility node, you can achieve a notable increase in speed.
- That not every expression is a good candidate for replacement with utility nodes – focus on simple expressions that are executed many hundreds or thousands of times as the scene is evaluated.
- That the *Node and Attribute Reference* is the definitive source for information about what utility nodes are available and what their input and output attributes do.

18

Installing MEL Scripts

In this chapter you will learn

- How to make your scripts available in all of your scenes.
- How to run a script whenever Maya starts.
- How to add a script to your scene as a script node, so that it stays with that scene as it is copied from machine to machine.
- How to create a custom menu item.
- How to add a MEL command as a shelf button and customize its icon.

Installing a Script to Make It Available in All Scenes

To make scripts available in all Maya scenes, you must first create a text file that contains your script and whose name ends in .mel. The easiest way to do this is to use the Script Editor's Save selected . . . command to save a selection into a .mel file.

You can use the source command by hand to run the contents of your .mel file wherever it is on disk. However, if you want to make it available without manually using source, you can install your script in the Maya *script path*.

The script path is the list of directories that Maya searches for MEL scripts that you have installed. By default, it points to a few standard places in your home directory and to a few standard places in the Maya installation directory.

You can look at the directories in the Maya script path by typing the following command in the Script Editor:

```
getenv "MAYA_SCRIPT_PATH";
```

Typically, the result will look something like the following (although it may vary based on operating system and what Maya options you have installed):

```
// Result: C:/Documents and Settings/mark/My
Documents/maya/projects/ default/mel;C:/Documents and
    Settings/mark/My
Documents/maya/4.0/scripts;C:/Documents and Settings/mark/My
Documents/maya/scripts;C:/Documents and Settings/mark/My
Documents/maya/4.0/presets;C:/Documents and Settings/mark/My
Documents/maya/4.0/prefs/shelves;C:/Documents and
    Settings/mark/My Documents/
maya/4.0/prefs/markingMenus;C: /AW/Maya4.0/scripts/
startup;C:/AW/Maya4.0/scripts/others;C:/AW/Maya4.0/scripts/AE
    Templates //
```

To install a script so that it is available in all of your scenes, take the following steps:

- Run `getenv "MAYA_SCRIPT_PATH"` in Maya to verify the directories in your script path.
- Make sure that the procedure you wish to make available is defined as a global procedure in a `.mel` file whose name is `<procedure name>.mel` (where `<procedure name>` is the name of your global procedure).
- Place this file in one of the directories in the script path.

Once a global procedure is installed in this way, you can run it without loading, sourcing, or otherwise running the `.mel` file by hand before you call the procedure.

Installing a Script to Run When Maya Starts

To make a procedure run whenever you start Maya, first install it in the script path as described in the previous section. Then, edit your `userPrefs .mel` file to include a call to the procedure. The commands in `userPrefs .mel` are run whenever you start Maya. This file is in the `maya/<version>/prefs` directory under your home directory (or in Windows, in your `My Documents` directory). The `<version>` part is the version of Maya you're running, such as 4.0. Once you have edited `userPrefs.mel`, you should quit Maya and start it again to run your edited `userPrefs.mel` script.

Installing a Script into a Script Node in a Scene

A *script node* is similar to an expression node, except that the script it contains is triggered by an event taking place, rather than by the directed graph's recalculation. To make a script node, open the Expression Editor by choosing Window > Animation Editors > Expression Editor. . . . In the Expression Editor menu bar, choose Select Filter > By Script Node Name. Once you do this, you are in script node editing mode (Figure 18.1).

If you want the script itself to run when your scene opens or closes, or when another event that can trigger a script node occurs (such as when a frame is about to be rendered), the script you type into the Expression Editor should be a series of MEL commands that are not enclosed in a procedure. Pick an option from the Execute On: menu to determine when your script will execute. Each of those events has a Before and an After script that can be run before or after the specified event starts or finishes, respectively.

If you want to define a procedure that can be called any time you have your scene open, set your script node to execute on Open/Close, and set the Script radio button to Before. Then, define a global procedure. When your scene opens, this global procedure will be defined, and you can use it

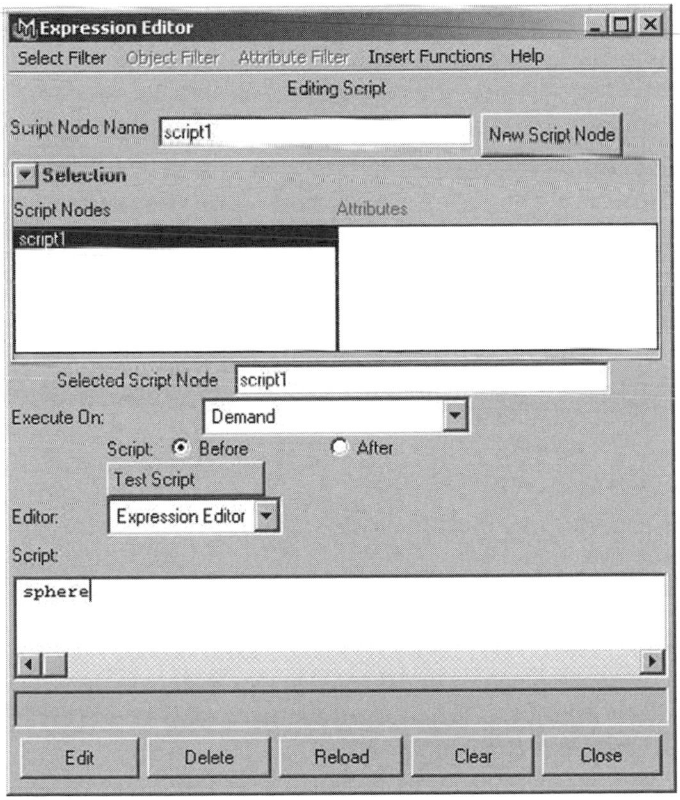

Figure 18.1 Expression Editor in script node editing mode.

whenever you like. However, since it is defined as a procedure and is not simply a series of MEL commands, it will not actually execute until you choose to run it, either by typing its name into the Script Editor and pressing Enter on the numeric keypad, or by calling it from another script.

Installing Custom Menus

Installing custom menus in the main menu bar works just like adding menus to a dialog box. However, instead of adding the menus to your dialog box window, you must add them to the main Maya window.

The name of the main Maya window object is stored in a global variable called $gMainWindow. You can use the setParent command to indicate that you want to add your menu items to the main window's menu bar by doing something like the following:

```
global string $gMainWindow;
setParent $gMainWindow;

  menu -label "Mark's Menu2";

    menuItem -label "Make a Sphere" -command "sphere";
    menuItem -divider true;
    menuItem -label "Make a Cone" -command "cone";
```

For example, you could put such code in a script node as an Open/Close script, or you could put it in a global procedure and install it in your scripts directory. However, chances are that you want this custom menu to be available at all times. The solution is to put the above commands into a file named userSetup.mel in your <home directory>/maya/scripts directory. Then, whenever Maya starts, your menu will be added.

Managing Button Shelves and Creating Custom Shelf Icons

You can select a MEL command in the Script Editor and middle-mouse-drag the command to the Tool Shelf to create a MEL button (Figure 18.2). To delete a MEL button, middle-mouse-drag it to the trash can icon on the right. To edit the menu items, click on the menu indicated by the downward-pointing arrow on the left, and then choose Shelf Editor . . . (Figure 18.3).

If you create your own shelf icon by creating a .xpm or .bmp image file, you can assign the icon to your MEL script using the Change Image . . . button in the Shelf Editor window. Using a simple icon as a visual reminder of what your script does can help you distinguish among the scripts on your shelf.

Figure 18.2 Tool shelf.

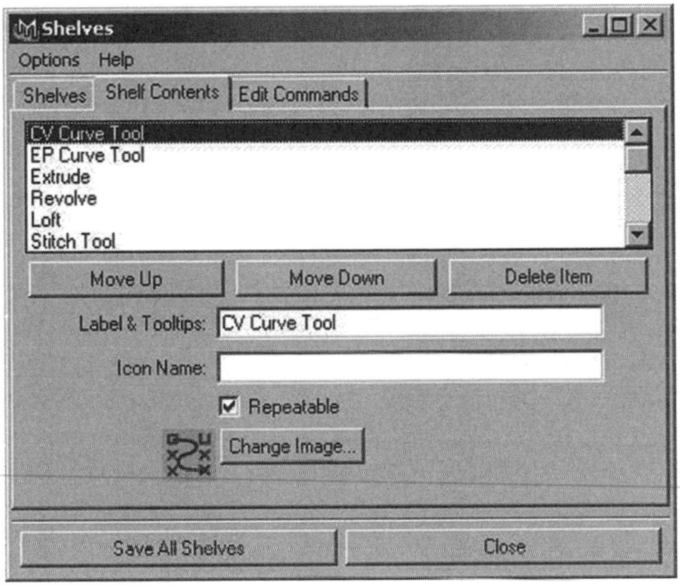

Figure 18.3 Shelf Editor.

What to Remember About Installing MEL Scripts

■ The first step to installing your MEL script is to put your global procedure definition in either a `.mel` file in the Maya script path or in a script
node in your scene.

■ Putting a script in a script node is most useful if you need the script to
go wherever your scene goes. Putting a script in the Maya script path
makes the most sense if it is a utility you want around for all of your
scenes.

■ You can add a menu and menu items by creating a `userSetup.mel` file
in your script path that finds the main Maya window from the
`$gMainWindow` global variable and adds new menus to it. Maya will
run this script when Maya starts up, installing your menu and menu
items.

■ You can middle-mouse-drag your commands to the shelf, and if you
like you can use the Shelf Editor to install a custom icon for your shelf
button.

19

Examples Using MEL with Particle Dynamics

As we saw in Chapter 4, you can use particle expressions to achieve fine control over the dynamics of particle systems by directly manipulating particles' positions, velocities, and accelerations.

An approach that is more useful in many circumstances, however, is to use MEL and expressions to manipulate particle goals. Using goals, you can use your scripts to influence particle motion while you still take advantage of fields and collisions. Rather than entirely bypassing the dynamics system as you do when you directly control particle position, velocity, or acceleration, by using goals to influence particles you can strike a suitable balance between your scripted behavior and the influence of collision objects and fields in your scene.

The examples in this chapter explore some of the ways that you can manipulate particle goals in your scripts.

Example 1: Introduction to Particle Goals

What are goals? Simply, a goal is like a "particle constraint" between different particle systems or between particle systems and objects. A goal relationship is like a controlled elastic cord that has an adjustable tension. To a greater or lesser degree, depending on the goal settings, a particle attempts to place itself where the goal is (Figure 19.1).

Goals can be more useful in controlling simulations than fields. Let's create a couple of particles and see how goals can be used to control them.

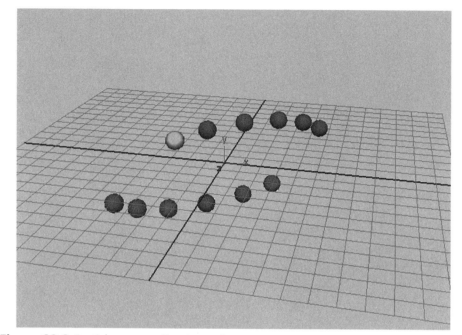

Figure 19.1 Particles responding to goals.

First, create two particles in the Script Editor, as follows:

```
particle -p -5 0 5 -name partOne;
particle -p 5 0 -5 -name partTwo;
```

(Remember to use the Enter key on the numeric keypad to execute MEL commands in the Script Editor, not the Return key on the main keyboard.)

The first `particle` command will create a particle system containing a single particle at position (`-p`) -5 in X, 0 in Y, and 5 in Z. The second will create a particle system containing a single particle at a mirrored position. Each particle system has a unique name. Now let's apply a goal from partOne to partTwo, as follows:

```
goal -goal partTwo -weight 0.5 partOne;
```

The above statement will make the particle in partOne try to follow the particle in partTwo. The weight flag will tell partOne how closely to follow partTwo. The weight attribute has a range from 0 to 1, with 0 representing no constraint on the particle's motion, and 1 representing an absolute constraint to particle2. Values between 0 and 1 cause the following particle to behave as though it were tied to the particle it follows by an elastic connection whose elasticity is established by the weight. A weight near 0 is highly elastic, and a weight near 1 is inelastic.

Before you play back the resulting animation, change the render type of the particles to the sphere type. To do this, you can use the following commands:

```
setAttr partOneShape.particleRenderType 4;
setAttr partTwoShape.prt 4;
```

The commands to change the render type for each of the different particle objects are the same, but in this instance we are using the short attribute name to set the particle render type for partTwoShape rather than the long attribute name used for partOneShape. For the remaining examples in this chapter, we will continue to use both the long and the short attribute names.

Make sure that your timeline has been set to end at frame 300 or so. If you want, you can set the timeline minimum and maximum frame using MEL, as follows:

```
playbackOptions -min 1 -max 300;
```

Now play back your animation (Figure 19.2). You should see partOne moving towards partTwo, overshooting it, and oscillating until it settles down exactly where partTwo is. The particle overshoots because of the weight attribute setting, which behaves like a tension control for the goal.

To see the effect of goal weight, try setting the goal weight to 1, rewind, and play back your animation again:

```
setAttr partOne.goalWeight[0] 1.0;
```

partOne will now stick to the position of partTwo.

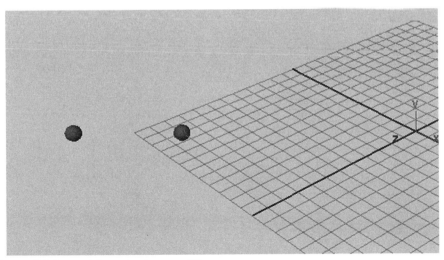

Figure 19.2 partOne chasing partTwo.

If we make partTwo a goal of partOne, we can watch the goals try to keep up with each other throughout the animation.

The attribute .goalWeight[0] is an array because an object system can have multiple goals. [0] would be the first; [1] would be the second, and so on.

Let's go back to the original weight of 0.5 and set a new goal between partTwo and partOne, as follows:

```
setAttr partOne.goalWeight[0] 0.5;
goal -w 0.5 -g partOne partTwo;
```

Now play back the scene one more time (Figure 19.3). partTwo and partOne are mutually attracted to each other until they finally settle down around where partOne originally was. The reason for this is the particle sampling order of goal assignment. Sampling can be thought of as how many "slices," or samples, are evaluated during the simulation. More samples increase the accuracy and detail in the motion of the simulation.

Adding Color and Radius

Let's add some color and use Maya's hardware shading so we can get a better idea of what's going on. We will also add a radius control to reduce the

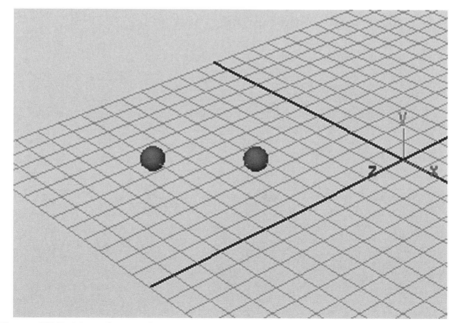

Figure 19.3 Mutual attraction.

size of the particle. First, in the Script Editor, let's add the color attribute for each particle:

```
addAttr -longName colorGreen -defaultValue 1
        -attributeType double partOneShape;
addAttr -ln colorRed -dv 1 -at double partTwoShape;
```

Be sure to set the Maya interface into shaded mode under the Shading menu in the perspective window. Previousl,y we set the particles to the "sphere" display model (particleRenderType4). Now let's add an attribute to control the radius of the displayed particle "sphere" and set its size to 0.5.

```
addAttr -longName radius -defaultValue 0.5 partOneShape;
addAttr -ln radius -dv 0.5 partTwoShape;
```

Note: A radius of 0.5 is a good viewing size for a Maya environment of grid size 5.0, subdivisions 5, and extent 12.0000. To use these settings, select Display > Grid ❐.

Adding Velocity

Let's also add some Y motion in both positive and negative directions to curve our particles' trajectories. We'll do this by adding a velocity to each of the particle systems, as follows:

```
particle -edit -id 0 -attribute velocity
         -vectorValue 0 2 0 partOne;
particle -e -id 0 -at velocity -vv 0 -2 0 partTwo;
```

A velocity *vector* for a particle has both a direction and a magnitude (or *speed*). Figure 19.4 shows a visualization of the number sets that were input in for partTwo.

Once again, let's change some of the two particles' attributes to make the animation a little more interesting. In the Script Editor, we are going to change the particle's goal weight, as follows:

```
setAttr partOne.goalWeight[0] 0.2;
setAttr partTwo.goalWeight[0] 0.2;
```

This will reduce the particle's attraction to one another and, therefore, the violence of the particle oscillation. Now rewind your animation and play (Figure 19.5).

As you can see, each particle's motion is controlled both by its velocity vector and also by the goals that we had set up before. Figure 19.6 shows a graph of how Maya assigns velocity to particles with goals.

Now we have all of the MEL code to make this simple goal example a stand-alone script that can be executed in Maya. Reproduced below is the full code for helloGoal.mel. Enter the code into a text file and save.

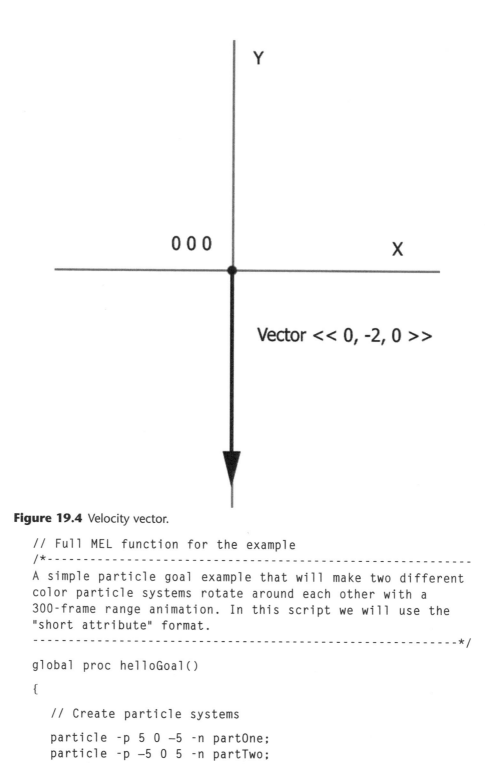

Figure 19.4 Velocity vector.

```
// Full MEL function for the example
/*-----------------------------------------------------------
A simple particle goal example that will make two different
color particle systems rotate around each other with a
300-frame range animation. In this script we will use the
"short attribute" format.
----------------------------------------------------------*/

global proc helloGoal()

{

    // Create particle systems

    particle -p 5 0 -5 -n partOne;
    particle -p -5 0 5 -n partTwo;
```

```
    // Set rendering type to sphere

    setAttr partOne.prt 4;
    setAttr partTwo.prt 4;

    // Set radius size

    addAttr -ln radius -dv 0.5 partOneShape;
    addAttr -ln radius -dv 0.5 partTwoShape;

    // Set particle colors

    addAttr -ln colorGreen -dv 1 -at double partOneShape;
    addAttr -ln colorRed -dv 1 -at double partTwoShape;

    // Add goals to each set of particles: 1 to 2, 2 to 1

    goal -g partTwo -w 0.2 partOne;
    goal -g partOne -w 0.2 partTwo;

    // Add velocity vectors to particles in +Y and −Y

    particle -e -at velocity -id 0 -vv 0 3 0 partOne;
    particle -e -at velocity -id 0 -vv 0 −3 0 partTwo;

    // Set goal smoothness for each goal
    // This will create a smooth "curved" transition
    // from one goal to another

    setAttr partOneShape.goalSmoothness 4.0;
    setAttr partTwoShape.goalSmoothness 4.0;

    // Set playback range to 1 − 300

    playbackOptions -min 1 -max 300;

}
```

Now that the script is in a text file, we need to *source* it in Maya. This process will define the function `helloGoal` within Maya. Open the Script Editor, and access the Source menu to load the script (Figure 19.7).

In the Script Editor, just type `helloGoal`, press Enter, and the example will load. That's it! You now have a function that Maya knows and can be used in other scripts.

Example 2: Particle Goals on a Surface

Now that we have talked about goals between particles, we will explore setting goals for particles on a NURBS surface (Figure 19.8). First, let's look at a patch and see how we can control particles on it by setting goals at particular U and V coordinates (UVs). Figure 19.9 shows how the UVs are arranged on a NURBS patch.

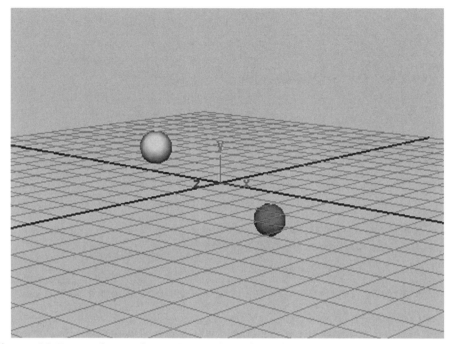

Figure 19.5 partOne and partTwo with goal weights.

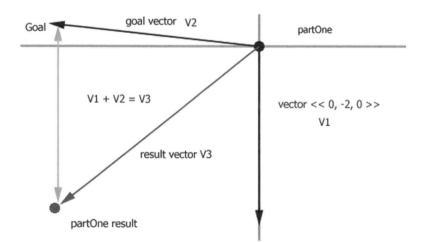

Figure 19.6 How Maya combines velocity vectors with goal attraction.

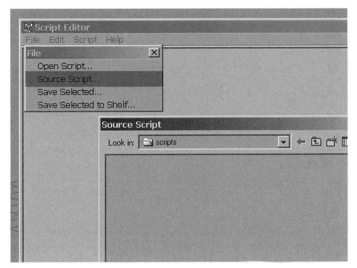

Figure 19.7 Script Editor's file menu.

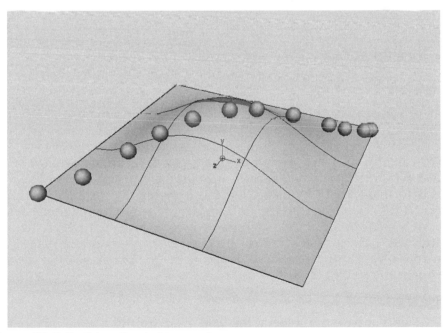

Figure 19.8 Particles attracted to a surface.

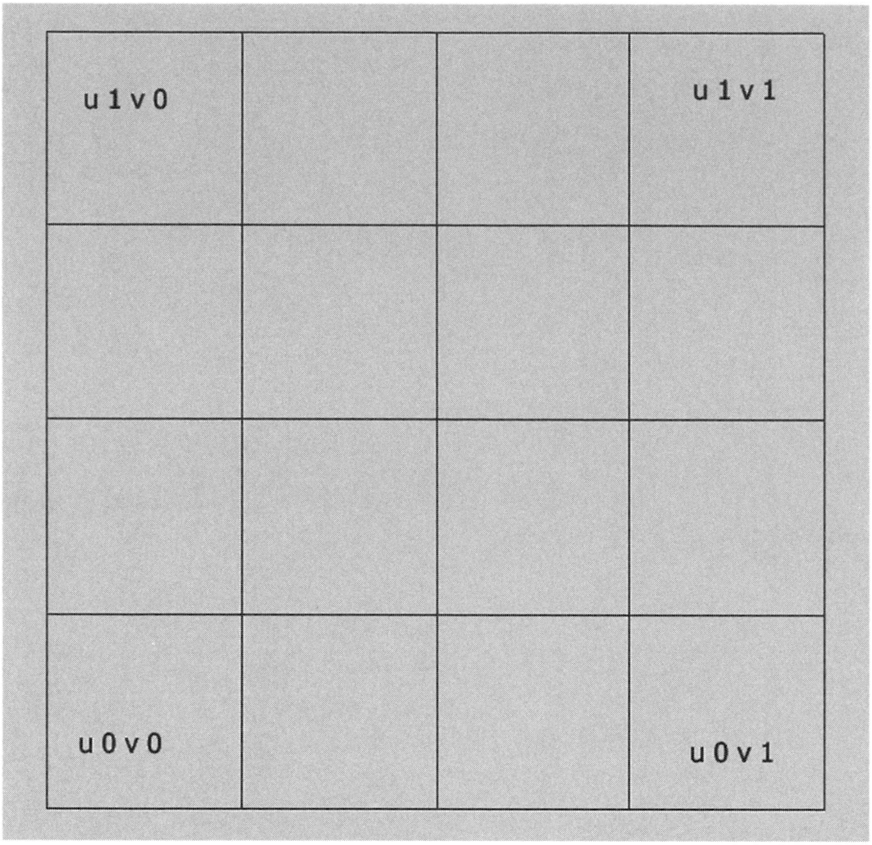

Figure 19.9 U and V parameters on NURBS patch.

If you have experience with texture mapping, you might be familiar with how texture mapping using UVs works. As you distort and manipulate the patch, the UVs stick to the surface, as shown in Figure 19.10.

We can attract a particle to a particular point on a surface selected by its U and V value by using two particle attributes, goalU and goalV. The first step is to make a NURBS plane. For this example, let's use the standard Maya NURBS plane because the UVs are guaranteed to be well behaved. If you use a plane or any other patch that you have made though an extrude or loft, you have to watch the construction of the curves and make sure that your UVs are properly placed. To create the NURBS plane, type the following in the Script Editor:

```
nurbsPlane -p 0 0 0 -ax 0 1 0 -w 1 -lr 1 -d 3 -u 1 -v 1 -ch 1;
```

(If you wish to see what some of the flags mean for this command, see the online MEL documentation.) Figure 19.11 shows the resulting plane. If

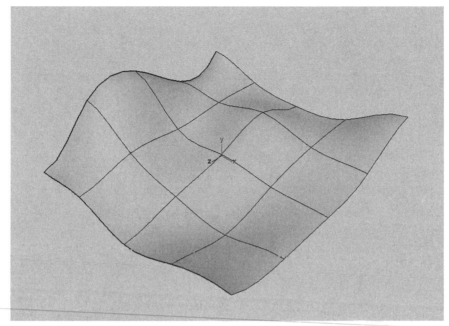

Figure 19.10 U and V parameters on a more complex surface.

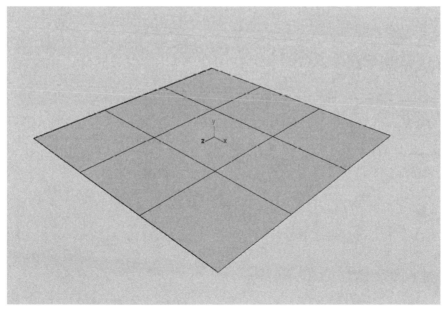

Figure 19.11 The resulting plane.

your plane looks too small, you can scale it up. The UVs will scale up with the surface. If you do not see the isoparams on your plane, select it and press "3" to set the display of the surface to full resolution.

Let's add an emitter with a rate of two particles per second. To do this, use the Maya interface rather than MEL. From the Particles menu in the Dynamics menu, go to the Create Emitter option box, making sure that the options are set to Omni with an emission rate of 2. Click Create to make the emitter.

Then, move the emitter up in Y 3 units to get it out of the way of the plane. Following is the MEL code to create the emitter, just for reference. As you can see, the Maya interface takes care of some relationships between the particles and the emitter.

```
emitter -type omni -pos 0 3 0 -r 2;
particle -n particle1;
connectDynamic -em emitter1 particle1;
```

Now, make the nurbsPlane the goal for the particles. Again, we can create the goal relationship from the Maya menu or make the connection in MEL. Select Window > Outliner. This a handy window to have up all the time since you can directly select objects inside hierarchies instead of hunting for them in the camera window. Select particle1, and then hold down the Ctrl key to select the nurbsPlane. Now go to the Particles window, and select the Goal section. Alternatively, if you would like to use MEL to set up the goal, type the following in the Script Editor, and press Enter:

```
goal -w 1.0 -utr 0 -g nurbsPlane1 particle1;
```

Now, let's set the particle render type to sphere, like before. Select the particle object, and open the Attribute Editor; click the Particle Render Type button, and then select sphere. Or, to set the render type in MEL, type the following in the Script Editor, and press Enter:

```
setAttr particle1Shape.particleRenderType 4;
```

Click the Current Render Type button to load the options for that type. Only one new render option, radius, will appear for the sphere render type. A setting of 0.5 should be fine. Remember the MEL code for doing this in Example 1?

```
addAttr -is true -ln radius -at "float" -min 0 -max 1
        -dv 0.5 particle1Shape;
```

To see how the patch goal (nurbsPlane) affects the particles, set your playback start time to 1 and your playback end time to 360 in the Maya interface and play, or use the following MEL command:

```
playbackOptions -min 1 -max 360;
```

Now play. Figure 19.12 shows the result.

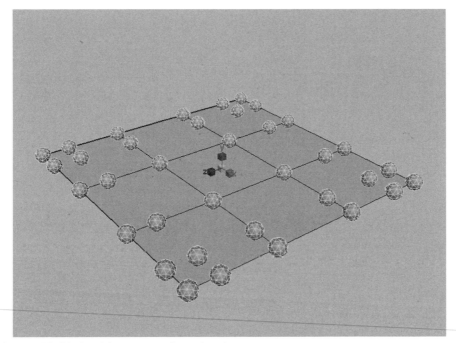

Figure 19.12 Particles attracted to plane's components.

If you select the nurbsPlane and switch to component mode by pressing F9, you can see that a particle will settle at each of the control vertices (CVs). The default UV goal assignment is to match up newly created particles to the UV locations of CVs on the goal surface sequentially. Because this usually will not produce the desired effect, we have to add some attributes to the particle system that will enable a more arbitrary UV to particle relation. With the particle system selected (particle1), open the Attribute Editor (Ctrl-A) to add some new attributes.

Per Particle Arrays

Access the Add Dynamic Attribute section, and click the General button. Now click the Particle tab. You should get a list of all sorts of new particle attributes, both per-particle and particle system attributes, that we can use. Look for the goalU and goalV attributes. Add them by selecting with the mouse and holding down the Ctrl key, which acts as a multiselect in the list (Figure 19.13). Click Add, and then Close. The attributes will now show up in the Per Particle (Array) Attributes section.
The MEL code for adding the attributes follows:

```
addAttr -ln goalU -dt doubleArray particle1Shape;
addAttr -ln goalU0 -dt doubleArray particle1Shape;
```

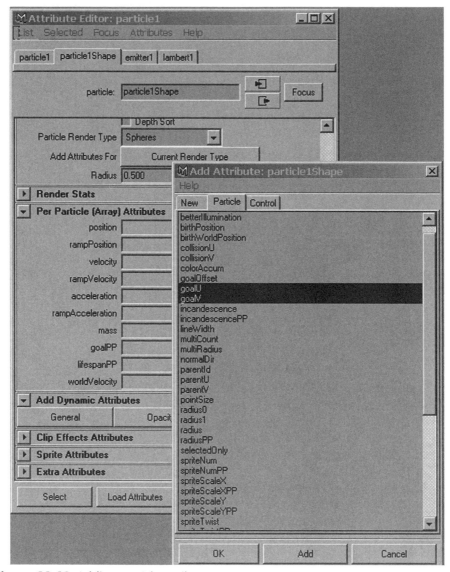

Figure 19.13 Adding particle attributes.

```
addAttr -ln goalV -dt doubleArray particle1Shape;
addAttr -ln goalV0 -dt doubleArray particle1Shape;
```

Initial States

The addAttr calls add the per-particle goalU and goalV attributes along with the per-particle attributes goalU0 and goalV0. In this instance, Maya adds `goalU0` and `goalV0` automatically. These attributes contain the initial values for `goalU` and `goalV`.

In order to start using the new attributes that we have just added, let's use expressions. For particles, expressions are divided into two different types: creation and runtime.

Expressions and the Expression Editor

Think of a creation expression as an expression that defines what the particle will do at birth time and the runtime expression as an expression that defines what the particle does once it is born. It's a good idea at the time you start entering the expression to put a comment at the top to remind you, as in

    // Runtime

or

    // Creation

When you're going back and forth between expressions, such a comment is a good visual note (Figure 19.14).

Select particle1 in the interface, and open the Attribute Editor. Scroll down the window to Per Particle (Array) Attributes. These are some of the attributes that you can set on a per-particle basis. The one that we need right now is the `goalU` attribute. With the right mouse button, select the blank box beside velocity, and hold down the mouse button. You will see the options *Creation Expression, Runtime Expression Before Dynamics, Runtime Expression After Dynamics,* and *Component Editor.*

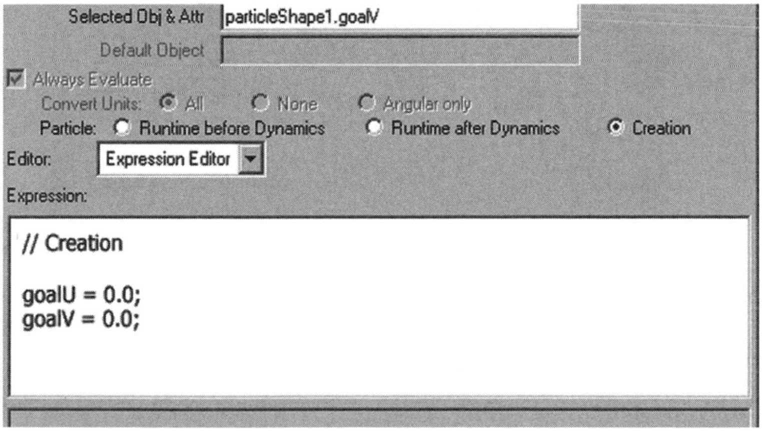

Figure 19.14 Editing the creation expression.

Choose Creation Expression, and the Expression Editor will open. Type in the following:

```
// Creation
goalU = 0.0;
goalV = 0.0;
```

Select the Create button to commit the expression, and click Close. We need to access Expression Editor again and enter our runtime expression, but we will do this from the Maya interface. Select Windows > Animation Editors > Expression Editor. In the Expression Editor, choose the Select Filter > By Expression pulldown menu option. This will show our current expression, so we should see `particleShape1` in the list (Figure 19.15). Select it, and we will be back where we were before in the Creation section.

Now select the Runtime After Dynamics option as shown in Figure 19.16.

Enter the runtime expression shown in Figure 19.17.

```
// Runtime
goalU = age;
goalV = age;
```

Click Create, and then Close again.

Age is a built-in attribute of the particle's age through time. Before we play the animation, let's distort the plane a bit so that we can see the particles forming to the surface UVs of the patch. In the Script Editor type the following code:

```
select -r nurbsPlane1.cv[1:2][1:2];
move -a 0 4.0 0;
```

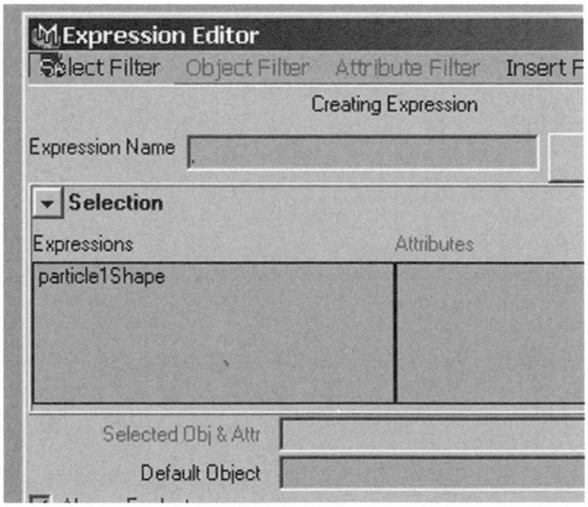

Figure 19.15 Selecting by expression in Expression Editor.

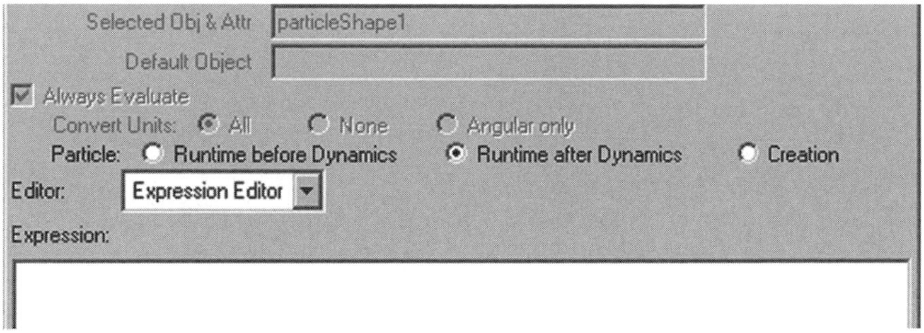

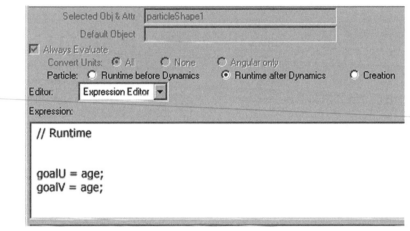

Figure 19.16 Picking the runtime option.

Figure 19.17 The runtime expression.

You might have to adjust the height in Y according to the scale you have set.

We are selecting the CVs on the surface and moving them 4.0 units in Y. The [1:2][1:2] syntax identifies the rows and columns on the surface. The -r flag in the select call means replace, and it ensures that nothing else is selected before we move the CVs. The -a flag means absolute instead of relative space. Figure 19.18 shows the results when you play this animation. This script will simply send the particles diagonally across the surface.

Watching Values of Particles

Let's watch the age change over the surface as the animation plays. To do this we need to set a new render type for the particles and tell them which attribute to display. Change the render type to numeric and the attribute name to age to watch age change over the surface UVs.

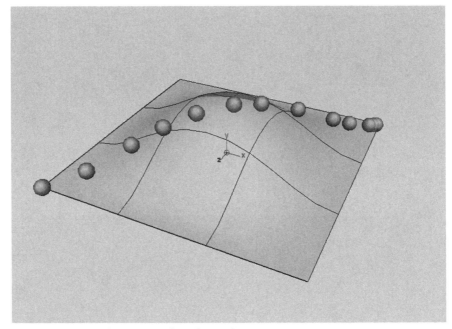

Figure 19.18 Particles attracted to the surface.

```
setAttr particle1Shape.particleRenderType 2;
addAttr -is true -ln pointSize -at long -min 1 -max 60
    -dv 2 particle1Shape;
addAttr -is true -ln selectedOnly -at bool
    -dv false particle1Shape;
addAttr -is true -dt "string" -ln attributeName particle1Shape;
setAttr -type "string" particle1Shape.attributeName age;
```

The above script can also be executed in the interface in the Attribute Editor as before (Figure 19.19).

We can also change the displayed attribute name to goalU or goalV and watch the particle values change. Try some others while you're there, such as velocity, position, and id. You will discover that it is very handy to visually see the values change over time instead of printing outputs and watching them in the Script Editor.

Now, access the Expression Editor in the Maya interface. Note how Maya fills in the name of the particle system. You will see goalU change to particleShape1.goalU. Your expressions will look like the following:

```
// Creation
// Start goals at 0

particle1Shape.goalU = 0.0;
particle1Shape.goalV = 0.0;
```

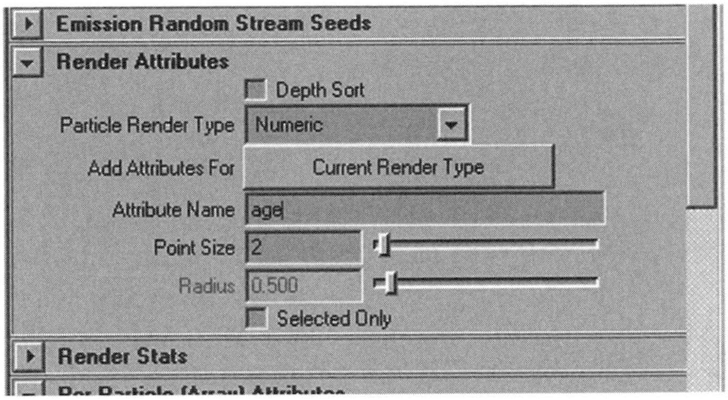

Figure 19.19 Setting the Numeric render type.

```
// Runtime
// Send goals across surface

particle1Shape.goalU = particle1Shape.age;
particle1Shape.goalV = particle1Shape.age;
```

Maya makes these changes to insure that your expressions are not ambiguous when you're looking at the expression code; it's always clear which particle objects are being manipulated.

Using a Lifespan per Particle

Play the animation again. As you can see, the particles bunch up after both the goalU and goalV get up to 1.0, the end of the UV settings on the patch. To solve this problem, you can make a simple "kill particles" condition using lifeSpanPP. Turn on the Lifespan Mode to lifespanPP only as shown in Figure 19.20.

Using MEL, you would type in

```
setAttr particle1Shape.lifespanMode 3;
```

Now add the following code to the runtime expression:

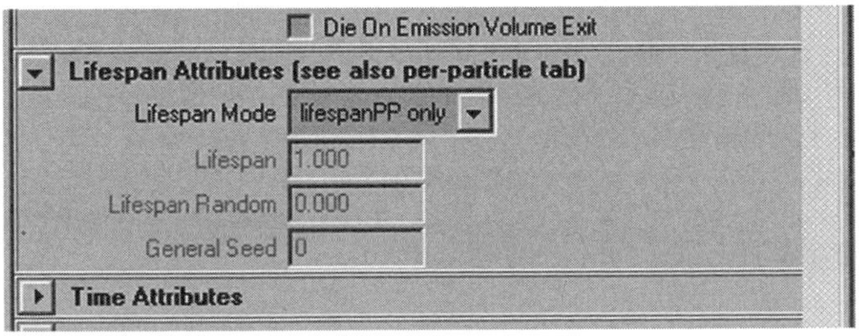

Figure 19.20 Setting Lifespan Mode.

```
// Simple kill expression
if (goalV > 1.0) {
    lifespanPP = 0.0;
}
```

Since both goalU and goalV are referencing age, we will just use goalV for our value in the if statement to set the lifespanPP to 0. Now play the animation (Figure 19.21).

Let's go back and make the movement of the particles a little more interesting by adding some math to the U and V travel.

Changing U and V with Math Functions

The runtime expression is evaluated every frame, which lets us change attributes over time. Using a sin (sine) function, we can vary the U to move in a wave pattern over the surface. We will explore this further in the next example, but for now suffice it to say that sin makes the U value oscillate from –1.0 to 1.0. We don't want negative U values, so we introduce the abs function to make the function go from 0.0 to 1.0 instead. The age

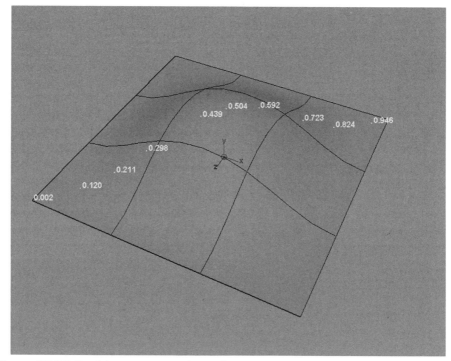

Figure 19.21 Particle ages across the surface.

attribute will act as before in moving the particles along, and the number 6 acts as a frequency for the wave.

> **Tip:** The default Maya setup does not have a hotkey for the Expression Editor. Either set one up using Window > Settings/Preferences > Hotkeys or capture the window call with the Shift + Ctrl combo when opening the window.

Return to the Expression Editor again, and enter the following code:

```
// Runtime
// Send goals across surface in waveform pattern

goalU = abs(sin(age * 6));
goalV = age;

// Simple kill for new UV travel

if (goalV > 1.0) {

    lifespanPP = 0.0;

}
```

Let's bring the emission rate up to a rate of 100 and switch the render type back to sphere.

```
setAttr emitter1.rate 100;
setAttr particle1Shape.particleRenderType 4;
```

Now play the animation (Figure 19.22).

As you can see, this technique of attracting particles to UVs on surfaces is a whole new way of thinking about methods for controlling particles. If you hide the target surfaces, you can "shape" particle patterns with geometry instead of using forces and emitters to get the job done.

Example 3: Using Goals on Multiple Surfaces

In this example, we use goal weights to control a single particle bouncing between two NURBS patches. We'll use the expression function from Example 2, but we will use it to control the goalWeights instead of the UVs. Also, we will add a custom attribute that will control the frequency at which the particle bounces. When we are finished, we'll be able to move the NURBS patches anywhere in the scene, but the bounce timing and target locations on the surfaces will remain constant (Figure 19.23).

Let's start by creating the scene. Add a nurbsPlane at 0 0 0 with the name plane1, as follows:

```
nurbsPlane -p 0 0 0 -ax 0 1 0 -w 1 -lr 1 -d 3 -u 1 -v 1
          -name plane1;
```

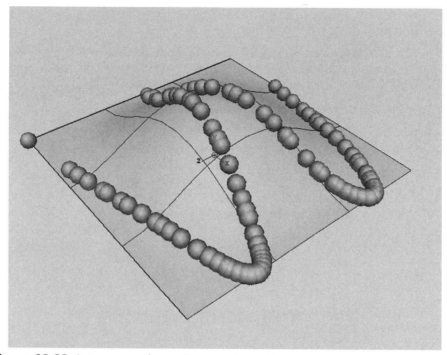

Figure 19.22 A more complex path across the surface.

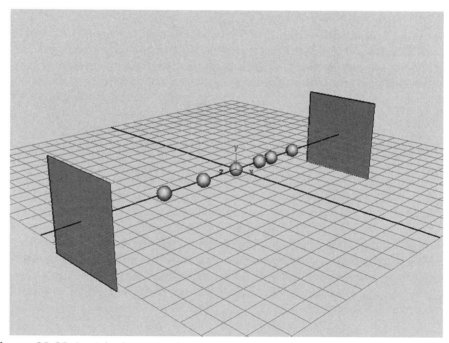

Figure 19.23 Particles bouncing between two planes.

Now move plane1 to 0 0 10, and scale up by 5. To do this, we can use the xform function, which allows us to move, transform, or scale, separately or all at once.

```
xform -scale 5 5 5 plane1;
xform -rotation 90 0 0 plane1;
xform -translation 0 0 10 plane1;
```

Let's add the other patch, plane2, and rotate it –90 degrees:

```
nurbsPlane -p 0 0 0 -ax 0 1 0 -w 1 -lr 1
           -d 3 -u 1 -v 1 -name plane2;
xform -scale 5 5 5 plane2;
xform -rotation –90 0 0 plane2; // reverse the rotation
xform -translation 0 0 –10 plane2;
```

The scene should look like Figure 19.24.

Now, create a single particle called ball, and change its render type to sphere with a radius of 0.4.

```
particle -p 0 0 0 -name ball;
setAttr ballShape.prt 4;
addAttr -is true -ln radius -at "float" -dv 0.4 ballShape;
```

Set the goals as follows:

```
goal  w 0.5 -utr 0 -g plane1 ball;
goal -w 0.5 -utr 0 -g plane2 ball;
```

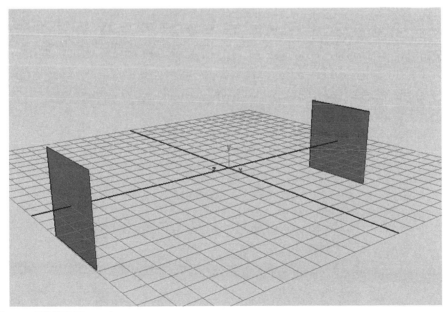

Figure 19.24 Two planes.

This time, set the playback range at 1 to 500, as follows:

```
playbackOptions -min 1 -max 500;
```

Add `goalU` and `goalV` to particle ball:

```
addAttr -ln goalU -dt doubleArray ballShape;
addAttr -ln goalU0 -dt doubleArray ballShape;
addAttr -ln goalV -dt doubleArray ballShape;
addAttr -ln goalV0 -dt doubleArray ballShape;
```

As we did it in Example 2, we first click the right mouse button on the General button under Add Dynamic Attributes in the Attribute Editor. Scroll until you find the `goalU` and `goalV` attributes (hold down the Shift key, and you can multiselect), and then click OK (Figure 19.25). Now let's make a creation expression for `goalU` and `goalV`. In the Attribute Editor, add the creation expression with the same technique as Example 2 by right-clicking over any of the Per Particle attributes.

Add the expression for Creation:

```
// Creation
ballShape.goalU = 0.5;
ballShape.goalV = 0.5;
```

The above code will place the particle in the center of the patches when the particle reaches them. Also, let's add an initial `goalWeight` for both goals that we have set up.

```
goalWeight[0] = 1.0;
goalWeight[1] = 0.0;
```

These statements will start the particle at plane1 at the beginning of the animation.

To add the creation expression, we can use MEL as we did in Chapter 5. Following is the MEL code for entering the last creation expression; note the layout of the syntax.

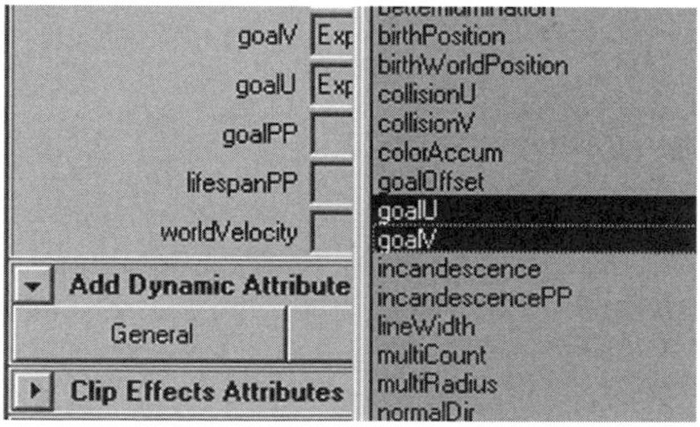

Figure 19.25 Adding the `goalU` and `goalV` attributes.

```
dynExpression -s (

    "// Creation\n" +
    "goalU = 0.5;\n" +
    "goalV = 0.5;\n" +
    "goalWeight[0] = 1.0;\n" +
    "goalWeight[1] = 0.0;"

) -creation ballShape;
```

Note that we use the dynExpression command to create expressions for dynamic objects, such as particles, instead of the expression command, which is only usable for nondynamic Maya objects. You can put the entire expression on one line, or you can spread the expression across multiple lines as we did here, which makes it more readable.

As you probably noticed when you entered these expressions in the Expression Editor, Maya tacks on the object's name ballShape to the attribute. This is a nice shortcut so that you can see the expression more clearly when you are working on it; thus, goalV turns into ballShape.goalV only after you open the expression with the Expression Editor.

Example 2 sin Function Revisited

Regarding the runtime expression, we are looking for a function that will make a nice transition for our goalWeights from 0.0 to 1.0. The sin (sine) function that we used in Example 2 should do just fine, as it will make a smooth oscillation (Figure 19.26).

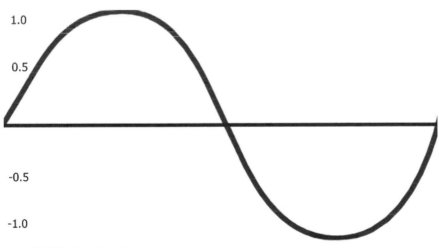

Figure 19.26 Sine function.

We also need a changing variable to drive the expression; let's use the built-in `time` attribute for that. Start out with a runtime expression in the Expression Editor, as follows:

```
// Runtime
goalWeight[0] = sin(time);
```

This statement will make our `goalWeight` values oscillate throughout the animation. To see the numbers in the Script Editor, let's add some print commands to our expression. To do this, add the following statements to the runtime expression:

```
print ("\n");
print ("Goal one = " + goalWeight[0] + "\n");
```

Now open the Script Editor and play the animation. Figure 19.27 shows the output.

We need the `goalWeight` values to stay in the positive range, so we will use the `abs` (absolute value) function again. In this case, the `abs` function will introduce discontinuities in the `sin` wave where it would normally cross the 0 value. This will cause the function to no longer be smooth, but later this will work for us in the animation to make it seem like the particle ball is being slowed and caught by the planes. In the Expression Editor, replace the above `goalWeight` expression with

```
ballShape.goalWeight[0] = abs(sin(time));
```

and press Enter. The output is shown in Figure 19.28.

Now we need to have another oscillating function that can be offset from the first. We could use `sin` again and offset it, but let's use the function `cos` (cosine) instead, which is already 90 degrees out of phase with `sin`. Figure 19.29 shows how `sin` and `cos` relate on a graph.

```
goal one = -0.9775301177

goal one = -0.9916838719

goal one = -0.9989549171

goal one = -0.999292789

goal one = -0.9926951426

goal one = -0.9792077685
```

Figure 19.27 Negative values for goal one.

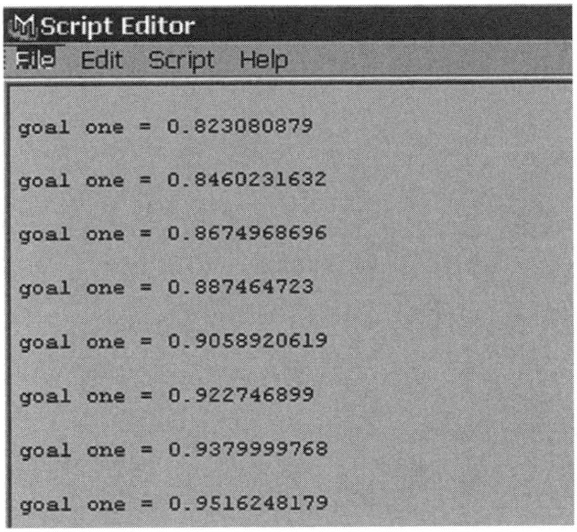

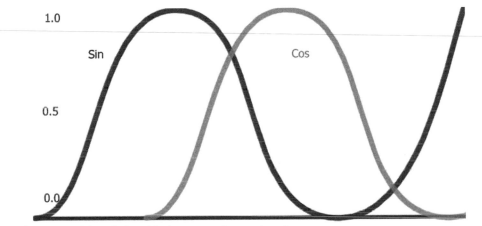

Figure 19.28 Positive values for goal one from `abs` function.

Figure 19.29 Relationship between sine and cosine.

We will simply apply the same function to `goalWeight[1]`. So now let's open the runtime expression and add the following code segment:

```
// Runtime

goalWeight[0] = abs(sin(time));
goalWeight[1] = abs(cos(time));

print("\n");
print ("goal one = " + goalWeight[0] + "\n");
print ("goal two = " + goalWeight[1] + "\n");
```

Figure 19.30 shows the results of playing the animation.

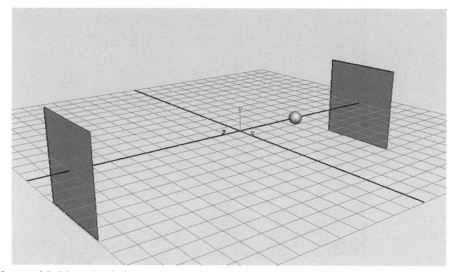

Figure 19.30 A single bouncing sphere.

Adding a Custom Attribute

The above script works, but we need to control the speed of the bounce. We can add our own custom attribute called `freq` and use it as a speed control that can be animated if needed.

We will do this in the Attribute Editor, using the Add Dynamic Attribute menu. Left-click the General button in the menu, and a new window will come up. This is where we can set up custom attributes that will show up in the Channel Box, attributes that we can reference and change in the Expression menu. Type `freq` in the Attribute Name box. Now we have to define the Data Type. We have a lot of options, but for now we will choose the Float type. Retain the Attribute Type as Scalar for now. Let's type in our default settings for the new attribute. In the Numeric Attribute Properties section, enter 1.0 for Minimum, 12.0 for Maximum, and 1.0 for the Default value in the window, as shown in Figure 19.31.

Click the Add and OK buttons: Maya now has added our attribute to `ballShape` particle. If you select the particle in the window and look at the Channel Box, you will see `freq` at the bottom of the attribute list.

Through MEL we can add the custom attribute as follows:

```
addAttr -ln freq -at double -min 1 -max 12 -dv 1.0 ballShape;
setAttr -e -keyable true ballShape.freq;
```

We can also have communication between our runtime expression and the Channel Box. Access the Expression Editor back, and add the new attribute to the runtime expression. Add the following statements:

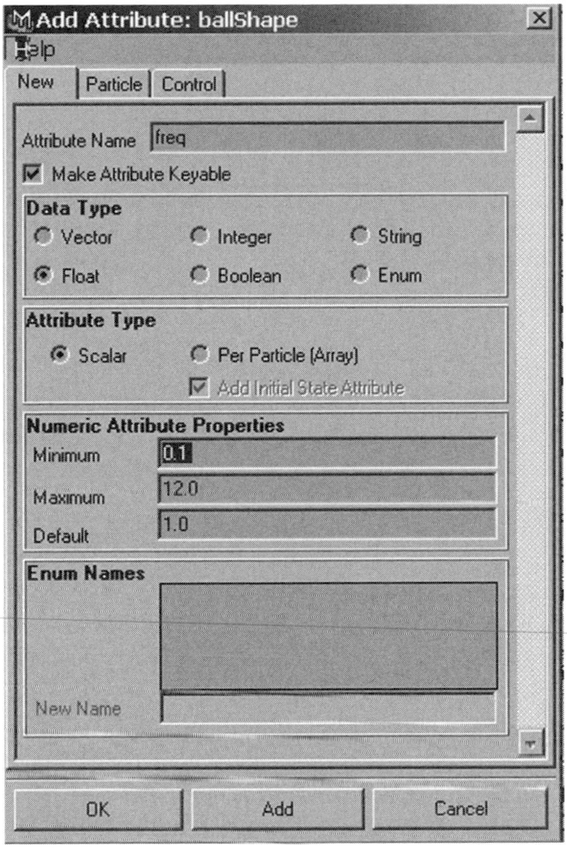

Figure 19.31 Adding the `freq` attribute.

```
// Runtime

goalWeight[0] = abs(sin(time * freq));
goalWeight[1] = abs(cos(time * freq));
```

Delete the print statements, which are not needed anymore and can slow things down. The print statements are really only useful for debugging your expressions. Click Edit and Close, and select the ball particle system. In the Channel Box, you should see freq listed at the end of the attribute list (Figure 19.32).

Now play the animation. During playback, you can change freq to other numbers, such as 4, 8, and 12, the maximum we put in when we added the attribute. You should see the ball change speed/frequency as you enter the numbers.

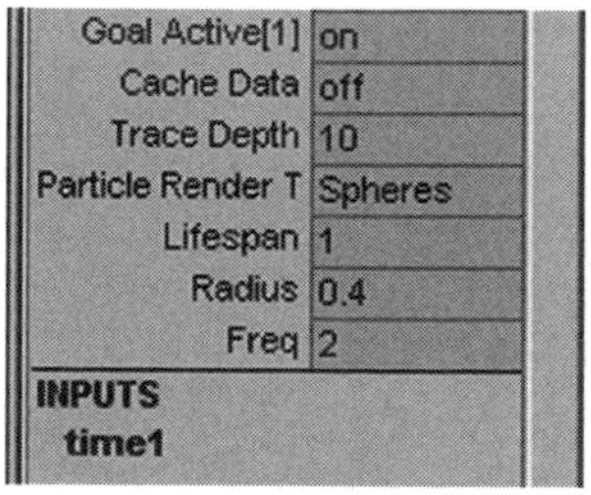

Goal Active[1]	on
Cache Data	off
Trace Depth	10
Particle Render T	Spheres
Lifespan	1
Radius	0.4
Freq	2
INPUTS	
time1	

Figure 19.32 `freq` attribute in Channel Box.

Extra

To see the control that you have set up in our fake simulation, animate the position of the planes. Also, try animating the `freq` attribute.

Example 4: Using Goals on Surfaces, Part 2

In this example, instead of building the scene from scratch, we will load in a scene that has been set up and animated and add to it. We will build a MEL script that makes a particle travel among four NURBS planes in a pre-determined order (Figure 19.33).

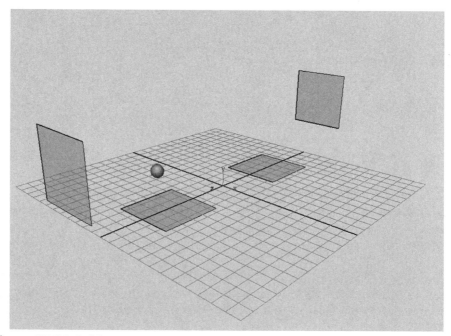

Figure 19.33 Ball bouncing among several surfaces.

Overview

Instead of manual animation, it's better sometimes to build scripts that create animation effects and maintain them throughout a production job for convenience and organization. If your production job requires hundreds or even thousands of particles or objects and has several scenes that reuse an effect repeatedly, implementing the effect via *procedures* may be the most efficient strategy. Also, if you are the person developing the effect, you will want to create something that you can hand over to other people that can be done the same way every time.

The following approach starts with small, easy-to-manage procedures and slowly builds them into a script that you can use or hand off to others.

Load the Scene

Load the scene in Maya as you normally would. Find the Maya scene chapter19.ma from the online resources page at *www.melscripting.com*. This scene has four animating planes from the frame range of 1 to 150, as shown in Figure 19.34. Now play the scene to see the planes moving apart

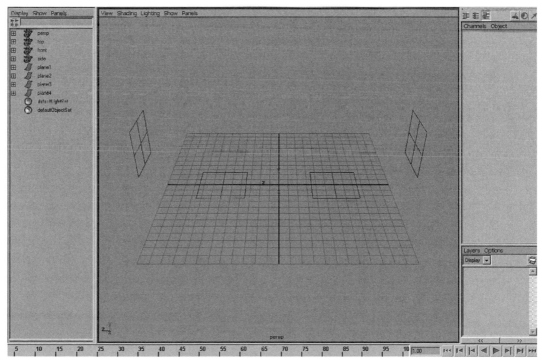

Figure 19.34 Four planes in the Outliner and the persp Panel.

at frame 50, then coming together again at frame 100, and then going to the opposite of frame 50 at frame 150.

We want a particle (Ball, as in Example 3) to go from plane1 to plane3 to plane4 to plane2 and then back to plane1. We will design the MEL script so that the plane order will be determined by the order in which we select the planes.

Add Particle Ball

We need to find where plane1 is positioned so that we can put our particle there. plane1 will be our starting point for the animation and our first goal. To do this, let's set up a float array variable to store the result of an xform call named $Pstart. Select plane1 in the scene.

As before, open the Script Editor using the Script Editor button in the Maya interface (Figure 19.35). Type the following statement:

```
float $Pstart[] = `xform -q -a -translation plane1`;
```

You'll see this message:

```
// Result: 0 5 14 //
```

The MEL command above stores the result in $Pstart. The -q flag means query, and the -a flag means that xform should return the absolute coordinate in three-dimensional space. If you want to see what's in $Pstart, use a print command:

```
print $Pstart;
```

MEL will print the following:

```
print $Pstart;
0
5
14
```

Three numbers are printed because $Pstart is an *array* of floats, or numbers that can have fractional parts. $Pstart, then, actually consists of $Pstart[0], $Pstart[1], and $Pstart[2] like the goalWeights array in the previous examples. $Pstart[0] is 0, $Pstart[1] is 5, and $Pstart[2]

Figure 19.35 Script Editor button.

is 14. These three elements of the $Pstart array represent the X, Y, and Z coordinates obtained from the xform command.

Now let's add our particle Ball to the scene with its position set to the X, Y, and Z values in $Pstart and set the render type to sphere. Type the following statements:

```
particle -n Ball -p $Pstart[0] $Pstart[1] $Pstart[2] -c 1;
setAttr BallShape.particleRenderType 4;
```

The particle Ball will now be at the center of plane1 (Figure 19.36).

Adding Goals for Particle and Planes Using String Variables

Let's add the goals in the same way that we did the particle position. We need to set a variable that will be a list of strings, to hold our plane's names in the order that we have selected them. We will create the goal relationship by substituting the array elements into the MEL command in the order that we pick the planes. In the Maya interface, select the plane1 in the order shown in Figure 19.37 while holding the Shift key and picking with the mouse.

In the Script Editor, type

```
string $planes[] = `ls -sl`;
```

ls -sl means list selected, and the result will be stored in the order the planes were selected. $planes is an array as before, but this time it's a list of strings. As before, let's check to see what is in $planes:

```
print $planes;
```

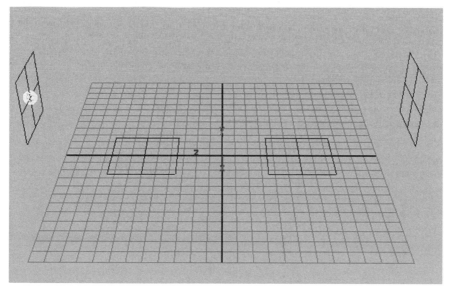

Figure 19.36 The four planes and a ball.

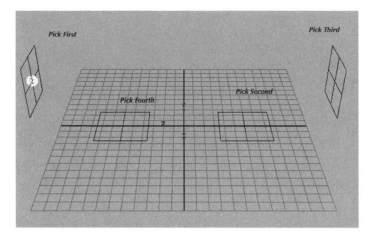

Figure 19.37 Pick the planes in this order.

The MEL results follow:

```
print $planes;
plane1
plane3
plane4
plane2
```

The order tells us that it's an array with $planes[0] being plane1, and $planes[3] being plane2. (Remember, array indices for a four-element array go from 0 to 3, not 1 to 4.) We also need to find two more properties for the variable $planes: size and type of objects in the list.

To find the size of an array in MEL, use the following command:

```
size($planes);
```

MEL returns the following:

```
size($planes);
// Result: 4 //
```

Tip: The whatIs command will tell you what type a variable is.

Type in

```
whatIs "$planes";
```

MEL responds as follows:

```
whatIs "$planes";
// Result: string[] variable //
```

Type in

```
whatIs "$Pstart";
```

MEL response:

```
whatIs "$Pstart";
// Result: float[] variable //
```

This command is handy if you're not sure what MEL has put in your variable. Note that the []'s after the variable indicate that it's an array variable—it contains a list of values, not just a single value. If the whatIs command had just printed // Result: float variable //, then we would know that the variable contained only a single value.

Now we need to add the goals. The following statements do this, using the $planes array to find the selected object names from the selection list.

```
goal -w 0 -utr 0 -g $planes[0] Ball;
goal -w 0 -utr 0 -g $planes[1] Ball;
goal -w 0 -utr 0 -g $planes[2] Ball;
goal -w 0 -utr 0 -g $planes[3] Ball;
```

The goals are now set up in the order in which we picked the planes.

Adding Creation Expressions to Particle Ball

Let's start with the creation expression first since that will be fairly straightforward. We first need to add the goalU and goalV to the particle as we did in Example 3. This time, we will do this using MEL only and not the Maya interface.

```
addAttr -ln goalU -dt doubleArray BallShape;
addAttr -ln goalU0 -dt doubleArray BallShape;
addAttr -ln goalV -dt doubleArray BallShape;
addAttr -ln goalV0 -dt doubleArray BallShape;
```

Now let's also add the creation expression through MEL. We'll set it up so that if we open the Expression Editor it will read easily, in case we want to add to it. Remember the syntax from Example 3? Type in the following statements:

```
dynExpression -creation -s (

    "// Creation \n\n" +
    "goalU = 0.5;\n" +
    "goalV = 0.5;\n\n"

) BallShape;
```

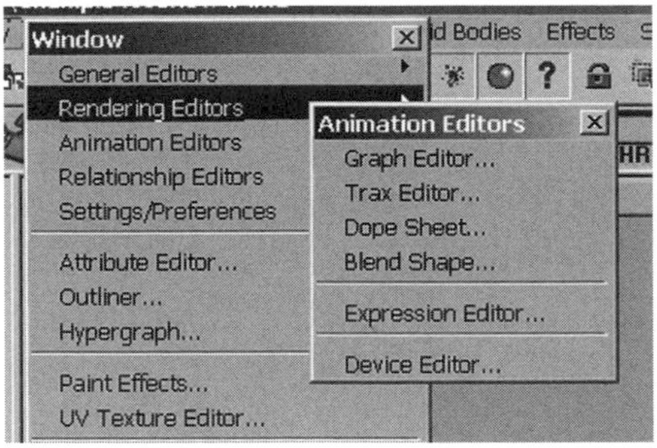

Figure 19.38 Opening Expression Editor.

The \n will make it easier to read by adding line breaks when you open the expression in the Expression Editor (Figure 19.38). Open the Expression Editor now.

Choose Select Filter > By Expression Name in the Expression Editor, and you'll see BallShape listed. Select it, and the expression will appear in the window (Figure 19.39). Note that all line breaks are in the expression where we had added \n.

Add Runtime Expression

Now we need to create an expression that will do the work for the travel from plane to plane. This is also where most of your work will be. We need goalWeights that change like we had before, but we need to have four of them working together. Let's start with the expression that we wrote in Example 3:

```
abs(sin(time));
abs(cos(time));
```

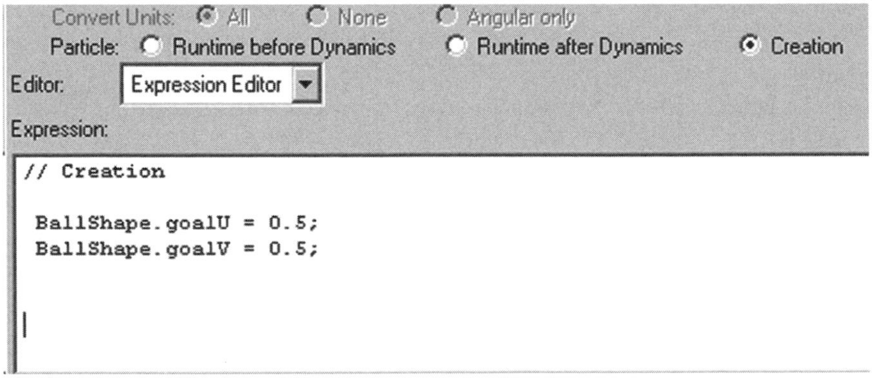

Figure 19.39 Goal expression in Expression Editor.

The above statements worked fine for two planes and the particle, but we need more now. Instead of relying on the absolute value of the sine and cosine functions, let's use a curve function that will give us more control. The function linstep (linear step) will work. The syntax for linstep follows:

```
linstep (value_from, value_to, percentage)
```

So let's change the expression for the goalWeights to

```
goalWeight[0] = linstep(0.0, 1.0, sin(time));
goalWeight[1] = linstep(0.0, 1.0, cos(time));
```

Figure 19.40 shows a plot of the sin, cos, and the linstep functions. When the sin and cos go negative, the linstep function waits until it starts getting positive numbers to go from 0.0 to 1.0 and then back from

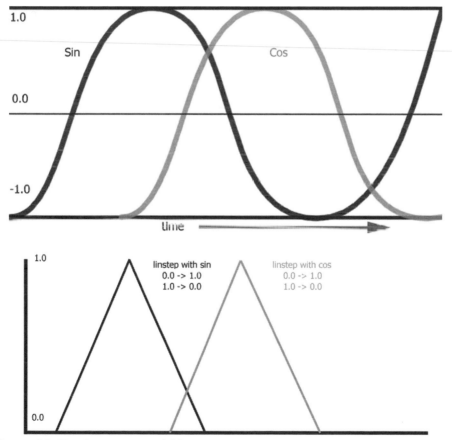

Figure 19.40 sin, cos, and linstep.

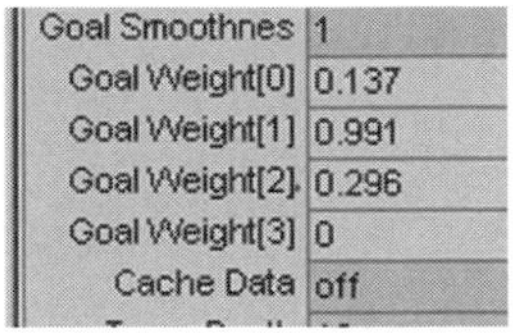

Figure 19.41 Goal Weight attributes in Channel Box.

1.0 to 0.0. This will buy us some time and let another set of sin and cos functions that are offset from the first pair make their transition from 0.0 to 1.0 and back to 0.0.

Now we need to offset the other two. These functions are set into motion through the use of the time command in Maya. So we need to offset time's output and feed it into the other set of sin and cos. Don't type it in yet, but the following code segment shows how we'll do that.

```
goalWeight[0] = linstep(0.0, 1.0, cos(time));
goalWeight[1] = linstep(0.0, 1.0, sin(time));
goalWeight[2] = linstep(0.0, 1.0, sin((time) + 24));
goalWeight[3] = linstep(0.0, 1.0, cos((time) + 46));
```

The two numbers 24 and 46 are the time shift numbers that will enable sin and cos to offset their waves. We arrived at these numbers by experimenting with the expression and watching the output in the Channel Box (Figure 19.41).

We also need to add our freq attribute as before, but this time we will put it in the expression and change it there if necessary. Add it in the (time) area. Our runtime expression thus far follows:

```
// Runtime
// Add freq and set it to 4
float $freq = 4.0;
// Main expression

goalWeight[0] = linstep(0.0, 1.0, cos((time * $freq)));
goalWeight[1] = linstep(0.0, 1.0, sin((time * $freq)));
goalWeight[2] = linstep(0.0, 1.0, sin((time * $freq) + 24));
goalWeight[3] = linstep(0.0, 1.0, cos((time * $freq) + 46));
```

Let's put the expression into MEL syntax and enter it:

```
dynExpression -runtimeAfterDynamics -s (

    "// Runtime \n\n" +
    "// Add $freq and set it to 4.\n\n" +
    "float $freq = 4.0;\n\n" +
    "// Main expression\n\n" +
```

```
"goalWeight[0] = linstep(0.0, 1.0, cos((time * $freq)));\n" +
"goalWeight[1] = linstep(0.0, 1.0, sin((time * $freq)));\n" +
"goalWeight[2] = linstep(0.0, 1.0, sin((time * $freq)
                    + 24));\n" +
"goalWeight[3] = linstep(0.0, 1.0, cos((time * $freq) + 46));"
) BallShape;
```

Now let's write the MEL script. In a text editor of your choice, enter the following code:

```
//
// MEL script: ballTravel
//
// Notes: This is designed to work with the scene chapter19.ma
//
// Usage: Select the four NURBS planes in the scene in the
   order that
// you want and execute the script
//
// Extra: The runtime expression variable $freq can be changed
   in the
// Expression Editor for travel speed changes

global proc ballTravel( ) {
    // Get the plane order from the selection
    string $planes[] = `ls -sl`;

    // Check to see if we have enough planes

    if (size($planes) != 4) {
    error "We need more planes\n"; // This will stop the script.
    }

    // Make a particle and place it at center of first
       selected plane
    float $Pstart = `xform -q -a -translation $planes[0]`;
    particle -n Ball -p $Pstart[0] $Pstart[1] $Pstart[2] -c 1;

    // Set particle to sphere type
    setAttr BallShape.particleRenderType 4;

    // Add goals in order of selection

    goal -w 0 -utr 0 -g $planes[0] Ball;
    goal -w 0 -utr 0 -g $planes[1] Ball;
    goal -w 0 -utr 0 -g $planes[2] Ball;
    goal -w 0 -utr 0 -g $planes[3] Ball;

    // Add goalU and goalV to Ball
```

```
addAttr -ln goalU -dt doubleArray BallShape;
addAttr -ln goalU0 -dt doubleArray BallShape;
addAttr -ln goalV -dt doubleArray BallShape;
addAttr -ln goalV0 -dt doubleArray BallShape;

// Expression section
// Add creation and runtime expressions

dynExpression -s (

"// Creation \n\n" +
"goalU = 0.5;\n" +
"goalV = 0.5;\n\n"

) -creation BallShape;

dynExpression -runtimeAfterDynamics -s (

    "// Runtime \n\n" +
    "// Add $freq and set it to 4.\n\n" +
    "float $freq = 4.0;\n\n" +
    "// Main expression\n\n" +
    "goalWeight[0] = linstep(0.0, 1.0, cos((time *
$freq)));\n" +
    "goalWeight[1] = linstep(0.0, 1.0, sin((time *
$freq)));\n" +
    "goalWeight[2] = linstep(0.0, 1.0, sin((time * $freq)
                   + 24));\n" +
    "goalWeight[3] = linstep(0.0, 1.0, cos((time * $freq)
    + 46));"

) BallShape;

// End the script and source it. Load scene and
// type ballTravel in Script Editor

} // End of global proc
```

Source the script; then select the four planes, and run it by typing ballTravel in the Script Editor. Then, rewind and play back your scene (Figure 19.42).

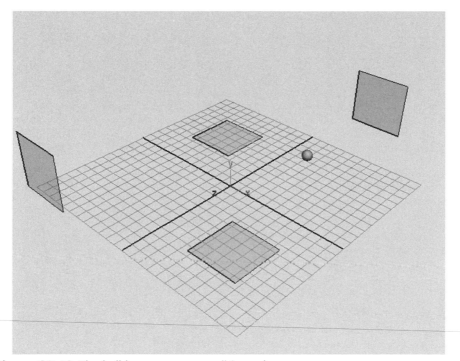

Figure 19.42 The ball bounces among all four planes.

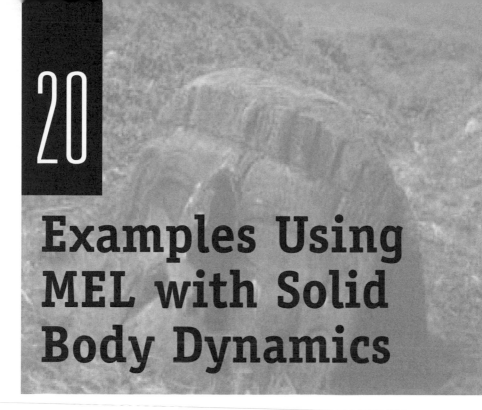

20

Examples Using MEL with Solid Body Dynamics

Unlike particles, solid bodies do not have a class of expressions all their own to aid in creating complex animation. However, MEL and expressions are still quite useful in setting up and controlling solid-body dynamics systems.

In the following examples, we'll explore how to use MEL to construct scenes that use solid body dynamics and how to use collision events to trigger behaviors both in scenes that only consist of solid bodies and in scenes that combine solid bodies with particles.

Example 1: Particle Collisions

In this example, we will look at particles and how they interact with surfaces. We can tell a particle, or particles in a system, to collide and react with a surface or groups of surfaces (Figure 20.1). These surfaces can be either NURBS or polygon objects.

Let's start off by making a simple collision with a polygon grid and some particles.

Create the Scene

Select Create > Polygon Primitives > Plane ❑. This will open the Polygon Plane Options window. Type in the settings for a 4 × 4 plane, as shown in Figure 20.2.

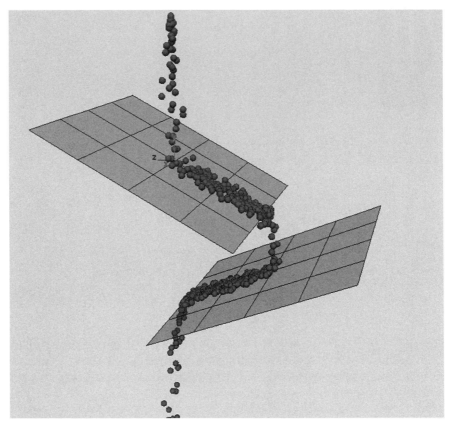

Figure 20.1 Particles cascading down two planes.

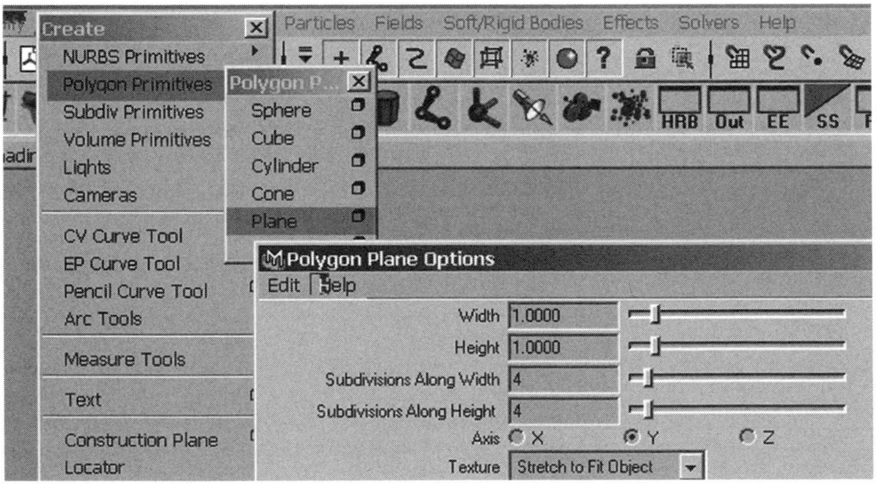

Figure 20.2 Polygon Plane Options window.

Or if you like, open the Script Editor (Figure 20.3) and enter the following MEL command:

```
polyPlane -width 1 -height 1 -subdivisionsX 4
          -subdivisionsY 4 -axis 0 1 0;
```

(Remember to press the Enter key on the numeric keypad to execute the command.)

We need to rename and scale up the plane, so select pPlane1 (it should be selected already), and enter 6 in the scale X, Y, and Z fields in the Channel Box. Now change the name of the plane to Floor in the Channel Box (Figure 20.4).

As we have seen before, we can do all of this in MEL using the rename and setAttr commands:

```
rename pPlane1 Floor;
setAttr Floor.scaleX 6;
setAttr Floor.scaleY 6;
setAttr Floor.scaleZ 6;
```

Toggle off the Grid in the Display menu so we can see our Floor better.

Now let's put in a directional type of emitter and hook up the collisions. First, create the emitter by accessing the Dynamics page and using the Particles > Create Emitter > ❑ (Figure 20.5).

Figure 20.3 Script Editor button.

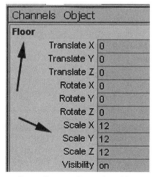

Figure 20.4 Renaming and scaling floor plane in Channel Box.

Figure 20.5 Creating an emitter with custom options.

Let's change some settings in the options window and add a name to our emitter (Figure 20.6). Set the Type to Directional, the Rate to 30, and the Directions to X = 0, Y = –1.0, and Z = 0. Also, change the Spread to 0.2. Move the emitter 4 units in Y to give us some time before the emitted particles intersect with the Floor.

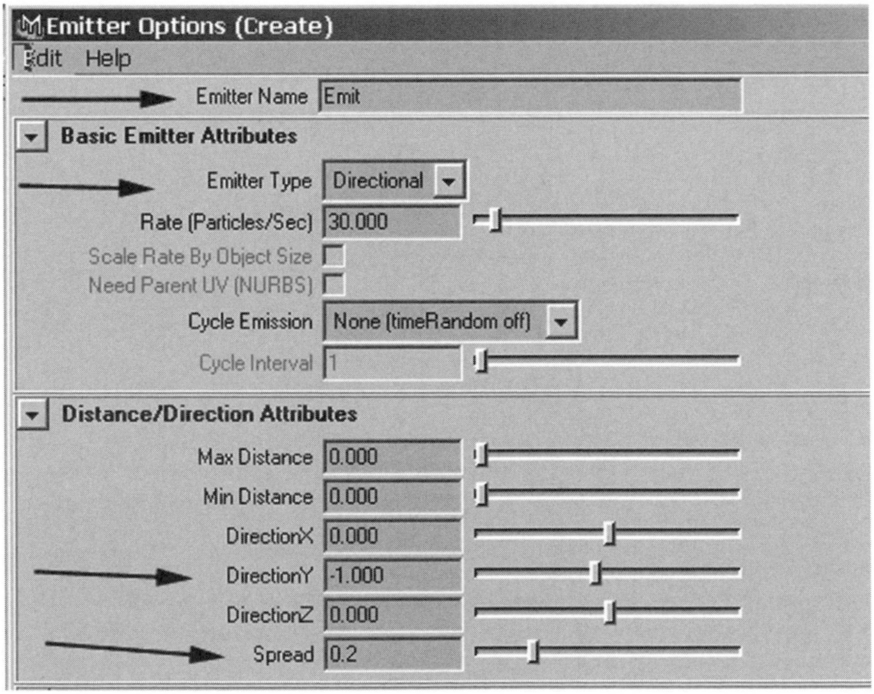

Figure 20.6 Emitter options to change.

Following is the MEL code for the emitter. Now, though, instead of moving the emitter in Y, we just use the -position flag. Let's also create a string array variable that will contain the results of the emitter creation command by using the single quote symbols to enclose the string. By doing this, the string array will contain the names of the nodes that were created. The name Emit will be in array position 0, and its shape node EmitShape will be in array position 1.

```
string $eObject [] = `emitter -position 0 4 0 -type direction
                    -name Emit -rate 30 -speed 1 -spread 0.2
                    -dx 0 -dy -1.0 -dz 0`;
```

When we create an emitter in the Maya interface, it's automatically connected to a particle object. In MEL, we must do this by hand. Here's how to create a particle object and make the connections so that the emitter knows which particle (particle1) to emit. Let's also again store the result name in another string array variable and then use the results in both strings to hook them together with connectDynamic.

```
string $pObject[] = `particle`;
connectDynamic -em $eObject[0] $pObject[0];
```

Now let's change our Playback start and end times to a range of 1 to 500. Then, move the perspective camera to center the scene in its panel, and play (Figure 20.7).

To set the start and end times, if you like, you can use the following MEL command:

```
playbackOptions -min 1 -max 500;
```

Collide the Particles

Select particle1. Then, hold down the Shift key, and select Floor. Go to the Particles menu, and select the Make Collide function (Figure 20.8).

The MEL code to make the floor a collision object for the particles follows:

```
collision -resilience 1.0 -friction 0.0 Floor;
connectDynamic -collisions Floor particle1;
```

The collision command makes a geoConnector node that gives the object Floor additional dynamic attributes related to collisions. Then, connectDynamic connects the particle1 object to Floor so that particles collide with the floor.

To take a look for yourself, choose Window > HyperGraph, and select Floor (Figure 20.9). Now click the Up and DownStream Connections icon (Figure 20.10). Figure 20.11 shows what you see in the Hypergraph.

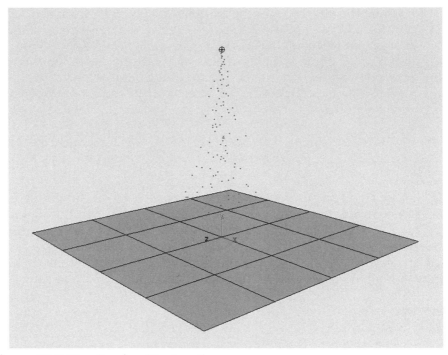

Figure 20.7 Directional emitter in action.

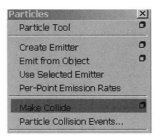

Figure 20.8 Make Collide menu item.

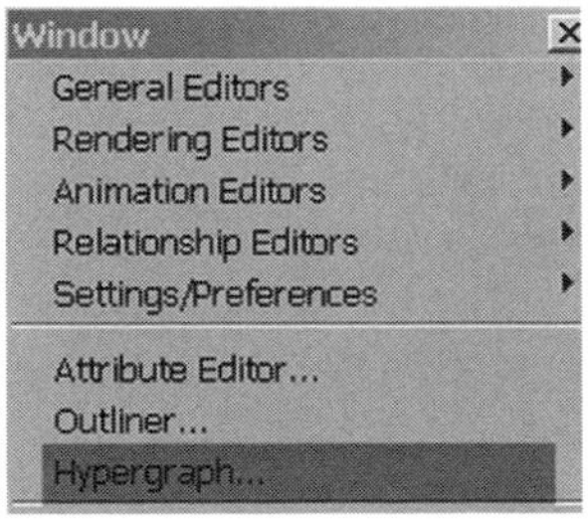

Figure 20.9 Hypergraph menu item.

Figure 20.10 Up and DownStream Connections button.

Now, play back the scene to see `particle1` bouncing off the floor without going through the floor (Figure 20.12).

Setting Controls for Collisions

Now we can use MEL to see more details about how the collisions occur. First, let's look at the `geoConnector1` that was created. If we select Floor in the Maya interface and look in the Channel Box, we will see the `geoConnector1`. Once it is selected, we will see an attribute called `Tessellation Factor` that is set to 200. This is how `Floor` is being subdivided for the dynamics solver. The higher the `tessellation` value, the more accurate the collision motion will be. This `tessellation` attribute controls how the dynamics engine breaks the surface down into triangles when calculating the collision motion (Figure 20.13).

Also, on the particle object there is a setting called `traceDepth`. The default `traceDepth` is set to 10. If it is set to 0, the particles will pass right through the surface. This setting controls how accurately Maya tracks the positions of the particles as it calculates collisions. You can also set a per-particle attribute called `traceDepthPP` that can control this on an individual particle basis. Changing these attributes can be a solution for problems with particle/surface collisions.

> **Tip:** We have been using a polygon surface for this example, but if we had used a NURBS surface, it would be the same. When you use a NURBS surface, Maya adds an extra step to the collision calculations because Maya will convert the NURBS to polygons.

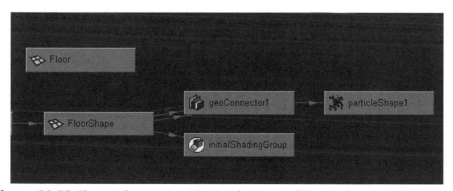

Figure 20.11 The `geoConnector` that implements collisions in hypergraph.

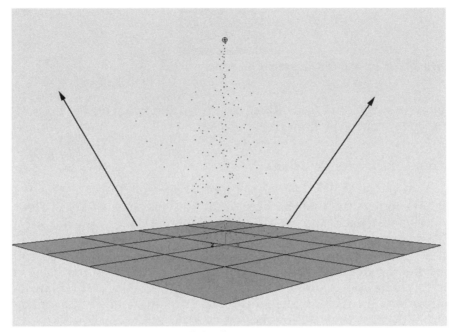

Figure 20.12 Particles bouncing off the floor.

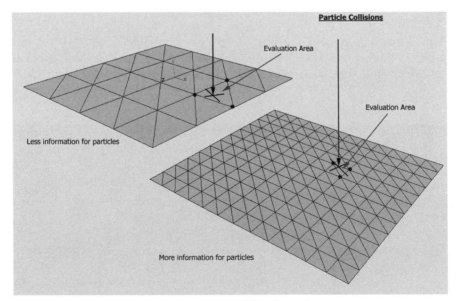

Figure 20.13 Effect of increasing the `tessellation factor`.

If you are using production-ready, high-resolution models, it's a good idea to make stand-in polygon objects for use in particle collisions instead of using a high-resolution model when you can. The calculations will be simpler, and you will save some time when you experiment with the scene.

Using Other Controls in geoConnector Node

Other control options that the `geoConnector` node provides are Resilience and Friction. You can think of resilience as a "bounce" setting and friction as a "slide" control. If we change the current settings on both of these controls, we can see the difference. Select the `Floor` object, and get a listing for `geoConnector1` in the Channel Box. Set Resilience to 0.0 and Friction to 0.5 (Figure 20.14).

You can set the resilience and friction controls in MEL as follows:

```
setAttr geoConnector1.resilience 0.0;
setAttr geoConnector1.friction 0.2;
```

Figure 20.15 shows the results of playback. The particles in `particle1` now slide over the surface.

Finish Scene Using MEL

Now let's finish the scene by adding a second `Floor` object and rotating it so that `particle1` particles slide off one floor to the other. We will also add a gravity field to the simulation so that the particles fall downward.

First rotate the `Floor` object −26.00 in X.

```
xform -rotation -26 0 0 Floor;
```

Copy `Floor`, and move it 3.0 units in Z, −3.0 units in Y. Then rotate it 26.0 units in X.

```
duplicate -name Floor1 Floor;
xform -a translation 0 -3 -3 Floor1;
xform -a rotation 26 0 0 Floor1;
```

OUTPUTS
geoConnector1
Tessellation Factor 200
Resilience 0
Friction 0.2

Figure 20.14 Dynamic collision settings for `geoConnector1` node.

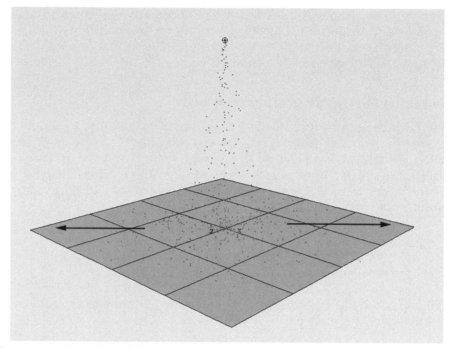

Figure 20.15 Particles sliding over surface.

We need to make particle1 collide with the new Floor1, so let's add a second geoConnector node and set its resilience and friction the same as geoConnector1.

```
collision -resilience 0 -friction 0.2 Floor1;
connectDynamic -collisions Floor1 particle1;
```

Attach a gravity field to particle1 so that it will fall and slide off the Floor objects.

```
gravity -magnitude 3 -attenuation 0.0;
connectDynamic -fields gravityField1 particle1;
```

Finally, make particle1 a sphere type, and set its radius to 0.2.

```
setAttr particle1.particleRenderType 4;
addAttr -longName radius -defaultValue 0.2 particleShape1;
```

Figure 20.16 shows the results of playback.

In this example, we have seen how collision objects interact with particle objects, and how to set up collision objects in MEL. In the next examples, we will look at how to use MEL to create more complex particle collision effects.

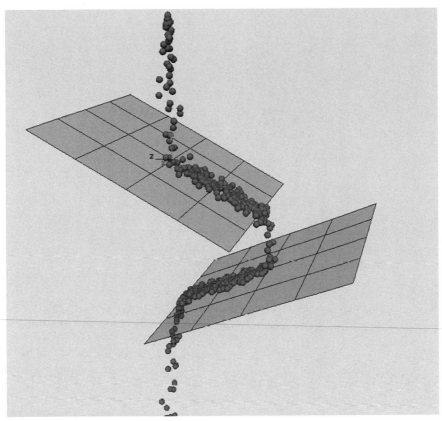

Figure 20.16 Resulting particle cascade.

Example 2: Collision Events

In this example, we will take a look at a method for triggering particle behavior with collisions, called an *event*. Figure 20.17 shows results of an event. Events can cause particles to do certain things when a particle collides with a surface, or a number of collisions have taken place. They also can be used to trigger MEL scripts.

Start by loading the example scene. Choose File > Open, and find the scene chapter20.ma in the archive on the Web site at *www.melscripting.com*.

The scene has three polygon objects named bucket1, bucket2, and bucket3. These were made by revolving a NURBS curve with the output set to Polygon in the Revolve options (Figure 20.18).

Overview

We will create an emitter, positioned such that the particles fall into the first bucket, bucket1, and then a collision event will make bucket1 spill the

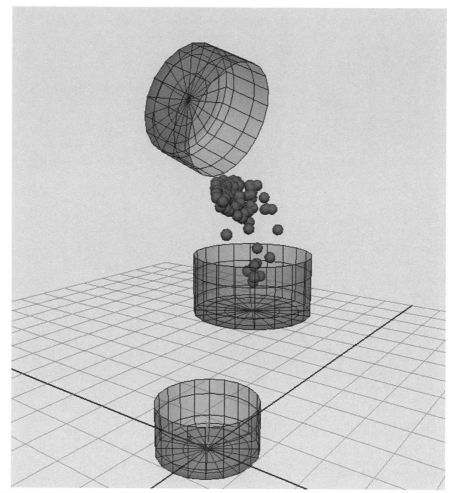

Figure 20.17 Particles in buckets.

particles into bucket2. Then another collision event will trigger bucket2 to spill into the last bucket, bucket3. The collision events will call a MEL expression that will make the buckets rotate and spill the particles.

Add Emitter and Particles

In the Dynamics page (Figure 20.19), create an emitter by choosing Particles > Create Emitter > ❑. This will be a directional emitter called waterEmit with an emission rate of 100, a direction of –1.0 in Y, and a spread of 0.2 (Figure 20.20).

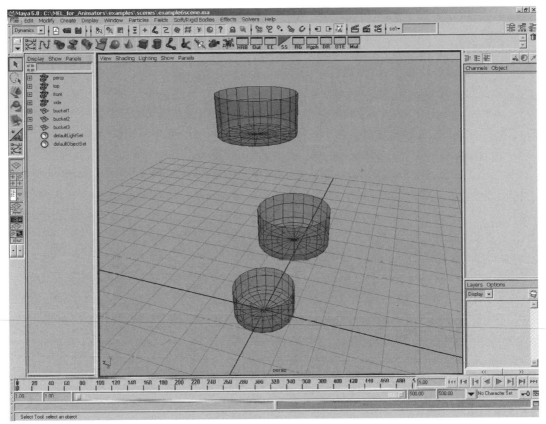

Figure 20.18 Contents of chapter20.ma.

In the side view, move the emitter above bucket1, perhaps to X = 0, Y = 9.0, and Z = 0. As before, we can simplify this process using MEL. Launch the Script Editor and enter the following:

```
string $eObject[] = `emitter -name waterEmit -position 0 9 0
        -type direction -rate 100
        -spread 0.2 -dx 0 -dy -1.0 -dz 0`;

string $pObject [] = `particle`;
connectDynamic -emitter $eObject[0] $pObject[0];
```

File	Edit	Modify	Create	Display	Window	Particles	
						Particle Tool	
						Create Emitter	
						Emit from Object	

Figure 20.19 Creat Emitter menu item.

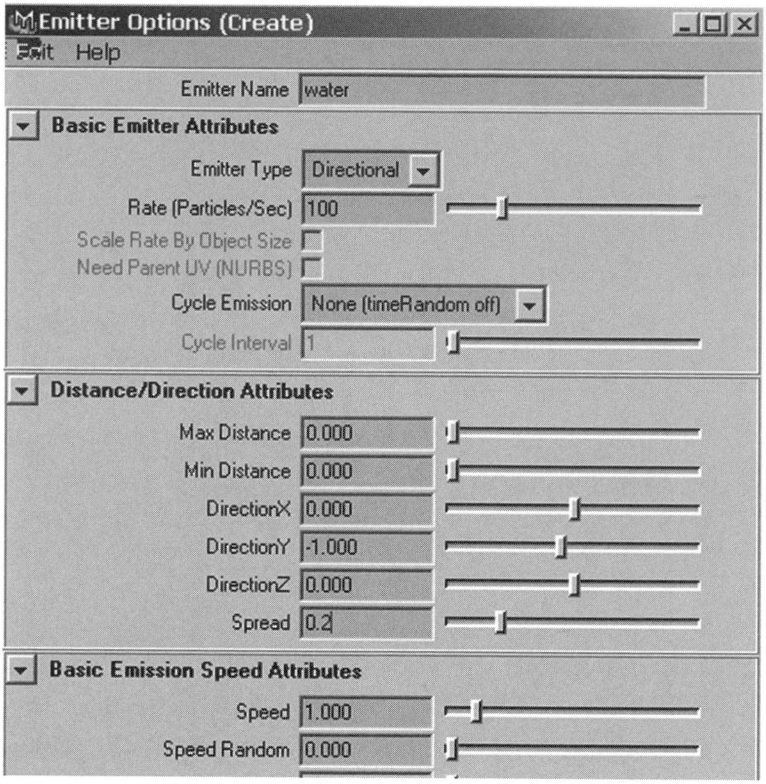

Figure 20.20 Emitter options.

Set the start and end frames in the timeline to 1 and 500, respectively, and then play. You should see the particles fall through bucket1 (Figure 20.21).

Let's make bucket1 a collision object and change the particle render type to sphere. Also, when we add the collision node, let's set the bucket's resilience to a small bounce and set friction to 0.

```
collision -resilience 0.3 -friction 0.0 bucket1;
connectDynamic -collisions bucket1 particle1;
setAttr particle1.particleRenderType 4;
addAttr -longName radius -defaultValue 0.1 particleShape1;
```

Now play. Figure 20.22 shows a side view of what you should see in your scene.

Dynamic Relationships

In Example 1, we saw how the menu item for making collision objects corresponded to MEL commands. Now, let's look at the menu equivalent to

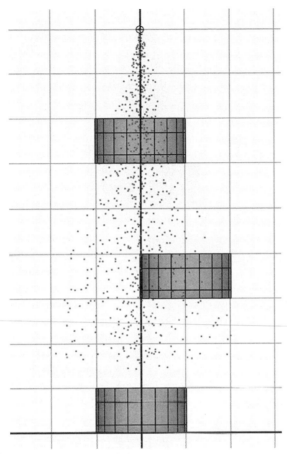

Figure 20.21 Particles falling through buckets.

the `connectDynamic` command. Choose Window > Relationship Editors > Dynamic Relationships (Figure 20.23).

Select `particle1` by clicking on its name in the object list. Then, click the Collisions option in the SELECTION MODES area. You will see `bucketShape1` in the list (Figure 20.24).

The operations you can perform in this window correspond to the function of the `connectDynamic` MEL command. This window is an interface for organizing and connecting fields, emitters, and collisions.

Limit Number of Particles and Add Gravity

We only want 150 particles to fall into the buckets. To do this, set the Max Count attribute of `particle1` to 150. You will find it in the Channel Box. (By default, this attribute is set to –1, which allows Maya to create

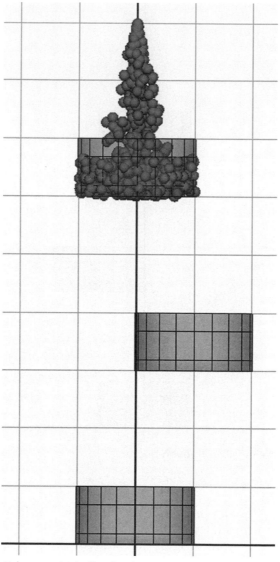

Figure 20.22 Particles caught in first bucket.

an infinite number of particles.) The corresponding MEL command
would be

```
setAttr particleShape1.maxCount 150;
```

If you prefer to set this attribute in MEL, type the above statement into the
Script Editor. Then, add a `gravity` field, and connect it to `particle1` by
typing the following MEL commands:

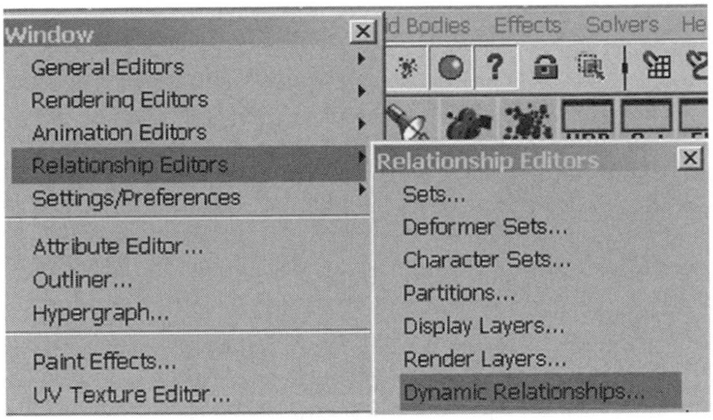

Figure 20.23 Dynamic Relationships editor menu item.

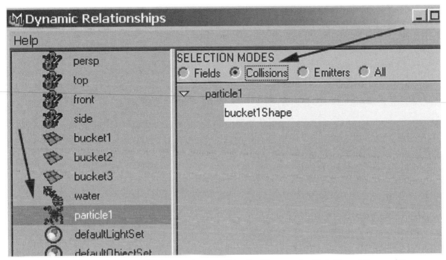

Figure 20.24 Creating a collision relationship in Dynamic Relationships editor.

```
gravity -magnitude 10 -attenuation 0.3 -dx 0 -dy −1 -dz 0;
connectDynamic -fields gravityField1 particle1;
```

Figure 20.25 shows the results of playback.

Now, only 150 particles will fall into bucket1, while the gravity field adds some force to particle1 to keep the particles under control while still retaining a small amount of bounce.

Add Other Collisions

Now, we'll add the other buckets (2 and 3) to the collisions. Let's use the same settings for resilience and friction as we did before. Enter the following MEL commands:

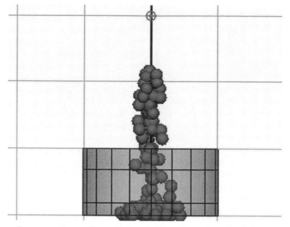

Figure 20.25 Smaller number of particles falling into bucket1.

```
collision -resilience 0.3 -friction 0.0 bucket2;
collision -resilience 0.3 -friction 0.0 bucket3;
connectDynamic -collisions bucket2 particle1;
connectDynamic -collisions bucket3 particle1;
```

The particles in particle1 will collide with the other buckets as they do with bucket1. You won't see this yet, though, because the particles bounce and come to a stop in bucket1.

Events

Usually, events are used to *split* or *emit* particles when collisions happen. This approach can be used to make splashes from rain particles when they collide with an object. In this example, instead, we will use the event command to launch a MEL procedure that will perform a task when an individual particle in the system has a collision with a particular bucket.

We start by creating an *event object,* which manages what Maya does when an event occurs. When we enter an event MEL command to create an event object for particle1, we will use the -proc flag to designate a MEL procedure that Maya will run when the event occurs. The syntax of the event command follows. Do not enter this command just yet.

```
event -name mainEvent -die 0 -count 0
      -proc eventProc particle1;
```

Before creating the object, though, we need to define the eventProc MEL script. The -name flag designates a name for the event object. The -die 0 flag establishes that the event should not delete the particles that collide. With a nonzero value, the -count flag tells event that it should wait for a particular collision, but by setting it to zero we can ensure that the event will take place every time the particle collides with a collision object.

A MEL procedure to be called by an event object, in this case named eventProc, must accept three parameters: first, a string for the particle object name; second, an integer for the particular particle Id; and third, a string for the name of the collision object. Thus, the procedure's definition must look like this:

```
global proc eventProc (string $particle, int $Id,
                       string $geoObj);
```

In a text editor of your choice, enter the code shown in Figure 20.26. The event will pass the procedure the name of particle system, the particle Id that is colliding, and the object that it is colliding with. This will execute every time a collision takes place.

Instead of defining some complex operation within this procedure that the collision events will trigger, we'll design it to set an attribute on each of the buckets that indicates that a collision has taken place. Then we will use expressions in the scene to generate the behavior we want when we see that the attribute has been set. Leave your text editor open for now; we will return to the eventProc procedure after we have created the buckets' custom trigger attributes.

In the Script Editor, type the following statements:

```
addAttr -ln collisionCheck -at long -min 0 -max 1 -keyable 1
        -dv 0 bucket1;
addAttr -ln collisionCheck -at long -min 0 -max 1 -keyable 1
        -dv 0 bucket2;
addAttr -ln collisionCheck -at long -min 0 -max 1 -keyable 1
        -dv 0 bucket3;
```

The above code will add a switch to the buckets that the eventProc procedure will change from 0 to 1 when a collision occurs. This will tell the buckets to rotate, making the particles fall into the next bucket. Once you

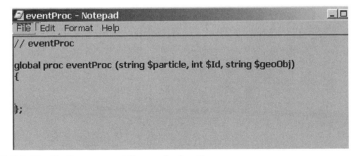

Figure 20.26 Shell of an eventProc declaration.

have created these attributes, you will see them in the Channel Box when you select each bucket.

Now, in the `eventProc` procedure, we will add the code that will set the trigger attribute. We'll use an `if` statement that will wait for the particle whose `Id` is 120 to strike `bucket1`. When this happens, we will change `bucket1.collisionCheck` from 0 to 1. Enter the code in Figure 20.27 into your `eventProc` procedure.

Note that the `"bucket1"` string has a space after the first double quote and before the word `bucket1`, due to the way the Maya passes arguments to the `eventProc`.

```
if ( ( $Id == 120) && ($geoObj == "bucket1") ) {
   set Attr ($geoObj + ".collisionCheck") 1;
}
```

Now we can add analogous code for each of the other buckets. Make your `eventProc` look like the following code block, and then save the file in your script directory. Save the file as `eventProc.mel` since Maya requires that the MEL file be named the same as the global proc you wish to call from your script path. Remember that you can find the directories in your script path by typing `getenv("MAYA_SCRIPT_PATH")` in the Script Editor. Just to make sure that Maya sees the script, we will define it manually, but if you want to have the script defined when you launch Maya, you must place it in the directories that are set in your environment.

```
// eventProc

global proc eventProc (string $particle, int $Id,
                         string $geoObj)
{
   if ( ( $Id == 120) && ($geoObj == " bucket1") ) {
      setAttr ($geoObj + ".collisionCheck") 1;
   }
}
```

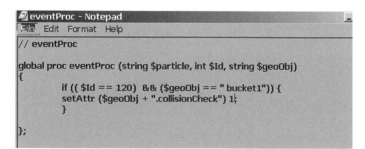

Figure 20.27 First bucket's part of the `eventProc` function.

```
    if ( ( $Id == 120) && ($geoObj == " bucket2") ) {
        setAttr ($geoObj +".collisionCheck") 1;
    }
    if ( ( $Id == 120) && ($geoObj == " bucket3") ) {
        setAttr ($geoObj +".collisionCheck") 1;
    }
};
```

Source the script from the Script Editor menu to define the global procedure eventProc (Figure 20.28). If you get an error, look over the script to see if you have any syntax problems. The way to source a script with MEL would be to type in the Script Editor:

```
source eventProc.mel;
```

Now, enter the previously discussed event command in MEL to define the event object that will call the eventProc, as follows:

```
event -name mainEvent -die 0 -count 0
      -proc eventProc particle1;
```

Expression for Buckets

Now that we have created attributes that get set to 1 when particle Id 120 collides with each bucket, we must create expressions to make the buckets tip when this attribute is set. This expression must do a couple of things. First, the expression must make sure to set all the collisionCheck attributes to 0 at frame 1. Without this, once the attribute is triggered there is no way to tell collisionCheck to go back to 0 when we rewind the scene. The second is to tell the bucket rotations to go back to rotation 0 0 0 at frame 1.

Open the Expression Editor by choosing Window > Animation Editors > Expression Editor (Figure 20.29).

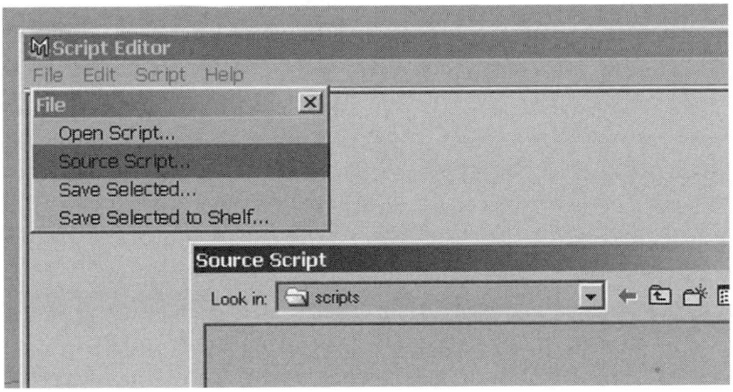

Figure 20.28 Source Script menu item.

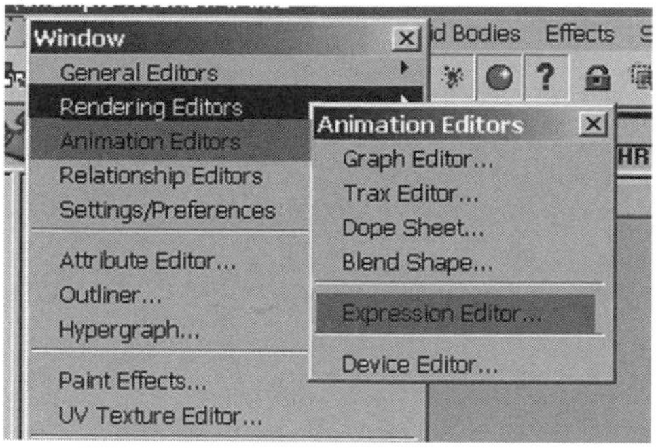

Figure 20.29 Opening the Expression Editor.

Enter the following code:

```
// Initialize the bucket(1-3).collisionCheck to 0 when on
   frame 1

if (frame == 1) {           // Check if we're back on frame 1
   setAttr bucket1.collisionCheck 0;
   setAttr bucket2.collisionCheck 0;
   setAttr bucket3.collisionCheck 0;
                           // Set all collisionChecks to 0
}

// Initialize the bucket to a rotation of 0 0 0

if (frame == 1) {           // Check if we're back on frame 1
   bucket1.rotateX = 0;
   bucket2.rotateX = 0;
   bucket3.rotateX = 0;        // Set all rotateX's back to 0
}
```

This part of the expression initializes the collisionCheck and rotate attributes when the animation is rewound. In the same expression, we need now to set up the actions that take place after the event triggers the collisionCheck attribute. Also, notice that we are using a setAttr command for the collisionCheck in order to avoid setting up a connection between the expression node and the collisionCheck attributes, which would make it impossible for the eventProc() callback to set that attribute at runtime. This is why we can't simply use bucket.collisionCheck = 1 syntax in the expression. We will rotate the buckets with a small increment to the rotateX attribute of each bucket when that bucket's collisionCheck attribute is set. The motion will not have any ease in/ease out, but it will suffice for now. In the same expression, after the code above, enter the following:

```
// Set up a triggered rotation with a += to the rotateX attrs

if (bucket1.collisionCheck != 0) {
                                // Check if the attr is not equal 0
    if (bucket1.rotateX > -111){
                                // If we are not at -111 rotateX
        bucket1.rotateX += -2; // Add the current X -2 each frame
    }
}

if (bucket2.collisionCheck != 0) {      // Same for bucket2,
                                        // only use positive
    if (bucket2.rotateX < 111) {        // numbers for reverse rotation
        bucket2.rotateX += 2;
    }
}

if (bucket3.collisionCheck != 0) {
                                        // Use the same sets as bucket1
    if (bucket3.rotateX > -111){
        bucket3.rotateX += -2;
    }
}
```

Now, commit the expression by clicking the Create button. Figure 20.30 shows the results of playback.

Edit Settings to Fix Problems

There are two things that we need to change. The first is to increase the tessellation factor in the geoConnectors to 600. We will get better collisions this way since some particles travel through the buckets every once in a while. Use the following statements in MEL:

```
setAttr geoConnector1.tessellationFactor 600;
setAttr geoConnector2.tessellationFactor 600;
setAttr geoConnector3.tessellationFactor 600;
```

We also want to change the friction in bucket2 to 0.2 so we can cut down on the sliding around in bucket2. Input the following statement:

```
setAttr geoConnector2.friction 0.2;
```

Speed

As you noticed, the scene does not play back in "real time" because of the collisions, to event, to expression calls. Pick a good camera position, and shoot a Playblast movie to see the animation at full speed. If you run into

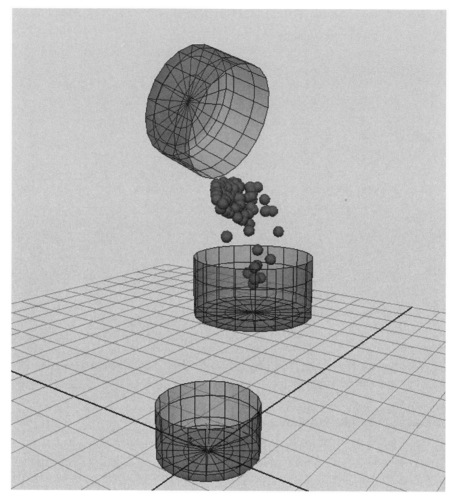

Figure 20.30 Finished digital bucket brigade.

memory problems, lower the Scale settings in the Playblast options. Playblast and its options are available by choosing Windows > Playblast ❏.

Example 3: Collisions Between Objects in Solid Dynamics

In Example 2, we looked at collisions between particles and objects. Solid dynamics allow similar object interactions but with much more control over how they react to each other. Figure 20.31 shows an example of the solid dynamics approach.

Start by building an array of polygonal planes in a 3 × 3 grid. Select Create > Polygon Primitives > Plane ❏, and make a plane with 4 subdivi-

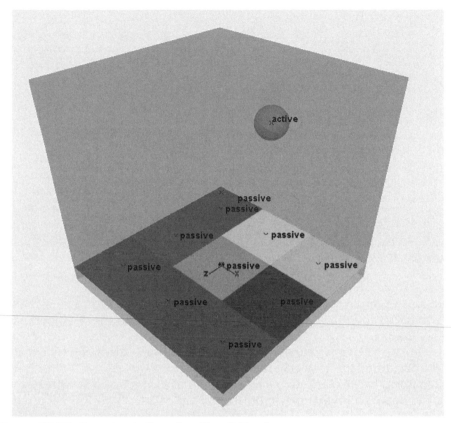

Figure 20.31 Bouncing ball made with solid bodies.

sions in width and height. Leave the rest of the Plane options at their default settings (Figure 20.32).

Rename the pPlane1 object to grid in the Channel Box, and set the X, Y, and Z scale values to 4, 4, and 4. To do this in the Script Editor, use the following statements:

```
rename pPlane1 grid;
xform -worldSpace -scale 4 4 4 grid;
```

Remember to look in the lower right corner of the screen for the Script Editor button.

Note: We have been using the xform command frequently in these examples because this command can complete several functions at once. Otherwise, you might have to make several calls to the move, scale, and rotate commands. In the long run, you will find it more useful to do all at once with xform.

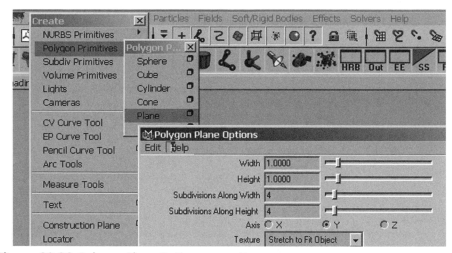

Figure 20.32 Polygon Plane Options menu item.

In this example, we will assign a *shader* to grid. To attach a shadingMap type material to grid, choose Windows > Rendering Editors > HyperShade (Figure 20.33).

Create a shadingMap shader from the Create Materials menu by clicking on the Shading Map icon (Figure 20.34).

Rename shadingMap1 to shadingMap in the Hypershade window by holding down the right mouse button on the shader icon for the rename option. Then, with grid selected, select the shadingMap icon, hold the right mouse down, and pick Assign Material to Selection. Now grid will use shadingMap for rendering. Also, each shader has a shading group that defines what objects it shades. Now that we have renamed the shader, rename the corresponding shading group as well.

```
rename shadingMap1SG shadingMapSG;
```

Write Small Duplicate and Position Script

Instead of just duplicating the grid eight times so that we get nine grids in the set, we can script it by using an array variable to store the grid positions

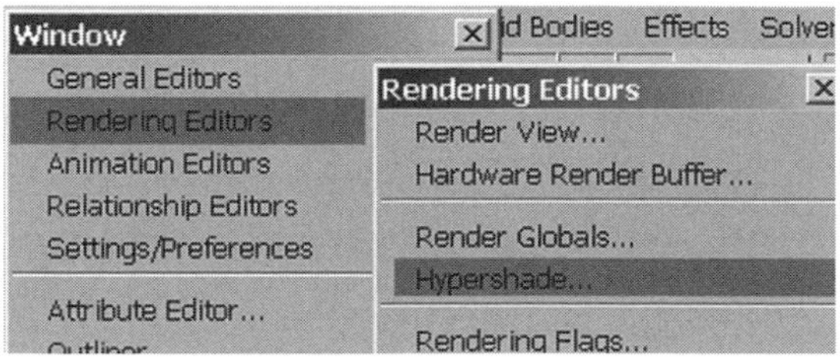

Figure 20.33 Hypershade menu item.

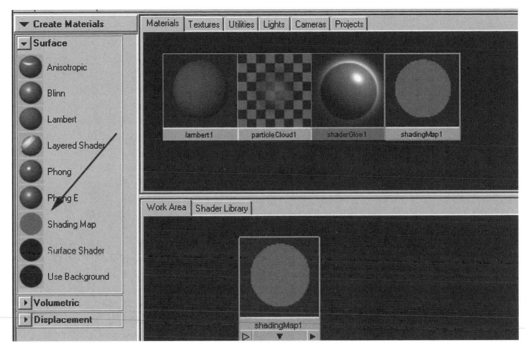

Figure 20.34 Shading Map icon in Hypershade window.

and move through the array as we duplicate. Our script will duplicate the grid using the array of positions, making a copy of shadingMap and assigning it to the new grids, using string substitutions. This way, each new grid will have its own shadingMap. Open your favorite text editor, and enter the following header:

```
global proc gridDup () {
```

Now enter the array of positions that we want the other grids to be:

```
$gridArray = {"-4 0 -4", "-4 0 0", "-4 0 4", "0 0 -4",
              "0 0 4", "4 0 -4", "4 0 0", "4 0 4"};
```

We will need to use the eval command to assemble a command with the extracted string from $gridArray since we cannot use the string of numbers directly in an xform command. Create the for loop that will duplicate the grid and the shadingMap shader, and assign the new shaders to the new grids. We are going to let Maya make the names of the new grids that are being duplicated and use them in the loop.

```
for ($i = 0; $i < 8; $i++) {
    // Duplicate grids and transform using array positions
      duplicate -rr grid;
```

```
$cmd = "xform -worldSpace -translation " +
        ($gridArray[$i] + " grid"+ ($i + 1) );
eval($cmd);

// Duplicate shadingMap shader group and assign to each grid
    duplicate -name ("shadingMap" + $i + "SG")
                -upstreamNodes shadingMapSG;
sets -e -forceElement ("shadingMap" + $i + "SG")
                            ("grid" + ($i + 1) );
    }// End loop
}; // End procedure
```

When we make the grid objects, they will be named grid1, grid2, grid3, and so on. Because $i starts at 0, we must use $i +1 when we refer to the grid objects. The loop starts $i at a 0, which is fine for moving through the array, but we know that the grid names will start with grid1 at the first duplicate. Note that using the variable $i this way in the object name will not affect the actual value of $i.

Common Mistakes in Assembling String Variables

Remember to make sure there is a space before the word " grid" in double quotes.

Save your text file, naming it gridDup.mel. In the Script Editor, source it, using the Source Script menu item (Figure 20.35). If you get any error messages, go back and check for syntax errors.

Tip: This is not really an interactive script that you can use to duplicate any object. Instead, it's a one-time script developed for this particular scene. Later, if you want

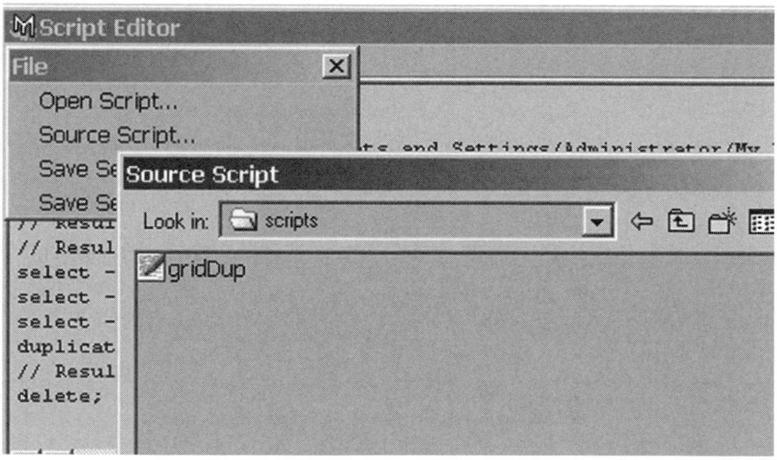

Figure 20.35 Source Script menu item.

to modify this script to be more generic, you can alter it to use string parameters in place of the hard-coded strings grid and shadingMap1.

Now, in the Script Editor, type gridDup without .mel, and press the Enter key on the numeric keypad. This will execute the script and link the new shaders to the new grid objects. Figure 20.36 indicates what you should see in the Maya interface; Figure 20.37, what you should see in the HyperShade window.

Create Collision Box

Now we need to create a polygonal box that will surround the grids. In the Script Editor, enter the polyCube command, as follows:

```
polyCube -name collisionBox. -w 1 -h 1 -d 1 -sx 1 -sy 1
                             -sz 1 -ax 0 1 0
                             -tx 1 -ch 1;
```

Next, scale and transform the box to surround the grids:

```
xform -worldSpace -scale 12 12 12 collisionBox;
xform -worldSpace -translation 0 5 0 collisionBox;
```

Turn on Shading > Smooth Shade All and Shade Options > WireFrame on Shaded in the persp Panel. We can't see through the box, but we can adjust the transparency parameter on its shader to fix this. Return to the Hypershade window, and adjust the transparency on the lambert1 shader, which was assigned to the collisionBox when it was created. Double-click the lambert1 icon, and move the Transparency slider almost all the way to the right (Figure 20.38). Figure 20.39 shows what you should see in the persp window.

Flip Normals on collisionBox

Select the collisionBox, and select the Display > Polygon Components > Normals (Figure 20.40). From this, you can see that the normals are pointing out. We need them reversed for correct collisions to happen within the box.

Now we can see the normals pointing out in the interface (Figure 20.41).

Let's flip the normals, using the polynormal command in the Script Editor.

```
polyNormal -normalMode 0 -ch 1 collisionBox.f[0:5];
```

We have to do this for each of the polygon faces; thus, the collisionBox.f[0:5]. This statement has changed our selection mode. To change it back to Object mode, click the Select by Object Type icon (Figure 20.42). Figure 20.43 shows the results of reversing the normals.

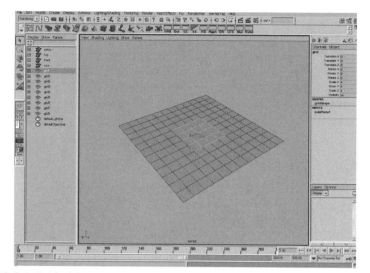

Figure 20.36 Grid objects in main window.

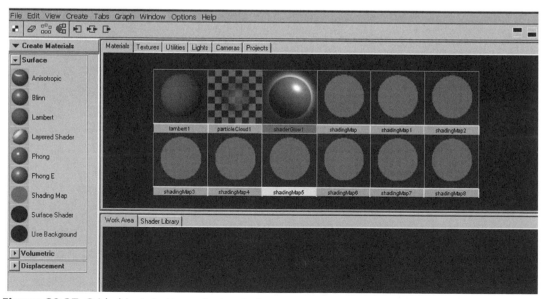

Figure 20.37 Grid objects in Hypershade window.

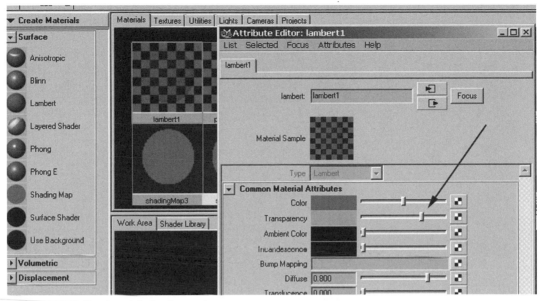

Figure 20.38 lambert1 shader options.

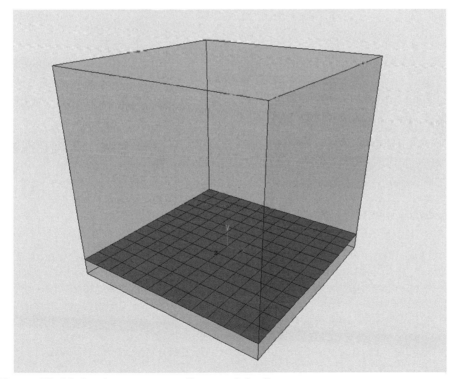

Figure 20.39 Semitransparent walls around the floor.

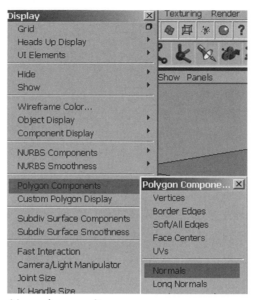

Figure 20.40 Show Normals menu item.

You can switch off the normal display by selecting menu item Display > Polygon Components > Normals with collisionBox selected.

Active and Passive Rigid Bodies

Now it's time to create a sphere and make it a dynamic object. First, create Ball. In the Script Editor, type the following code:

```
polySphere -name Ball -r 1 -subdivisionsX 12 -subdivisionsY 12
        -ax 0 1 0 -tx 1 -ch 1;
xform -worldSpace -scale 1.0 1.0 1.0;
xform -worldSpace -translation 0 5 0;
```

In the Dynamics menu group, select Ball, and choose Soft/Rigid Body > Create Active Rigid Body > ☐. As you can see, the solid dynamics options for objects are quite extensive. The Ball will be an active rigid body while the collisionBox will be a passive rigid body. The difference is that an active body acts and reacts to its dynamics and that of others, including active and passive rigid bodies. Passive rigid bodies do not react to active rigid bodies. Passive rigid bodies are instead fixed objects with which active rigid bodies can collide.

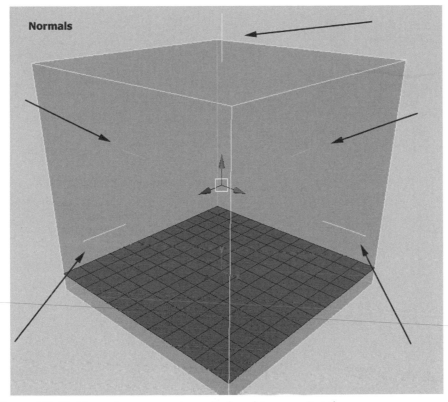

Figure 20.41 Normal components as displayed in persp Panel.

Figure 20.42 Select by Object Type icon.

Settings for Ball are shown in Figure 20.44. The attributes we are looking for are Static Friction, 0.1; Bounciness, 0.8; and Damping, 0.1.

In the Initial Settings frame, we want to add the settings shown in Figure 20.45. Specifically, set Initial Spin to 0, 0, and 360, and Initial Velocity to 12, 0, and −12. Then, in Performance Attributes, set Stand In to Sphere (Figure 20.46).

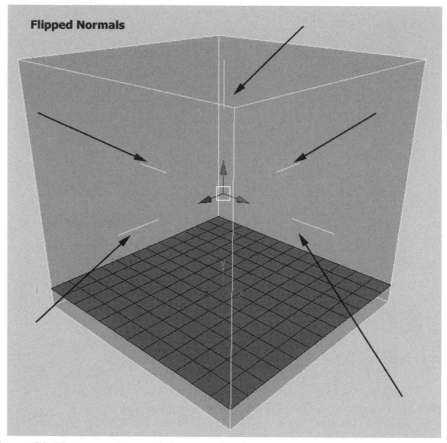

Figure 20.43 Reversed normals in persp Panel.

To set all of the above options, the MEL command statement follows:

```
rigidBody -active -m 1 -dp 0.1 -sf 0.1 -df 0.2 -b 0.8 -1 0
           -tf 600
           -iv 12 0 -12
           -iav 0 0 360 -c 0 -pc 0 -i 0 0 0 -imp 0 0 0
           -si 0 0 0
           -sio sphere Ball;
```

If we take a look in the Hypergraph, we will see all the connections that setting up rigid bodies creates (Figure 20.47).

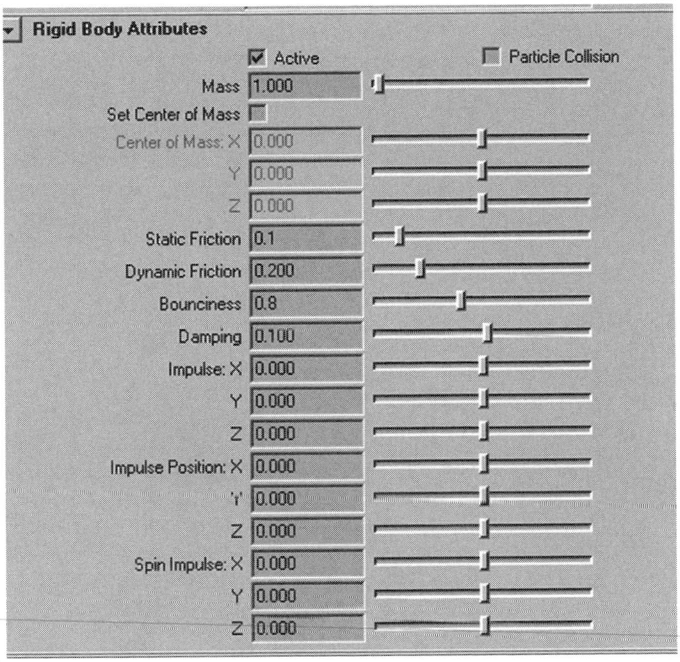

Figure 20.44 Rigid Body Attributes for Ball.

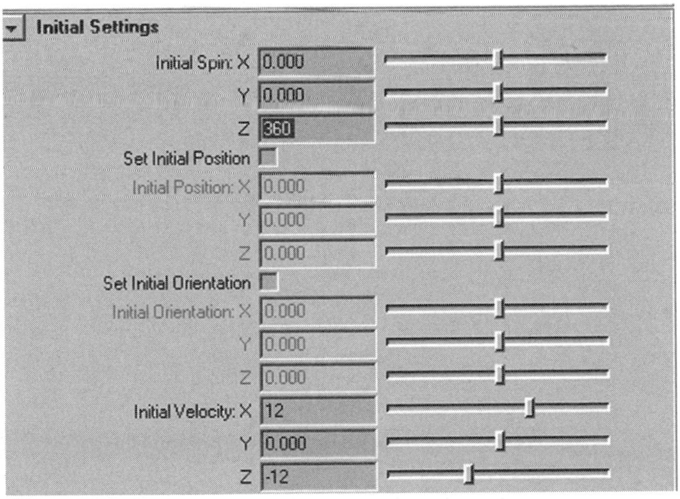

Figure 20.45 Initial Settings for Ball.

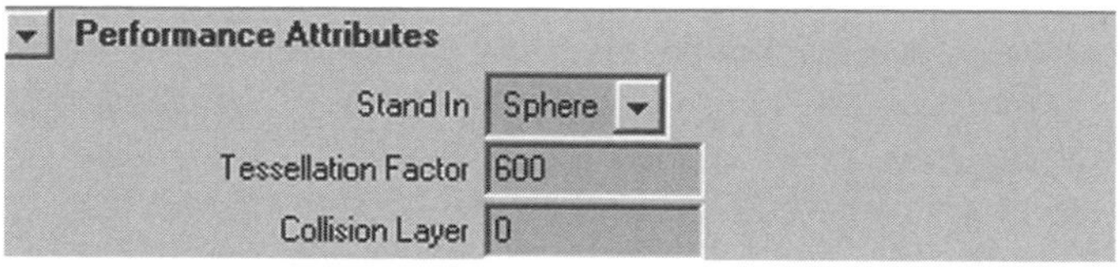

Performance Attributes

Stand In | Sphere
Tessellation Factor | 600
Collision Layer | 0

Figure 20.46 Performance Attributes for `Ball`.

Now we need to make `collisionBox` a passive rigid body. Select the `collisionBox`. From the same menu that we used to make `Ball` an active rigid body, select the menu choice Passive Rigid Body > ❏. Make the settings the same as you did for the active rigid body, except set Stand In to none, and set all Initial Settings to 0.

The equivalent MEL command follows:

```
rigidBody -passive -m 1 -dp 0.1 -sf 0.2 -df 0.2 -b 0.7 -l 0
          -tf 600 -iv 0 0 0
          -iav 0 0 0 -c 0 -pc 0 -i 0 0 0 -imp 0 0 0 -si 0 0 0
          -sio none collisionBox;
```

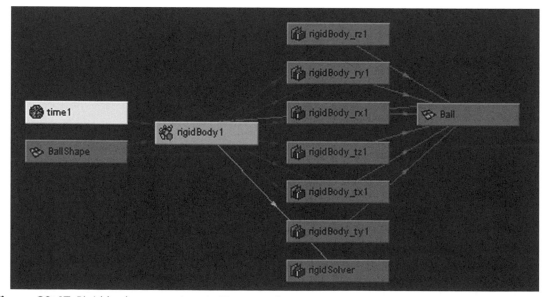

Figure 20.47 Rigid body connections in Hypergraph.

Before you play back the scene, add a `gravity` field with a magnitude of 3 and a `turbulenceField` with a magnitude of 20. Both will have an Attenuation of 0 since we want the effect of these fields to be instant. Following are the MEL commands to do this. (If you choose to use Maya's menus instead, remember to select the `Ball` first so that the fields will automatically connect to `Ball`.)

```
gravity -pos 0 0 0 -m 3 -att 0 -dx 0 -dy -1 -dz 0 -mxd -1;
turbulence -pos 0 0 0 -m 20 -att 0 -f 1 -mxd -1;
connectDynamic -f gravityField1 Ball;
connectDynamic -f turbulenceField1 Ball;
```

Now set the playback start; end at 1 to 300, and play.

```
playbackOptions -min 1 -max 300;
```

The playback should resemble a bee-in-a-box animation in which the `Ball` bounces around in the `collisionBox`. If you get the following warning message in the Script Editor,

```
// Warning: Cycle on 'Ball.worldMatrix[0]' may not evaluate
as expected. (Use 'cycleCheck -e off' to disable this
warning.) //
```

just type `cycleCheck -e off` in the Script Editor.

Now, we will make the grids Passive Rigid Bodies for the `Ball` to collide with.

Make Each Grid a Passive Collision Object

There are two ways in MEL to make the grids passive collision objects for the `Ball`. The easiest is to select all the grids and run the `rigidBody` command.

```
select -r grid grid1 grid2 grid3 grid4 grid5 grid6 grid7 grid8;

rigidBody -passive -m 1 -dp 0.1 -sf 0.2 -df 0.2 -b 0.7 -l 0
          -tf 600
          -iv 0 0 0 -iav 0 0 0 -c 0 -pc 0 -i 0 0 0 -imp 0 0 0
          -si 0 0 0 -sio none;
```

The other is to use a `for` loop, as we did when we duplicated the grids. While using the loop is not as simple in this instance, if you needed to run other MEL commands as you were making each grid a passive collision object, you could place them in the loop to ensure that they are run at the same time.

You have one object named `grid` and a series named `grid1` through `grid8`, so let's make `grid` a passive collision object without using a loop, since it does not a have number added at the end of its name. In the Script Editor, type the above `rigidBody` command, but this time specify the object by name rather than relying on the selection, as follows:

```
rigidBody -passive -m 1 -dp 0.1 -sf 0.2 -df 0.2 -b 0.7 -l 0
        -tf 600
        -iv 0 0 0 -iav 0 0 0 -c 0 -pc 0 -i 0 0 0 -imp 0 0 0
        -si 0 0 0 -sio none grid;
```

Now make the for loop:

```
for ($i = 1; $i < 9; $i++) {
    rigidBody -passive -m 1 -dp 0.1 -sf 0.2 -df 0.2 -b 0.7
            -l 0 -tf 600 -iv 0 0 0
            -iav 0 0 0 -c 0 -pc 0 -i 0 0 0 -imp 0 0 0 -si 0 0 0
            -sio none ("grid" + $i);
}
```

When you play back the above script, the Ball should now bounce off the grids and not the bottom of the collisionBox. If you want, go to the menu Solvers > Rigid Body Solver and turn on the Display Label option. This will tell you which colliders are passive and which are active (Figure 20.48).

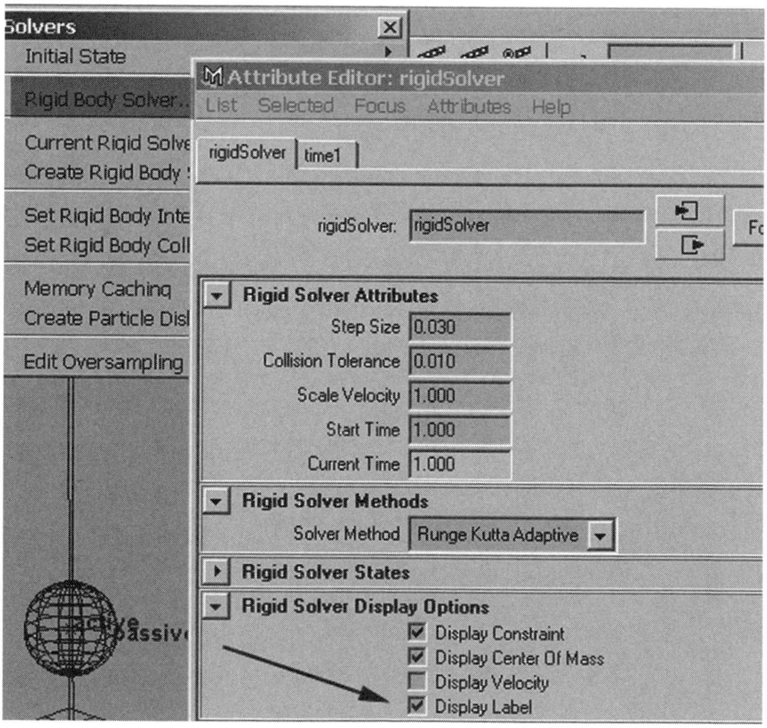

Figure 20.48 Rigid Body Solver's Display Label option.

In the persp window, select Shading > Shade Options, and turn off the Wireframe on Shaded option (Figure 20.49).

Turn on Collision Data Options

Since we will be working with collision data, we need to turn on that option in the Attribute Editor for the `rigidSolver` object. Select Solvers > Rigid Body Solver, and click the option Contact Data in the Rigid Solver States section (Figure 20.50). This is not on by default since it will slow the simulation down from the regular performance. In this simulation, we will not see a difference.

Change Color of Grids with Collisions

Now we'll add an expression that will send a random RGB color to the `Ball`'s `shadingMap` shader when `Ball` collides with one of the grids. We will start by adding the expression to grid's rigid body object, and then

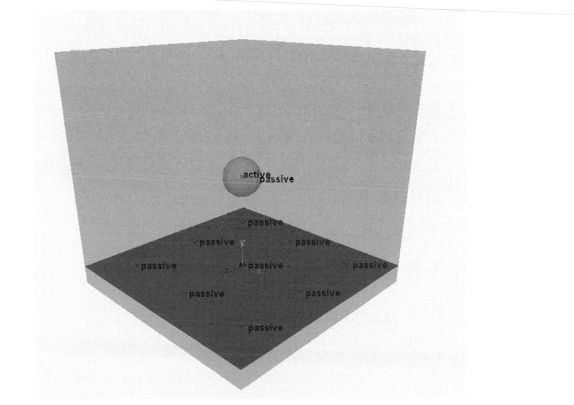

Figure 20.49 Scene with wireframe display turned off.

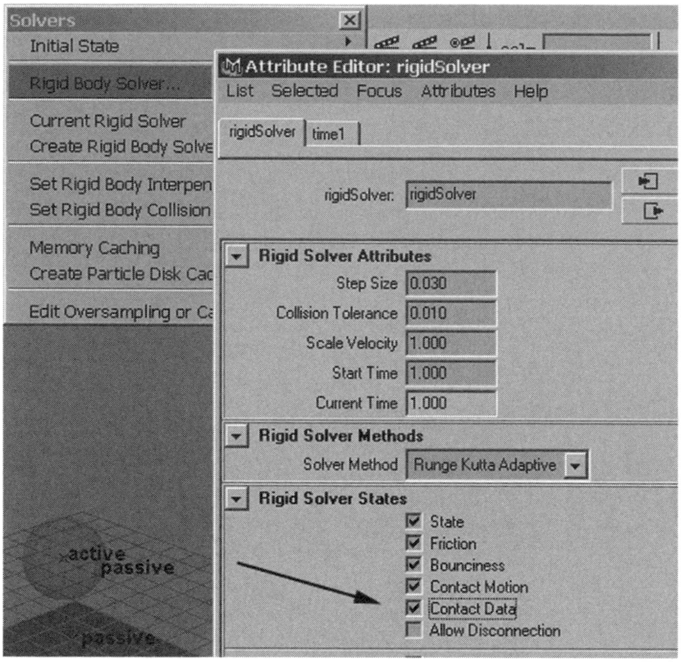

Figure 20.50 Contact Data options in rigid body Solver attributes.

we'll add the expression to the numbered grids' rigid body objects. In other words, we are going to attach the expressions to `rigidBody3` through `rigidBody11`.

With `rigidBody3` selected, open the Expression Editor with Windows > Animation Editors > Expression Editor. If you want an easy way to get to `rigidBody3`, use the Outliner with the Display Shapes option. Then open the + icon to see what is under the selected node (Figure 20.51).

In the Expression Editor, type the following code:

```
// Check to see if we are at frame 1 and
// set the color to grey

if (frame == 1) {
   setAttr shadingMap.shadingMapColor -type double3 0.5 0.5 0.5 ;
};

// Check if Ball has hit and capture first collision
// Change color to random RGB value

if ( rigidBody3.contactCount > 0 ) {
  setAttr shadingMap.shadingMapColor -type double3 (rand(0,1))
                                  (rand(0,1)) (rand(0,1));
};
```

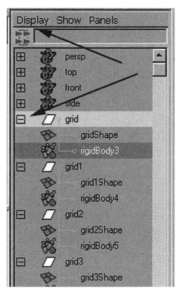

Figure 20.51 Using display shapes and expanding the outline to see `rigidBody3`.

The nice thing about a rigid body's `contactCount` attribute is that it will remain 0 until the collision. Then it will change to 1, then to 2, and so on with each collision. Thus, we only need to check that it's 0 to know that a collision has occurred.

Create the expression by clicking the Create button. Before we click on Play, let's change the initial velocity and spin settings that we gave to the `Ball` and change the magnitude of the turbulence. To do this, type the following code in the Script Editor:

```
setAttr rigidBody1.initialVelocityX 0;
setAttr rigidBody1.initialVelocityZ 0;
setAttr rigidBody1.initialSpinZ 0;
setAttr turbulenceField1.magnitude 0;
```

Then, in the persp window, go to the Shading menu, and turn on Hardware Texturing so that we can see the color changes (Figure 20.52). Also, turn off the grid from the Display > Grid menu so that we can see more clearly. Figure 20.53 shows the results of playback.

The `grid` will now change to a random color each time that `Ball` hits it. Now we need to make another `for` loop to create the same expression for each of the other grids, to control the other `shadingMap` shaders. We can attach this expression to each grid node using a MEL script, by assembling

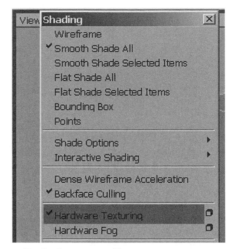

Figure 20.52 Hardware Texturing menu item.

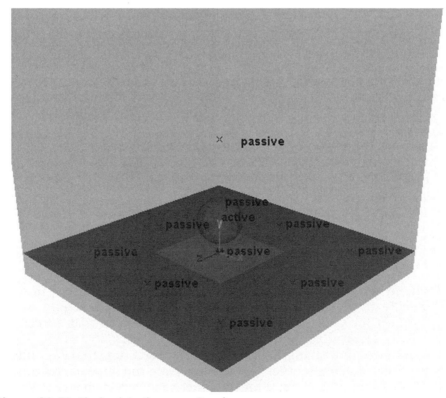

Figure 20.53 Playback in the persp Panel.

the expression in a variable called $expstring and then passing that string to the MEL expression command. Remember that we need to start off with rigidBody4 and end at rigidBody11, with each expression manipulating a different shadingMap from shadingMap1 to shadingMap8.

In the Script Editor, type in this double for loop, which increments both $i and $j each time through the loop.

In the Script Editor, type in the following double for loop:

```
for ($i = 4, $j = 1; $i < 12, $j < 9; $i++, $j++) {

    $expstring = "\nif (frame == 1) {\n";
    $expstring += "setAttr ";
    $expstring += ("shadingMap" + $j + ".shadingMapColor");
    $expstring += "-type double3 0.5 0.5 0.5;\n";
    $expstring += "};\n";
    $expstring += "if (";
    $expstring += ("rigidBody" + $i + ".contactCount");
    $expstring += " > 0) {\n";
    $expstring += "setAttr ";
    $expstring += ("shadingMap" + $j + ".shadingMapColor");
    $expstring += "-type double3 (rand(0,1)) (rand(0,1))
                                 (rand(0,1));\n";
    $expstring += "};";

    // Execute the expressions
    expression  s $expstring -o ("expression" + $j)
             -ae true -uc all;
};
```

If you are assembling strings like the above code, you can test the script first by assembling the string, and then printing it to see if it is what you want. To test this, try commenting out the expression command by adding a at the beginning of the line, and replace it with

```
print $expstring
```

Enter the command by pressing Enter.

Before you play the scene, set the values for the initial velocities and spins for the Ball and also the turbulence magnitude back to their initial values.

```
setAttr rigidBody1.initialVelocityX 12;
setAttr rigidBody1.initialVelocityZ -12;
setAttr rigidBody1.initialSpinZ 360;
setAttr turbulenceField1.magnitude 20;
```

Figure 20.54 shows results of playback. Now, when the ball strikes the grids, their colors change. Try different settings for the ball's rigidBody1 initial velocities, bounciness, and turbulence magnitude to experiment with variations.

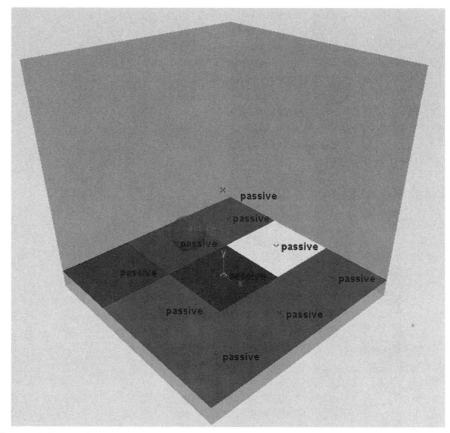

Figure 20.54 Changing grid colors in response to bounding ball.

Example 4: Solid Dynamics and Particles

In this example, we are going to use particle collisions to act on multiple solid bodies with added expressions. Figure 20.55 shows the results of such a strategy. Also, we'll create a small MEL window to control the direction for particle emission.

Let's start by constructing the scene. In the Script Editor, create a NURBS plane, as follows:

```
nurbsPlane -name panel -p 0 0 0 -ax 0 1 0 -w 1 -lr 1 -d 3
            -u 1 -v 1 -ch 1;
    xform -worldSpace -scale 20 20 20 panel;
    xform -worldSpace -rotation 0 0 -90 panel;
```

These commands will place the panel in the center of the world and point the normals in the positive X direction, which will be important for the collisions.

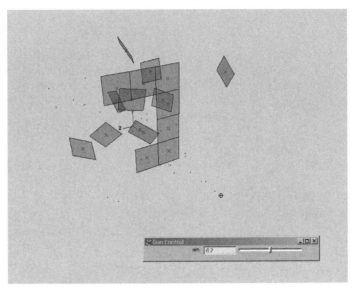

Figure 20.55 Particle gun knocks away solid bodies.

Now we need to create a directional emitter called gun. In the Script Editor, type the following:

```
emitter -pos 25 0 0 -type direction -name gun -r 30 -spd 50
        -mxd 0
        -dx -1
         dy 0 -dz 0 -sp 0;
particle;
connectDynamic -em gun particle1;
```

Set the timeline's start and end to 1 and 300, respectively, and hit Play. Figure 20.56 shows the result.

Create Interface Window for Aim Control Using MEL

Let's create a floating MEL slider in a window that we will hook up to the gun's Y rotation so that we can control the direction of the particles. First, we have to determine the limits that we want on the rotation. A range of −30 to 30 should be fine since we do not always want the particles to hit the panel throughout the simulation. Also, we want to use floating-point numbers and not integers since the floats will give a smoother transition between −30 and 30.

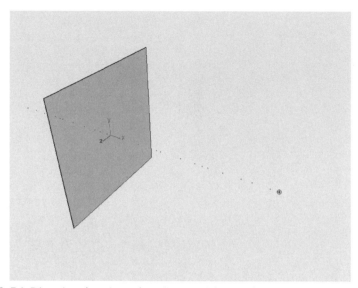

Figure 20.56 Directional emitter shooting particles at plane.

Open your favorite text editor for MEL scripting. In this editor, we will develop the MEL commands to build the window. Enter the following commands:

```
window -title "Gun Control" -width 400 -height 50;
  columnLayout;
  floatSliderGrp -label "aim" -field true
    -minValue -30.0 -maxValue 30.0 rotY;

connectControl rotY gun.rotateY;
showWindow;
```

After we look at how these commands work, we will paste them into the Script Editor and execute them to see what the window looks like and how it functions.

The above commands and their parameters should be familiar from Chapter 14.

`window -title "Gun Control"` is the name of the window as it appears on the interface.

`-width` and `-height` specify a 400 • 50 pixel window. Although the user can resize it, this will be the default window size.

`columnLayout` creates the layout of the rest of the settings called after it in a single column.

Figure 20.57 Gun Control window.

floatSliderGrp will make a slider and an associated floating-point field.

-label defines the name of the slider.

-minValue and -maxValue set the range of the slider.

rotY is the name of the slider that floatSliderGrp creates.

connectControl rotY gun.rotateY connects the control rotY to the attribute gun.rotateY, so that dragging the slider changes the attribute.

showWindow displays the window in the Maya interface.

To make the window, select the text in the text editor, and cut and paste (Ctrl+C and then Ctrl+V in Windows) into the Script Editor. Press Enter. Figure 20.57 shows the window that you will see.

Now, play back the scene while you move the slider back and forth to see the effect it has on the gun emitter (Figure 20.58).

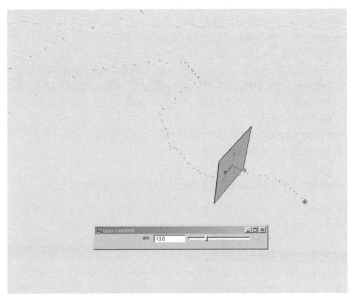

Figure 20.58 Erratic spray of particles from rotating gun.

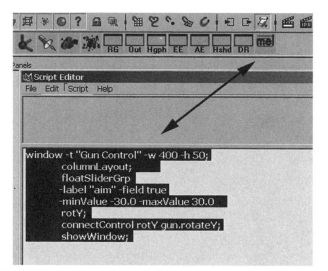

Figure 20.59 Installing script as MEL shelf button.

Add New Window Control to Shelf

We can add the script to make the window we created and put it in Maya's shelf so that it can be executed with the click of a button. In the Script Editor, paste the selected text that you copied from the text editor (it's probably still in the system text buffer). Select the text in the Script Editor, and hold down the middle mouse button. With the button held down, drag it into the shelf in the Maya interface (Figure 20.59).

Close the Gun Control window, and click the new MEL icon on the shelf. The window will return. If you want to name the icon, use the Shelf Editor, available from the pop-up menu indicated by the triangle icon at the left side of the shelf.

Save the scene as ex8start in your project scenes directory (default); we are going to return to it later.

Convert Panel to Polygons and Break Up into Pieces

Later in the example, we will create a script that will convert the panel to polygons and break it into smaller pieces. First, to become familiar with the steps involved, select the panel and choose Modify > Convert > NURBS to Polygons > ❐ (Figure 20.60).

Change 3D Delta to 0.13 and Type to Quads, and then click Apply. You will end up with a nice polygonal grid with even distribution of square

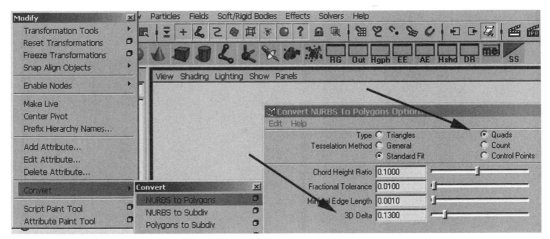

Figure 20.60 Converting NURBS to polygons.

faces. Change the name of the resulting object in the Outliner window to
polyPanel. The MEL equivalent follows:

```
nurbsToPoly -name polyPanel -polygonType 1 -delta 0.13 panel;
```

To break the panel into pieces, we need to break it up into individual
polygons per face. Hide the original panel by selecting panelL in the
Outliner and using the default key mapping Ctrl-H. Or, in the Script Editor,
type

```
hide panel;
```

Figure 20.61 shows the results.

To break the panel up, we need to select its faces. Using MEL, we can do
this in a way that returns the number of faces that are selected. First, we
will use the select command but with "*" wildcard syntax. The following
statement will select all the faces in polyPanel.

```
select -r polyPanel.f["*"];
```

Now we will use the filterExpand command with the -selectionMask
34 flag to get the faces that are selected and store them in a variable called
$faceList. filterExpand looks at the selection and returns to your script
a list of all of the selected objects of a given type, designated by the
selectionMask number. Looking in the MEL Command Reference in the
filterExpand page, we can see that a selectionMask of 34 returns selected
polygon faces.

```
$faceList = `filterExpand -sm 34`;
```

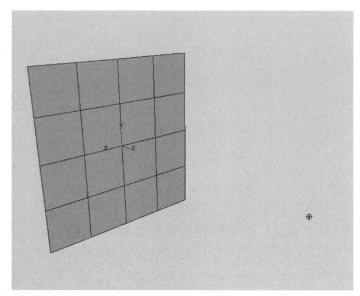

Figure 20.61 With the NURBS panel hidden, only the polygon panel remains visible.

Now we can find the number of faces with the `size( )` function:

```
size($faceList);
```

If you run the above command in the Script Editor, you will see the following:

```
size($faceList);
// Result: 16 //
```

To break up the surface, you will need to know the number of faces are in `polyPanel`. The number of elements in `$faceList` tells us that there are 16 faces, or 0 to 15 in the `polyPanel.f[]` array. Now that we have the face count, let's extract the faces with the `polyChipOff` command, which makes them individual objects. In the Script Editor, type the following:

```
polyChipOff -keepFacesTogether 0
polyPanel.f[0:(size($faceList) + 1)];
```

Now separate the faces so that each gets its own node. Type in

```
polySeparate -name smPanels polyPanel;
```

You should see each of them under the `polyPanel` node in the Outliner window (Figure 20.62).

Since the above command leaves the original object, we can delete smPanels from the list. We just want the individual, separated polygon objects of smPanels1 to 16. Use the following command:

```
delete smPanels;
```

Add Dynamics and Expressions to Pieces

We will use a for loop to give smPanels1 to 16 dynamic properties, to connect them to particle collisions, and then to expressions. Listed below are the actions we want to perform on each piece.

1. Make each a solid body with an initial setting to react to a particle collision.
2. Connect each with particle1 to enable collisions with its particles.
3. Assign an expression to each piece that will turn off particle collisions once the piece reacts to a particle striking it, and that will send the piece in positive X and negative Z to simulate a wind force.

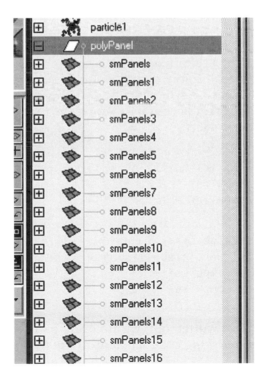

Return to your favorite text editor to assemble the following script so that you can later copy and paste it into the Script Editor. In the text editor enter the following:

```
for ($i = 1; $i <= size($faceList); $i ++ ) {

rigidBody -active -damping 1 -collisions 0 -particleCollision 1
        ("smPanels" + $i);
collision -r 0.2 -f 0.2 ("smPanels" + $i);
connectDynamic -c ("smPanels" + $i) particle1;
```

Note that we have not yet completed the loop. Before we finish, we will add an expression.

The first command turns smPanel + $i into a rigidBody with particle collisions on, and the next command makes it a collision object. Finally, the third command connects the collision object with particle1. We don't want collisions between the smPanels for the sake of speed, so we need to set -collisions to 0, or off, in the rigidBody command.

Now assemble the expression that will give the smPanel piece an impulse if its velocity is less than 0 in X (in the negative X direction). When this happens, our expression will set the impulse velocity in X to 2 and in Z to –2. This will send the piece forward and to the right. We also need to turn the rigid body particle collisions off because the particles will keep hitting the piece and pushing in negative X through dynamics. Once this attribute is turned off, the particles will still bounce off the pieces but not affect the panel's dynamics. And of course we need to reset the settings when we rewind to the beginning, frame 1.

Following is the expression as we would type it in directly to the Expression Editor. What we will actually do is build this expression in a string and use the expression command to create an expression node connected with the panel object.

```
if (frame == 1) {
    rigidBody1.particleCollision = 1;
    rigidBody1.impulseX = 0;
    rigidBody1.impulseZ = 0;
};

if (rigidBody1.velocityX < 0) {
        rigidBody1.particleCollision = 0;
        rigidBody1.impulseX = 2;
        rigidBody1.impulseZ = –2;
};
```

With the expression written out, we are ready to assemble it in a string. To do this, add the following code segment to the loop that we have been editing.

```
$expstring = "\nif (frame == 1) {\n";
$expstring += ("rigidBody" + $i + ".particleCollision");
$expstring += " = 1;\n";
$expstring += ("rigidBody" + $i + ".impulseX");
$expstring += " = 0;\n";
$expstring += ("rigidBody" + $i + ".impulseZ");
$expstring += " = 0;\n";
$expstring += "};\n";
$expstring += "\nif (";
$expstring += ("rigidBody" + $i + ".velocityX");
$expstring += " < 0) {\n";
$expstring += ("rigidBody" + $i + ".particleCollision");
$expstring += " = 0;\n";
$expstring += ("rigidBody" + $i + ".impulseX");
$expstring += " = 2;\n";
$expstring += ("rigidBody" + $i + ".impulseZ");
$expstring += " = -2;\n";
$expstring += "};\n";

expression -s $expstring -o ("expression" + $i)
                          -ae true -uc all;
```

Finally, end the loop with a curly bracket and a semicolon:

```
};
```

Now select the text from the text editor, and copy and paste into the Script Editor. Press Enter on the numeric keypad to execute it.

Finally, we need to adjust the life span of particle1 so that the particles will not live forever in the scene. Type the following:

```
setAttr particleShape1.lifespanMode 1;
```

```
setAttr particleShape1.lifespan 1.0;
```

Access the window that we created earlier by clicking the icon on the shelf. This will bring back the Gun Control slider (Figure 20.63).

Now, play the scene, moving the slider to the left side so that it reads 30, and then move it to the right (Figure 20.64).

Create Full MEL Script

Now that we have tested all the parts, let's assemble the full MEL script in the text editor so that we can load the saved scene and run the script on the panel object. The full script follows:

```
global proc panelBreakup( ) {

    print "Converting panel to polys\n";
    nurbsToPoly -name polyPanel -polygonType 1 -delta 0.13 panel;
```

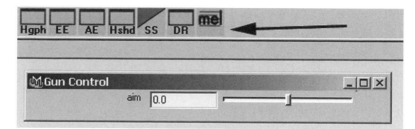

Figure 20.63 Clicking on the MEL button reveals Gun Control window.

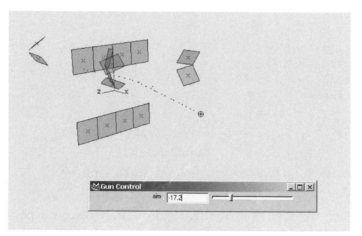

Figure 20.64 Knocking away solid bodies with the gun.

```
print "Selecting face and creating individual poly pieces\n";
select -r polyPanel.f["*"];
$faceList = `filterExpand -sm 34`;

polyChipOff -keepFacesTogether 0
            polyPanel.f[0:(size($faceList) + 1)];
polySeparate -name smPanels polyPanel;

print "Clean up conversion\n";
delete smPanels;

print "Convert poly pieces to rigidBodies and attach
    expressions\n";
for ($i = 1; $i <= size($faceList); $i ++ ) {

    rigidBody -active -damping 1 -collisions 0 -
            particleCollision 1 ("smPanels" + $i);
```

```
        collision -r 0.2 -f 0.2 ("smPanels" + $i);
        connectDynamic -c ("smPanels" + $i) particle1;
        $expstring = "\nif (frame == 1) {\n";
        $expstring += ("rigidBody" + $i + ".particleCollision");
        $expstring += " = 1;\n";
        $expstring += ("rigidBody" + $i + ".impulseX");
        $expstring += " = 0;\n";
        $expstring += ("rigidBody" + $i + ".impulseZ");
        $expstring += " = 0;\n";
        $expstring += "};\n";
        $expstring += "\nif (";
        $expstring += ("rigidBody" + $i + ".velocityX");
        $expstring += " < 0) {\n";
        $expstring += ("rigidBody" + $i + ".particleCollision");
        $expstring += " = 0;\n";
        $expstring += ("rigidBody" + $i + ".impulseX");
        $expstring += " = 2;\n";
        $expstring += ("rigidBody" + $i + ".impulseZ");
        $expstring += " = -2;\n";
        $expstring += "};\n";

        expression -s $expstring -o ("expression" + $i) -ae true
                    -uc all;
    };
    print "Set up scene environment\n";
    hide panel;
    setAttr particleShape1.lifespanMode 1;
    setAttr particleShape1.lifespan 1.0;
    setAttr gun.spread 0.2; // Adjust gun spread to hit more
    pieces
    cycleCheck -e off;
    playbackOptions -min 1 -max 300 -loop continuous;

    print "Call up the Gun Control window and play....\n";
};
```

Save the text file as panelBreakup.mel in your scripts directory, and source it by choosing File > Source Script in the Script Editor (Figure 20.65).

Load in Scene and Run Script

Load the scene ex8start that we saved earlier by choosing the menu item File > Open Scene (Figure 20.66).

Now open the Script Editor, and run the panelBreakup script:

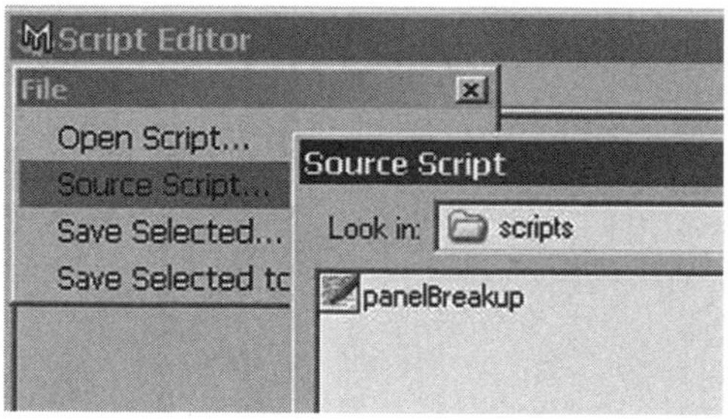

Figure 20.65 Source Script menu item.

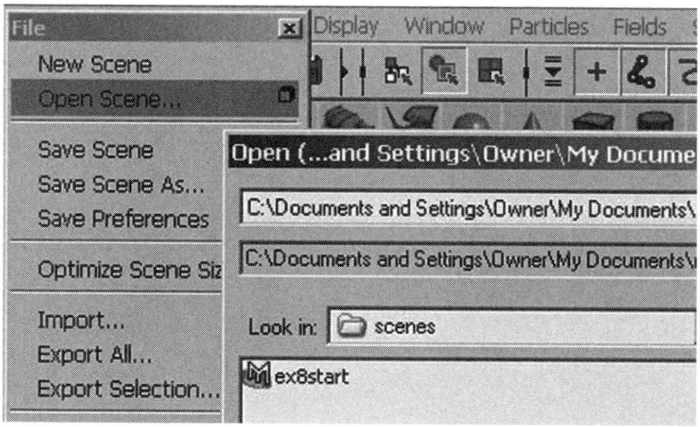

Figure 20.66 Opening the scene.

```
panelBreakup;
```

Figure 20.67 shows the results of scene playback.

If you want to change the number of pieces, change the -delta flag in the script's conversion to polygons to a smaller number. This will affect the performance of the playback.

Pass a Float into panelBreakup

You can change the function to accept a float parameter and pass it to the -delta setting. In the panelBreakup function header, add the following:

```
global proc panelBreakup (float $myDelta)
{
```

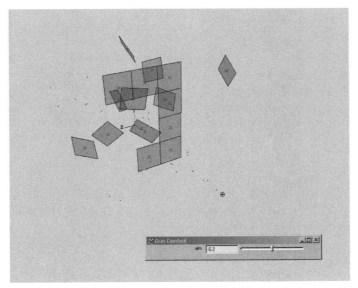

Figure 20.67 Results of panelBreakup script.

In the script body, add:

```
nurbsToPoly -name polyPanel -polygonType 1 -delta $myDelta
panel;
```

Save the script, and re-source it. If the script is in one of the Maya environment script path directories, you can simply type and execute it in the Script Editor as follows:

```
source panelBreakup;
```

Load the scene ex8start again, and type

```
panelBreakup 0.1;
```

You will get an error if you do not give the function a float number after typing panelBreakup.

```
// Error: panelBreakup; //
// Error: Wrong number of arguments on call to panelBreakup. //
```

21

Example of a Simple Crowd System

Sometimes you will need to create a tool that can be used throughout the course of a long production. In this chapter's four examples, we will create a crowd system tool that will use Maya's solid dynamics system and MEL scripts to implement an interface and crowd behavior. Our goal will be to make it robust enough for others to use. The end result of this project is shown in Figure 21.1.

Our discussion of this crowd system's design will start with basics and then move on to the more complex. By the end, we will have a complete procedure that constructs a scene with a number of crowd "vehicles" that will have their own rules to follow describing how to interact with the environment and other vehicles that can be interactively controlled by the user. We will build the crowd system with the assumption that the vehicles will move in the XZ plane.

Example 1: Creating a Vehicle

First, we need to make what we will call a "vehicle." This vehicle will be constructed from a polygonal cube that we'll make a solid dynamic object so that we can rely on Maya's dynamics engine to compute its motion. Later on, we will add other parameters to give it a personality (Figure 21.2).

Before starting, set some grid settings that will help you to build your vehicle. Choose Display > Grid > ❑ menu item, and set your options as shown in Figure 21.3.

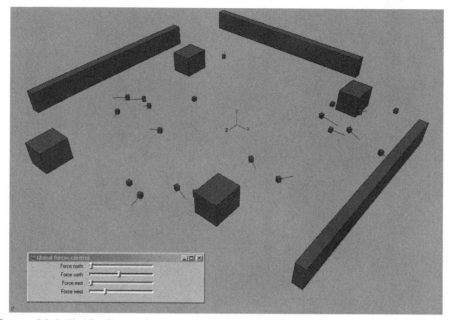

Figure 21.1 Finished crowd system.

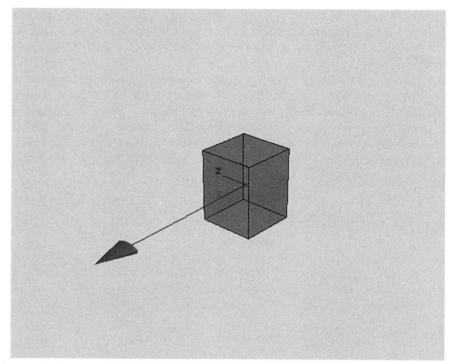

Figure 21.2 A simple vehicle.

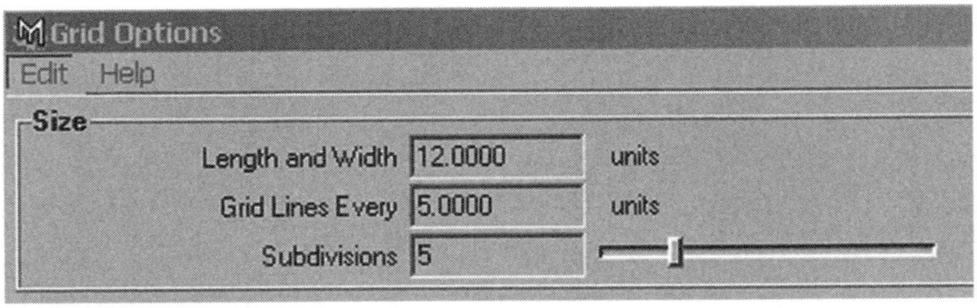

Figure 21.3 Grid Options.

Also, create a four-view window environment by selecting Window > View Arrangement > Four Panes (Figure 21.4). Figure 21.5 shows the resulting four-pane display.

Now, let's create the polygonal cube that will become a vehicle (Figure 21.6). In the Script Editor, execute the following command:

```
polyCube -name vehicle_1 -width 2 -height 2.5 -depth 2;
```

This command will create our `vehicle_1` cube with a size of 2 in X, 2.5 in Y, and 2 in Z. Note that we have chosen a naming convention that ends our object name with _1, since we will want to control the naming and numbering of vehicles later on, rather than having Maya do it for us.

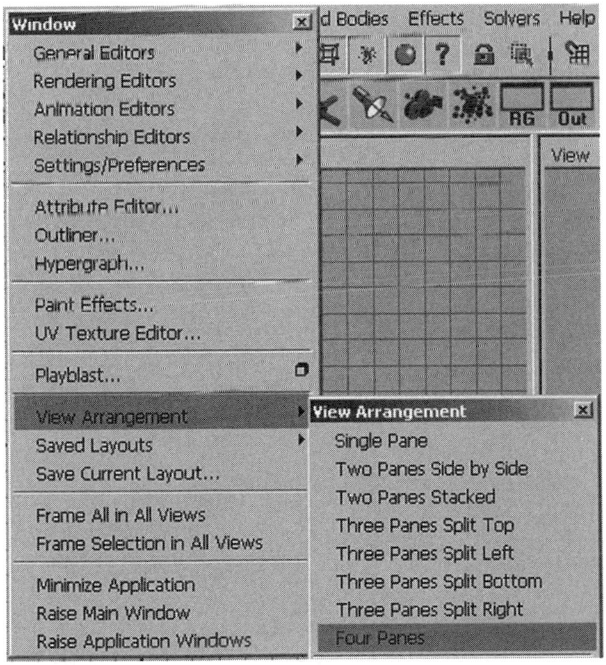

Figure 21.4 Four Panes menu item.

Make Vehicle a Solid Dynamic Object

In this section, we will attach a `rigidBody` node to `vehicle_1` called `rigidVehicle_1`. We will also add an initial position and *impulse* (an instantaneous force with a direction of motion) to `rigidVehicle_1`. Everything else will be default. In the Script Editor, type the following:

```
rigidBody -name rigidVehicle_1 -active -mass 1 -bounciness 0
          -damping 1.5 -position -10 0 0
          -impulse 0.15 0.0 0.0 vehicle_1;
```

This command will add the `rigidBody` to `vehicle_1` with the position −10, 0, and 0 in X, Y, and Z, respectively and an impulse direction of 0.15 in X. Note the result from the MEL command:

```
// Result: rigidSolver //
// Result: rigidVehicle_1 //
```

A `rigidSolver` node was created, and `rigidVehicle_1` was connected to it. We will need to connect all the other vehicles later to the `rigidSolver` so that their dynamics can interact. Later, we will create the `rigidSolver` and manually assign the `rigidVehicles` to it, but we'll let Maya do it for now. Let's open the Solvers > Rigid Body Solver window in Maya's Dynamics section and click the Rigid Solver Display Options section. Select the Display Velocity box (Figure 21.7).

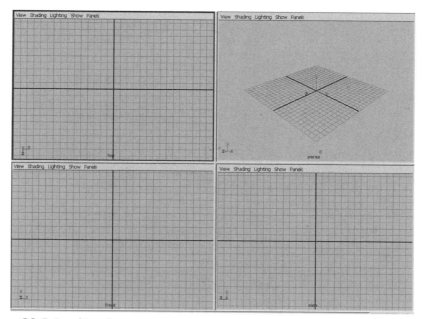

Figure 21.5 Resulting four panes.

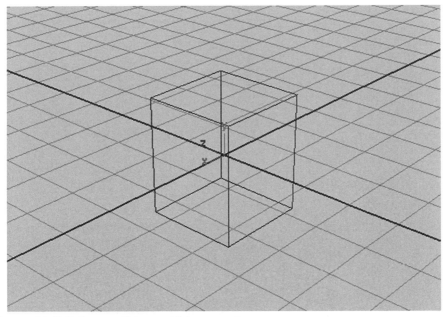

Figure 21.6 Polygon cube as vehicle geometry.

The vector icon within the vehicle_1 object is displayed, showing us which way it is going to travel. If we wished to use MEL to do this, we could use the following command:

```
setAttr rigidSolver.displayVelocity 1;
```

Let's change the rigid body solver scale velocity to 0.5 to scale back the effect of the impulse settings. At the same time, let's set the frame number of the playback range at 1 to 300.

```
setAttr rigidSolver.scaleVelocity 0.5;
playbackOptions -min 1 -max 300;
```

Now play the scene (Figure 21.8). You will see vehicle_1 traveling in the X direction with an impulse force of 0.15. If you get the may not evaluate as expected warning, type cycleCheck -e off in the Script Editor to disable the warning.

Changing the Vehicle's Direction

When vehicle_1 was created, we gave it an impulse of 0.15 0 0. Open the Outliner window by choosing Window > Outliner, and select vehicle_1. In the Channel Box under the Shapes section, we can see the controls for the rigidVehicle_1's impulses. Change Impulse Z to –0.15, and hit the

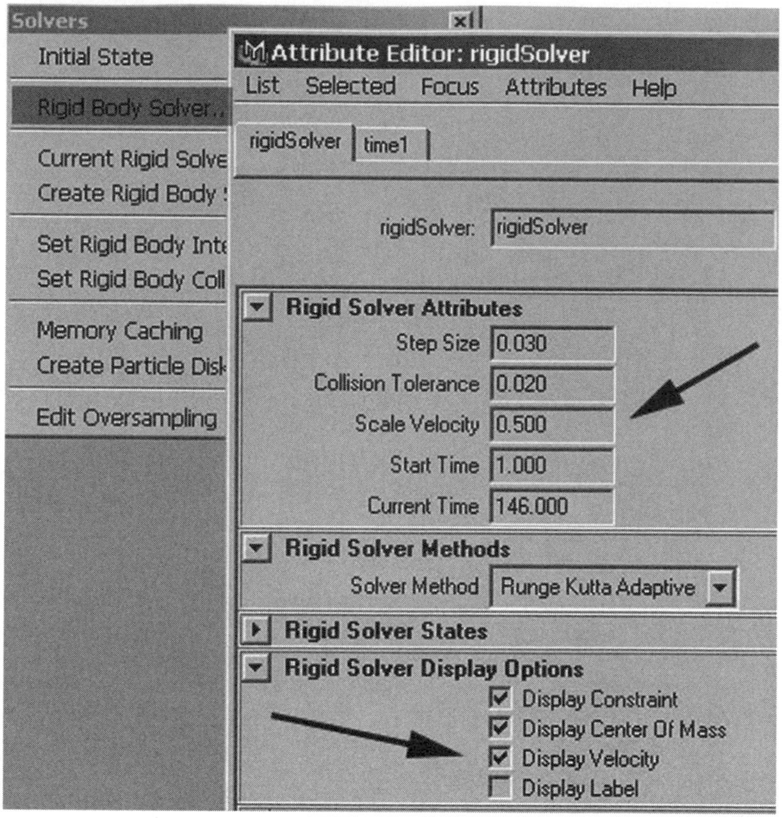

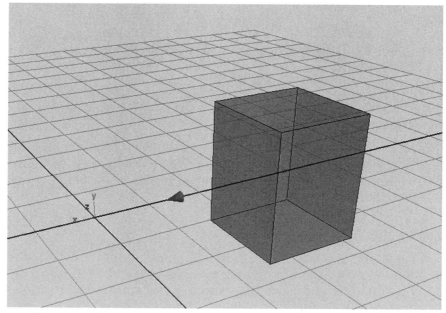

Figure 21.7 Rigid Body solver options.

Figure 21.8 A single moving vehicle.

Rewind button on the transport controls. To do this in MEL, you can use the following `setAttr` command:

```
setAttr rigidVehicle_1.impulseZ -0.15;
```

Figure 21.9 shows the results of the above command. Note that the direction vector icon will reflect the new direction that `vehicle_1` travels.

Try some different numbers for Impulse X and Impulse Z. You'll get best results if you enter numbers in the 0.1 to 1.0 range in either positive or negative directions (Figure 21.10).

Change Motion of vehicle_1 with Expression

Right now, `vehicle_1` motion doesn't change its course as you play back the simulation. Let's add an expression that will change its course over time. Select Window > Animation Editors > Expression Editor. Enter the following expression for `rigidVehicle_1`:

```
rigidVehicle_1.impulseX = sin(time);
```

Name the expression `wander` in the Expression Name box (Figure 21.11).

Click the Create button within the Expression Editor. Click on the Top view panel; press the space bar to fill the screen, and then play the scene (Figure 21.12). (The dots indicate the path of motion for the vehicle.)

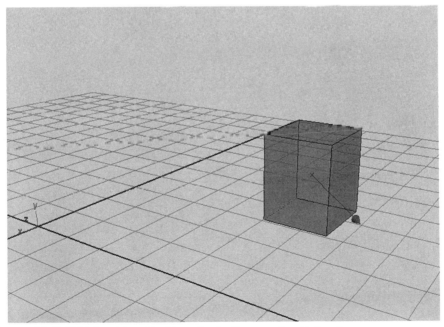

Figure 21.9 Vehicle with added impulse in the negative Z direction.

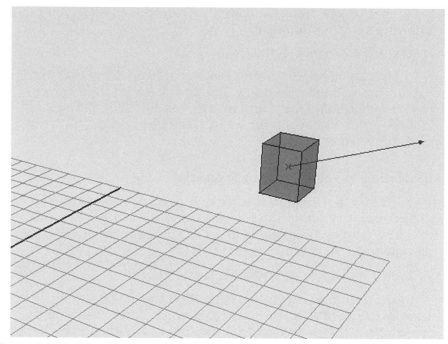

Figure 21.10 Direction vector lengthens as impulse increases.

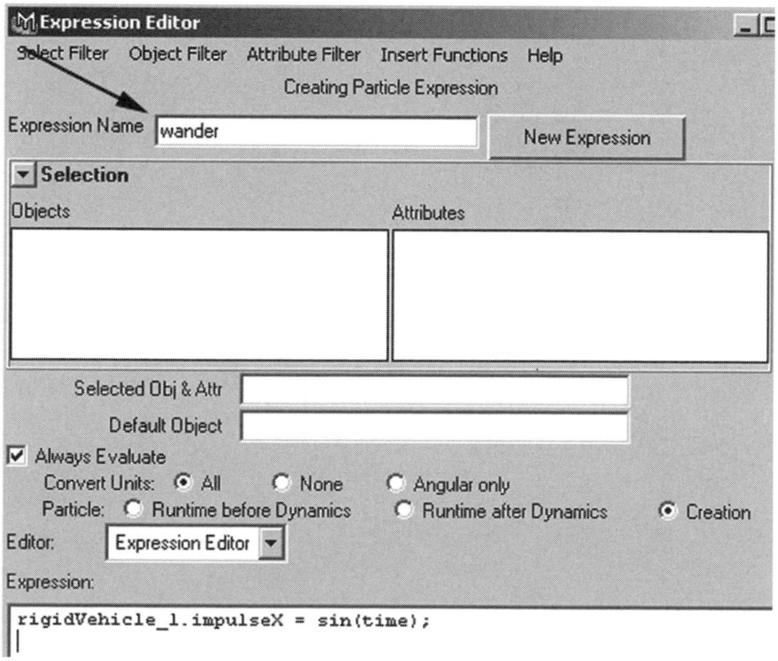

Figure 21.11 The wander expression.

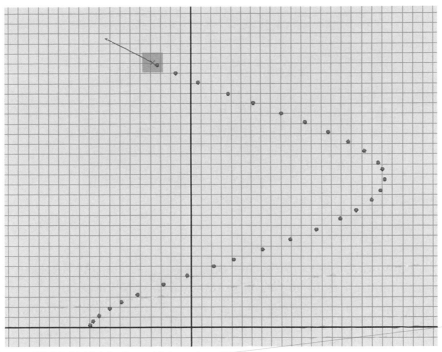

Figure 21.12 Vehicle's sinusoidal motion.

Now, the attached `rigidVehicle_1` node's Impulse X expression gives `vehicle_1` small "kicks" back and forth in X, creating a sine wave pattern in its motion. We'll do the same for the Z direction. Open the Expression Editor again, and choose Select Filter > By Expression Name (Figure 21.13).

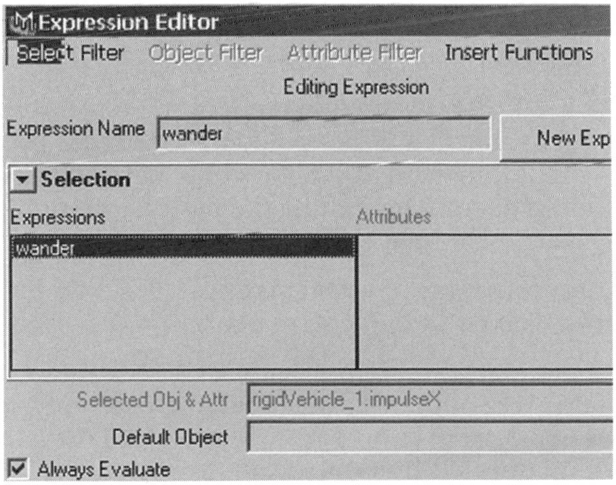

Figure 21.13 Finding `wander` expression in Expression Editor.

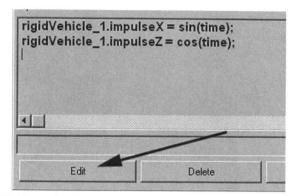

```
rigidVehicle_1.impulseX = sin(time);
rigidVehicle_1.impulseZ = cos(time);
```

Edit   Delete

Figure 21.14 Clicking Edit changes expression in editor.

In the Expressions window, you should see wander listed. Select it, and add an Impulse Z assignment to the expression, as follows:

```
rigidVehicle_1.impulseX = sin(time);
rigidVehicle_1.impulseZ = cos(time);
```

Click Edit (Figure 21.14). Instead of a sine pattern, the vehicle now follows a circular motion (Figure 21.15).

Now, edit the expression once again. This time, change the expression to create a figure-eight motion, as follows:

```
rigidVehicle_1.impulseX = sin(time);
rigidVehicel_1.impulseZ = cos(time * 2);
```

Click Edit, and play back the scene (Figure 21.16).

Create Wander Motion

We can also give vehicle_1 a pseudo-random impulse by using the noise function. The noise function is called "pseudo random" because you may be able to see a repeating pattern after a while, but generally the resulting motion will seem random. This will be the basic expression motion for all vehicles as we create them later. In the Expression Editor, type the following:

```
rigidVehicle_1.impulseX = sin(time);
rigidVehicle_1.impulseZ = noise(time);
```

Click Edit, and play back the scene (Figure 21.17).

Now that vehicle_1 appears to be wandering randomly, let's add a couple of variables called $xMult and $zMult that we can use later to give each vehicle its own motion. We'll multiply $xMult by time for X, and multiply $zMult by the noise result for Z.

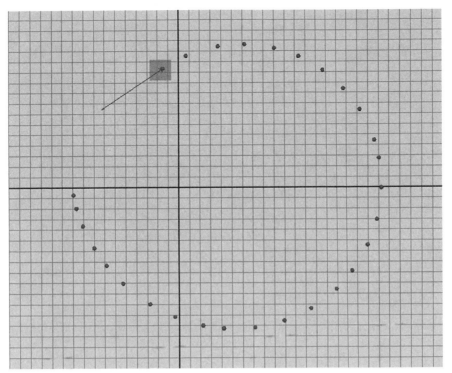

Figure 21.15 Sinusoidal motion in X and Z makes a circle.

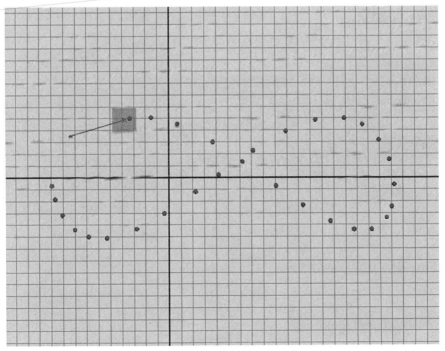

Figure 21.16 Doubling frequency in Z yields figure eight.

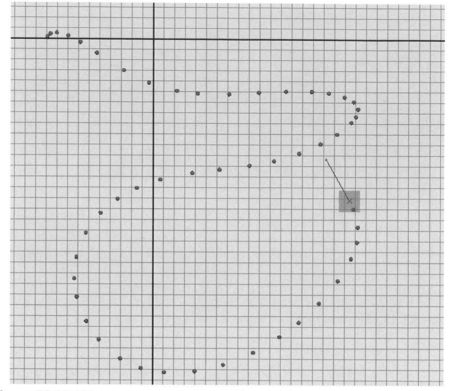

Figure 21.17 Using `noise` as `impulse` yields wandering.

In the Expression Editor, change your expression as follows:

```
// Set random motion of vehicle and add multipliers.

float $xMult = 2.0;
float $zMult = 1.5;
rigidVehicle_1.impulseX = sin(time * $xMult);
rigidVehicle_1.impulseZ = (noise(time) * $zMult);
```

Click Edit, and play the scene once more (Figure 21.18).

Later, as we create each vehicle, we will use the `rand()` function to set each $xMult and $zMult differently.

Orient vehicle_1's Direction with Its Motion

When `vehicle_1` moves, we notice that its orientation always stays the same. Now, we'll add code to an expression on `vehicle_1` that keeps the vehicle rotated to match the direction of its motion. To do that, we have to disconnect the Y rotation channel on `vehicle_1` that is currently controlled by `rigidVehicle_1`. First, open the Attribute Editor for

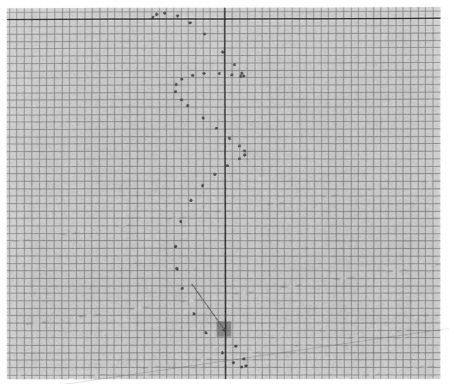

Figure 21.18 Multipliers control relative influence of X and Z impulse expressions.

rigidVehicle_1 by selecting it in the Outliner under vehicle_1 and pressing Ctrl-A. Select the Allow Disconnection option box under the Rigid Body Attributes selection; without this setting turned on, you cannot disconnect the connections between the geometry object (vehicle_1) and the rigid body object (rigidVehicle_1) (Figure 21.19).

To do this with a setAttr command in MEL, use the following statement:

```
setAttr rigidSolver.allowDisconnection 1;
```

Now we can disconnect the rigidVehicle_1's connection to the rotateY attribute with this command:

```
disconnectAttr rigidVehicle_1ry.output vehicle_1.rotateY;
```

You should see the Rotate Y channel in the Channel Box change color to indicate that it's no longer connected. You can now rotate vehicle_1's transform node in Y without affecting the dynamics of rigidVehicle_1. Make sure, though, that you rewind the simulation when you change the rotation value if you are using the Rotate tool instead of typing numbers into the Channel Box. If you don't, Maya will interpret the rotation you select as the initial state for the beginning of the simulation, which may not be what you intend.

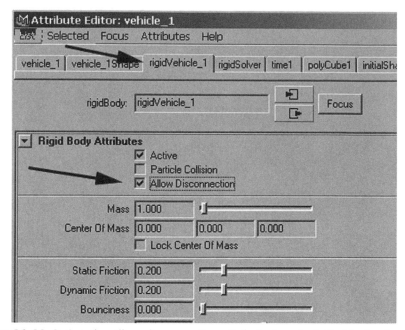

Figure 21.19 Seting the Allow disconnection attribute for `rigidVehicle_1`.

In Figure 21.20, you can see how the transform node and the rigid body node control the vehicle object. The transform node controls explicit rotations, while the rigid body node responds to impulses in X and Z.

Let's disconnect the X and Z rotation as well, since we will need them for the part of our expression that orients the cube in the direction that it's moving. Type the following statements:

```
disconnectAttr rigidVehicle_1rx.output vehicle_1.rotateX;
disconnectAttr rigidVehicle_1rz.output vehicle_1.rotateZ;
```

Open the Expression Editor, and select the wander expression, using the Select Filter > By Expression Name view. Add the following code after the impulse motion section. We'll examine how each section of the expression works after you type it. (New code is **boldface**.)

```
// Set random motion of vehicle and add multipliers

float $xMult = 2.0;
float $zMult = 1.5;
rigidVehicle_1.impulseX = sin(time * $xMult);
rigidVehicle_1.impulseZ = (noise(time) * $zMult);

// Set orientation of vehicle according to velocity direction

float $fVel[ ] = `getAttr rigidVehicle_1.velocity`;

vehicle_1.rotateX = 0;
```

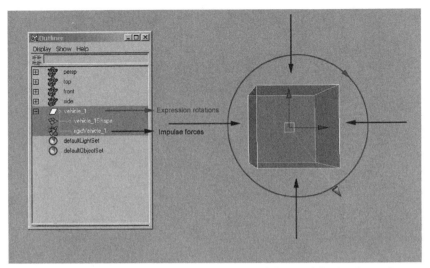

Figure 21.20 Transform node controls rotation while rigid body dynamics control translation.

```
vehicle_1.rotateY = atan2d( $fVel[0], $fVel[2] );
vehicle_1.rotateZ = 0;
```

Click Edit to change the expression. Now, before you play it back, let's go over each new line from the beginning of what you've added.

```
float $fVel[ ] = `getAttr rigidVehicle_1.velocity`;
```

The above statement defines a float array $fVel, and it retrieves the current velocity of rigidVehicle_1 in X, Y, and Z. It then stores it in the new array. Note that Maya represents velocity object attributes as arrays of floats, while it represents velocity particle attributes as vectors.

```
vehicle_1.rotateX = 0;
```

This statement assigns a value of 0 for the X rotation.

```
vehicle_1.rotateY = atan2d( $fVel[0], $fVel[2] ) );
```

This statement calculates the arctangent (inverse tangent), using the velocity Z component and velocity X velocity component, and it assigns it to the Y rotation, which will orient the cube in the direction of its motion in the XZ plane.

```
vehicle_1.rotateZ = 0;
```

Assign a value of 0 for the Z rotation so that the top and bottom remain oriented with the XZ plane in which vehicle_1 moves.

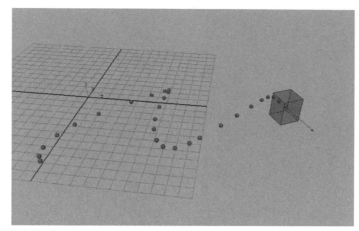

Figure 21.21 Final vehicle wandering motion.

Play back the scene to see the resulting motion (Figure 21.21).

How do you come up with these kinds of expressions on your own? Experiment, read the examples in the online documentation, and take every opportunity you can to read other MEL scripts from friends, from Alias Wavefront's examples, *from Highend3D.com,* or other sources. Sometimes, clever mathematical code that was not originally written in MEL can be adapted to MEL with the built-in functions that Maya provides. You can find further information on `atan2d` and the other trigonometric functions in *Using Maya: Expressions.*

Tip: It's a good idea to collect functions that you might use frequently in a separate text file that you can reference as needed.

Example 2: Vehicle Interaction

Now that we have a basic vehicle model, let's look at how two vehicles will react to each other. For our crowd system, we will develop two behaviors: the first behavior establishes each vehicle's tendency to avoid collisions with others, and the other establishes that some of the vehicles, which our script will define as "followers," tend to follow other vehicles, defined as "leaders." Figure 21.22 shows the end result of this exercise.

Create Script to Automate Creating Vehicle in Example 1

First, make a new, empty scene by choosing the File > New Scene menu item. The equivalent MEL command is

```
file -force -new;
```

Let's start by slightly modifying the MEL code from Example 1 to create a script that will generate one vehicle in a scene. Open your favorite text editor, and assemble the MEL commands that create the `rigidSolver`, a basic vehicle model, the associated rigid body object, and the expressions that cause the object to wander in the XZ plane.

```
// Create a master crowdSolver for all vehicles

rigidSolver -create -current -name crowdSolver
            -velocityVectorScale 0.5
-displayVelocity on;
setAttr crowdSolver.allowDisconnection 1;

// Basic vehicle model

polyCube -name vehicle_1 -width 2 -height 2.5 -depth 2;

// Make the vehicle a rigid body

rigidBody -name rigidVehicle_1 -active -mass 1 -bounciness 0
          -damping 1.5 -position -10 0 0 -impulse 0.0 0.0 0.0
          -solver crowdSolver vehicle_1;

disconnectAttr rigidVehicle_1ry.output vehicle_1.rotateY;
disconnectAttr rigidVehicle_1rx.output vehicle_1.rotateX;
disconnectAttr rigidVehicle_1rz.output vehicle_1.rotateZ;

// Create expression for vehicle

$expString = "// Set wander motion of vehicle and add multipliers.\n";
$expString += "float $xMult = 2.0;\n";
$expString += "float $zMult = 1.5;\n";
$expString += "rigidVehicle_1.impulseX = sin(time * $xMult);\n";
$expString += "rigidVehicle_1.impulseZ = (noise(time) * $zMult);\n\n";
$expString += "// Set orientation of Vehicle according to the velocity direction.\n";
$expString += "float $fVel[ ] = `getAttr rigidVehicle_1.velocity`;\n\n";
$expString += "vehicle_1.rotateX = 0;\n";
$expString += "vehicle_1.rotateY = atan2d( $fVel[0], $fVel[2] );\n";
$expString += "vehicle_1.rotateZ = 0;\n";

expression -s $expString -name wander -alwaysEvaluate true
           -unitConversion all;

cycleCheck -e off;
```

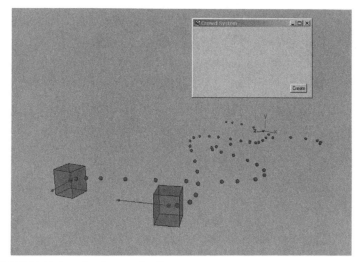

Figure 21.22 Vehicles chasing each other.

Save the above script as `SingleVehicle.mel`. Don't source the file you just created yet. Instead, cut and paste the script into the Script Editor (if you are not using the Script Editor for your text editing), and press Enter (Figure 21.23). This script should produce the same results as your work in Example 1. Keep the script open in your editor so that we can continue to add to it.

Add Radial Field to vehicle_1 to Repel Other Vehicles

Each vehicle should try to maintain its personal space. To implement this, we'll add a radial field to each vehicle so that if another vehicle comes near, each will repel the other. In combination with the collision behavior that comes with the rigid body simulation, the vehicles will display a useful combination of avoidance and collision behavior. We can also control the strength of each *radial field* on a per-vehicle basis.

In the section of the script labeled `// Basic vehicle model`, add the radial field creation immediately after the `polyCube` command.

```
// Basic vehicle model

polyCube -name vehicle_1 -width 2 -height 2.5 -depth 2;

// Add a vehicle force field
radial -position 0 0 0 -name vehicleForce_1 -magnitude 50
        -attenuation 0.3 -maxDistance 8.0;
parent vehicleForce_1 vehicle_1;
```

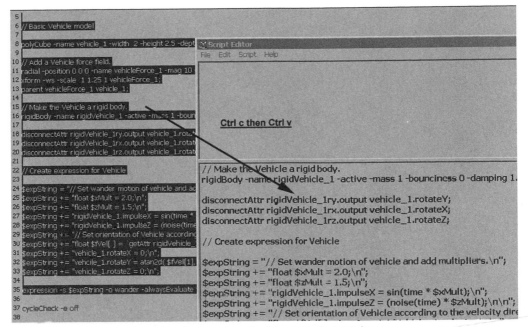

Figure 21.23 Copying and pasting from external editor into Script Editor.

The first command creates a radial field with a maximum force distance that is outside the boundary of vehicle_1. This gives us a repulsive force that will push away other vehicles that come close to it. In the second command, the field is parented to vehicle_1's hierarchy so that the field will move with the vehicle.

Use File > New Scene to create a new, empty scene. Copy the MEL code from the text editor into the Script Editor, and press Enter on the numeric keypad to execute it.

You will not see any obvious results on playing back the scene because there isn't another vehicle to react to, but you can see the field in the Outliner and its icon in your camera views (Figure 21.24).

Now that we have created the first vehicle and the radial field that will implement its collision avoidance behavior, we will modify the script to create another vehicle.

Add Another Vehicle

In the text editor, we will add another section to the script for a leader vehicle, and we will alter the existing code to create a follower vehicle. We'll

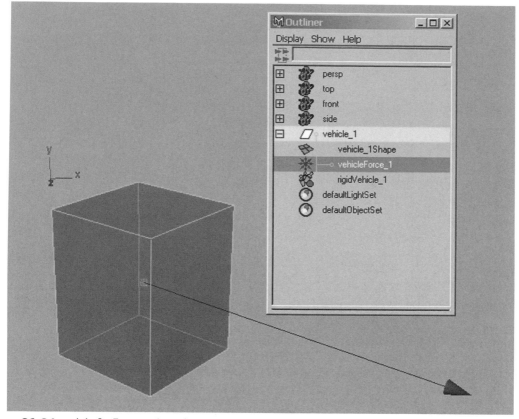

Figure 21.24 vehicleForce_1 node parented to vehicle.

implement the leading and following behavior by adding a second, attractive radial field to the new leader that is global in influence and has no maximum distance setting. This will allow it to affect any solid body in the scene. Also, our script will connect the fields to the solid bodies so that they have the desired effect.

The modified code for these changes follows. (New code is **boldface**.)

```
// Vehicle creation for crowd system

// Create a master crowdSolver for all vehicles

rigidSolver -create -current -name crowdSolver
          -velocityVectorScale 0.5 -displayVelocity on;
setAttr crowdSolver.allowDisconnection 1;

// Basic vehicle model type: follower

polyCube -name vehicleF_1 -width 2 -height 2.5 -depth 2;
```

```
// Add vehicle force field for follower

radial -position 0 0 0 -name vehicleFForce_1 -magnitude 50
       -attenuation 0.3 -maxDistance 8.0;
parent vehicleFForce_1 vehicleF_1;

// Make vehicle a rigid body

rigidBody -name rigidVehicleF_1 -active -mass 1 -bounciness 0 -damping
          1.5 -position -10 0 0 -impulse 0.15 0.0 0.0 -standInObject
          cube -solver crowdSolver vehicleF_1;

disconnectAttr rigidVehicleF_1ry.output vehicleF_1.rotateY;
disconnectAttr rigidVehicleF_1rx.output vehicleF_1.rotateX;
disconnectAttr rigidVehicleF_1rz.output vehicleF_1.rotateZ;

// Create expression for VehicleF_1

$expString = "// Vehicle type: Follower";
$expString += "// Set wander motion of vehicle and add multipliers.\n";
$expString += "float $xMult1 = 2.0;\n";
$expString += "float $zMult1 = 1.5;\n";
$expString += "rigidVehicleF_1.impulseX = sin(time * $xMult1);\n";
$expString += "rigidVehicleF_1.impulseZ = (noise(time) * $zMult1);\n\n";
$expString +=
"// Set orientation of Vehicle according to the velocity direction.\n";
$expString += "float $fVel1[];\n";
$expString += "$fVel1 = `getAttr rigidVehicleF_1.velocity`;\n\n";
$expString += "vehicleF_1.rotateX = 0;\n";
$expString += "vehicleF_1.rotateY = atan2d( $fVel1[0], $fVel1[2]);\n";
$expString += "vehicleF_1.rotateZ = 0;\n";

expression -s $expString -name wanderF_exp1
           -alwaysEvaluate true -unitConversion all;

// Basic vehicle model type: leader

polyCube -name vehicleL_1 -width 2 -height 2.5 -depth 2;

// Add vehicle force field for leader

radial -position 0 0 0 -name vehicleLForce_1 -magnitude 50
       -attenuation 0.3 -maxDistance 8.0;
parent vehicleLForce_1 vehicleL_1;

// Add leader field
```

```
radial -position 0 0 0 -name vehicleLeadGlobalForce_1
        -magnitude -1 -attenuation 1.2;
parent vehicleLeadGlobalForce_1 vehicleL_1;

rigidBody -name rigidVehicleL_1 -active -mass 1 -bounciness 0
        -damping 1.5 -position 10 0 0 -impulse 0.15 0.0 0.0
        -standInObject cube -solver crowdSolver vehicleL_1;
disconnectAttr rigidVehicleL_1ry.output vehicleL_1.rotateY;
disconnectAttr rigidVehicleL_1rx.output vehicleL_1.rotateX;
disconnectAttr rigidVehicleL_1rz.output vehicleL_1.rotateZ;

// Create expression for VehicleL_1

$expString = "// Vehicle type: Leader";
$expString += "// Set wander motion of vehicle and add multipliers.\n";
$expString += "float $xMult2 = -2.0;\n";
$expString += "float $zMult2 = 2.5;\n";
$expString += "rigidVehicleL_1.impulseX = sin(time * $xMult2);\n";
$expString += "rigidVehicleL_1.impulseZ = (noise(time) * $zMult2);\n\n";
$expString += "// Set orientation of Vehicle according to the velocity direction.\n"
$expString += "float $fVel2[];\n";
$expString += "$fVel2 = `getAttr rigidVehicleL_1.velocity`;\n\n";
$expString += "vehicleL_1.rotateX = 0;\n";
$expString += "vehicleL_1.rotateY = atan2d( $fVel2[0], $fVel2[2] );\n";
$expString += "vehicleL_1.rotateZ = 0;\n";

expression -s $expString -name wanderL_exp1
        -alwaysEvaluate true -unitConversion all;

// Hookup dynamics, both collisions and fields

// Forces
connectDynamic -fields vehicleLForce_1 rigidVehicleF_1 ;
connectDynamic -fields vehicleLeadGlobalForce_1 rigidVehicleF_1 ;
connectDynamic -fields vehicleFForce_1 rigidVehicleL_1 ;

cycleCheck -e off;
```

Save the script as TwoVehicles.mel; cut and paste the code from the text editor to the Script Editor, and press the Enter key. Once you have fixed any typos, play the scene (Figure 21.25). The leader wanders back and forth while the follower tries to follow, despite the fact that it has its own wander expression.

As you can see, we have several influences that affect both the leader and follower. Each has its own of the original wander expression, and each has the effect of the radial fields that are parented to both vehicles acting on it as well. When the follower hits the leader, we can see both the collision

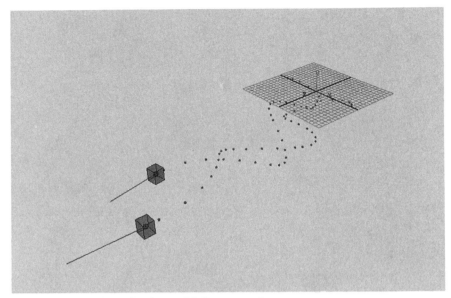

Figure 21.25 Resulting leader and follower motion.

reaction and also the repulsive effect. Each affects the post-collision motion of both, giving the illusion of the vehicles directing their own motions.

Also note the changes we applied to the original code to have two vehicles in the scene. We had to add variables that were local in scope to each vehicle's expressions. This will reduce the performance of the simulation as we add more vehicles; we will return to address those performance issues later. For now, let's put the script we have created into a procedure definition and add a blank dialog box with a Create button. Later, we will add controls to this dialog box as we flesh out our simulation further.

Add Simple MEL Interface

In the text editor, let's add the code to create a dialog box. For this dialog box, we will use the `formLayout` command so that we can control the precise layout of the box's contents. At the top of the existing script, add a procedure definition for a `global proc` called `createCrowd`. At the end of the existing script, add a curly bracket to end the procedure. The `createCrowd` procedure is your script's main body. As we develop the crowd system further, this procedure will be controlled by a separate user interface procedure called `crowdSystem`. Your changes should look like the following code segment. (New code is **boldface**.)

```
// createCrowd

global proc createCrowd ( )
{

   // Create master crowdSolver for all vehicles

   .......
   .......(TwoVehicles.mel body)
   .......

   cycleCheck -e off;

}
```

At the bottom, add the `crowdSystem` procedure to create our one-button dialog box.

```
// Interface

global proc crowdSystem ( )
{
   window
      -title "Crowd System"
      -widthHeight 300 200
         crowdWin;

   // Create button
   string $button1 = `button -label "Create"`;

   // Place button in window
   formLayout -edit
      -attachForm          $button1 "bottom" 10
      -attachForm          $button1 "right" 10
       formLayout;

   // Add command to button to call createCrowd function and
   // then kill window after script has been executed

   button -edit -command ("createCrowd; deleteUI crowdWin;") $button1;

   showWindow crowdWin;
}
```

Save and Source Script

Save the new text file in your scripts directory as `crowdSystem.mel`. To test your script, create a new scene by choosing File > New Scene, or enter the following command in the Script Editor:

```
file -f -new;
```

If you have placed the new script in your command path, all you need do to execute the new script is to execute the following commands:

```
source crowdSystem;
crowdSystem;
```

The dialog box that we described in the script should appear (Figure 21.26). Now click the Create button. After the script runs, click the Close box to close the window.

Now we have a basic structure within which we can add additional features in the next sections. If you build your script in stages and test at each stage (ensuring that the script is divided up into meaningfully distinct procedures), you'll find it easier to read, test, change, or fix your script more efficiently. We break the procedures down into even smaller chunks in subsequent examples.

Create Wrapper Script and Place on Shelf

In the Script Editor, type the following commands to source your .mel file along with the call to your main entry point procedure, but do not execute them.

```
source crowdSystem;
crowdSystem;
```

These commands source the script that you have saved (crowdSystem.mel) and then execute the identically named crowdSystem global procedure defined in that script. You can add parameters to your main entry point

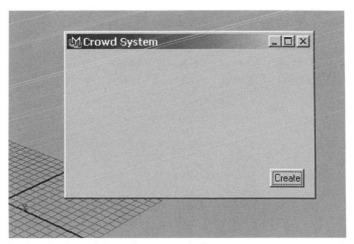

Figure 21.26 Beginning of Crowd system window.

procedure to customize the way a script runs. Once your script is stable, if it's installed in your script path, you could call the procedure without first using the source command. However, while you are continuing to develop it, you should always source the script before calling the main entry point procedure. Once Maya has automatically sourced your script, it will not see changes you have made to your MEL file unless you manually source it again. These two lines of code are a simple "wrapper" script, meaning a script that adds additional code before or after a call to another script that performs the main body of a useful function; hence, one script wraps around another.

Select the two lines with the mouse, and middle-mouse drag the lines to the shelf (Figure 21.27).

Now we can launch the script with a mouse click. If you want to name the script icon, choose the Shelf Editor menu item on the shelf's menu, which is accessed by clicking on the triangle at the left.

The code for the full script to this point follows:

```
// createCrowd

global proc createCrowd ( )
{
    // Vehicle creation for crowd system

    // Create master crowdSolver for all vehicles

    rigidSolver -create -current -name crowdSolver
            -velocityVectorScale 0.5 -displayVelocity on;
    setAttr crowdSolver.allowDisconnection 1;

    // Basic vehicle model type: follower

    polyCube -name vehicleF_1 -width 2 -height 2.5 -depth 2;

    // Add vehicle force field for follower

    radial -position 0 0 0 -name vehicleFForce_1 -magnitude 50
            -attenuation 0.3 -maxDistance 8.0;
    parent vehicleFForce_1 vehicleF_1;
```

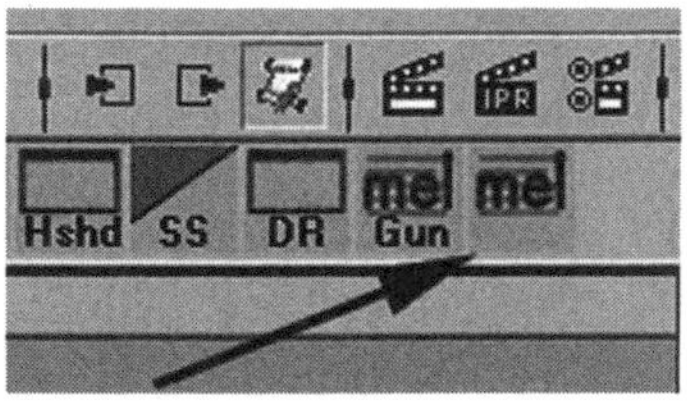

Figure 21.27 Dragging MEL script to shelf.

```
// Make vehicle a rigid body

rigidBody -name rigidVehicleF_1 -active -mass 1
          -bounciness 0 -damping 1.5 -position -10 0 0
          -impulse 0.15 0.0 0.0 -standInObject cube
          -solver crowdSolver vehicleF_1;

disconnectAttr rigidVehicleF_1ry.output vehicleF_1.rotateY;
disconnectAttr rigidVehicleF_1rx.output vehicleF_1.rotateX;
disconnectAttr rigidVehicleF_1rz.output vehicleF_1.rotateZ;

// Create expression for VehicleF_1

$expString = "// Set wander motion of vehicle and add multipliers.\n";
$expString += "float $xMult1 = 2.0;\n";
$expString += "float $zMult1 = 1.5;\n";
$expString += "rigidVehicleF_1.impulseX = sin(time * $xMult1);\n";
$expString += "rigidVehicleF_1.impulseZ = (noise(time) * $zMult1);\n\n";
$expString += "// Set orientation of Vehicle according to the velocity direction.\n";
$expString += "float $fVel1[];\n";
$expString += "$fVel1 = `getAttr rigidVehicleF_1.velocity`;\n\n";
$expString += "vehicleF_1.rotateX = 0;\n";
$expString += "vehicleF_1.rotateY = atan2d( $fVel1[0], $fVel1[2] );\n";
$expString += "vehicleF_1.rotateZ = 0;\n";

expression -s $expString -name wanderF_exp1 -alwaysEvaluate true
           -unitConversion all;

// Basic vehicle model type: leader

polyCube -name vehicleL_1 -width 2 -height 2.5 -depth 2;

// Add vehicle force field for leader

radial -position 0 0 0 -name vehicleLForce_1 -magnitude 50
       -attenuation 0.3 -maxDistance 8.0;
parent vehicleLForce_1 vehicleL_1;

// Add leader field

radial -position 0 0 0 -name vehicleGlobalLeadForce_1
       -magnitude -1 -attenuation 1.5;
parent vehicleGlobalLeadForce_1 vehicleL_1;

rigidBody -name rigidVehicleL_1 -active -mass 1 -bounciness 0
          -damping 1.5 -position 10 0 0 -impulse 0.15 0.0 0.0
          -standInObject cube -solver crowdSolver vehicleL_1;
```

```
disconnectAttr rigidVehicleL_1ry.output vehicleL_1.rotateY;
disconnectAttr rigidVehicleL_1rx.output vehicleL_1.rotateX;
disconnectAttr rigidVehicleL_1rz.output vehicleL_1.rotateZ;

// Create expression for VehicleL_1

$expString = "// Set wander motion of vehicle and add multipliers.\n";
$expString += "float $xMult2 = -2.0;\n";
$expString += "float $zMult2 = 2.5;\n";
$expString += "rigidVehicleL_1.impulseX = sin(time * $xMult2);\n";
$expString += "rigidVehicleL_1.impulseZ = (noise(time) * $zMult2);\n\n";
$expString +=
"// Set orientation of Vehicle according to the velocity direction.\n";
$expString += "float $fVel2[];\n";
$expString += "$fVel2 = `getAttr rigidVehicleL_1.velocity`;\n\n";
$expString += "vehicleL_1.rotateX = 0;\n";
$expString += "vehicleL_1.rotateY = atan2d( $fVel2[0], $fVel2[2] );\n";
$expString += "vehicleL_1.rotateZ = 0;\n";

expression -s $expString -name wanderL_exp1
           -alwaysEvaluate true -unitConversion all;

// Hook up the fields

connectDynamic -fields vehicleLForce_1 rigidVehicleF_1 ;
connectDynamic -fields vehicleGlobalLeadForce_1 rigidVehicleF_1 ;
connectDynamic -fields vehicleFForce_1 rigidVehicleL_1 ;

cycleCheck -e off;

}
// Interface
global proc crowdSystem ( )
{

  window
    -title "Crowd System"
    -widthHeight 300 200
      crowdWin;

  string $form = `formLayout`;
  // Create button
  string $b1 = `button -label "Create"`;

  // Place button in window
  formLayout -edit
    -attachForm          $b1 "bottom" 10
    -attachForm          $b1 "right" 10

  $form;
```

```
    // Add command to button
    button -edit -command ("createCrowd") $b1;
    showWindow crowdWin;
}
```

Example 3: Vehicle Environment

In this section, we'll add the ability to turn selected objects into obstacles for our crowd's vehicles. We will also give the script the ability to add a user-controllable *global field* that affects all of the objects uniformly. Figure 21.28 shows the end result of this exercise.

Launch crowdSystem.mel

We assume that you have completed Examples 1 and 2, and you have a working script saved in your Maya project script directory or elsewhere in your script path. We also assume that you have the `script crowdSystem.mel` open and ready to edit in your favorite text editor. Finally, we assume that you have created a `crowdSystem` MEL script icon on your shelf.

First, open the Script Editor, and type

```
file -f -new;
```

To resume where we left off, click the MEL script icon that you created in Example 2 to create a crowd (Figure 21.29). Close the Crowd System window (Figure 21.30) after you have created the crowd. We'll modify our script to close the window when it creates a crowd later on.

Add Boundary Obstacles

Now let's create a few polygonal cubes that will become obstacles in the scene. To make a positive Z obstacle object, place a `polyCube` at 0 0 20 in XYZ, and scale it to 50 4 1 with the name `ob1`. In the Script Editor, type the following:

```
polyCube -name ob1 -sx 2 -sy 2 -sz 1;
```

As in the previous examples, `-sx`, `-sy`, and `-sz` control the number of subdivisions along each axis. By increasing the number of subdivisions in X and Y to 2, we'll ensure that Maya more accurately calculates the effects of collisions. Now, translate `ob1` to 0 0 20, and scale it to 50 4 1. To do this in one step, type the following statement in the Script Editor:

```
xform -worldSpace -translation 0 0 20 -scale 50 4 1 ob1;
```

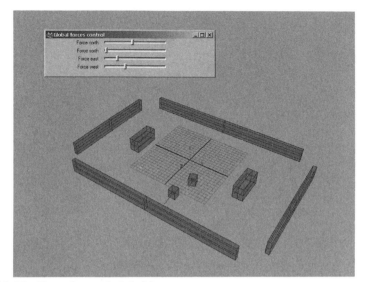

Figure 21.28 Obstacles and global forces.

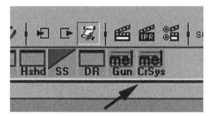

Figure 21.29 Clicking on the MEL script shelf icon.

Now we need to make ob1 a passive rigidBody (Figure 21.31). Following is a rigidBody call that we can use to do this:

```
rigidBody -passive -name ob1RigidB1 -bounciness 2.0 ob1;
```

We have set the bounciness to 2.0 to make vehicles recoil nicely off the obstacle. Because the script uses the -current flag when it creates the crowdSolver, new rigid bodies will automatically be connected to it. This means that they'll be able to interact dynamically with each other without having to make any further connections by hand in your script.

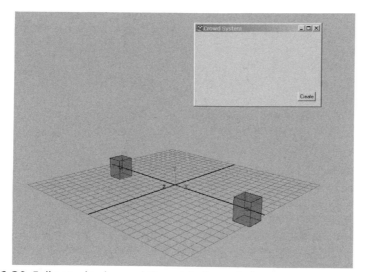

Figure 21.30 Follower, leader, and Crowd System window.

Play the scene to see how the vehicles react to your new object (Figure 21.31). Remember to check your playback min and max to give it enough frames; 1 to 500 should be fine. Also, make sure that you adjust your camera to see how the vehicles react when they collide with ob1.

Initially, the vehicles move as they did before, but when they collide with each other or ob1, they react both to collision dynamics and to the wander expression.

To create the feel of a crowd, we'll exploit this further by adding more obstacles, vehicles, and global fields.

Create More Obstacles

Let's rewind the simulation and place some more obstacles in the scene. For now, we will place them in the pattern shown in Figure 21.33.

To create the obstacles with MEL commands, type

```
polyCube -name ob2 -sx 2 -sy 2 -sz 1;
polyCube -name ob3 -sx 2 -sy 2 -sz 1;
polyCube -name ob4 -sx 2 -sy 2 -sz 1;
xform -worldSpace -translation 0 0 -20 -scale 50 4 1 ob2;
xform -worldSpace -translation 30 0 0 -scale 30 4 1
      -rotation 0 90 0 ob3;
xform -worldSpace -translation -30 0 0 -scale 30 4 1
      -rotation 0 -90 0 ob4;
```

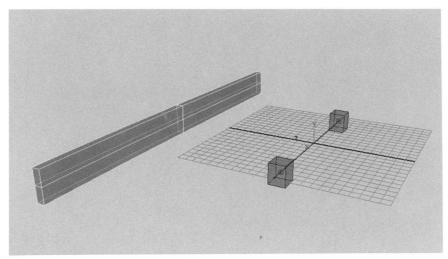

Figure 21.31 Adding a passive rigid body obstacle.

Now, let's add two more in the middle:

```
polyCube -name ob5 -sx 2 -sy 2 -sz 1;
polyCube -name ob6 -sx 2 -sy 2 -sz 1;
xform -worldSpace -translation 17 0 0 -scale 3 4 8 ob5;
xform -worldSpace -translation -17 0 0 -scale 3 4 8 ob6;
```

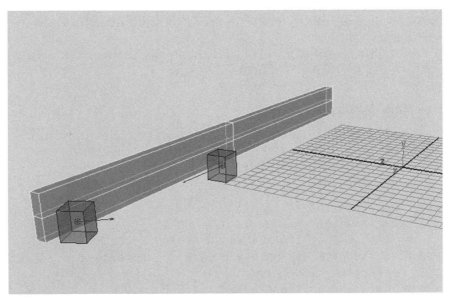

Figure 21.32 Objects bouncing off rigid body obstacle.

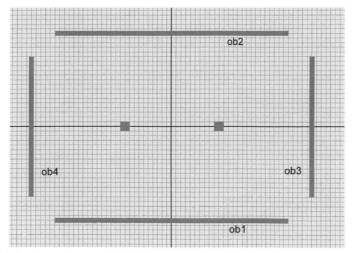

Figure 21.33 Four walls.

Figure 21.34 shows ob5 and ob6.

As we said before, it's really not important to place the obstacles precisely in the scene. Ultimately, we'll modify crowdSystem.mel to make rigid bodies from obstacles that you've placed anywhere in the scene.

Convert New Obstacles into Passive Rigid Bodies

In the Script Editor, or in a separate text file, let's start building a chunk of MEL code that we will use later in a global proc called collectObstacles.

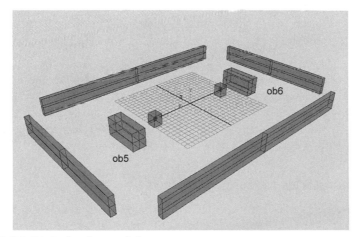

Figure 21.34 Obstacles five and six.

First, we assume that all of the newly created polyCubes (other than ob1) are selected. We will use ls to capture the selected objects' names into a string array, and then loop over them using a for loop to make them rigid bodies. Select the new polyCubes in the Maya interface with the mouse, and place them in the array $collectObjects by typing the following:

```
string $collectObjects[ ] = `ls -sl`;
print $collectObjects[0];
```

Execute these commands one by one. You should see the following response:

```
string $collectObjects[ ] = `ls -sl`;
// Result: ob4 ob2 ob6 ob5 ob3 //
print $collectObjects[0];
ob4
```

The order in which you selected the obstacles determines the order that ls lists them. For what we're doing, order won't matter, but since we are using a for loop to turn each into a rigid body object, we'll need to know how many there are. Our script can determine this with by calling the size() function. Try typing

```
size($collectObjects);
```

The response follows:

```
size($collectObjects);
// Result: 5 //
```

Following is a for loop that we can use to convert each object to a passive rigid body, using the same settings that we did for ob1:

```
for ( $i = 0; $i
size($collectObjects); $i++) {
rigidBody -passive -name ($collectObjects[$i] + "RigidB" + $i)
        -bounciness 2.0 ($collectObjects[$i]);
};
```

Execute the loop. Now, open the Outliner window to see whether the loop did what we expected by looking for the rigid body nodes that go with each obstacle (Figure 21.35).

Figure 21.36 shows the results of playback. The vehicles now will bounce off the new obstacles, just as they bounced off of ob1.

Add collectObstacles to crowdSystem.mel

Open crowdSystem.mel in a text editor and add a new global proc called collectObstacles after the global proc createCrowd. (New code is **boldface**.)

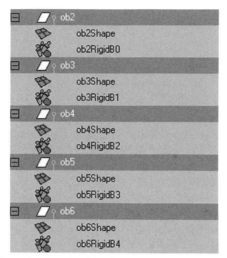

Figure 21.35 Each obstacle as a rigid body.

```
connectDynamic -fields vehicleFForce_1 rigidVehicleL_1;

cycleCheck -e off;

} // End of createCrowd

global proc collectObstacles() {

    string $collectObjects[] = `ls -sl`;

    for ( $i = 0; $i < size($collectObjects); $i++) {
        rigidBody -passive -name ($collectObjects [$i] + "RigidB" + $i)
                -bounciness 2.0 ($collectObjects [$i]);
    };

}
```

Save crowdSystem.mel. Later in Example 4, we'll add an option to our dialog box to determine whether to call the collectObstacles procedure when we run our script. We will also add a warning to the user if he or she has not selected anything.

At this point, save the current scene as ex3Tmp.ma because we will be adding another procedure using what we have done to this point.

Create Global Forces

Now we'll add some global forces that influence all of the vehicles. To do this, we'll place four radial fields around the crowd area and create an interface to control the magnitude of the fields. Let's place the four fields 150 units from the center in X, –X, Z, and –Z. The radial fields' influence on the vehicles will have an infinite maximum distance.

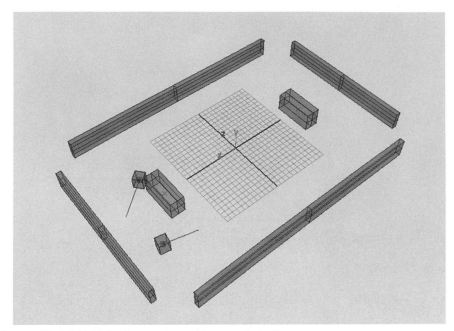

Figure 21.36 Vehicles interacting with new obstacles.

Create Matrix Variable to Use for Placement

A *matrix* is a two-dimensional array of floats; the floats can be accessed by referring to their row and column index. You specify the size of a matrix at creation, and unlike an array variable, it can't be resized once it's created. Matrices are often used to represent transformations because the matrix can represent a combination of translation, scale, and rotation all at the same time. You can also perform math functions on the entire matrix in a fast and efficient way.

For this example, though, we'll use each of four columns of a matrix to represent the X, Y, and Z positions of one of our forces. In the Script Editor type

```
matrix $gFp[4][3] = << 0, 0, -150; 0, 0, 150; 150, 0, 0;
        -150, 0, 0 >>;
```

Following is another way to type the same matrix assignment that makes the relationship of rows and columns more visually obvious:

```
matrix $gFp[4][3] = << 0, 0, -150;
                0, 0, 150;
                150, 0, 0;
                -150, 0, 0 >>;
```

The above commands will create a 4 \cdot 3 matrix, of 4 rows and 3 columns, as illustrated below.

0	0	−150
0	0	150
150	0	0
−150	0	0

Now we can access one of the floats in the matrix by typing

```
print $gFp[0][0];
```

This command will print out 0, the value in the first row and first column. Remember that row and column numbering starts at 0. Now, try this:

```
print $gFp[3][0];
```

This command will print out –150, the value in the 4th row and 1st column.

Now place the radial fields by creating a for loop that will move through the matrix and create a radial from the positions. First, let's do this in a text editor and cut and paste the node to try it out. We also need to create a string variable called $compassForce so we can add a position name at the end of the field. Type this in the text editor:

```
matrix $gFp[4][3] = <<0, 0, -150; 0, 0, 150; 150, 0, 0; -150, 0, 0>>

string $compassForce[] = {"N", "S", "E", "W"};

for ($i = 0; $i < 4; $i++) {
    radial -name ("Gforce" + $compassForce[$i])
            -position $gFp[$i][0] $gFp[$i][1] $gFp[$i][2] -m 0 -att 0;
}
```

Using a matrix this way may be overkill, but it's a good way to see how creating and accessing a matrix works. Cut and paste the new code into the Script Editor, and press Enter.

By default, we want our radial fields' magnitude -m to be 0, which will create no effect. The attenuation -att is set at 0 so that the field will have a constant influence on all the vehicles, no matter how far they are from the field object. Figure 21.37 shows a top view of our scene thus far.

Let's connect the fields to the vehicles. When we add the following segment to our script later, we'll add these connections to the loop that connects other fields to the vehicles.

```
connectDynamic -fields GforceN rigidVehicleF_1 ;
connectDynamic -fields GforceS rigidVehicleF_1 ;
connectDynamic -fields GforceE rigidVehicleF_1 ;
connectDynamic -fields GforceW rigidVehicleF_1 ;
```

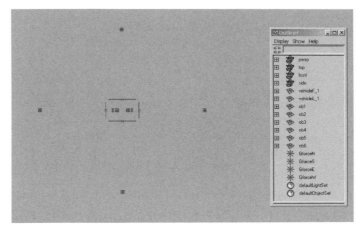

Figure 21.37 Positioning global force objects.

```
connectDynamic -fields GforceN rigidVehicleL_1 ;
connectDynamic -fields GforceS rigidVehicleL_1 ;
connectDynamic -fields GforceE rigidVehicleL_1 ;
connectDynamic -fields GforceW rigidVehicleL_1 ;
```

Create Control Slider Interface

Now, let's construct a slider window similar to the one that controlled the gun in Chapter 17. Because we are using radial fields, when you increase the northernmost field, the force will make the vehicles go south, because the radial field pushes away the objects that it affects. To create a dialog box that offers a north slider to control how hard the vehicles are pushed north, we'll have to connect the north slider to the magnitude of the field located to the south of the vehicles. We will make south, east, and west sliders as well.

Type the following in your text editor, and then do a cut and paste into the Script Editor since this segment is quite long and we will be using it again.

```
string $window =
    `window -t "Global forces control" -w 450 -h 150 GforceWin`;

columnLayout;

floatSliderGrp -label "Force north" -field false -minValue 0.0
               -maxValue 0.3 -value 0.0 magForceN;

floatSliderGrp -label "Force south" -field false -minValue 0.0
               -maxValue 0.3 -value 0.0 magForceS;

floatSliderGrp -label "Force east" -field false -minValue 0.0
               -maxValue 0.3 -value 0.0 magForceE;
```

```
floatSliderGrp -label "Force west" -field false -minValue 0.0
              -maxValue 0.3 -value 0.0 magForceW;

// Connect control sliders with fields
connectControl magForceS GforceS.magnitude;
connectControl magForceN GforceN.magnitude;
connectControl magForceW GforceW.magnitude;
connectControl magForceE GforceE.magnitude;
showWindow $window;
```

Figure 21.38 shows the control window created by the above script. We have set the min and max to only 0.0 to 0.3 so that the effect of our radial fields won't get out of control.

Play the animation, and adjust the sliders. Since there are only two vehicles, the result will not be that exciting, but you should be able to see the effect of the new global forces.

Add Global Forces Procedure to crowdSystem.mel

After the global proc collectObstacles(), add the following code to the evolving crowdSystem.mel script. (Bold statements represent new code.)

```
rigidBody -passive -name ($collection[$i] + "RigidB" + $i)
          -bounciness 3.0 ($collection[$i]);
   };

} // End of collectObstacles
```

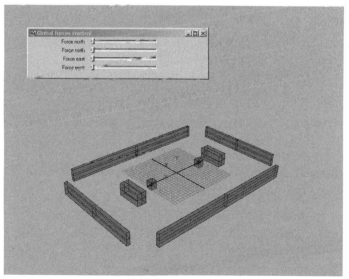

Figure 21.38 Global Force Control window.

```
global proc makeGforces() {
    // Edit matrix for position changes
    matrix $gFp[4][3] = <<0, 0, -150; 0, 0, 150; 150, 0, 0; -150, 0, 0>>
    string $compassForce[] = {"N", "S", "E", "W"};

    for ($i = 0; $i < 4; $i++) {
    radial -name ("Gforce" + $compassForce[$i]
    -position $gFp[$i][0] $gFp[$i][1] $gFp[$i][2] -m 0 -att 0;
    }

    // Use createCrowd proc for dynamic connections

    // Launch window control

    string $window =
    `window -t "Global forces control" -w 450 -h 150 GforceWin`;

    columnLayout;

    floatSliderGrp -label "Force north" -field false
                   -minValue 0.0 -maxValue 0.3
                   -value 0.0 magForceN;

    floatSliderGrp -label "Force south" -field false
                   -minValue 0.0 -maxValue 0.3
                   -value 0.0 magForceS;

    floatSliderGrp -label "Force east" -field false
                   -minValue 0.0 -maxValue 0.3
                   -value 0.0 magForceE;

    floatSliderGrp -label "Force west" -field false
                   -minValue 0.0 -maxValue 0.3
                   -value 0.0 magForceW;

    // Connect sliders to the fields' magnitude

    connectControl magForceS GforceS.magnitude;
    connectControl magForceN GforceN.magnitude;
    connectControl magForceW GforceW.magnitude;
    connectControl magForceE GforceE.magnitude;
    showWindow $window;

}
```

Save crowdSystem.mel.

If you close the window to control the sliders, you can display it again by cutting and pasting the commands that make up the //Launch window control procedure into the Script Editor and pressing Enter. Cut from the first code line shown below to the last.

```
string $window = `window -t "Global forces control"
                            -w 450 -h 150
. . . . . . . . . .
. . . . . . . . . . . . . .
. . . . . . . . . . . . . . . . . . . .
showWindow $window;
```

Example 4: Fine Tuning and Completing the Script

In this section, we'll bring all the elements together to complete the script by connecting our procedures into a unified structure. We will also add some errors and warnings to provide better feedback to the user when things don't go as expected. Figure 21.39 shows the completed crowd system.

Make a new scene, and check the script by clicking on the crowdSystem .mel icon that you have saved to your shelf (Figures 21.40 and 21.41).

The two new procedures that were added in Example 3, collectObstacles() and makeGforces(), will not run yet, because we haven't added a call to those procedures to the script, but the source statement in the button's MEL code ensures that they are being defined when the crowdSystem.mel file is sourced. Keep an eye out for errors in the Script Editor that might indicate typos in the script.

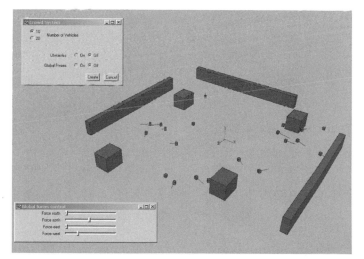

Figure 21.39 Completed crowd system.

Figure 21.40 Clicking on CrSys shelf icon.

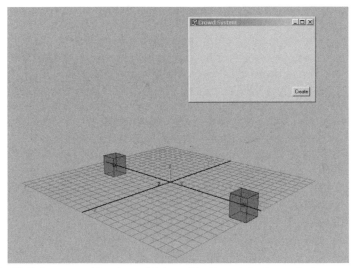

Figure 21.41 Folower and leader vehicles with Crowd System window.

Add New Features to User Interface

First, we'll add controls to the dialog box that give the user a choice between having 10 and 20 vehicles in the simulation.

■ A 20-vehicle simulation will have 4 leaders and 16 followers.

A 10-vehicle simulation will have 2 leaders and 8 followers.

Let's start by adding these options to the `global proc crowdSystem()` window procedure. We will be able to test the window by cutting and pasting the changes into the Script Editor. Look through the script to find the code to define the window.

```
// Interface
global proc crowdSystem ( )
{
window
    -title "Crowd System"
    -widthHeight 300 200
    crowdWin;
    string $form = `formLayout`;
```

Immediately under the `string $form = `formLayout`;` let's add a couple of radio buttons and some text to give the user an option for 10 or 20 vehicles. We'll make 10 the default with the `select` flag in the `radioCollection` command.

Instead of using a `radioButtonGrp` object, we'll build our own collection of radio buttons:

```
string $txt;
$txt = `text -label "Number of Vehicles"`;
string $collection = `radioCollection`;
string $radiob1, $radiob2;
$radiob1 = `radioButton -label "10"`;
$radiob2 = `radioButton -label "20"`;
setParent ..; setParent ..;

radioCollection -edit -select $radiob1 $collection;
// Select the 10 for default

formLayout -edit
        -attachForm        $txt        "top" 20
        -attachForm        $txt        "left" 70

$form;
formLayout -edit
        -attachForm        $radiob1        "top" 10
        -attachForm        $radiob1        "left" 20
        -attachForm        $radiob2        "top" 30
        -attachForm        $radiob2        "left" 20

$form;
```

Cut and paste into the Script Editor a section of the script from the `window` line to `showWindow crowdWindow;` and then press Enter (Figures 21.42 and 21.43).

If you have executed the code repeatedly to find problems, you may get errors because of Maya's renaming the window to prevent you from creating two windows with the same name. Later, we will discuss a way to check

```
window
        -title "Crowd System"  ⟵——————————————————
        -widthHeight 300 200
        crowdWin;

string $form = `formLayout`;
string $txt;
        $txt = `text -label "Number of Vehicles"`;
        string $collection = `radioCollection`;
        string $radiob1, $radiob2;
        $radiob1 = `radioButton -label "10" -onCommand "int $vNumber = 10"`;
        $radiob2 = `radioButton -label "20" -onCommand "int $vNumber = 20"`;
        setParent ..; setParent ..;

radioCollection -edit -select $radiob1 $collection;

formLayout -edit
        -attachForm            $txt    "top" 20
        -attachForm            $txt    "left" 70
$form;
formLayout -edit
        -attachForm            $radiob1   "top" 10
        -attachForm            $radiob1   "left" 20
        -attachForm            $radiob2   "top" 30
        -attachForm            $radiob2   "left" 20
$form;

// Create button
string $b1 = `button -label "Create"`;

// Place button in the window
formLayout -edit
        -attachForm        $b1 "bottom"  10
        -attachForm        $b1 "right"   10
        $form;


// Add the command to the button.
button -edit -command ("createCrowd") $b1;


showWindow crowdWin;  ⟵——————————————————
```

Figure 21.42 Enter this region of the script.

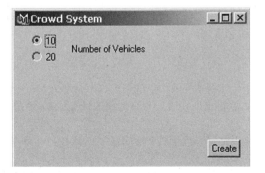

whether the window is already there and then delete it, if necessary, before making a new window. For now, if you encounter this problem, type

```
deleteUI -window crowdWin;
```

and run the script again.

You can now switch between 10 and 20 by selecting radio buttons with the mouse. One way to read the value of the radio buttons is to use the `radioButton -query` command. Another, which we'll use in this example, is to set a command that executes when each button turns on; it sets a variable that our script can read. In the `$radiob1` = and `$radiob2` = lines, add the `-onCommand` flag, as follows:

```
$radiob1 = `radioButton -label "10" -onCommand "$vNumber = 10"`;
$radiob2 = `radioButton -label "20" -onCommand "$vNumber = 20"`;
```

Cut and paste the script again into the Script Editor, and press Enter. With the dialog box displayed, turn on the 10 `radioButton`, and examine the variable with a print statement, as follows:

```
print $vNumber;
```

The result from Maya follows:

```
print $vNumber;
10
```

Now, select the radio button labeled 20, and look at the value of `$vNumber` with another print statement.

```
print $vNumber;
```

The result from Maya follows:

```
print $vNumber;
20
```

Note that when the dialog box first appeared, the value 10 was selected. We used the following statement to turn on the 10 option when the window was created:

```
radioCollection -edit -select $radiob1 $collection;
```

Add Checkbox Options

Now that we have radio buttons to let the user choose the number of vehicles, let's add some radio buttons to offer options for obstacles and global forces. After the `setParent` commands but before the `radioCollection` command that we just added, insert the code for the new radio buttons. (In the following, new code is **boldface**.)

```
$radiob2 = `radioButton -label "20" -onCommand "int $vNumber = 20"`;
setParent ..; setParent ..;

    string $txtOB = `text -label "Obstacles"`;
    string $collection2 = `radioCollection`;
    string $radiob3, $radiob4;
    $radiob3 = `radioButton -label "On"
            -onCommand "$obst = 1"`;
    $radiob4 = `radioButton -label "Off"
            -onCommand "$obst = 0"`;
    setParent ..;setParent ..;

    string $txtGF = `text -label "Global Forces"`;
    string $collection3 = `radioCollection`;
    string $radiob5, $radiob6;
    $radiob5 = `radioButton -label
            "On" -onCommand "$gforces = 1"`;
    $radiob6 = `radioButton -label "Off"
            -onCommand "$gforces = 0"`;
    setParent ..; setParent ..;

radioCollection -edit -select $radiob1 $collection;
radioCollection -edit -select $radiob4 $collection2;
radioCollection -edit -select $radiob6 $collection3;
```

Now, add the following code segment just after the layout section for the $radiob2 radio button. (New code is **boldface**.)

```
                -attachForm    $radiob2    "left" 20
$form;

// Place environment options
formLayout -edit
                -attachForm    $txtOB        "top" 80
                -attachForm    $txtOB        "left" 80
$form;
formLayout -edit
                -attachForm    $radiob3      "top" 80
                -attachForm    $radiob3      "left" 150
                -attachForm    $radiob4      "top" 80
                -attachForm    $radiob4      "left" 190

$form;
formLayout -edit
                -attachForm    $txtGF        "top" 110
                -attachForm    $txtGF        "left" 63

$form;
formLayout -edit
```

```
-attachForm      $radiob5      "top"  110
-attachForm      $radiob5      "left" 150
-attachForm      $radiob6      "top"  110
-attachForm      $radiob6      "left" 190
```

```
$form;
```

Now, copy and paste the new dialog box procedure into the Script Editor, and press Enter to run it (Figure 21.44).

Use `print` statements to see the new values of `$obst` and `$gforces` in the Script Editor, as follows:

```
print $obst;
print $gforces;
```

Each of these variables contains a value of 0, corresponding to the default Off selection, set by the `radioCollection -select $radiob4` and `$radiob6` calls. If you choose the On setting for either `radioButton` and then run the `print` statements again, you'll see that the radio button you've changed now contains a value of 1, for On.

Add Cancel Button

To close the window, thus far we have been using the Close box at the top of the window, which is provided automatically. To be consistent with Maya's dialog boxes, we should add a Cancel button next to the existing Create button that also closes the window without changing the scene. In addition, because our dialog box's operation should be run only once in the scene, we want the window to close after the script is run. To do this, we'll use the `deleteUI` command to tell Maya to close the window when the Cancel button is pressed.

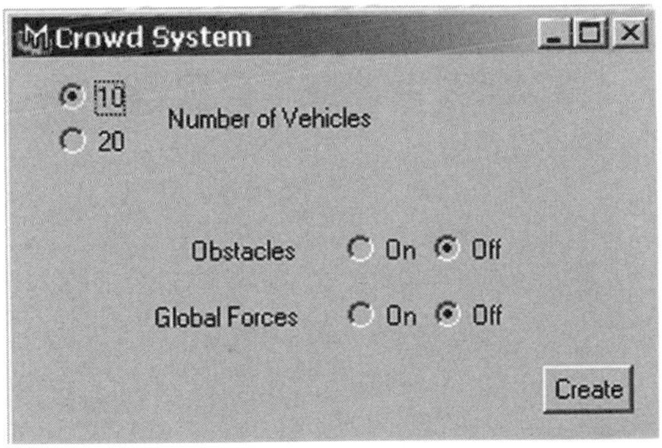

Figure 21.44 More controls in Crowd System window.

Under the `// Create` buttons section from the original window that we created, enter the **boldface** lines shown below.

```
// Create buttons
string $button1 = `button -label "Create"`;
string $button2 = `button -label "Cancel"`;
```

In the section just under the previous one for `$button1`, enter the following code:

```
formLayout -edit
          -attachForm   $button2 "bottom"   10
          -attachForm   $button2 "left"     215

    $form;

// Add commands to the buttons
button -edit -command ("createCrowd; deleteUI crowdWin;")
       $button1;
button -edit -command ("deleteUI crowdWin;") $button2;
```

Once again, paste the script into the Script Editor (Figure 21.45).

Window Standards

When compared against Maya's standards for button placement, the Cancel and Create buttons are reversed. To correct this, switch the numbers in the `formLayout -edit` area for the buttons. The resulting MEL code follows:

```
formLayout -edit
          -attachForm              $button1 "bottom"   10
          -attachForm              $button1 "left"     215
```

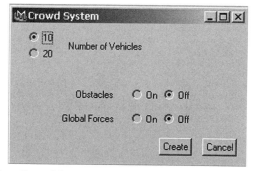

Figure 21.45 Adding Cancel button.

```
$form;

formLayout -edit
          -attachForm          $button2 "bottom"     10
          -attachForm          $button2 "right"      10

$form;
```

Because we're using the `formLayout` layout type, we have nearly complete control over the placement of the buttons in the window. These `-attachForm` flags tell Maya how far to space the buttons you've created from the edges of the form. If you like, you can place them relative to any of the window edges, named `left`, `right`, `top`, and `bottom`.

Save `crowdSystem.mel`, and clear the scene via File > New, or type

```
file -f -new;
```

Run the script from the icon on your shelf to make sure you are getting the latest version that you have saved in your script path. You should see the new interface options in the dialog box. The entire script for the dialog box as assembled thus far follows:

```
// Window launch
//_____
global proc crowdSystem()
{

window
  -title "Crowd System"
  -widthHeight 300 200
  crowdWin;

string $form = `formLayout`;
  string $txt = `text -label "Number of Vehicles"`;
  string $collection = `radioCollection`;
  string $radiob1, $radiob2;
  $radiob1 = `radioButton -label "10" -onCommand "$vNumber = 10"`;
  $radiob2 = `radioButton -label "20" -onCommand "$vNumber = 20"`;
  setParent ..; setParent ..;

  string $txtOB = `text -label "Obstacles"`;
  string $collection2 = `radioCollection`;
  string $radiob3, $radiob4;
  $radiob3 = `radioButton -label "On" -onCommand "$obst = 1"`;
  $radiob4 = `radioButton -label "Off" -onCommand "$obst = 0"`;
  setParent ..;setParent ..;

  string $txtGF = `text -label "Global Forces"`;
```

```
        string $collection3 = `radioCollection`;
        string $radiob5, $radiob6;
        $radiob5 = `radioButton -label "On" -onCommand "$gforces = 1"`;
        $radiob6 = `radioButton -label "Off" -onCommand "$gforces = 0"`;
        setParent ..; setParent ..;

    radioCollection -edit -select $radiob1 $collection;
    radioCollection -edit -select $radiob4 $collection2;
    radioCollection -edit -select $radiob6 $collection3;
    // Place vehicle options
    formLayout -edit
                -attachForm         $txt         "top" 20
                -attachForm         $txt         "left" 70

    $form;
    formLayout -edit
                -attachForm         $radiob1     "top" 10
                -attachForm         $radiob1     "left" 20
                -attachForm         $radiob2     "top" 30
                -attachForm         $radiob2     "left" 20

    $form;

    // Place environment options
    formLayout -edit
                -attachForm         $txtOB       "top" 80
                -attachForm         $txtOB       "left" 80

    $form;
    formLayout -edit
                -attachForm         $radiob3     "top" 80
                -attachForm         $radiob3     "left" 150
                -attachForm         $radiob4     "top" 80
                -attachForm         $radiob4     "left" 190

    $form;
    formLayout -edit
                -attachForm         $txtGF       "top" 110
                -attachForm         $txtGF       "left" 63

      $form;
      formLayout -edit
                -attachForm         $radiob5     "top" 110
                -attachForm         $radiob5     "left" 150
                -attachForm         $radiob6     "top" 110
                -attachForm         $radiob6     "left" 190
```

```
$form;

// Create buttons
string $button1 = `button -label              "Create"`;
string $button2 = `button -label              "Cancel"`;

// Place buttons in window
formLayout -edit
           -attachForm        $button1 "bottom"   10
           -attachForm        $button1 "left"      215

$form;
formLayout -edit
           -attachForm        $button2        "bottom"   10
           -attachForm        $button2        "right"    10

$form;

// Add commands to buttons
button -edit -command ("createCrowd;deleteUI crowdWin;")
       $button1;
button -edit -command ("deleteUI crowdWin;") $button2;

showWindow crowdWin;

} // End of crowdSystem proc
```

Add More Vehicles

Now that we have added an option to create either 10 or 20 vehicles, let's redesign the code to create them. We not only need to modify the code to add the number entered by the user, but also to distribute the vehicles over a wider area in the scene. Whether the user chooses to make 10 or 20 vehicles, we'll need to create them over a larger area than we did in Example 3. In that example, we located the obstacles at 30 and −30 units in X, and 20 and −20 units in Z. To allow for more vehicles, this time we'll place them at 120 and −120 units in X and Z.

To add vehicles, we will have to edit the vehicle creation section of createCrowd(). In your text editor, load the script crowdSystem.mel, and find the lines at the top of the script where it creates the crowdSolver node. Making the necessary name changes in the expression section can get tedious, but once we get it working, we can copy and paste the section for the leader vehicles, changing only the names.

Let's use a switch statement to handle both choices for the Number of Vehicles radio buttons, assigning the appropriate values for $FvNumber and $LvNumber, depending on whether $vNumber is 10 or 20. Enter the following new code in the proc createCrowd(). (New code is **boldface**.)

```
rigidSolver -create -current -name crowdSolver
            -velocityVectorScale 0.5 -displayVelocity on;
setAttr crowdSolver.allowDisconnection 1;

// Get total number of vehicles from interface options

int $FvNumber;
int $LvNumber;

switch ($vNumber)
{

   case 10:
      $FvNumber = 8;        // Followers
      $LvNumber = 2;        // Leaders
      break;

   case 20:
      $FvNumber = 16;       // Followers
      $LvNumber = 4;        // Leaders
      break;

}

// Basic vehicle model type: follower

for ($i = 0; $i < $FvNumber; $i++) {
   polyCube -name ("vehicleF_" + $i) -width 2 -height
   2.5 -depth 2;

   // Add vehicle force field for follower

   radial -position 0 0 0 -name ("vehicleFForce_" + $i)
          -magnitude 50 -attenuation 0.3 -maxDistance 8.0;
   parent ("vehicleFForce_" + $i) ("vehicleF_" + $i);

   // Make vehicle a rigid body with random placement

   rigidBody -name ("rigidVehicleF_" + $i) -active -mass 1
             -bounciness 0 -damping 1.5 -position
   (rand(-120,120)) 0 (rand(-120,120)) -impulse 0 0 0
             -standInObject cube   -solver
   crowdSolver ("vehicleF_" + $i);
   disconnectAttr ("rigidVehicleF_" + $i + "ry.output")
      ("vehicleF_" + $i + ".rotateY");
   disconnectAttr ("rigidVehicleF_" + $i + "rx.output")
      ("vehicleF_" + $i + ".rotateX");
   disconnectAttr ("rigidVehicleF_" + $i + "rz.output")
      ("vehicleF_" + $i + ".rotateZ");
```

```
// Create expression for VehicleF with a random multiplier added to
// expression

float $randX = rand(-3,3);
float $randZ = rand(3,-3);

$expString =
        "// Set wander motion of vehicle and add random multipliers.\n";
$expString += ("rigidVehicleF_" + $i + ".impulseX");
$expString += " = sin(time * ";
$expString += ($randX);
$expString += ");\n";
$expString += ("rigidVehicleF_" + $i + ".impulseZ");
$expString += " = (noise(time) * ";
$expString += ($randZ);
$expString += ");\n\n";
$expString +=
"// Set orientation of Vehicle according to the velocity direction.\n";
$expString += "float $fVel" + $i + "[];\n";
$expString += "$fVel" + $i +" = `getAttr rigidVehicleF_" + $i +
   ".velocity`;\n\n";
$expString += "vehicleF_" + $i + ".rotateX = 0;\n";
$expString += "vehicleF_" + $i + ".rotateY = atan2d( $fVel" + $i
   + "[0], $fVel" + $i + "[2] );\n";
$expString += "vehicleF_" + $i + ".rotateZ = 0;\n";

expression -s $expString -name ("wanderF_exp" + $i)
            -alwaysEvaluate true -unitConversion all;

} // End of follower creation
```

One new feature of this version of our script is that we use the rand function to place the follower vehicles. Also, this version picks a random multiplier for the sine functions in each follower vehicle's wander expression, and it inserts the number into the wander expression string creation. This is more efficient than having the expression refer to the global variables $xMult and $zMult, and it will allow the simulation to run faster.

Now, let's move on to the leader creation code. To create this, we can just cut and paste the code to create the followers and add a line for the extra radial field that distinguishes leaders from followers. Also, we'll change the vehicle's name to include L for leader instead of F for follower. In the expression, we also give a new name to the float array variable $fVel, so that each follower can have its own copy of the variable. We'll name this variable $fVelL<n>[] instead, where <n> is the number of the follower. For example, the first vehicle's $fVelL variable will be called $fVelL1[]; the second will be called $fVel2[], and so on.

The other new feature that we'll add is to create a `GlobalLeadForce` radial field as part of the leader hierarchy. It needs to be a more subtle effect than before, so we need to give it an area of influence that will limit its effect to followers that come within a certain distance. To do this, we'll need to change the `attenuation` and add a `maxDistance` of 50 units.

The new leader creation section follows. (New code is **boldface**.)

```
} // End of follower creation

// Basic vehicle model type: leader
//_____
for ($i = 0; $i < $LvNumber; $i++) {
    polyCube -name ("vehicleL_" + $i) -width 2 -height 2.5 -depth 2;

// Add vehicle force field for leader

radial -position 0 0 0 -name ("vehicleLForce_" + $i) -magnitude 50
        -attenuation 0.3 -maxDistance 5.0;
parent ("vehicleLForce_" + $i) ("vehicleL_" + $i);

// Add leader field

radial -position 0 0 0 -name ("vehicleGlobalLeadForce_" + $i )
        -magnitude -1 -attenuation 0.2 -maxDistance 50;
parent ("vehicleGlobalLeadForce_" + $i) ("vehicleL_" + $i);

// Make vehicle a rigid body with random placement

rigidBody -name ("rigidVehicleL_" + $i) -active -mass 1
        -bounciness 0 -damping 1.5 -position
(rand(-120,120)) 0 (rand(-120,120)) -impulse 0 0 0 -standInObject cube
        -solver crowdSolver ("vehicleL_" + $i);

disconnectAttr ("rigidVehicleL_" + $i + "ry.output")
    ("vehicleL_" + $i + ".rotateY");
disconnectAttr ("rigidVehicleL_" + $i + "rx.output")
    ("vehicleL_" + $i + ".rotateX");
disconnectAttr ("rigidVehicleL_" + $i + "rz.output")
    ("vehicleL_" + $i + ".rotateZ");

// Create expression for VehicleL with random multiplier added to expression

float $randX = rand(-3,3);
float $randZ = rand(3,-3);

// Changed $fVel[ ] to $fVelL[ ] in expression

$expString = "// Set wander motion of vehicle and add multipliers.\n;
$expString += ("rigidVehicleL_" + $i + ".impulseX");
$expString += " = sin(time * ";
```

```
$expString += ($randX);
$expString += ");\n";
$expString += ("rigidVehicleL_" + $i + ".impulseZ");
$expString += " = (noise(time) * ";
$expString += ($randZ);
$expString += ");\n\n";
$expString +=
"// Set orientation of Vehicle according to the velocity direction.\n";
$expString += "float $fVelL" + $i + "[];\n";
$expString += "$fVel" + $i +" = `getAttr rigidVehicleL_" + $i +
             ".velocity`;\n\n";
$expString += "vehicleL_" + $i + ".rotateX = 0;\n";
$expString += "vehicleL_" + $i + ".rotateY = atan2d( $fVelL" + $i +
             "[0], $fVelL" + $i + "[2] );\n";
$expString += "vehicleL_" + $i + ".rotateZ = 0;\n";

expression -s $expString -name ("wanderL_exp" + $i)
          -alwaysEvaluate true -unitConversion all;

} // End of leader creation
```

Add Integer Pass from One Procedure to Another

Before we test the script, we need to add a parameter to the `createCrowd()` global procedure that will allow us to pass the number of vehicles to the procedure. (New code is **boldface**.)

```
// createCrowd
// _____
global proc createCrowd(int $vNumber)
                              // Pass ints from interface
```

We also need to change the call to `createCrowd` in the button command for Create. At the bottom of the window launch section in the `global proc crowdSystem()`, make the following change. (New code is **boldface**.)

```
// Add commands to buttons
button -edit -command ("createCrowd $vNumber; deleteUI crowdWin;")
    $button1;
```

This change will pass the `int` variable `$vNumber` as a parameter to the proc `createCrowd()`.

At this time, it would be a good idea to save the `crowdSystem.mel` script if you have not been doing so. To test our changes to the script so far, click the MEL icon on your shelf. Click Create in the dialog box that appears; if everything went well, you should get the appropriate number of vehicles. Open the Outliner to see the names of the new vehicle objects (Figure 21.46).

You probably will get a warning that there is a "New procedure defini-tion for createCrowd." This warning tells you that you've changed the parameters to the createCrowd function, which can be a serious mistake if you do not intend it. Since this was an intentional change, we'll ignore the warning. This will happen again later as we add parameters for global forces and using obstacles.

Make sure that both the 10 and 20 options work. Remember to create a new scene before trying a different option.

Play the scene. You will see the vehicles moving around, controlled by their individual wander expressions.

Connect Radials for Both Leaders and Followers Together with "Nested" Loops

Now we need to set up some "nested" loops that will connect the fields to the vehicles. We also have to pass another int out of crowdSystem(), which will tell createCrowd() to generate global forces and connect them as well.

In the // Hook up the fields section, delete the code from Example 3, and replace it with the following code:

```
for ($i = 0; $i < $LvNumber; $i++ ) {
   // Connect leaders to followers, both fields
   for ( $j = 0; $j < $FvNumber; $j++) {
      connectDynamic -fields ("vehicleLForce_" + $i)
                             ("rigidVehicleF_" + $j);
      connectDynamic -fields ("vehicleGlobalLeadForce_" + $i)
                             ("rigidVehicleF_" + $j);
   }
}

for ($i = 0; $i < $FvNumber; $i++) {
   // Connect Followers to Leaders
   for ($j = 0; $j < $LvNumber; $j++) {
      connectDynamic -fields ("vehicleFForce_" + $i)
                             ("rigidVehicleL_" + $j) ;
   }
}
```

The above segment uses a for loop to loop through each set of vehicles. Each leader is connected to all followers in the first loop, and each follower is connected to all leaders in the second loop.

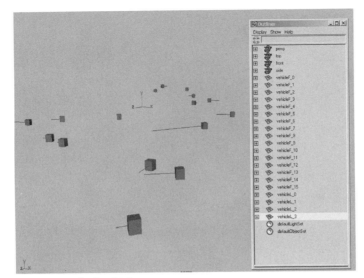

Figure 21.46 A crowd of vehicles.

Save the crowdSystem.mel script, and clear the scene again. Click on the MEL icon, and view the result (Figure 21.47).

We get a nice subtle effect as each of the followers starts to pursue the leaders as the leaders approach. They then go on their way if they fall out of the leader's influence distance.

Now we need to connect the follower fields to the followers and leader fields to the leaders so that we can get the same avoidance behavior that we saw in Example 3. To do this, we need another nested loop. Enter the following loops in the script, right under the previous loops:

```
// Connect same type vehicles to each other. Disconnect vehicle from itself

for ($i = 0; $i < $LvNumber; $i++) {
        // Connect leaders to leaders
        for ($j = 0; $j < $LvNumber; $j++) {
                connectDynamic -fields ("vehicleLForce_" + $i)
                                        ("rigidVehicleL_" + $j);

        }

                connectDynamic -delete -fields ("vehicleLForce_" + $i)
                                        ("rigidVehicleL_" + $i);

}
```

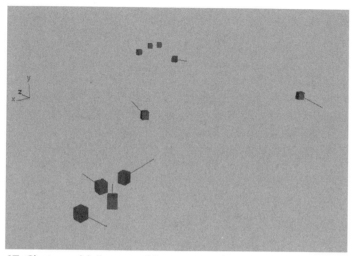

Figure 21.47 Clusters of followers with respective leaders.

```
for ($i = 0; $i < $FvNumber; $i++) {
// Connect followers to followers
for ($j = 0; $j < $FvNumber; $j++) {
   connectDynamic -fields ("vehicleFForce_" + $i)
                          ("rigidVehicleF_" + $j);

}

   connectDynamic -delete -fields ("vehicleFForce_" + $i)
                                  ("rigidVehicleF_" + $i);

}
```

At the end, we have to disconnect (-delete) the force field from its owner so that the vehicles do not try to repel themselves. In this instance, there would be no noticeable effect if we didn't disconnect these fields, but when using dynamics it's generally a good idea to ensure that no connections exist that don't make sense physically, since such connections may have unintended results.

Now you will start to see that the motions are becoming quite natural for the vehicles as they travel along their paths, avoiding each other and pursuing the leaders.

Add Global Forces Function to Main Script

At this juncture, we need to check the $gForces variable to decide whether to call makeGforces(). We need to execute the global proc `makeGforces()` early so that they will be there when we connect them in the `// Hook up fields` section. First, we need to check whether the option in the interface was selected. After the `switch` statement for the number of vehicles, add the following line to the code. (New code is **boldface**.)

```
        break;

    }

    if ($gforces == 1) makeGforces; // Check global forces option

    // Basic vehicle model type: follower
```

Now we will add an `int` parameter to the `createCrowd()` procedure that the `crowdSystem()` procedure will pass in. Edit the `createCrowd()` procedure definition to accept the new integer parameter as follows:

```
    global proc createCrowd(int $vNumber, int $gforces)
    {
```

In the `crowdSystem()` procedure, add `$gforces;` as follows. (New code is **boldface**.)

```
    button -edit -command
            ("createCrowd $vNumber $gforces; deleteUI crowdWin;")
            $button1;
```

Now we need to add code to connect the global fields in the loop section if `$gforces` is set to 1 (meaning the user turned on the Global Fields option). In the `// Hook up fields` section, add the following `if` statement, and loop. (New code is **boldface**.)

```
    connectDynamic -delete -fields ("vehicleFForce_" + $i)
                                    ("rigidVehicleF_" + $i);

    }

    // Connect global forces to both types of vehicles if option is on

    if ($gforces == 1) {

        string $compass[4] = { "N", "S", "E", "W" };
        for ($i = 0; $i < $LvNumber; $i++) {
            for ($c = 0; $c < size($compass); $c++) {
                connectDynamic -fields ("Gforce" + $compass[$c])
                                        ("rigidVehicleL_" + $i);

            }
        }
        for ($i = 0; $i < $FvNumber; $i++) {
            for ($c = 0; $c < size($compass); $c++) {
```

```
                    connectDynamic -fields ("Gforce" + $compass[$c])
                                           ("rigidVehicleF_" + $i);
          }
      }
  }
```

This code segment is a variation of the nested loops that we used before, except that we create a $compass array containing the four cardinal directions, and we use those strings to build each field's name.

Test Global Forces Option

We should test the script again to make sure that the Global Forces option correctly controls the creation and connection of the fields that implement global forces. Save the script, and click the MEL icon on the shelf. When the dialog box appears, turn on Global Forces, and click Create (Figure 21.48).

Move the sliders to use the global fields to push the vehicles in the different directions. If you want to check to see that all field connections are correct, select Window > Relationship Editors > Dynamic Relationships . . . (Figure 21.49).

Now, select vehicleF_0 from the list to view all corresponding fields (Figure 21.50).

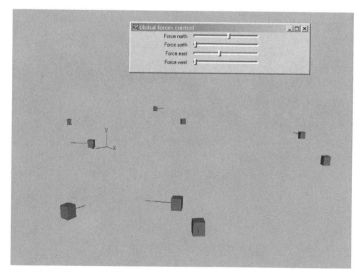

Figure 21.48 Global forces influence all vehicles.

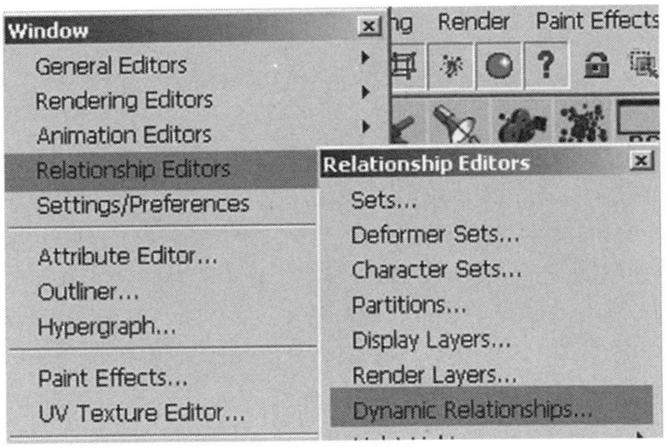

Figure 21.49 Dynamic Relationships menu item.

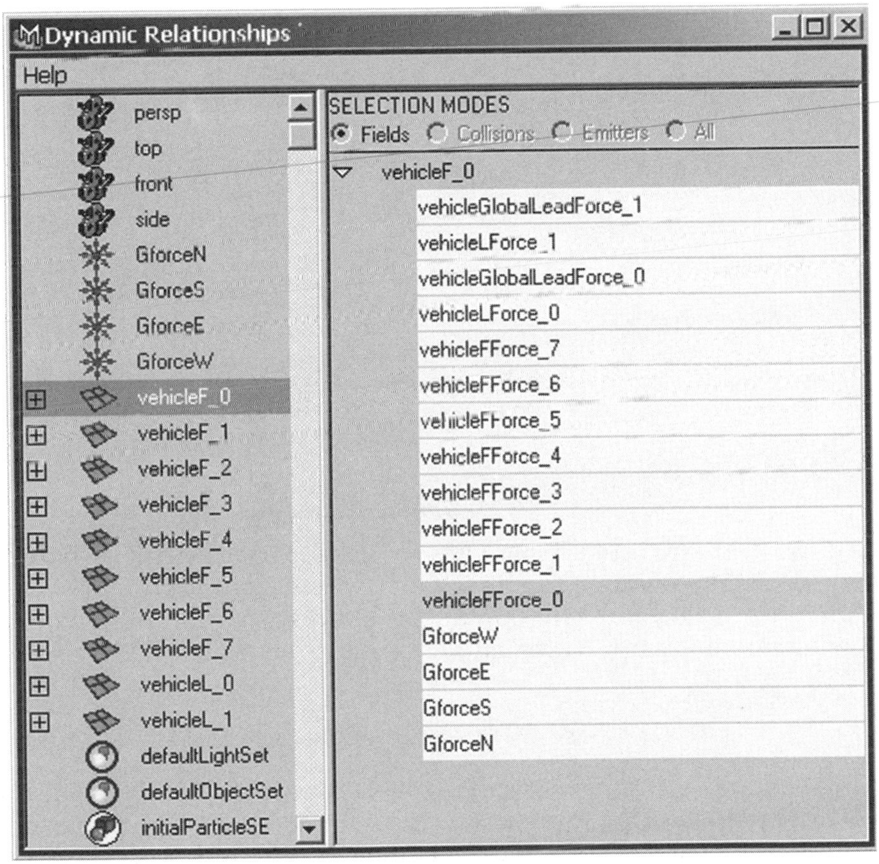

Figure 21.50 Fields that influence `vehicleF_0`.

Add Main Launch Procedure

We want to add a Main procedure to our script that will serve two functions. First, it will initialize a *global string array* that will contain a list of names of the selected objects in the Maya interface at the time the script launches. Later, we'll add code that will make these selected objects obstacles. Second, the Main procedure will add a test to see whether the window already exists. If it does, an old window from a previous execution of the script is still open, and a previous crowd system may exist. After the makeGlobalForces proc(), add the following code to the script:

```
// Main
// _____
global proc crowdMain()
{

    global string $collectObjects[]; // Initialize global string that
                                     // all procs can see

    if (`window -exists crowdWin`) { // Check to see if window is open

        confirmDialog -t "Already running!"
                -m "Please close Crowd System window and create a New Scene";
    } else {

        $collectObjects = `ls -sl`; // Collect objects that are selected

        crowdSystem; // Run crowdSystem proc

    }

}
```

We use confirmDialog to provide an error message if the window is already open. The script quits after the user presses Confirm. If you want to see the error dialog box without running the script, cut and paste the following into the Script Editor, and press Enter (Figure 21.51).

```
confirmDialog -t "Already running!"
        -m "Please close Crowd System window and create a New Scene";
```

Creating the global variable $collectObjects to hold the list of selected objects is often a poor way to share data between procedures; usually, passing data as a procedure parameter is a better choice. However, in a large script it can be reasonable to use global variables for data like

Figure 21.51 Resulting warning dialog.

the initial selection list that may need to be available at many places in the code.

Because we now want the entry point to our script to be the crowdMain() procedure, we need to replace the call to crowdSystem() in our MEL script shelf button with a call to crowdMain(). Middle-mouse drag the shelf button that you have been using to run the script to the shelf's trashcan to delete it. Now, enter the following lines into the Script Editor, and middle-mouse drag them to the shelf to give us a new shelf button that calls our new entry point procedure.

```
source crowdSystem;
crowdMain;
```

Add collectObstacles to Script

Let's add a new collectObstacles procedure to the script. It makes any selected objects into obstacles, if the obstacles feature is turned on in the dialog box. After the createCrowd procedure, add the following code. (New code is **boldface**.)

```
cycleCheck -e off;

} // End of createCrowd proc

// Build obstacles
//__  _

global proc collectObstacles() {

    global string $collectObjects[];
    // Re-declare global array for obstacles

        if (size($collectObjects) == 0) {

            warning "No obstacle objects were selected.";

        } else {

        for ( $i = 0; $i < size($collectObjects); $i++) {

            rigidBody -passive -name ($collectObjects[$i] + "RigidB" + $i)
                    -bounciness 2.0 ($collectObjects[$i]);

        }
```

```
    }
} // End of collectObstacles proc
```

The above procedure starts by declaring the global variable $collectObstacles to make it accessible to the code in the procedure. Then, the procedure loops over the objects listed in the $collectObstacles variable to convert the objects into rigid bodies so that the vehicles can collide with them. The rigidBody commands automatically connect the new rigid bodies to crowdSolver because it's still the *current* solver. Also, we've added a warning that appears when nothing is selected when the script runs:

```
warning "No obstacle objects were selected.";
```

The warning notifies the user that the Obstacles On option was selected in the interface, but there was nothing selected and stored in the $collectObstacles array. The warning will not stop the script, but it will only print a warning in the status line at the lower right corner of the Maya interface. Cut and paste the warning line into the Script Editor to see what it does (Figure 21.52).

Add Objects to Scene and Run Script

Let's place some objects in the scene and test the Obstacles option. Make a new scene, and place several polyCubes in it (Figure 21.53).

Place the cubes wherever you like, but remember that the vehicles will be distributed between –120 and 120 in X and Z. Select the cubes, and click the shelf button (Figure 21.54).

In the dialog box, turn on both Obstacles and Global Forces, and then click Create. After the script has executed and the Global Forces window has appeared, play back the scene (Figure 21.55).

Move some of the sliders while you watch the vehicles wander around, avoid each other, bounce off the obstacles, and react to the global forces you control with the sliders. Congratulations!

Note: Sometimes, you may see a warning because two or more vehicles have been placed either within an obstacle or within another vehicle. Because the obstacles and vehicles will mutually repel each other, this problem will correct itself within a few frames. This problem is a result of using the rand function to place the vehicles without checking for intersections before placing them.

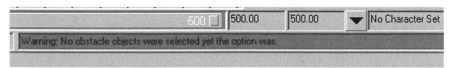

Figure 21.52 Warning in status line.

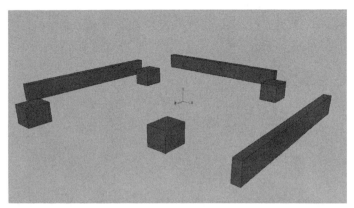

Figure 21.53 Cubes as obstacles.

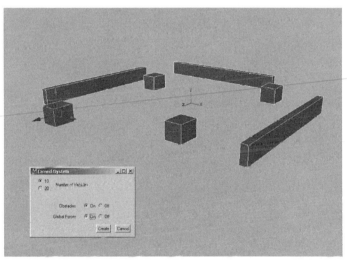

Figure 21.54 Crowd System window with new obstacles.

Full Script Reference: crowdSystem.mel

Note: The hide command has been added to the vehicles and global forces routines to visually clean up the scenes.

```
// createCrowd
// _____

global proc createCrowd(int $vNumber, int $gforces, int $obst)
// Bring in ints and string from interface
```

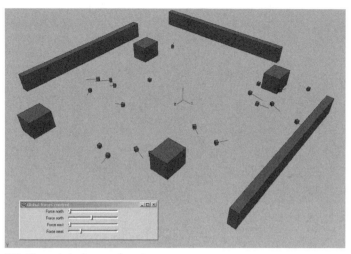

Figure 21.55 Completed crowd system.

```
{
    // Vehicle creation for crowd system

    // Create a master crowdSolver for all vehicles

    rigidSolver -create -current -name crowdSolver
                -velocityVectorScale 0.5 -displayVelocity on;
    setAttr crowdSolver.allowDisconnection 1;

    // Get total number of vehicles from interface options

    int $FvNumber;
    int $LvNumber;

    switch ($vNumber)
    {
    case 10:
        $FvNumber = 8;                  // Followers
        $LvNumber = 2;                  // Leaders
        break;
    case 20:
        $FvNumber = 16;                 // Followers
        $LvNumber = 4;                  // Leaders
        break;
    }
```

```
if ($gforces == 1) makeGforces; // Check Global Forces option

// Basic vehicle model type: follower
//_____

    for ($i = 0; $i < $FvNumber; $i++) {
        polyCube -name ("vehicleF_" + $i) -width 2 -height 2.5 -depth 2;

    // Add vehicle force field for follower

    radial -position 0 0 0 -name ("vehicleFForce_" + $i)
            -magnitude 50 -attenuation 0.3 -maxDistance 8.0;
    parent ("vehicleFForce_" + $i) ("vehicleF_" + $i);
    hide ("vehicleFForce_" + $i);

    // Make vehicle a rigid body with random placement

    rigidBody -name ("rigidVehicleF_" + $i) -active -mass 1 -bounciness 0
            -damping 1.5 -position

    (rand(-70,70)) 0 (rand(-70,70)) -impulse 0 0 0 -standInObject cube
                                    -solver crowdSolver ("vehicleF_" + $i);
    disconnectAttr ("rigidVehicleF_" + $i + "ry.output") ("vehicleF_" +
                $i + ".rotateY");
    disconnectAttr ("rigidVehicleF_" + $i + "rx.output") ("vehicleF_" +
                $i + ".rotateX");
    disconnectAttr ("rigidVehicleF_" + $i + "rz.output") ("vehicleF_" +
                $i + ".rotateZ");

    // Create expression for VehicleF with random multiplier
    // added to expression

    float $randX = rand(-3,3);
    float $randZ = rand(3,-3);

    $expString =
    "// Set wander motion of vehicle and add random multipliers.\n";
    $expString += ("rigidVehicleF_" + $i + ".impulseX");
    $expString += " = sin(time * ";
    $expString += ($randX);
    $expString += ");\n";
    $expString += ("rigidVehicleF_" + $i + ".impulseZ");
    $expString += " = (noise(time) * ";
    $expString += ($randZ);
    $expString += ");\n\n";
    $expString +=
    "// Set orientation of vehicle according to the velocity direction.\n";
```

```
            $expString += "float $fVel" + $i + "[];\n";
            $expString += "$fVel" + $i +" = `getAttr rigidVehicleF_" + $i +
                     ".velocity`;\n\n";
            $expString += "vehicleF_" + $i + ".rotateX = 0;\n";
            $expString += "vehicleF_" + $i + ".rotateY = atan2d($fVel" + $i +
                     "[0], $fVel" + $i + "[2]);\n";
            $expString += "vehicleF_" + $i + ".rotateZ = 0;\n";

            expression -s $expString -name ("wanderF_exp" + $i)
                     -alwaysEvaluate true -unitConversion all;

      } // End of follower creation

      // Basic vehicle model type: leader

      //_____

      for ($i = 0; $i < $LvNumber; $i++) {
      polyCube -name ("vehicleL_" + $i) -width 2 -height 2.5 -depth 2;

      // Add vehicle force field for leader

radial -position 0 0 0 -name ("vehicleLForce_" + $i) -magnitude 50
            -attenuation 0.3 -maxDistance 8.0;
parent ("vehicleLForce_" + $i) ("vehicleL_" + $i);
hide ("vehicleLForce_" + $i);

// Add leader field

radial -position 0 0 0 -name ("vehicleGlobalLeadForce_" + $i ) -magnitude
            -1 -attenuation 0.2 -maxDistance 50;
parent ("vehicleGlobalLeadForce_"+ $i) ("vehicleL_" + $i);
hide ("vehicleGlobalLeadForce_"+ $i);

// Make vehicle a rigid body with random placement

rigidBody -name ("rigidVehicleL_" + $i) -active -mass 1 -bounciness 0
            -damping 1.5 -position
(rand(-70,70)) 0 (rand(-70,70)) -impulse 0 0 0 -standInObject cube
                              -solver crowdSolver ("vehicleL_" + $i);

disconnectAttr ("rigidVehicleL_" + $i + "ry.output") ("vehicleL_" + $i +
            ".rotateY");
disconnectAttr ("rigidVehicleL_" + $i + "rx.output") ("vehicleL_" + $i +
            ".rotateX");
disconnectAttr ("rigidVehicleL_" + $i + "rz.output") ("vehicleL_" + $i +
            ".rotateZ");
```

```
// Create expression for VehicleL with random multiplier added to
// expression

float $randX = rand(-3,3);
float $randZ = rand(3,-3);

// Changed $fVel[ ] to $fVelL[ ] in expression
$expString = "// Set wander motion of vehicle and add multipliers.\n";
$expString += ("rigidVehicleL_" + $i + ".impulseX");
$expString += " = sin(time * ";
$expString += ($randX);
$expString += ");\n";
$expString += ("rigidVehicleL_" + $i + ".impulseZ");
$expString += " = (noise(time) * ";
$expString += ($randZ);
$expString += ");\n\n";
$expString += "// Set orientation of vehicle according to the velocity direction.\n";
    $expString += "float $fVelL" + $i + "[];\n";
    $expString += "$fVelL" + $i +" = `getAttr rigidVehicleL_" + $i +
                ".velocity`;\n\n";
    $expString += "vehicleL_" + $i + ".rotateX = 0;\n";
    $expString += "vehicleL_" + $i + ".rotateY = atan2d ( $fVelL" + $i +
                "[0], $fVelL" + $i + "[2] );\n";
    $expString += "vehicleL_" + $i + ".rotateZ = 0;\n";

    expression -s $expString -name ("wanderL_exp" + $i)
            -alwaysEvaluate true -unitConversion all;

} // End of leader creation

// Connect fields' nested loops

// _____

for ($i = 0; $i < $LvNumber; $i++ ) {
// Connect leaders to followers both fields
    for ( $j = 0; $j < $FvNumber; $j++) {
    connectDynamic -fields ("vehicleLForce_" + $i) ("rigidVehicleF_" +
                        $j);
     connectDynamic -fields ("vehicleGlobalLeadForce_" + $i)
                        ("rigidVehicleF_" + $j);
    }
}
```

```
for ($i = 0; $i < $FvNumber; $i++) { // Connect followers to leaders
   for ($j = 0; $j < $LvNumber; $j++) {
        connectDynamic -fields ("vehicleFForce_" + $i) ("rigidVehicleL_"
                               + $j) ;
     }
}

// Connect same type vehicles to each other. Disconnect vehicle from
   // itself

for ($i = 0; $i < $LvNumber; $i++) { // Connect leaders to leaders
   for ($j = 0; $j < $LvNumber; $j++) {
        connectDynamic -fields ("vehicleLForce_" + $i) ("rigidVehicleL_"
                               + $j) ;
     }
        connectDynamic -delete -fields ("vehicleLForce_" + $i)
                                       ("rigidVehicleL_" + $i);

   }

for ($i = 0; $i < $FvNumber; $i++) { // Connect follower to followers
     for ($j = 0; $j < $FvNumber; $j++) {
          connectDynamic -fields ("vehicleFForce_" + $i)
                                 ("rigidVehicleF_" + $j) ;
       }
        connectDynamic -delete -fields ("vehicleFForce_" + $i)
                                       ("rigidVehicleF_" + $i);
     }

   // Connect global forces to both types of vehicles if option is on

   if ($gforces == 1) {

      string $compass[4] = { "N", "S", "E", "W" };

        for ($i = 0; $i < $LvNumber; $i++) {
           for ($c = 0; $c < size($compass); $c++) {
              connectDynamic -fields ("Gforce" + $compass[$c])
                                     ("rigidVehicleL_" + $i);

           }

        }

        for ($i = 0; $i < $FvNumber; $i++) {
           for ($c = 0; $c < size($compass); $c++) {
```

```mel
                connectDynamic -fields ("Gforce" + $compass[$c])
                                ("rigidVehicleF_" + $i);

        }

      }

    }

    // Build obstacles if option is selected

    if ($obst == 1) collectObstacles;
    // Disable warning

    cycleCheck -e off;

} // End of createCrowd proc

// Build obstacles

//_____

global proc collectObstacles() {

    global string $collectObjects[];
    // Declare global array for obstacles

    if (size($collectObjects) == 0) {

        warning "No obstacle objects were selected.";

      } else {

    for ( $i = 0; $i < size($collectObjects); $i++) {
        rigidBody -passive -name ($collectObjects[$i] + "RigidB" + $i)
                -bounciness 2.0 ($collectObjects[$i]);

      }

    }
} // End of collectObstacles proc

// Make global forces with an interface
//_____ _____

global proc makeGforces() {

// Edit matrix for position changes

matrix $gFp[4][3] = <<0, 0, -150; 0, 0, 150; 150, 0, 0; -150, 0, 0>>;

string $compassForce[] = {"N", "S", "E", "W"};
```

```
for ($i = 0; $i <4; $i++) {
    radial -name ("Gforce" + $compassForce[$i])
          -position $gFp[$i][0] $gFp[$i][1] $gFp[$i][2]
          -m 0 -att 0;
    hide ("Gforce" + $compassForce[$i]);
    };

// Set flag in createCrowd for dynamic hookups
// Launch window control
if (`window -exists GforceWin`) // If window is there, delete and
                                // create new
    deleteUI -window GforceWin;

string $window = `window -t "Global forces control" -w 450 -h 150
                 GforceWin`;
                 columnLayout;
                 floatSliderGrp
                 -label "Force north" -field false -minValue 0.0
                  -maxValue 0.3
                 -value 0.0 magForceN;
                 floatSliderGrp
                 -label "Force south" -field false -minValue 0.0
                  -maxValue 0.3
                 -value 0.0 magForceS;
                    floatSliderGrp
                    -label "Force east" -field false -minValue 0.0
                     -maxValue 0.3
                    -value 0.0 magForceE;
                    floatSliderGrp
                    -label "Force west" -field false -minValue 0.0
                     -maxValue 0.3
                    -value 0.0 magForceW;

// Connect sliders to fields' magnitude
// Swap control sliders with fields

connectControl magForceS GforceS.magnitude;
connectControl magForceN GforceN.magnitude;
connectControl magForceW GforceW.magnitude;
connectControl magForceE GforceE.magnitude;
showWindow $window;

} // End of makeGforces proc
```

```
// Main
// _____

global proc crowdMain()
{
      global string $collectObjects[];

   if (`window -exists crowdWin`) {

      confirmDialog -t "Already running!"
                -m "Please close Crowd System window and create a New Scene";

   } else {

      $collectObjects = `ls -sl`;

      crowdSystem;

         }
}

// Window launch
//_____
global proc crowdSystem()
{

   window
         -title "Crowd System"
         -widthHeight 300 200
         crowdWin;

string $form = `formLayout`;
   string $txt = `text -label "Number of Vehicles"`;
   string $collection = `radioCollection`;
   string $radiob1, $radiob2;
   $radiob1 = `radioButton -label "10"
                           -onCommand "$vNumber = 10"`;
   $radiob2 = `radioButton -label "20"
                           -onCommand "$vNumber = 20"`;
   setParent..; setParent..;

   string $txtOB = `text -label "Obstacles"`;
   string $collection2 = `radioCollection`;
   string $radiob3, $radiob4;
   $radiob3 = `radioButton -label "On"
                           -onCommand "$obst = 1"`;
```

```
        $radiob4 = `radioButton -label "Off"
                            -onCommand "$obst = 0"`;
        setParent ..;setParent ..;

        string $txtGF = `text -label "Global Forces"`;
        string $collection3 = `radioCollection`;
        string $radiob5, $radiob6;
        $radiob5 = `radioButton -label "On"
                            -onCommand "$gforces = 1"`;
        $radiob6 = `radioButton -label "Off"
                            -onCommand "$gforces = 0"`;
        setParent ..; setParent ..;

    radioCollection -edit -select $radiob1 $collection;
    radioCollection -edit -select $radiob4 $collection2;
    radioCollection -edit -select $radiob6 $collection3;

    // Place vehicle options
    formLayout -edit
            -attachForm         $txt            "top" 20
            -attachForm         $txt            "left" 70
    $form;
    formLayout -edit
            -attachForm         $radiob1        "top" 10
            -attachForm         $radiob1        "left" 20
            -attachForm         $radiob2        "top" 30
            -attachForm         $radiob2        "left" 20
    $form;

    // Place environment options
    formLayout -edit
            -attachForm         $txtOB          "top" 80
            -attachForm         $txtOB          "left" 80
    $form;
    formLayout -edit
            -attachForm         $radiob3        "top" 80
            -attachForm         $radiob3        "left" 150
            -attachForm         $radiob4        "top" 80
            -attachForm         $radiob4        "left" 190
    $form;
    formLayout -edit
            -attachForm         $txtGF          "top" 110
            -attachForm         $txtGF          "left" 63
    $form;
```

```
formLayout -edit
        -attachForm                 $radiob5              "top" 110
        -attachForm                 $radiob5              "left" 150
        -attachForm                 $radiob6              "top" 110
        -attachForm                 $radiob6              "left" 190
$form;

// Create buttons
string $button1 = `button -label "Create"`;
string $button2 = `button -label "Cancel"`;

// Place buttons in window
formLayout -edit
        -attachForm                 $button1              "bottom" 10
        -attachForm                 $button1              "left" 185
$form;

formLayout -edit
        -attachForm                 $button2              "bottom" 10
        -attachForm                 $button2              "right" 10
$form;

// Add commands to buttons

button -edit -command
    ("createCrowd $vNumber $gforces $obst; deleteUI crowdWin;")
        $button1;
button -edit -command ("deleteUI crowdWin;") $button2;

showWindow crowdWin;
} // End of crowdSystem proc
```

22

Examples Using MEL in Character Rigging

Using MEL does not revolutionize character setup, but it can make animating your characters easier by giving you useful tools for working with features of your character setup. Expressions can simplify animation; user interfaces can make manipulating the character easier, and other tools can be developed that will automate common tasks.

In production, many of the most useful MEL scripts and expressions perform simple tasks, such as managing animation curve data, selecting parts of the character, and so on. Almost everything that character-related MEL scripts do can be done by hand in the interface; the advantage of using MEL is that by scripting these tasks they can be repeated and in many cases performed much more quickly.

In the following examples, we'll explore how to use Maya's expression language to create high-level animation controls on a simple skeleton. We will then move on to look at how to create a user interface that eases the animator's interaction with the character rig. These examples are based on the assumption that you are familiar with basic character setup in Maya. Figure 22.1 shows the character developed in the examples.

Example 1: Character Controls

In this example, we'll look at a setup for a bipedal character based on a human skeleton, and we'll examine how we can add to the character high-level animation controls that use expressions to drive complex motion. In Example 2, we'll add a user interface to simplify animation.

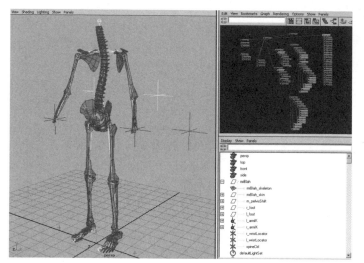

Figure 22.1 Example character.

Load Scene

First, load the scene `mrBlah.mb`. From the File > Open Scene menu, select the scene `mrBlah.mb` in the archive on the Web site.

Figure 22.2 shows what you should see once the scene loads. Depending on your preferences in Maya, the joints might look different. You can change the size of the joints by choosing Display > Joint Size > 25%.

You can zoom out a little in the Hypergraph panel on the upper right side of the screen to get a better view of the nodes that make up the character.

Overview of Scene

The character `mrBlah` is an example of a biped character that is already equipped with bones and skin. The skin consists of a polygonal skeleton model called `mrBlah_skeleton` that was used to lay out the joints for `mrBlah`. Let's look at the joints alone by going to the persp panel's menu Show and deselecting the Polygon option (Figure 22.3). This will hide the `mrBlah_ skeleton` model so that you see only the joints, IK handles, and locators.

Overview of mrBlah's Controls

Let's start by organizing the character's animation controls. Then, we'll create some custom attributes and expressions for `mrBlah` that will aid in animating him.

The character has some foot controls that are already set up. Zoom in the persp panel to the right foot area, and look for a locator just to the right

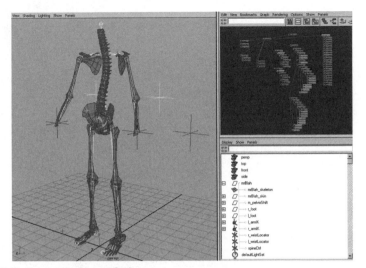

Figure 22.2 Contents of `mrBlah.ma`.

of the foot. Select it; then move it up and down and back and forth with the Transform tool to see what it does (Figure 22.4).

This control can also be found in the Outliner window under the name r_foot. Find it in the Outliner window, and open the entire hierarchy beneath it (Figure 22.5). (Remember that you can open the entire hierarchy all at once by holding down the Shift key while clicking the + symbol.)

In the r_foot hierarchy, you will see a hidden node called r_toePivot. Select it, and "unhide" it by choosing Display > Show > Show Selection from the menu. The IK relationships that were created in setting up the foot are displayed in Figure 22.6.

A custom attribute added to the foot's top node r_foot is called Roll. When you select the node r_foot and open the Attribute Editor (Ctrl-a), you will see the attribute Roll under the Extra Attributes tab (Figure 22.7). The Set Driven Key feature was used to control the rotations of the foot structure by using the Roll attribute in r_foot as an input. Move the slider to see the results (Figure 22.8).

If you want to view how the Roll attribute drives the foot's motion, open the Graph Editor by selecting Windows > Animation Editors > Graph Editor, and then select the r_heelPivot, r_toePivot, and r_ankle nodes in the Outliner. In the Graph Editor, you'll see the curve values that were used on the RotateX channels for each node (Figure 22.9).

Set the Roll attribute back to 0; then select the r_toePivot node, and hide it once again (using the Hide Selection menu item or Ctrl-h). The right foot and left foot are set up the same way.

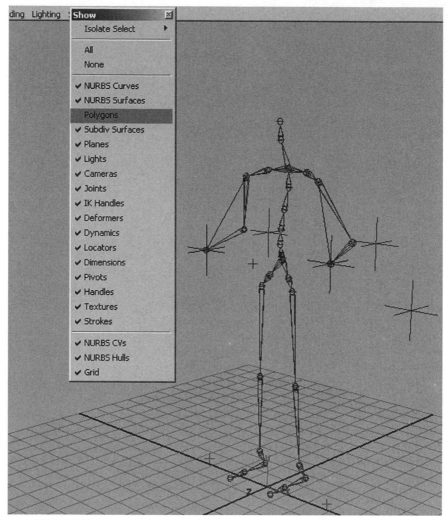

Figure 22.3 Hiding the polygon model.

Locking Attributes

Before you close the Attribute Editor for `r_foot`, note that the Scale channels have been locked to 1.0. This was done to preserve the hierarchy's scale transform by preventing the animator from changing it or setting keys for it. If you look in the Channel Box, you will notice that the Scale channels will not be displayed in the window. Using locking and range of motion limitations can help the animator avoid modifying attributes that will break the character setup.

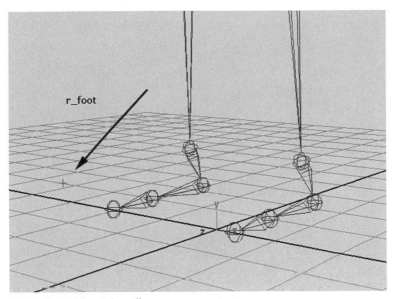

Figure 22.4 The `r_foot` handle.

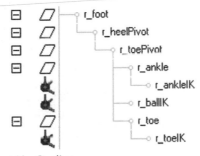

Figure 22.5 `r_toePivot` in Outliner.

Arm Controls

The character setup in the example scene features two simple arm controls—wrist control and an elbow control—each of which is manipulated with a locator next to each arm. The locators for the right arm are called `r_wristLocator` and `r_elbowLocator`. The `r_wristLocator` is under the main `mrBlah` hierarchy, and the `r_elbowLocator` is under the `m_pelvisShift` hierarchy. The character was built this way because `m_elbowLocator`'s transform will move with `mrBlah`'s spine and orient itself correctly with respect to his backbone. Move these locators around with the Move tool to see how they work. Make sure that you select `r_wristLocator` in the Outliner window when you want to move it (Figure 22.10).

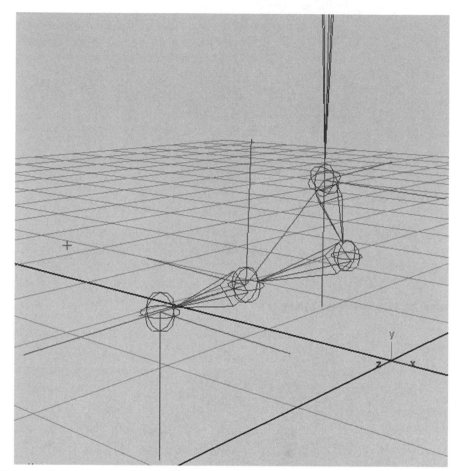

Figure 22.6 IK relationships in foot.

▶	**Node Behavior**		
▼	**Extra Attributes**		
	Roll	0.000	▬▬▬▭▬▬▬

Figure 22.7 Roll custom attribute in Attribute Editor.

In the Hypergraph window, find the IK node for the right arm, called `r_armIK`. Select it, and you will see the two constraints that are used to control the arm (Figure 22.11).

This control uses a `point` constraint and a `poleVector` constraint to control the arm.

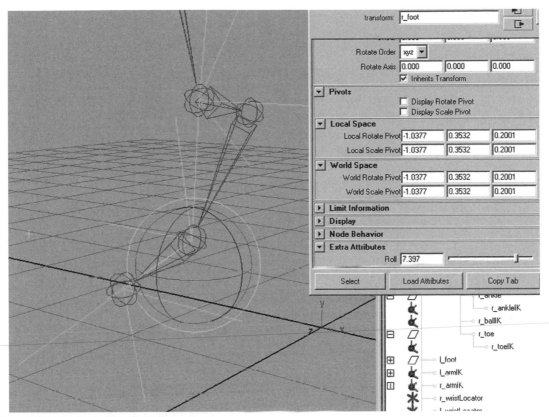

Figure 22.8 Effect of Roll attribute.

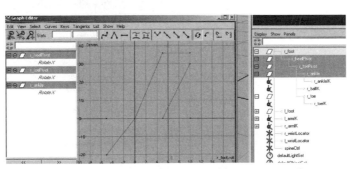

Figure 22.9 Curves that allow a Roll attribute to drive rotate attributes.

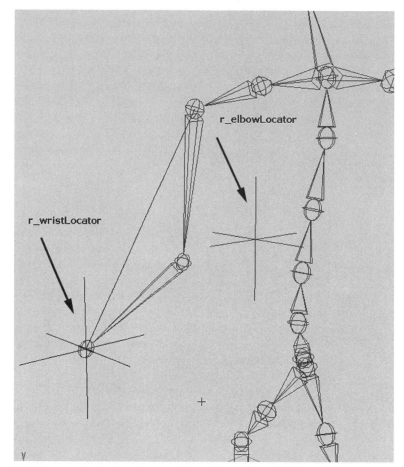

Figure 22.10 `r_wrist_locator` and `r_elbow_locator`.

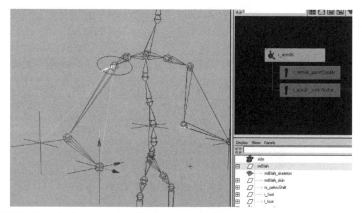

Figure 22.11 Constraints used to limit arm motion.

Set Up mrBlah's Backbone Controls

Let's set up some controls for the character's backbone. To do this, we first need to add some custom attributes on a locator that is in the scene. Open the Outliner window, and find the locator called `spineCtrl` in the Outliner window at the top level of mrBlah's hierarchy at the bottom of the list (Figure 22.12 and Figure 22.13).

In the Script Editor, we'll add the custom attributes using MEL that we will later use in our expressions. Type the following MEL command, and use the Enter key on the numeric keypad to execute it.

```
addAttr -ln Side -at double -keyable 1     mrBlah spineCtrl;
```

Note that we use the | symbol to separate the names of the nodes along the way from the top of the hierarchy to the node that we want to manipulate. This is essential if your scene has multiple identically named objects in it, but is not necessary if each node is named uniquely.

At this point, we need to add two more attributes that will control twisting and bending of the spine. We are not going to specify minimum and maximum values since we will later create a slider control to these attributes for the animator, and we can place limits on the slider to control the minimum and maximum. In the Script Editor, execute the following commands:

```
addAttr -ln Twist -at double -keyable 1     mrBlah    spineCtrl;
addAttr -ln Bend -at double -keyable 1      mrBlah    spineCtrl;
```

Select the `spineCtrl` locator in the Attribute Editor, and open the Extra Attributes tab (Figure 22.14).

Now we need to enter expressions that allow the attributes to control the backbones. Figure 22.15 shows how the backbones, m_back0 to m_back4, are set up.

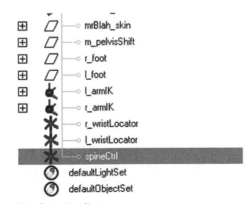

Figure 22.12 `spineCtrl` in Outliner.

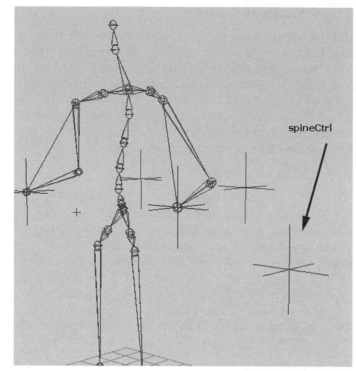

Figure 22.13 `spineCtrl` in persp panel.

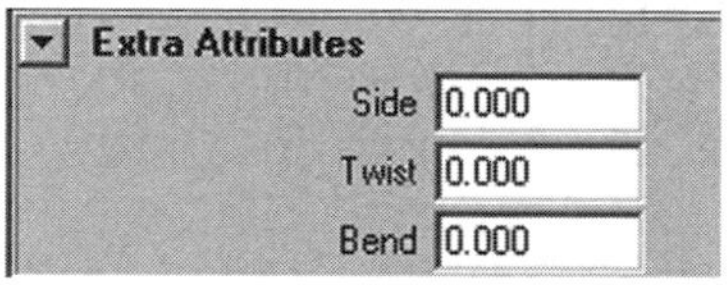

Figure 22.14 Side, Bend, and Twist attributes in Attribute Editor.

We'll need our expression to control the individual rotations of X, Y, and Z for each bone 0 to 4. Open the Expression Editor by choosing Window > Animation Editors > Expression Editor, and then enter in the following expression:

```
// Control each backbone's rotation with the attrs Side,
// Twist, and Bend

m_back0.rotateZ = -spineCtrl.Bend;
m_back1.rotateZ = -spineCtrl.Bend;
m_back2.rotateZ = -spineCtrl.Bend;
m_back3.rotateZ = -spineCtrl.Bend;
m_back4.rotateZ = -spineCtrl.Bend;
```

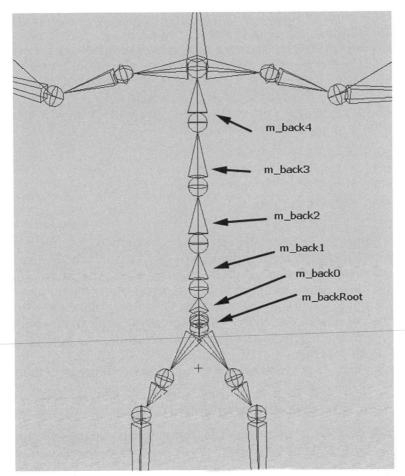

Figure 22.15 Backbone joints.

```
m_back0.rotateX = spineCtrl.Twist;
m_back1.rotateX = spineCtrl.Twist;
m_back2.rotateX = spineCtrl.Twist;
m_back3.rotateX = spineCtrl.Twist;
m_back4.rotateX = spineCtrl.Twist;

m_back0.rotateY = -spineCtrl.Side;
m_back1.rotateY = -spineCtrl.Side;
m_back2.rotateY = -spineCtrl.Side;
m_back3.rotateY = -spineCtrl.Side;
m_back4.rotateY = -spineCtrl.Side;
```

Type the name mrBlah_expression into the Expression Name box at the top of the window, and click Create (Figure 22.16).

Select the spineCtrl locator, and select the Side channel's name (Figure 22.17). In the persp panel, hold down the middle mouse button, and move the mouse from side to side to emulate a slider control (Figure 22.18). Try this for the other channels as well.

Let's look at the first part of the expression and see how it adjusts the joints when you modify the Bend attribute.

```
m_back0.rotateZ = -spineCtrl.Bend;
m_back1.rotateZ = -spineCtrl.Bend;
m_back2.rotateZ = -spineCtrl.Bend;
m_back3.rotateZ = -spineCtrl.Bend;
m_back4.rotateZ = -spineCtrl.Bend;
```

As you change the value for Bend, it will rotate each of the m_back joints in the negative direction around the Z axis, or counterclockwise as you look in the positive Z direction. As each joint is rotated, the parent-child relationships of the joints add each joint's transform to the joint above, causing a cascading, increasing rotation as you travel up the chain. Twist will do it with a positive value to the X rotation, and Side will do another negative value to the Y. This is a simple expression that does not rely on complex IK to do the trick.

Set the Bend, Twist, and Side attributes back to 0 before moving on.

Create Sway Effect When Picking Up Feet

Let's add a sway expression to mrBlah so that when you pick up either foot, the upper body will shift its weight to the other side. Open the Expression

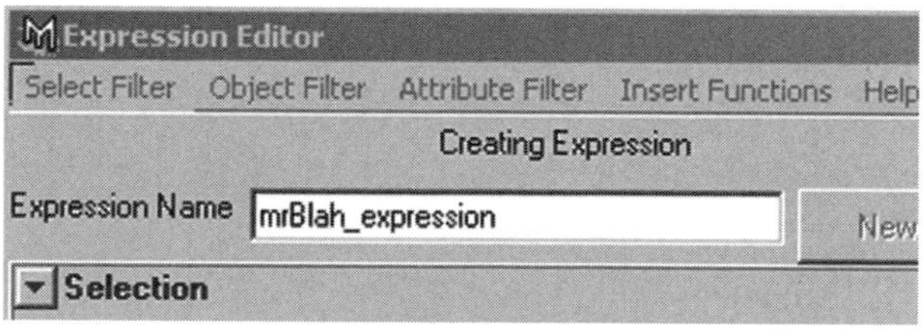

Figure 22.16 Creating mrBlah_expression in Expression Editor.

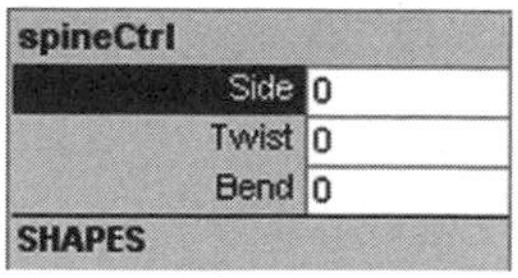

Figure 22.17 Side attribute in Channel Editor.

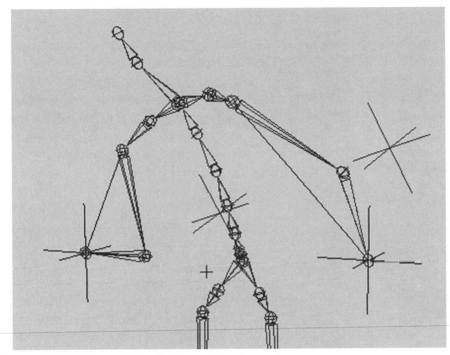

Figure 22.18 Effect of Side, Twist, and Bend on spine.

Editor again, and choose Select Filter > By Name. Pick the expression
mrBlah_expression (Figure 22.19).

Now, add the following two lines to the end of the other expression that
we entered earlier.

```
// Cause sway when moving feet

m_backRoot.rotateY = ( l_foot.translateY * 2)
                    -(r_foot.translateY * 2);
m_backRoot.translateX = (-l_foot.translateY / 4)
                    -(-r_foot.translateY / 4);
```

Click Edit to accept the changes to the expression. Select the r_foot
locator; then use the Move tool to move the locator up in Y
(Figure 22.20).

Now the skeleton sways to its left as we lift the right foot. This happens
because when r_foot or l_foot is moved in Y, the expression multiplies
each foot's Y translation by 2, and then it subtracts the results to find how
far to rotate the root joint in Y. The body tends to rotate away from
whichever foot is higher.

Then the negated Y translations of r_foot and l_foot are divided by 4,
and right is subtracted from left to translate the back away from the foot

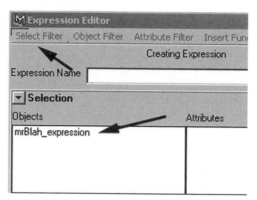

Figure 22.19 Selecting `mrBlah_expression` by name.

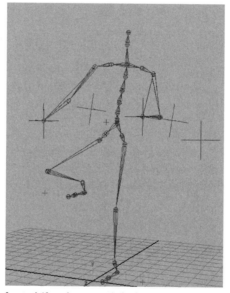

Figure 22.20 Raising foot shifts character's balance.

that's higher. This completes the effect of shifting the character's weight onto the lower foot.

Turn on the skeleton model that we turned off in the beginning by going back to the persp panel and selecting the Polygon option from the Show menu (Figure 22.21).

Finally, Save the scene in your projects directory so that you have it for the next example. In Example 2, we will build some user interface tools to make animating `mrBl ah` easier.

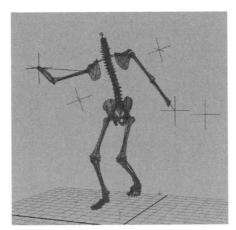

Figure 22.21 Get up and dance!

Example 2: Building a Character User Interface

In this example, we'll build on the previous example by adding a user interface to control mrBlah. This user interface will be a window containing sliders (for our high-level Bend, Twist, and Side attributes) and selection buttons (for all of the most-used body part controls). Also, the window will contain display control buttons to allow the user to select whether to display joints only, low-resolution geometry, or high-resolution geometry. Finally, the window will contain controls that allow the user to set keyframes from within the window (Figure 22.22).

Load Saved mrBlah Scene

From the projects directory into which you saved the mrBlah scene at the end of Example 1, load the scene by selecting File > Load Scene, and then choose mrBlah.ma.

Turn off the skeleton polygonal model as before so that you can concentrate on the joints only. This time, we'll hide the model instead of turning off the display for all the polygonal models that might be in the scene. In the Script Editor type

```
hide mrBlah_skeleton;
```

Check to see that all the expressions that you added in Example 1 are there by choosing Windows > Animation Editors > Expression Editor > Select Filter, and then select By Name. You should see mrBlah_expression in the list (Figure 22.23).

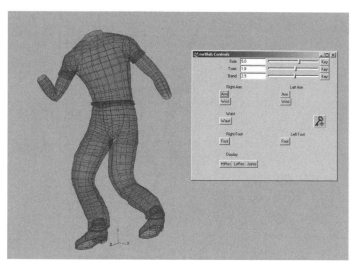

Figure 22.22 Finished user interface for character.

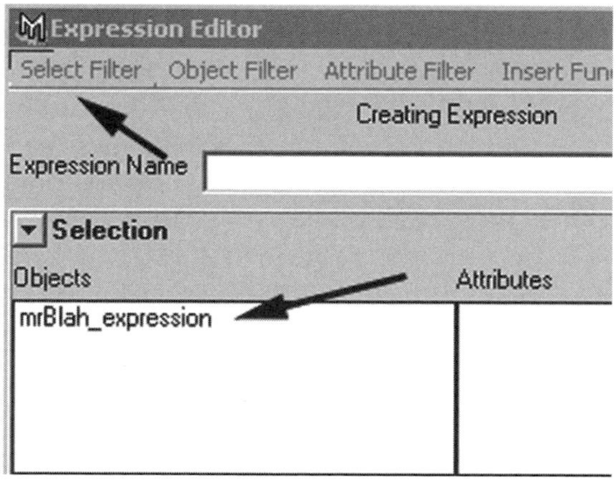

Figure 22.23 Selecting `mrBlah_expression` by name.

Organize Controls for Users

If you're developing a character that will be animated by someone else, the first step in developing user interfaces for the character is to meet with your audience and discuss how they would like to control the character. However, since we are setting up this character for ourselves, let's first make a list of what interface options we want. Besides buttons to select control handles and set keyframes, we also will want to allow ourselves to use our user interface window to switch between displaying the two different versions of the model that are already contained in the setup.

Figure 22.24 shows the layout of controls in the character. Following is a map of where we want to place buttons in our user interface window to help manipulate those controls.

```
r_wristLocator      move    l_wristLocator    move
r_elbowLocator      move    l_elbowLocator    move
r_foot              move    l_foot            move
m_backRoot          move    spineCtrl         select to display
                                              Side, Twist, and
                                              Bend controls
```

Figure 22.24 Overview of mrBlah controls.

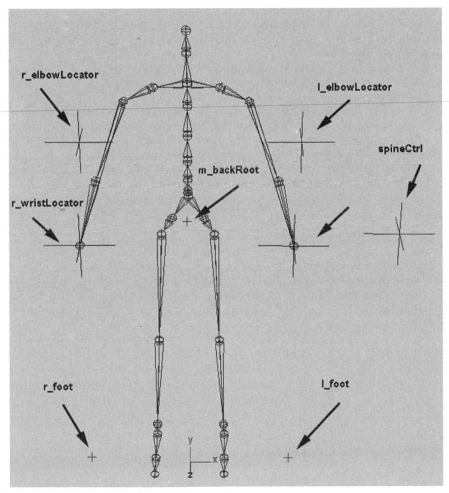

Figure 22.24 Overview of mrBlah controls.

A button to select each of these handles or locators will make up the main part of the window. Additionally, we'd like to be able to use buttons in our user interface window to move around among the following.

- HiRes: Display high-resolution NURBS model that is smooth skinned to the joints.
- LoRes: Display low-resolution polygonal pieces that are rigid skinned to the joints, plus the joints themselves.
- Joints: Display joints only.

Finally, we want to include a Key option in the interface window so that the user can directly set keyframes to the items that are selected.

Create mrBlahControls.mel

Open your favorite text editing program, and start building the script mrBlahControls.mel. At the top of the file, start writing the global proc mrBlahControls().

```
global proc mrBlahControls ( ){
    window
        -title "mrBlah Controls"
        -widthHeight 450 450
        MBcontrols;
```

This first command in the mrBlahControls procedure will give us the framework and title for the window.

Now, let's create the static text headings to form sections for the buttons.

```
string $form = `formLayout`;

// Interface text
string $txt1 = `text -label "Right Arm          Left Arm"`;
string $txt2 = `text -label "Waist"`;
string $txt3 = `text -label "Right Foot          Left Foot"`;
string $txt4 = `text -label "Display"`;
```

The string $form will contain the name of the formLayout object that the formLayout command creates. When you enter the text strings containing "Right Arm and Left Arm", make sure that there are 49 spaces between the end of Right Arm and the beginning of Left Arm—spacing is important because we'll be placing buttons precisely to align with those names.

To create the necessary buttons, enter the following code:

```
// Create buttons

// Right arm
```

```
string $b1 = `button -label "Arm"
               -command "select -r r_wristLocator r_elbowLocator"`;
string $b2 = `button -label "Wrist"
               -command "select -r r_wristLocator"`;

// Left arm
string $b3 = `button -label "Arm"
               -command "select -r l_wristLocator l_elbowLocator"`;
string $b4 = `button -label "Wrist"
               -command "select -r l_wristLocator"`;

// Waist
string $b5 = `button -label "Waist" -command "select -r m_backRoot"`;

// Right foot
string $b6 = `button -label "Foot" -command "select -r r_foot"`;

// Left foot
string $b7 = `button -label "Foot" -command "select -r l_foot"`;

// Display buttons
string $b8 = `button -label "HiRes"
               -command "int $dis = 1;displayFunc($dis)"`;
string $b9 = `button -label "LoRes"
               -command "int $dis = 2;displayFunc($dis)"`;
string $b10 = `button -label "Joints"
        -command "int $dis = 3;displayFunc($dis)"`;
```

The -command flags in the button creation section set up a select command for each button that will be executed when that button is clicked. The Arm buttons will select both the wrist and the elbow for movement. The next section's display buttons -command flags introduce a new variable $dis and a function called displayFunc. When these buttons are clicked, the variable is given a value of 1, 2, or 3 and then passed to displayFunc.

We have not yet defined this function, so at the top of the file, above the global proc mrBlahControls, enter the following:

```
global proc displayFunc(int $dis) {
int $dis;
switch ($dis) {

    case 1:
       HideJoints;
       hide "*_stdin";
       select -r mrBlah_skin; showHidden -a; select -d;
    break;

    case 2:
       hide mrBlah_skin;
```

```
        select -r "*_stdin";
        showHidden -a; select -d;
     break;

     case 3:
        hide mrBlah_skin;
        hide "*_stdin";
        ShowJoints;
     break;
     default:
   }

 }
```

The function passes the value of $dis into a switch function to determine what display mode we have chosen. The case 1 displays high-resolution geometry, hides all joints, and hides all the stand-in objects that are bound to the joints. These are low-resolution polygon objects that help give users an impression of where the high-resolution version of mrBlah's skin will be. We use the wildcard format "*_stdin" to hide all the stand-in objects, because they've all been named to end with _stdin. Then, the last command selects the high-resolution skin, unhides it, and then de-selects it.

As you can see, in the other case structures we use similar commands to swap the displays. The case 2 hides the high-resolution geometry and displays the low-resolution geometry, while case 3 hides both high- and low-resolution geometry, leaving only joints displayed.

Under // Display buttons in the main global proc, let's create a Key button that will allow us to keyframe the transforms of the locators that are selected in the window. Following is the MEL code to create this button:

```
// Keyframe button
string $KEYframe = `symbolButton -image "setKey.xpm"
                   -parent $form
                   -command setkeys`;
columnLayout;
```

This new symbolButton type will display the standard Maya key icon, whose picture is in the image file "setKey.xpm" as the button (Figure 22.25).

The file setKey.xpm is one of Maya's standard icons used for its interface, so an explicit path is not necessary for Maya to find the file. However, if you preferred, you could substitute your own icon in xpm format to replace it.

Figure 22.25 setKey.xpm button image.

The button section is closed with the final columnLayout call. The keyframe button's -command flag tells the button to call a new function setkeys when it's clicked. Again, at the top of the script that we've been working on, enter the following global proc:

```
global proc setkeys() {

    string $names[ ] =`ls -sl`;
      if ($names[0] != "m_backRoot") {
          string $name;
            for ($name in $names) {
            setKeyframe ($name + ".tx");
            setKeyframe ($name + ".ty");
            setKeyframe ($name + ".tz");
            }
        } else {
            setKeyframe m_backRoot.ty;
            setKeyframe m_backRoot.tz;
    }
  }
```

The setkeys procedure gets the selected locator from the scene by using ls -sl to store the selection list in an array variable called $names[ ]. Then, it checks to see whether the locator m_backRoot is selected; if it is, the script will not be able to set a keyframe for the X channel.

If m_backRoot is not in the first [0] position of the array, the script loops through the array by using a for-in loop. This for-in loop sets a keyframe for the x, y, and z channels of each selected locator. The setkeys button needs to loop over a selection list instead of just keying the first selected locator because the Arm selection option that we are putting in the interface selects two locators (both the elbow and the wrist), so we will need to set keyframes for both.

If our test at the beginning found the name m_backRoot at the start of the array, it bypasses the loop and skips directly to the last section, where the control gets its y and z channels keyed.

Create Sliders to Control spinCtrl Attributes

Let's create a slider interface to control values for the spine's Bend, Key, and Twist attributes. In the area under the last columnLayout call, enter the following:

```
// Sliders for spineCtl

floatSliderButtonGrp -label "Side" -field true
                     -buttonLabel "Key"
```

```
                           -buttonCommand
                            "select -r spineCtrl; setKeyframe spineCtrl.Side"
                           -minValue -20.0 -maxValue 20.0
                           -value 0.0 Side;
                           connectControl Side spineCtrl.Side;

floatSliderButtonGrp -label "Twist" -field true
                           -buttonLabel "Key"
                           -buttonCommand
                            "select -r spineCtrl; setKeyframe spineCtrl.Twist"
                           -minValue -20.0 -maxValue 20.0
                           -value 0.0 Twist;
                           connectControl Twist spineCtrl.Twist;

floatSliderButtonGrp -label "Bend" -field true
                           -buttonLabel "Key"
                           -buttonCommand
                            "select -r spineCtrl; setKeyframe spineCtrl.Bend"
                           -minValue -45.0 -maxValue 45.0
                           -value 0.0 Bend;
                           connectControl Bend spineCtrl.Bend;
```

The sliders will each have their own Key button, so they will not need to use the `setkeys` global procedure. Also, we added a `select -r` before the `setKeyframe` command. This selection is not needed to perform the set key; instead, it's there because by selecting it the user will get visual feedback on the timeline of at what frames keys exist for the selected control (Figure 22.26).

Create Layout for Window Controls

Now we will add the MEL code that lays out the text and the buttons that will appear in the window. We'll use the `formLayout` layout type, anchoring the items to the "top" and "left" sides to keep the code simple. Under the slider section, add the calls to `formLayout -edit` that will add the text items to the layout, as follows:

```
// Text layouts

formLayout -edit
            -attachForm        $txt1        "top" 80
            -attachForm        $txt1        "left" 100
            -attachForm        $txt2        "top" 160
            -attachForm        $txt2        "left" 100
            -attachForm        $txt3        "top" 220
```

Figure 22.26 Keyframes in timeline.

```
            -attachForm        $txt3        "left" 100
            -attachForm        $txt4        "top" 280
            -attachForm        $txt4        "left" 100
    $form;
```

In the next section, where we will lay out the buttons, let's create three variables for offsets. We can position some of our buttons by using some of the same positions that we used before for the text, but with an added offset. Enter the following code:

```
// Button layouts
int $bOffsetW = 180;
int $bOffsetH1 = 80;
int $bOffsetH2 = 140;

formLayout -edit
            -attachForm        $b1        "top" 98
            -attachForm        $b1        "left" 80
            -attachForm        $b2        "top" 120
            -attachForm        $b2        "left" 80
    $form;

    formLayout -edit
            -attachForm        $b3        "top" 98
            -attachForm        $b3        "left" (80 + $bOffsetW)
            -attachForm        $b4        "top" 120
            -attachForm        $b4        "left" (80 + $bOffsetW)
    $form;

    formLayout -edit
            -attachForm        $b5        "top" (98 + $bOffsetH1)
            -attachForm        $b5        "left" 80
    $form;

    formLayout -edit
            -attachForm        $b6        "top" (98 + $bOffsetH2)
            -attachForm        $b6        "left" 80
    $form;

    formLayout -edit
            -attachForm        $b7        "top" (98 + $bOffsetH2)
            -attachForm        $b7        "left" (80 + $bOffsetW)
```

```
        $form;
        formLayout -edit
                -attachForm        $b8        "top" 305
                -attachForm        $b8        "left" 80
                -attachForm        $b9        "top" 305
                -attachForm        $b9        "left" 118
                -attachForm        $b10       "top" 305
                -attachForm        $b10       "left" 158
        $form;
        formLayout -edit
                -attachForm        $KEYframe        "top" 170
                -attachForm        $KEYframe        "left" 360
        $form;
        showWindow MBcontrols;
    }
```

The final command, showWindow, will launch the window. Save the MEL file as mrBlahControls.mel in your default scripts directory so that Maya will know where to look when you source the file.

Test Window

In the Script Editor window, source the script, and launch the window so that we can see if everything is there and whether it works.

```
    source mrBlahControls;
    mrBlahControls;
```

Figure 22.27 shows what you should see if everything went well.

Try out the buttons and sliders. Use the Move tool to transform what you select in the window. Also, try the Display buttons and the Key icon button to make sure that everything is in order. If you are getting errors and need to delete the window, type in

```
    deleteUI MBcontrols;
```

Display Only What You Want User to See

Let's hide all the locators, handles, and IK handles in the scene to reduce the temptation for the user to select them in the interface. We can do this by using the Show menu in the persp panel. Enlarge the persp panel to full screen by pressing the space bar with the mouse over the window. Now go to the Show menu, and turn off the options shown in Figure 22.28 by de-selecting them from the list.

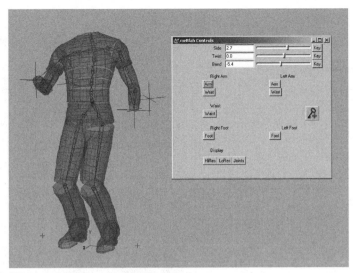

Figure 22.27 User interface for `mrBlah`.

Create Script Node for Window

We did not put a Close button in the interface because this window was designed to be open all the time and only "stowed" if the user wants to hide it temporarily. The window will be automatically launched when the scene is loaded. This will be done using a `scriptNode` that the scene will execute as it loads. In the Script Editor, enter the following command:

```
scriptNode -beforeScript "source mrBlahControls;mrBlahControls;"
    -n Controls;
setAttr Controls.scriptType 2;
```

Setting the `scriptType` to 2 will open the window only when Maya's interface is used to load the scene. It will not execute the script if the scene is batch rendered.

Now choose File > Save Scene As, and call the file `mrBlahAnimation.mb` in the `scenes` directory (Figure 22.29).

Close the `mrBlah` Controls window, and choose File > New Scene to clear out the scene. Now choose File > Open Scene, and select the `mrBlahAnimation.mb` file. When the scene is loaded, the custom window pops up, and the scene is ready to animate.

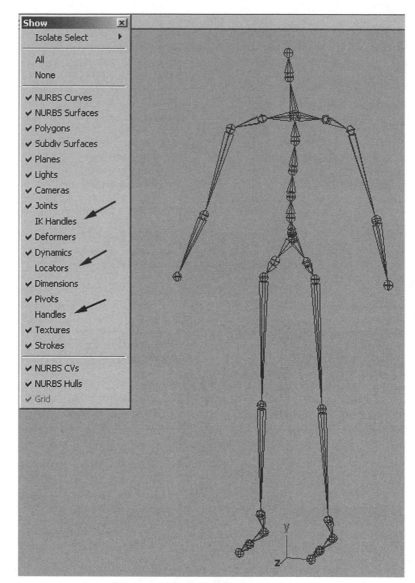

Figure 22.28 Turning off extraneous object display.

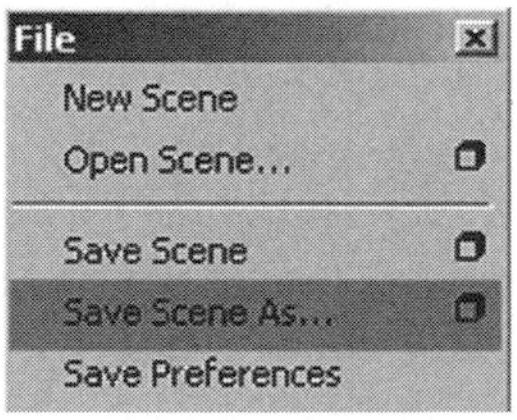

Figure 22.29 Save Scene As . . . menu item.

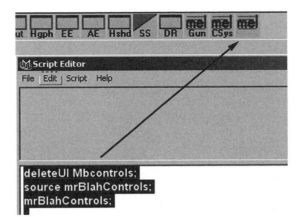

Figure 22.30 Making shelf button to open `mrBlah` user interface.

Create Shelf Icon to Reopen Window When Closed

To give the user a means to open the window if he or she accidentally closes it, create an icon on the shelf that will reopen it, even if it's just stowed. In the Script Editor, enter the following:

```
if (`window -exists Mbcontrols`) deleteUI MBcontrols;
source mrBlahControls;
mrBlahControls;
```

Do not execute the commands now; instead, select the text with the mouse, and middle-mouse drag it to the shelf (Figure 22.30).

Full Text of mrBlahControls.mel

```
global proc setkeys() {

    string $names[] =`ls -sl`;
      if ($names[0] != "m_backRoot") {
         string $name;
         for ($name in $names) {
            setKeyframe ($name + ".tx");
            setKeyframe ($name + ".ty");
            setKeyframe ($name + ".tz");
         }
      } else {
            setKeyframe m_backRoot.ty;
            setKeyframe m_backRoot.tz;
      }
   }
```

```
global proc displayFunc(int $dis) {
   int $dis;
   switch ($dis) {

      case 1:
         HideJoints;
         hide "*_stdin";
         select -r mrBlah_skin; showHidden -a;select -d;
      break;

      case 2:
         hide mrBlah_skin;
         select -r "*_stdin";
         showHidden -a; select -d;
      break;
   case 3:
      hide mrBlah_skin;
      hide "*_stdin";
      ShowJoints;
   break;
   default:
   }
}

global proc mrBlahControls ( ){
   window
      -title "mrBlah Controls"
      -widthHeight 450 450
      MBcontrols;
      string $form = `formLayout`;

   // Interface text
   string $txt1 = `text -label "Right Arm Left Arm"`;
   string $txt2 = `text -label "Waist"`;
   string $txt3 = `text -label "Right Foot Left Foot"`;
   string $txt4 = `text -label "Display"`;

   // Create buttons

   // Right arm
   string $b1 = `button -label "Arm" -command
               "select -r r_wristLocator r_elbowLocator"`;
   string $b2 = `button -label "Wrist" -command
               "select -r r_wristLocator"`;

   // Left arm
   string $b3 = `button -label "Arm "-command
               "select -r l_wristLocator l_elbowLocator"`;
```

```
      string $b4 = `button -label "Wrist" -command
                  "select -r l_wristLocator"`;

      // Waist
      string $b5 = `button -label "Waist" -command "select -r m_backRoot"`;

      // Right Foot
      string $b6 = `button -label "Foot" -command "select -r r_foot"`;

      // Left Foot
      string $b7 = `button -label "Foot" -command "select -r l_foot"`;
// Display buttons
string $b8 = `button -label "HiRes" -command
            "int $dis = 1;displayFunc($dis)"`;
string $b9 = `button -label "LoRes" -command
            "int $dis = 2;displayFunc($dis)"`;
string $b10 = `button -label "Joints" -command
            "int $dis = 3;displayFunc($dis)"`;

// Keyframe button
string $KEYframe = `symbolButton -image "setKey.xpm"
                    -parent $form -command setkeys`;
columnLayout;

// Sliders for spineCtl
floatSliderButtonGrp -label "Side" -field true -buttonLabel "Key"
   -buttonCommand "select -r spineCtrl; setKeyframe spineCtrl.Side"
   -minValue -20.0 -maxValue 20.0
   -value 0.0 Side;
   connectControl Side spineCtrl.Side;
floatSliderButtonGrp -label "Twist" -field true -buttonLabel "Key"
   buttonCommand "select -r spineCtrl; setKeyframe spineCtrl.Twist"
   -minValue -20.0 -maxValue 20.0
   -value 0.0 Twist;
   connectControl Twist spineCtrl.Twist;
floatSliderButtonGrp -label "Bend" -field true -buttonLabel "Key"
   -buttonCommand "select -r spineCtrl; setKeyframe spineCtrl.Bend"
   -minValue -45.0 -maxValue 45.0
   -value 0.0 Bend;
   connectControl Bend spineCtrl.Bend;
```

```
// Text layouts
formLayout -edit
-attachForm          $txt1      "top" 80
-attachForm          $txt1      "left" 100
-attachForm          $txt2      "top" 160
-attachForm          $txt2      "left" 100
-attachForm          $txt3      "top" 220
-attachForm          $txt3      "left" 100
-attachForm          $txt4      "top" 280
-attachForm          $txt4      "left" 100
$form;
    // Button layouts
    int $bOffsetW = 180;
    int $bOffsetH1 = 80;
    int $bOffsetH2 = 140;
    formLayout -edit
       -attachForm    $b1     "top" 98
       -attachForm    $b1     "left" 80
       -attachForm    $b2     "top" 120
       -attachForm    $b2     "left" 80
    $form;

    formLayout -edit
       -attachForm    $b3     "top" 98
       -attachForm    $b3     "left" (80 + $bOffsetW)
       -attachForm    $b4     "top" 120
       -attachForm    $b4     "left" (80 + $bOffsetW)
    $form;

    formLayout -edit
       -attachForm    $b5     "top" (98 + $bOffsetH1)
       -attachForm    $b5     "left" 80
    $form;

    formLayout -edit
       -attachForm    $b6     "top" (98 + $bOffsetH2)
       -attachForm    $b6     "left" 80
    $form;

    formLayout -edit
       -attachForm    $b7     "top" (98 + $bOffsetH2)
       -attachForm    $b7     "left" (80 + $bOffsetW)
    $form;
```

```
formLayout  -edit
    -attachForm     $b8        "top"  305
    -attachForm     $b8        "left" 80
    -attachForm     $b9        "top"  305
    -attachForm     $b9        "left" 118
    -attachForm     $b10       "top"  305
    -attachForm     $b10       "left" 158
$form;

formLayout  -edit
    -attachForm     $KEYframe       "top"  170
    -attachForm     $KEYframe       "left" 360
$form;

showWindow MBcontrols;
}
```

Index